A Trouser-wearing Character

A Trouser-wearing Character

The Life and Times of Nancy Spain

ROSE COLLIS

CASSELL

For a catalogue of related titles in our Sexual Politics/Global Issues list
please write to us at the address below:

Cassell
Wellington House
125 Strand
London
WC2R 0BB

P.O. Box 605
Herndon
VA 20172

First published 1997

British Library Cataloguing-in-Publication Data
A catalogue record for this book is available from the British Library.

ISBN 0–304–32879–0

Front cover photograph: © Karsh of Ottawa/Camera Press London

Typeset by York House Typographic, London

Printed and bound in Great Britain by Biddles Ltd, Guildford, Surrey

Contents

In memory of my beloved grandmother
Narcissa Florence Tann Austin
(1885–1973)

★ ★ ★

For my mother
Dorothy Austin Collis

★ ★ ★

And for my niece
Sarah Ann Austin

★ ★ ★

'Children have more need of models than of critics'
Joubert, *Pensées*, No. 261

Foreword

by

Tony Warren

Author of *Behind Closed Doors* and creator of *Coronation Street*

The warning bells rang loudly. First of all there was a note from somebody at my own publishers: 'Did you know that Rose Collis is doing a biography of Nancy Spain for Cassell?' Then came the telephone call from a magazine editor who is also a friend: 'You will talk to Rose, won't you?' Finally there was a letter from the would-be biographer herself.

My first thought was to pull up the drawbridge. Since Nancy's death, I have been somewhat startled by the revelations of secrets which she thought she'd taken to the grave. And I was still guarding a few of her old confidences myself. Dietrich was dead so that one wouldn't matter . . . But I too had loved Nancy. Not that we were ever lovers. No. But I still remembered the glow of sincerest pleasure that I'd felt, as a very young man, when she said to my mother, 'I understand him because we are the same person'.

So why let a biographer in? When I was a child I wanted to be famous, and one of my avowed rewards would be that I was going to become a friend of Nancy Spain's. And after I invented *Coronation Street* (which she loathed) we did become friends, and Nancy could have given lessons in friendship.

Oh how I miss her! She wasn't just Britain's most famous journalist, top of the list of big television personalities, court jester to the remains of an older tightly knit group of international stars of the 1930s; she was somebody who made every moment in her presence seem diamond-sharp. Life was for living to the full. Joy was not a sin.

The sin is that Nancy Spain is virtually forgotten. So that's why I allowed Rose Collis into my house. And she charmed first my dogs and then me – to an extent where I trusted myself to remember aloud. She's worked the same spell on many others. Over the past two years, Rose's latest news of her almost fanatical search into the past has brought me whole hours of telephone pleasure. It has also brought a few shocks. All is revealed in this gloriously worthwhile book.

Nancy Spain was Britain's official 'tomboy'. Heavy was the conjecture about her sexuality. Times have changed, to an extent where we have 'The Lesbian, Gay, Bisexual and Transgender Communities'. If she was alive today, Nancy would have learned to zip off the phrase in one triumphant recitation. Then she would have mocked it, lightly but firmly. And then, when lights were low and hearts were open, she might have wondered aloud, 'But which section do I fall into?' Darling Nancy, three of them certainly – if not all four! *That* is what your biographer has found out.

Acknowledgements

I would like to thank Ernest Hecht, for his initial co-operation in getting this book started. I am especially indebted to the co-operation, encouragement and kindness shown to me by Lady Liz Hulse, Nick Werner Laurie, Tom Carter and Dick Laurie. I am grateful to Tony Warren for his foreword, and for his encouragement. I would like to thank the following for sharing their memories of Nancy, in person, by telephone and by letter:

Mrs M.W. Ackroyd; Michael Barker; Alan Beck; Bentley Bridgewater; Tom Carter; Mrs Eileen Chadwick; Mrs Pamela Clatworthy; Mrs Joan Cockburn; Mrs Helen Cottee; Mrs Kathleen Davey; Richard E. Deems; the late Noel Dyson; Frank Ellul; Anne Clements Eyre; Mrs Rosemary Fellowes; the late Lady Patsy Fisher; Michael Foot; Jackie Forster; Christina Foyle; Alan Freeman; Violet Fulford; Alison Hennegan; Mrs Betty Hodges; Lady Liz Hulse; David Jacobs; Beatrice Jewell; Dick Laurie; Brian Masters; John Kennedy Melling; Denis Norden; Sir Edward Pickering; Valerie Hobson Profumo; Mrs Shirley Roberts; Roy Rutherford; Anne Scott James; Alice Sewell; Roger Storey; Tony Warren; Nick Werner Laurie; Sandy Wilson; Geoffrey Wright.

Unless otherwise stated, all quotations in the text are taken from personal and telephone interviews with the author, and correspondence.

I am also grateful to the following individuals, institutions and libraries for their assistance in gaining access to relevant material and dealing with my enquiries:

Architectural Association; Mrs Jane Hardie, Association of Wrens; Jeff Walden, Jacquie Kavanagh and the staff of the BBC Written Archive Centre; British Architectural Library; the staff of the British Library Reading Room and the British Newspaper Library, Colindale; Alan Beale and J.I. Parvin, Central Newcastle High School for Girls; Mrs B.J. Hanbury, Chair of School Governors, Chailey School, Sussex; Nicky Badman, Gerald Duckworth and Co. Ltd; K.V. Bligh and the staff of the House of Lords Record Office; Caroline Theakstone, Hulton Getty Picture Library Collection; Julie Robertshaw, Department of Printed Books and Paul Kemp, Picture Library, Imperial War Museum; E. Michael, Jesmond Library; Andrew Thynne, Lancashire Record Office; Margaret Proctor, Merseyside Record Office, Preston; Modern Record Office, Liverpool; Susannah Van Langernberg and the staff of the Library, National Magazine Company;

Clive Powell, National Maritime Museum; Lesley Jane Bradshaw, Original Photographs Collection, National Portrait Gallery; the National Sound Archive, London; Maria Hoy, Barbara Heathcote and the staff of the Newcastle Central Library; Mrs C. Orlebar, Old Roedeanians' Association; Michael Bott, Library of the University of Reading; Lesley Thomas, Royal Naval Museum; Mrs Deborah Buckenham, Headmistress, Runton and Sutherland School; G.A. Smith and Naval Secretary, Second Sea Lord and Commander-in-Chief Naval Home Command, Portsmouth; Bernard Nurse, Society of Antiquaries; the Southport Coroner; Elizabeth Rees and the staff of the Tyne and Wear Archive Service; W.J. West; Dominic Young of News International.

Thanks also go to the following individuals for providing me with valuable snippets of information or contacts, and answering my queries:

Vicky Blake; Stephen Bourne; Brian Braithwaite; Peter Burton; Kate Charlesworth; Mrs Corbett; Margaret Drabble; Robert Edwards; Margaret Forster; Tony Garrett; Victoria Glendinning; Pamela Griffiths; Joan Hirst; Philip Hoare; Merlin Holland; Sue Laurie; Andy Medhurst; John Kennedy Melling; Lord Northbourne; Tom Sargant; Liz Sich; Geoffrey Wright.

I am grateful to Nicholas Werner Laurie, of the estate of the late Nancy Spain and the estate of the late Joan Werner Laurie, for kind permission to quote from their published and unpublished writings; the Beaverbrook Papers are in the custody of the House of Lords Record Office and I am grateful for kind permission from the Clerk of the Records, who acts on behalf of the Beaverbrook Foundation Trustees, to quote from these documents. I am grateful to the BBC Written Archives Centre for their kind permission to quote from BBC documents in the Nancy Spain files; Graham Payn and the estate of the late Noel Coward for kind permission to quote from *Waiting in the Wings* and the Noel Coward diaries; Nicky Badman and Gerald Duckworth and Company Ltd for permission to quote from the introduction to *Minutes to Midnight* by the late Arthur Marshall; to Merlin Holland for permission to quote from the unpublished diaries of his late father, Vyvyan Holland. Extracts from the letters of Evelyn Waugh are reprinted by permission of the Peters Fraser and Dunlop Group Ltd.

If, through oversight or failure to trace the present owners, copyright material has been included without acknowledgement, apologies are offered to all concerned and we will happily include acknowledgement in any future editions.

I am grateful to Dick Laurie and Roger Storey for kindly permitting me to publish photographs from their personal collections and I am grateful to News International for photographs numbers 19 and 20. Photograph number 18 is by courtesy of the National Portrait Gallery, London.

At this point, authors usually thank their secretary, researcher, typist, transcriber, agent, therapist or other such assistants. However, throughout the years it took to produce this book, I have never enjoyed the services of such people (apart from one tape – thanks Thea), though some of my friends are saying that a psychiatrist would have enjoyed analysing why Nancy and I remained inseparable for so long . . .

What I have had is a patient, enthusiastic and supremely supportive editor, with whom I've talked (endlessly), argued, laughed and planned. Roz Hopkins must be as relieved as I am (probably more) that the pain of Spain will not be felt again. I would also like to thank Steve Cook, who originally commissioned the book, and to everyone in production and publicity at Cassell, especially Helena Power and Malcolm O'Brien.

I regard 'biographers' who cannot be bothered to do their own research as cheats: if they're not sufficiently interested in their subject to do so, then they should never have embarked on such a project. Apart from any copy-editing mistakes, I take the blame and credit for this book – errors and omissions, facts and figures, chapter and verse – warts and all.

Throughout the years it has taken me to complete this book, I have been fortunate enough to be swept along on a tide of goodwill, support and encouragement. There have been innumerable people who, at different times, have been kind enough to ask, 'How's Nancy coming along?', offering words of kindness, encouragement and support, bottles of wine, meals, tear-mopping tissues, pats on the hand and pats on the back. And, although I have parted company with some, I would still like to acknowledge their contributions:

Firstly, I owe a debt of gratitude to all my former colleagues at the late, great *City Limits* (vintage 1985–90). It was thanks to their wit, wisdom, patience and support that I became a writer.

John and Ros Austin; Neil Bartlett; Sarah Barnett; Sarah Bennett; everyone at BDS, but especially Jen Hollveg, Paula Morris and Nicola Povey; Vicky Blake; Stephen Bourne; Jeanie Brehant; Philippa Brewster, Pat Finn and Candida Lacey, formerly of Pandora Press, for (very) early encouragement; Colin Brownlee of the Cheviot View Guesthouse in Newcastle, especially for his formidable breakfasts; the Brussels Bunch: Jo Brew, Janet McEvoy and Corinne Mulongo; Jane Chomeley and Sue Butterworth of Silver Moon Books; Tim Cole; Fiona Cooper; Sas Elinor; Berta Freistadt; James Gardiner; Liz Gibbs; the GLR Gay and Lesbian London team; Paula Graham; the late Michael Griffiths, *Time Out*; Annabel Hands; Jane Hanna; Alison Hennegan; Chris Holt in Boston; Keith Howes; everyone at the *National Aids Manual*; Jill, Linda and Margaret in Brighton; Julia Jones; the late Brian Kennedy; Liz Kettle; Steve Madison; Mandy McCartin; Lucy McPhail; the late Don Melia; Chris Moller; Nancy Moller; the late Robin Moonie; Sheridan Nye; Gerald Ornstein and Cora Vesey and everyone at Fisher Phillips, on whom I truly 'count'; Jan Ponsford; Lisa Power; Caroline Rees; Colin Richardson; Sarah Schulman; Linda Semple; Ian Shaw; Bill Short; Alan Sinfield; Richard Smith; Karen Stripp; Sophia Chauchard-Stuart; my friends in Toronto, especially Paul Boyd, Andrew Zealey and Lynn Fernie; the late Tom Wakefield, and Frances Williams . . . and to all the other countless people who, over the years, have bothered to keep asking the question, 'How's Nancy coming along?'

Now, at last, you can find out.

And, finally, immeasurable love and thanks go to the current members of my own, purpose-built immediate family, who have loved and supported me through various stages of this book, and without whom little of what I do, or who I am, would be possible:

Thea Bennett, Sharon Boyd, Sue Brearley, Peter Burton, Mark Bunyan and Andrew Craig – 'I knew I should succeed' – Helen Dady, Robert Devcik, Linda Gibson, Tom Robinson, Tom Sargant – 'You can imaaagine' – Val Wilmer . . . and Max and Radcliffe.

'Your Friend is Your Needs Answered'

Introduction

When a funny thing happened to 'a trouser-wearing character called N. Spain' on the way to the Grand National on 21 March 1964, her name, her achievements and her exploits filled the headlines and the airwaves, as they had done throughout her life. The sense of loss was felt not only by those who knew and loved her but by those who had always taken it for granted that they had known her, and that, somehow, she had loved them too: her public.

During the week following her death, the *News of the World*, for whom she had been on assignment when she died, was inundated with letters from ordinary readers, expressing their sorrow. A pensioner from Berkshire said he was 'completely stunned and unashamedly in tears' when he learned of her death. A couple from Liverpool described her as 'a first class reporter. Her articles were so practical and so full of human understanding'. From Bristol, another reader told the paper, 'Through your columns her humour and understanding would penetrate the gloom, rain and mists of many a Sunday afternoon. She was more than a contributor, she was an adornment'. A Belgian admirer described how 'She always gave you the impression she was writing for you personally', while from Dublin one man expressed the sentiments of many: 'We readers have lost a friend; journalism one who brought lustre to her profession'. From Sale, Cheshire, came this more spiritual declaration: 'The dauntless soul of Nancy Spain surely can never die. It is eternal'. And two women in Dewsbury, Yorkshire, sent the simplest of messages: 'We loved her, too'.

The news of her sudden, horrific but spectacular ending left dozens of the nation's finest writers and broadcasters struggling for the words that could capture what one called 'The spirit of Nancy Spain'. When her final book was published posthumously in 1964, the *Sunday Times* reviewer, Jeremy Clive, made his own attempt to sum up what she had meant to so many people:

When Nancy Spain and Joan Werner Laurie were killed seven weeks ago, a few hours after Brendan Behan died in the hospital in Dublin, one had the feeling ... that the individual lights were going out, and that the passing of two of the gayest and most gallant temperaments of our time did indeed diminish life by more than just a degree or so.[1]

It is significant that Clive referred to 'two' and not 'three' temperaments – in death, Joan Werner Laurie was by Nancy's side but, as had been the case throughout their life together, she failed to capture the spotlight, the appreciation or the widespread affection that her life partner had. This wouldn't have come as a surprise to them, or to most of the people who knew them. Indeed, in different circumstances, it was the sort of thing they would have probably had a good giggle about. Only they really appreciated the discrepancy between their perceived public roles and their private arrangements: in public, Nancy may have worn the trousers, but behind the scenes, it was Joan who wore the pants.

If anyone asks the simple question, 'Who was Nancy Spain?', it is impossible to give an equally simple answer. How could it not be, for someone who was a successful amateur sportswoman, cub reporter, radio actress, member of the armed forces, broadcaster, crime novelist, biographer, autobiographer, lecturer, television and radio panellist, book critic, gossip columnist, children's author and illustrator and cookery writer? As well as a loyal friend, a passionate lover of people, places and things and an unlikely co-parent, she was also one of the great communicators of her time, delivering whatever she had to say in an exceptional voice and manner which never sought to patronize or exclude. Her public were generally denied access to the glamorous and eccentric personalities, places and events that were part and parcel of her everyday life. However, she did give them the next best thing: an insider's view of it all which, ironically, was relayed by someone who was herself something of an outsider but who had managed to get under the wire.

Where Nancy Spain went, she took her audience with her. She was like an old friend, who they could enjoy a good gossip with. She instinctively knew what they would want to know, hear, see – and what they would not. With admirable astuteness, she applied the same rules when letting them in to take a peek into her own life and career.

During the course of researching this book, someone who met her only a few times said to me, 'You know, Nancy Spain wasn't that important . . . '. The fact that she would have been the first to agree with him doesn't alter the fact that they were both wrong. Nancy had no sense of her position in the scheme of things, or any great visions of her destiny. She was always looking upwards, but rarely forwards.

It was not simply who she was, or even the diversity of what she did, that made her important; it was the manner in which she – a very particular kind of female personality – did it all, and the framework within which she operated. Subconsciously she sent out far-reaching messages to all the other 'trouser-wearing' characters (male and female) about being themselves, and highlighted the pleasures and perils of balancing a life lived both in the spotlight and the twilight.

During Nancy's lifetime, there were very few male media personalities who could hold a candle to her, let alone women. Essentially, however, she regarded herself as neither – she was, she declared, a trouser-wearing character called N. Spain. Over the years, she offered several explanations for her notorious image: economy, practicality, even self-security were cited as reasons for her eye-catching appearance. However, she was careful to add the rider that 'If I thought that putting a woman into trousers would make a "Nancy Spain" of her, then I would give them up today'. In the 1990s, there has been much talk of 'Indie girls' – young women displaying fiercely independent, idiosyncratic traits, who 'have it all'. If anyone was the original 'Indie girl', then it was Nancy Spain.

Oscar Wilde once said, 'It is personalities, not principles, that move the age'. This was as true of the 1950s and 1960s as it was of the Victorian times he lived in. The *Sunday Mirror* described Nancy as 'one of the outstanding eccentrics of our eccentric times', to which the late Nicholas Tomalin, in the *Sunday Times*, added that she 'was the first real professional Celebrity, in its purest sense', her style 'a mixture of masculine force and girlish chat'. It was this mixture – unique for a woman of her time – that made her so successful, so special and so memorable.

Although she was a notable female product of Britain's postwar era, she would not have been a natural creature of the 1960s. She would have been out of sorts with the decade's dominant themes of satire, scandal and sexual liberation. Symbolically, in October 1964, the year she died, the wind of change blew in Harold Wilson's Labour government, and put an end to what the new Prime Minister called 'the 13 wasted years of Tory rule'. On the other hand, she had always found ways to adapt and thrive, whatever the prevailing mood of the times. Indeed, some of those closest to her felt that she had had enough of England and Europe and was looking for new horizons. One even suggested that she might have followed the hippy trail to India and the Far East; others, that she wanted to develop her career in America.

Certainly, the 1960s would have called for some professional and, possibly, personal readjustment on her part. To what extent she would have continued to enjoy a glittering career would have largely depended on how far she was willing to bend with the prevailing breeze. All the signs were, however, that she would have continued fairly unabated. She had, after all, come out of the steam radio era, adapting with ease to each popular medium of the day – 8-shilling detective novels, radio parlour games, the populist daily broadsheets of Fleet Street, trendsetting and pioneering women's magazines, the compulsive panel shows of the new television era.

George Harrison, reflecting on the parallel careers of the Beatles and Peter Sellers (who himself lampooned Nancy), observed that, unlike the rest of English showbusiness, 'who were happy to rub shoulders with Vera Lynn, we just kept on going for the ultimate experience, and Peter was like that . . . he wasn't just this person from the radio or *I'm Alright Jack*'. Nor was Nancy Spain just 'that woman from the radio' – and she also just 'kept on going'.

Her life and work are the stuff of which biographers' dreams are made. They have everything: celebrity, glamour, humour, unconventionality, gossip, hidden secrets and, ultimately, a tragic and dramatic twist at the end of the tale. But she would also turn out to be a biographer's nightmare: when she went, she left very little behind her, only the simplest of markers which pointed to records of her long and diverse career and one or two aspects of her private life.

The search for Nancy Spain was long and taxing, and it all began, quite unintentionally, in the summer of 1985, at the home of Lisa Power. During dinner she brandished a large, colourful book at me. 'Look what I got for 50p in that charity shop at Highbury Corner!', she said, waving the thing at me. On closer inspection, I saw that it was a copy of something called *The Nancy Spain Colour Cookery Book.*

'Who's Nancy Spain?' I asked. Miss Power stopped in her tracks and regarded me with a look of pure incredulity. 'Don't you *know* about Nancy Spain?!'

I knew there was a double meaning in that word 'know' — it was bad enough that I hadn't heard of this Nancy Spain, but it was obviously much worse that I didn't 'know' about her. From then on, I made it my business to get to 'know' her.

Within a couple of weeks, I too had acquired my own copy of *The Nancy Spain Colour Cookery Book.* Suddenly, bargain-priced copies of Spain books appeared to leap from the shelves of every charity and second-hand book-shop I set foot in. A first-edition copy of *Thank You — Nelson*, still in its original dust-jacket, priced 10p, was found lurking behind a row of books at the rear of one shop. Friends also joined the search on my behalf, at car boot sales, jumble sales and provincial bookshops. For my part, I became an avid index-reader, hunting for the slightest reference to 'Spain, Nancy' or 'Laurie, Joan Werner' in volumes of biographies, memoirs, letters, diaries and historical studies. The most surprising discovery, however, was that no one had written a biography of Nancy Spain.

I should point out that, when all this began in 1985, I was not even a practising journalist, let alone an experienced biographer. The journalism began a little later that year; by 1987, serious — though, at the time, misguided — suggestions were being made that I should write the Spain biography. A publisher expressed interest in commissioning the book, providing I carried out some initial research and put a proposal together. Having made a start, however, other commitments meant that I had to leave Miss Spain on the back-burner — a position she would not have appreciated. But she never really left me. I still kept finding copies of the books and other relevant snippets of information. I visualized a large cardboard box, full of Spain documents, cuttings and photographs that, one day, I would be handed temporary custody of. What I didn't know then — and perhaps it's just as well I didn't — was that although there would indeed be such a box, I would have to find almost the entire contents myself.

When, in 1993, I began work on this book in earnest, the inventory of the original Nancy Spain 'archive' consisted of a couple of telegrams from Lord Beaverbrook; one letter written by Joan Werner Laurie; another from Valerie Profumo; photographs of Joan on her wedding day and ill in bed; a copy of the official crash report from the Department of Aviation; an album containing photographs of Nancy in the WRNS and on holiday; a service sheet from Nancy's memorial and a pair of her cufflinks. Her books, most of them out of print for decades, were only available to peruse in the British Library. Her copious journalism lay tucked away, unindexed, in the bowels of the British Newspaper Library at Colindale. There were no books of cuttings, no diaries, no personal documents, no manuscripts.

In life, this woman appeared to live mostly in the public eye. Yet, as was to become apparent, in death, as in life, many of her tracks had been well covered. Uncovering them involved treading a path that led to many unusual journeys, ludicrous coincidences, remarkable strokes of luck, occasional disappointments and moments of pure, unadulterated triumph.

Investigating the connection between Angus Wilson and Nancy set me on a trail of research which eventually led not only to one of her oldest friends but to her sister, Lady Hulse. Contacting ex-Wrens who had known Nancy during the war in turn led me to women who had been at various schools with her, and to other members of her family. Nancy's appearance at a Foyle's literary luncheon in 1956 resulted in my attendance at one of these events in 1995, sitting five seats away from Margaret Thatcher – one of the strangest threads in this rich tapestry.

It has been said of biography that it can take six months to write one sentence. Doubt this at your peril. It is true, Nancy's second and third volumes of memoirs provided a rough blueprint of her life and work, but they were often irritatingly – and doubtless deliberately – short on specific details and dates of key events. She told us she was editor of *Books of Today*, but neglected to say during which years. Similarly, we knew she worked for the *Daily Express* during the 1950s, but, again, she didn't say in which year she started, or when she left the paper. She even managed to write an autobiography which failed to give her date of birth. There were often wild discrepancies between who, according to Nancy's writings, she appeared to know well and who was actually close to her.

Even material that should have been straightforward to locate took months to find. Take, for example, the reviews of her books: after thirty years, they were no longer in the possession of her publishers, and most of the books only bore their year of publication, not the month. This meant scouring an entire year's worth of Sunday papers for reviews of N. Spain's latest work. Once the month of publication was ascertained, it was then possible to look for reviews in weekly and daily publications. A simple task – except, of course, Nancy wrote twenty-three books . . .

American writer Judith Mayne, the biographer of film director Dorothy Arzner, found a snapshot of Marlene Dietrich, holding a cat, taken in the courtyard of Arzner's house. During the course of her research, Mayne could find no written or other evidence 'of a friendship, an acquaintanceship or an attachment between the two . . .'. Eventually, she came to regard this photograph as a good thing: 'it reminds me that no individual life is completely knowable by everyone else'. The same is true of Nancy Spain.

In 1957, she declared that 'History . . . is nothing but legend, gossip and hearsay'. In rediscovering the life and times of Nancy Spain, I have tried to go well beyond this traditional triumvirate. In doing so, I have inevitably raised some ghosts. But, as Nancy herself once wrote, somewhat rhetorically, 'It is the truth that is important, surely?' I couldn't agree more. I hope, then, that with this book, I have also managed to lay some ghosts to rest.

Rose Collis, May 1996
London

'Nancy ... A Gipsy Name'

Charles Williams, *The Greater Triumphs*

Trouser-wearing characters are mostly born, not made. Towards the end of her life, Nancy Spain was quite happy to accept both credit and blame for the creation of 'a trouser-wearing character called N. Spain'. But, as she was growing up, and being educated and groomed to don the apparel of what she called 'the role of young lady from the provinces',[1] she was waiting for an opportunity to slip into something more comfortable.

The appearance of 'square-peg' children in families is often initially greeted with acknowledgement and a protective nurturing only to be replaced by attempts to force them into round holes once adulthood beckons. 'Where did they come from?', goes the cry, as though the family themselves have played no part in producing the child's quirks and quaint-nesses. But no family throws up someone with a razor-sharp brain, a versatile pen, seductive charm, unconventionality and boundless energy without the existence of prominent forerunners. Nancy Spain's case was no different.

At first sight, hers seemed like any other solid, northern middle-class Conservative family – inheritors of a strong sense of patriotism and duty, and dividing their energies between farming, industry and military service. Nancy certainly shared some of these values but, in truth, her family could boast a fulsome share of unorthodox and notable personalities and talents. It is not simply that she was, as Sarah Freeman in her 1977 biography of Isabella and Samuel Beeton said, merely continuing the family's 'long tradition of black sheep'. She was a composite character, formed out of all the more outstanding features of her forebears. There were the more traditional virtues so beloved of families like the Spains: industriousness, loyalty, patriotism, artistic talents and an affectionate nature. But there was also ambition, rebelliousness and a maverick streak that embraced all things emotional and sexual – and, of course, her image, that visual trademark which virtually guaranteed lifelong notoriety. As one of her closest friends was to say, 'Nancy looked like a gypsy boy – and she behaved like one, too. She was a pirate'.

This particular pirate waged war against a predetermined destiny, carved in stone for generations of young ladies of respectable middle-class North-umberland families. She would have none of it. 'Newcastle was always reality to me', she wrote. 'My main root is there, drawing strength from my rebellion against middle-class provincial society, against the giving and taking of merchandise in marriage, the pathetic routine of bridge party and back-biting, jealousy and "keeping up with the Joneses"'.[2] Her admiration lay elsewhere.

> The North Country working class have always been my heroes and heroines. . . . I know I am in danger of romanticizing these men and their women, and their blind obstinacy in staying put, jobless and unyielding, living like slobs on the dole in the only place that is real to them. But I love them deeply, with all their faults.[3]

Nancy Spain loved the city in which she was born, displaying a characteristic Geordie loyalty and pride that stretched back through the centuries of Newcastle's existence, from when the Romans built a bridge across the Tyne in AD 122 with a fort at one end of it, as part of the defence of Hadrian's Wall. Eventually, the conquering Romans were replaced by the conquering Saxons and, after the conquering William took the crown of England, the town was fortified by his son Robert who built a new fort, the 'New Castle', in 1080. Apart from a ten-week occupation by the invading Scots, Newcastle flourished through the centuries as a city of commerce and industry, with coal and shipbuilding at the centre of its prosperity. In the nineteenth century W.G. Armstrong established his armaments and shipbuilding businesses at Elswick; George Stephenson set up the first ironworks on Tyneside in 1826 and the Durham and Sunderland Railway was opened in 1836.

By the end of the eighteenth century, its wealthier citizens had begun to move out of central Newcastle and into suburban areas such as Westgate. This trend continued into the nineteenth century, when other suburbs developed, including Heaton and Jesmond.

Jesmond had originally been called Jessemuth, then Jesumound. In the mid 1200s, the Grenville family of Jesmond built St Mary's Chapel on the site of a holy well and the Shrine of Our Lady of Jesmond subsequently developed into a place of pilgrimage. Jesmond became part of the city of Newcastle in 1835. Before then it was merely a village, until Tyneside's more affluent families started to move there in droves: between 1851 and 1911, Jesmond's population rose from 2,100 to 21,400, becoming one of the more desirable suburbs of the city. It was home to many of the city's prominent shipbuilders in the late nineteenth century: Charles Mark Palmer, Charles Mitchell, Henry Swan and G.B. Hunter. Its fields were transformed into streets of substantial brick houses, which became a feature of the area. In 1836, Jesmond Cemetery was built on the main Jesmond Road. The final resting place of many nineteenth-century local dignitaries – architects, writers, engineers and artists – it became known as the 'Tyneside Père Lachaise'.

The beginning of Jesmond is marked by the Parish Church, erected in 1861 and subsequently the place of worship for the Spain family. Jesmond was an all-faith district, boasting a synagogue, a Lutheran Church, a Church of Scotland, a Presbyterian church and a Quaker meeting place. Children born in Jesmond Vale were well spoken, with soft Tyneside accents. Their parents would tell them cautionary tales of the Boojum of Jesmond Vale, a large mysterious animal that was reputed to stalk the local parks. Brindle-coloured, slim and agile, with a head like an Alsatian, it was rumoured to be a cross between a wild dog and a deer and its legend terrified generations of Jesmond children.

The focal point of the area was, and is, Jesmond Dene Park. It was adapted from the natural dene of the Ouseburn into a park of outstanding beauty by Lord Armstrong, who lived in Jesmond Dene House. He subsequently made a gift of it to the Newcastle Corporation in 1883. The park was officially opened by the Prince and Princess of Wales in 1884; since then, it has remained a popular local day out for generations who have walked by its hanging woods, rocky gorge, waterfall, stepping stones, rare shrubs and the ruins of the thirteenth-century Old Mill. The Armstrong Road Bridge was built at one end of the park, linking Jesmond Dene and Heaton, 65 feet above the dene. But while the Dene represented a green, spacious, exciting day out for most Jesmond youngsters, the children of one of its families also had a vast area of Northumberland as their extended playground. For one of them, it was the manor unto which he was born.

Nancy's father, George Redesdale Brooker Spain, was born in the Redesdale Arms in the village of Horsley, by the River Rede, on 23 June 1877. He was the second son, and youngest child, of George and Georgiana Louisa Spain. Their eldest son, Walter Smitheyt, was then nine; their first daughter, Katherine Stewart Spain, was eight and their second, Mary Palliser Spain, seven. At thirty-three, George Spain had married 24-year-old Georgiana Stewart on 26 June 1866 at St Clement's Church, Sandwich, in Kent. They both had distinguished fathers: Smitheyt Spain was an eminent gentleman farmer of Hacklinge, and Thomas Dilnot Stewart was a captain in the Royal Navy, who had discovered the mutineers from the *Bounty* living on the Pitcairn Islands.

George Spain was born and raised in Kent, where he worked for his father. He was also a captain and adjutant of a volunteer corps, which served under its major, the then Lord Northbourne, Walter Henry James. In 1873, Spain was appointed the land agent to the Northbourne estate, a position he held for the rest of his life. The estate, which included thousands of acres of land in the Redesdale Valley area of Northumberland, was run from an office in Mosley Street, Newcastle, and for many years, George and his family lived at 10 Victoria Square, on the edge of Jesmond.

He was a solid Church of England conservative who became a high-ranking Freemason and 'As a lecturer on the craft, he was well-known in the North of England'.[4] He and his family lived in one of the city's most prosperous streets: their neighbours included corn, wine, timber and glass merchants, solicitors, shipbrokers and doctors.

The family divided their time between their country home at Otterburn, near Horley, the town house in Jesmond and Smitheyt Spain's farm in Kent. As a boy, George Spain junior spent much of his childhood fishing – often accompanied by a tame pig which followed him everywhere – and shooting on the estate which his father ran. His gentler hobbies included a lifelong love of history (particularly Roman) and antiquities: in 1901, he joined the

Newcastle upon Tyne Society of Antiquaries, remaining a member for over sixty years. He also had a love of poetry (a quality later passed on to his youngest daughter) and wrote verse. One poem was a love song to the countryside he was born and raised in:

> Here where the dark cloud shadows flit
> And dreams of sunshine alternate.
> The curlew trills her liquid note
> Unto her distant wheeling mate.
> Again in Spring   The little burns
> Dance down to join the ancient Tyne
> And all along the old Black Dyke
> There is a stirring in the land. If only we
> Could understand the dreams of old Northumberland.[5]

His mother, Georgiana, wrote on country matters in a series of articles for a publication called *Our Quarterly Record*. A collection of these pieces was published in 1910 by Mawson, Swan and Morgan as *Jottings from a Corner*. It was dedicated to Lord Northbourne, and illustrated with paintings by his son, the Hon. Walter J. James. The pieces dealt mostly with gardening, birds and bee-keeping. She also wrote about her two cats, Donner and Blitzen.

George junior grew into a tall, though short-sighted, young man. He was educated at Eastbourne College then, in 1898, aged twenty-one (despite his bad eyesight) he became a second lieutenant in the 3rd Volunteer Battalion of the Northumberland Fusiliers, a regiment dating back to the late seventeenth century. His brother Walter would also serve as a major in the army, before leaving for Rhodesia, where he first worked for the Chartered Company and later joined the Rhodesian police force.

During the latter stages of the Boer War, in July 1902, George was made a captain and commanded the 4th Volunteer Service Company of the Northumberland Fusiliers, part of the Infantry Brigade, in action in Natal. The Fusiliers had served throughout the conflict, suffering losses at Belmont, Klerksdorp and, most notably, at Nooitgedacht in December 1900. The 300 men were ambushed by the Boers in the mountains; 100 of them were killed and the rest taken prisoner when their commanding officer, Captain Yatman, surrendered. George acquitted himself honourably and was awarded the Queen's Medal with five clasps and, with his comrades, was made an Honorary Freeman of the City of Newcastle. A war memorial was erected in 1907 in Newcastle's Haymarket to the Fusiliers who fell during the Boer War.

Meanwhile, his sister Katherine was pursuing a more unconventional career: she became an actress, adopting the stage name of Katherine Stewart, and left for an acting career in America. At one time, she shared a flat with Faith Stone, later Faith Compton Mackenzie, wife of the writer Sir Compton Mackenzie. Mary Palliser Spain, or 'Aunt Maimie' as she would become known to Nancy, was 'the last of the English gentlewomen'.[6] She always dressed in black, carried a parasol in summer and was an avid consumer of the *Sunday Times* crossword. She had been friends with Aubrey Beardsley's sister, Mabel. 'There are few of us, looking back to our childhood, who cannot recollect the figure of some well-loved maiden aunt',[7] her famous niece would later observe.

George Spain senior died on 10 September 1906 at home in Newcastle. He had been staying in Bellingham the week before, when he was taken ill. He was brought back to Newcastle, but emergency surgery failed to save him. He was cremated and his ashes interred in what was to become the family grave at Holy Trinity Church, Horsley. He left an estate worth £11,284 to be administered by Georgiana, George and his nephew, Frank Smitheyt Hodsoll. He left his wife 'all watches, jewels, trinkets, wearing apparel, furniture, plated goods, books, glass, manuscripts . . . wines . . . consumable stores' and £500. Walter was bequeathed his shares in Taylor's Malabele Gold Fields Ltd; George received the unprincely sum of £100, while nephew Frank was left £50. After his debts and funeral expenses were settled, the residuary of George's estate was, after his wife's death, to be placed in trust for his two daughters, who would receive an income while they remained unmarried.

George junior succeeded his father as full-time land agent for the Northbournes. Georgiana continued to live at Netherhouses, a small house on the estate. Her near neighbours included Lord Redesdale and his six daughters, better known as the Mitford sisters. George now spent most of his time in Northumberland and, during a weekend shooting party in 1910, he met a young woman whose remarkable family would provide the other essential threads that combined to produce its most outstanding – and trouser-wearing – character.

Nancy's mother's family, the Smiles, included among its many strands the author of the world's most famous cookery book; an admiral; a philosophizing engineer who would pen a book later to prove inspirational for Britain's first woman prime minister; and an MP who would drown in an infamous shipping accident and be succeeded in Parliament by his daughter.

The story really begins with Henry Dorling, the Master of Epsom racecourse. He married twice, first to Emily, with whom he had two sons and a daughter. Then, with his second wife, Elizabeth, he raised an enormous family of thirteen: seven daughters (Charlotte, Helen, Lucy, Alice, Edith, Eliza and Amy) and six sons (William, Alfred, Frank, Walter, Lionel and Horace). From her first marriage, to Benjamin Mayson, who had died in 1841, Elizabeth also had a boy and three daughters: John, Bessie, Esther – and Isabella Mary.

Henry and Elizabeth Dorling's oldest daughter Charlotte, born in 1843, was to start quite an impressive mini-dynasty herself. She married General Charles McMahon and their daughter, Edith, became the wife of T.H. Keyes in 1909. Edith subsequently had five children: Rory (1910), Rosemary (1911), Lavender (1914), Patrick (1918) and Michael (1921). Their uncle was Admiral Lord Keyes and their cousin, Lieutenant-Colonel Geoffrey Keyes, later became a hero of the Second World War, leading a famous attempt to capture General Rommel in the Western Desert in November

1941. Keyes was fatally wounded in the attack and posthumously awarded the Victoria Cross.

Charlotte would take her children to see their unmarried Mayson aunts, Bessie and Esther, who had pronounced London accents and wore chains around their waists on which hung keys and small purses, which they would dip into to 'tip' the visiting children with presents of money.

Lucy was a bridesmaid when her half-sister Isabella Mary married Samuel Orchart Beeton on 10 July 1856. Her new husband was an enterprising publisher: from his premises in 18 Bouverie Street, he launched the *English Woman's Domestic Magazine* in 1852. This monthly magazine was a pioneer of the middle-class women's magazine market. It included reports from Paris on the styles and fashions of the day, even offering an exclusive pattern service for readers so they could make their own *haute couture*. After her marriage to Sam, Isabella began to contribute to the magazine, writing on domestic matters. Sam Beeton eventually sold the magazine to Ward, Lock and Tyler in 1879. In 1861 the Beetons began publishing *The Queen* (Queen Victoria herself gave them permission to use the regal half of her name, and the masthead boasted a drawing of Windsor Castle). It was a magazine aimed at wealthy women of leisure, covering such items as top society news, clothes and travel. Still in circulation a century later, it was merged with *Harper's Bazaar* in October 1970.

But, of course, it was the modestly titled book, published in 1861, that would make a legend of the name Beeton. Beeton's *Book of Household Management* (1861) started life as a series of articles in the *English Woman's Domestic Magazine*, spread out over twenty-four monthly parts between 1859 and 1861. 'Edited by Mrs Isabella Beeton', it was a 46-chapter book that included not only 3,000 recipes but all the information and basic skills required of the middle-class Victorian wife and hostess, from 'Arrangement and Economy of the Kitchen' to 'The Art of Carving at Table'. It is a popular, and misinformed, late-twentieth-century myth that Mrs Beeton's recipes were all about 'traditional', hearty Victorian English fare. In fact – decades before her time – she included sections on a diversity of culinary culture, including vegetarian, South African, Italian, Indian, even Australian. *The Book of Household Management* was an instant success, selling 60,000 copies in its first year, no small achievement for a 21-year-old woman who was still recovering from the death of her first child.

Of all her relatives, it was her great-aunt Isabella Nancy was particularly proud of and whom she would refer to most frequently in her own published works. She said of the Beetons:

> I think they both had the sort of charm that goes with sincerity. Both were hard workers, never procrastinated an hour, or dawdled away an idle day. For her relations, who had always depended so much on her vitality, Isabella left a gap that no one could fill.[8]

She was, of course, appreciating the very qualities which she shared with them and recognized in herself. But, for all his talents, Sam Beeton was also something of a fickle entrepreneur, always living beyond his means and looking for a way of escaping from his circumstances. When Isabella was pregnant with her last child, Mayson, Sam left her to carry most of the burden of their publishing work while he fought to avoid bankruptcy – a burden which almost certainly contributed to her premature death shortly after Mayson's birth. When she first became ill, Sam would still go into her sickroom and bring her up to date with the latest news of his financial problems. He was, however, genuinely heartbroken when Isabella died on 6 February 1865, aged just twenty-eight; he survived her by only twelve years.

Isabella's half-sister, Lucy Dorling, married into another family of industry and 'big' ideas. Her husband was the second son of one of the men who came to personify the values and ideals of his age, Samuel Smiles, described by his granddaughter Aileen Smiles as 'a real Victorian'.[9]

Samuel 'Self-Help' Smiles was born in 1812, in Haddington, East Lothian, the third child of Samuel Smiles, a merchant, and his wife Janet Wilson. Smiles senior died of cholera in 1832, leaving his widow with eleven children to raise (three others had died in infancy). In 1843, Samuel junior eloped and married Sarah Anne Holmes Dixon; they had three sons and two daughters. Samuel abandoned his aspiration to be a painter and instead studied to be a surgeon at Edinburgh University, subsequently practising medicine for several years in Haddingtonshire.

In 1838, he switched careers and became editor of the *Leeds Times*, a job he held until 1842. He eventually became secretary of the Leeds and Thirsk Railway, then of the South-Eastern Railway from 1854 to 1866. However, his first book was devoted to quite a different subject: *Physical Nurture and Education of Children* was published in 1835 as an antidote to the then high infant mortality rate (one-third of all children died before they were five years old). Smiles advocated plenty of fresh air, exercise and vitamins.

He became friends with Charlotte Cushman, the American-born actress and her partner, the poet Eliza Cook, exchanging many letters about health. The two women were described as 'a pair of those women friends, so common in the old days . . . [who] would solemnly give each other Mizpah rings'.[10] The friendship with Smiles was an unlikely one: Cushman was 'big and masculine looking with a deep voice. She had no sex appeal'.[11] While this may have been true for men, it certainly was not for Cushman's succession of female lovers, including Cook.

Samuel started writing leading articles for the *Edinburgh Weekly Chronicle* and began to travel – first Germany, then London – continuing to produce books on a regular basis. The *Lives of George and Robert Stephenson* was published in 1857 and he also wrote a five-volume work, *Lives of the Engineers*. Then, in 1859, came the book he would become synonymous with: *Self-Help*. Its origins lay in a series of evening talks he used to give to the working men who became his patients when he returned to life as a provincial doctor in 1855. 'Every human being has a vast destiny to accomplish', he told them. 'Knowledge is of itself one of the highest enjoyments'.[12]

The Smiles philosophy was built on one main ethos: that hard work equalled success. *Self-Help* was full of thoughts along these lines, such as ' "It can't be done" is the ruin of men and of nations' and 'Energy accomplishes more than genius'. On the subject of popular literature, Smiles had this to say:

> There is almost a mania for frivolity and excitement which exhibits itself in many forms in our popular literature. To meet the public taste our books and periodicals must now be highly spiced, amusing, and comic, not disdaining slang, and illustrative of breaches of all laws, human and divine.[13]

No doubt his great-granddaughter's books would not have received the Smiles seal of approval.

Self-Help became one of the most popular books of the Victorian era, selling 20,000 copies in its first year. At just one annual trade dinner, to which publishers would invite booksellers, 10,000 copies were sold. By 1889, it had sold 150,000 copies and been translated into seventeen languages. In Hungary it was called *Smiles' Pearls*; in Italy *To Will and Be Able*; and in Argentina, *The Social Gospel*.

Smiles's philosophy of 'self-help' was put to the test when, in his sixties, he suffered a stroke and had to relearn how to speak, read and write. This accomplished, he went on to write thirteen more books. He died on 16 April 1904, aged ninety-one, at his house in Pembroke Gardens, Kensington. Three days later, he was buried in Brompton Cemetery where his tombstone reads, 'Samuel Smiles, author of Self-Help'.

Lucy Dorling married William Holmes Smiles, Samuel's second and least favourite son, in 1874 at St Saviour's Church in Pimlico. They settled into a gabled Edwardian villa called 'Westbank' in Strandtown, a suburb of Belfast, where Willy had become a tea agent. He subsequently set up an insurance company, Lowson and Smiles, and then went on to build the Belfast Rope Works. But he and his family were never considered to be good enough to be accepted as 'grandees', part of Belfast's elite society.

Lucy and Willy had eleven children, eight boys and three girls. They were, according to Nancy, 'a flamboyant family . . . with mad enthusiasms and enormous personal attraction'.[14] The fifth son, Walter, was the epitome of the Smiles ethos of self-improvement and achievement: he won two DSOs, was knighted for his work in India and became an MP, posthumously succeeded by his daughter, Patricia. The youngest girl in this enormous family was Norah Elizabeth, born on 23 March 1886 in Strandtown. With dark hair and green eyes, she was, according to Nancy, 'the beauty of the Smileses'.[15]

Lucy loved the outdoor life and Willy was a devotee of swimming, particularly sea-bathing. 'If the Downs are good for young horses, they're good for young children', she declared.[16] So, in true Smiles fashion, there were lots of long, healthy walks and frequent visits to the seaside, where the large family would go for walks along White Rocks Sands at Portrush. Grandfather Samuel loved the company of his numerous grandchildren and always had plenty of buckets and spades at the ready to use on their days out. He was always concerned about their health, occasionally with good cause: little Norah lost one of her fingers in an accident involving a mowing machine.

Still keen to be accepted by Belfast's elite 'grandees', Willy Smiles vetted some four hundred English girls' schools before finding one he considered suitable for his daughters. He eventually settled on the Wimbledon House School for Girls – known as Roedean – in Brighton, Sussex. The Smiles sisters all went there in turn. Norah's sister Lily, a keen pianist, stayed on to become one of the junior music staff at the school, even composing its song, 'Wimbledonia':

> Cricket, tennis, swimming, drilling
> Thy dear colours, blue and white
> 'Public Spirit' is thy motto
> School of love and school of might
> Wimbledonia – fair and free
> Health and strength belong to thee
> Felix Wimbledonia.[17]

It proved to be her swansong: Lily died, aged just eighteen, of rheumatism of the heart.

Her father Willy was not destined for a long life either: he died at Newcastle Golf Club, aged just fifty. Lucy continued to live at Westbank. Norah and her second oldest sister, Aileen, played hockey for Ulster. Aileen led a somewhat nomadic life: she drove through Eastern Europe on her own, worked as a pastry cook in New York and as a cook-cum-laundress in Australia before, at the age of seventy-seven, writing the life story of her grandfather Samuel.

According to their eldest daughter, George Spain and Norah Smiles met at a shooting party held at Hesleyside, a small Northumberland village to the west of Bellingham, in the valley of the North Tyne river: 'My mother was at school with the hostess and my father was friendly with the family'. The couple were married, at St Mark's Parish Church, Dundela, not far from Lucy Smiles's house, on 14 July 1910. Norah was given away by her eldest brother, John Holmes Smiles; George's sister, Katherine, was one of the witnesses. The lavish reception was held in a marquee on the Smileses' rose-festooned lawn at Westbank. They returned to Newcastle and set up home at 18 Haldane Terrace, Jesmond, a few minutes walk from where George's parents had lived in Victoria Square. It was here that their first daughter, Lucy Elizabeth Smitheyt Spain, was born, on 13 August 1911.

Life for the new Spain family was secure and happy. Norah looked after their house and daughter (throughout their married life, she never worked outside the home). According to her eldest daughter, 'She never had a job and I think she should have had. She was quite clever'. George carried out his duties for Lord Northbourne and became more involved with the Newcastle Society of Antiquaries, going on excavations and giving talks.

But the indications of events that would shatter the Spains' tranquil life were already emerging. In 1912, George became a lieutenant-colonel of the 6th Battalion of the Northumberland Fusiliers (TA). Being the officer of a battalion of volunteer soldiers at that time may not have seemed like a hazardous enterprise. But no one then could have foreseen how much the

British Empire would depend on its volunteer regiments during its worst crisis, nor what a terrible price they would pay for their courage and loyalty.

In January 1914, the British Regular Army comprised fewer than 250,000 men throughout the Empire. Thus, when war was declared on 4 August 1914, the basic units of the 'New Army' were the 'Service' battalions, consisting of volunteers who signed up for three years or the duration of the war, whichever was the longest. These battalions were attached to already existing, six-section regiments. The 1st and 2nd Battalions were Regular Army; the 3rd and 4th Reserve; and the 5th and 6th were designated Territorial Force (TF). The Territorials were part-timers who trained at their local drill halls in the evenings and weekends and at summer camps. By 1910, over 250,000 men had joined TF units. Officers, like George, and non-commissioned officers came from the Volunteer Regiments.

On 10 August 1914, the TF units were invited to volunteer for overseas service and, by the spring of 1915, many of them were already on active service abroad. By the end of the war, 318 TF units had served in the field. George and his battalion were to undergo a terrible baptism by fire: they were sent to fight in the second battle being waged outside a town in Belgium whose name had already become synonymous with the worst of what war could offer: Ypres. The first battle of Ypres had taken place throughout October and November 1914, accounting for much of the Regular Army, plus some of the new Territorial battalions. In all, over 50,000 British soldiers had perished. With this grim statistic still fresh in their minds, George and his battalion of volunteers left for the killing fields. With him was his batman, Fred Powell, whose wife, Tilda, became nanny to the Spain baby, Elizabeth.

The second Battle of Ypres was fought during April and May 1915. The Allies had learned that the Germans were installing chlorine gas in the forest behind their lines. They chose to ignore this information, and on 22 April 1915 at 5 p.m., the Germans duly released the gas and advanced, halting just outside St Julien, a small village near Ypres. The next night, the Allies mounted a counter-attack, and on 24 April, the Battle of St Julien commenced, involving fierce house-to-house fighting. George led his men of the 6th up the line, under heavy shell-fire, into battle. At 4 a.m. that morning the Germans released more chlorine gas. It attacked the lungs and bronchial tubes, causing vomiting, violent coughing and shortage of breath. In some cases, the lung tissues deteriorated quickly, causing a dreadful, painful death. Others affected by it died a slower death, which sometimes took years.

On 25 April, German artillery shelled the Allies throughout the day and eventually the Germans took St Julien. On the night of 12/13 May, the Reserve Divisions pushed forward again. The Germans released more gas on 24 May, but the British line held – at a cost. The casualties numbered 59,275 British, 34,933 German.

Ypres was a shattering experience, even for the most battle-hardened troops. Years after George's death, Nancy wrote that only then had she begun 'to have any understanding of the gay, imperious, romantic character who went so cheerfully to war and returned, uncomplaining but deeply shocked . . . '.[18]

On Tyneside, the horrors of war were being brought closer to home: in April and June that year, the German airships L9 and L10 dropped nearly one hundred bombs. They fell mainly on the South Shields area, killing eighteen civilians and causing extensive damage. Meanwhile, George's terrible year continued with the death of his mother. Georgiana died at Netherhouses, Otterburn, on 27 July 1915 and was interred in the family grave at Horley. She left George her furniture; everything else in her meagre £972 estate went to her daughter, Mary. The dividends and interest on her stocks and shares in the Royal Assurance Company were to go to her sister, Mary Campbell Stewart.

In the spring of 1916, more of Britain's New Volunteer Army arrived in France and were sent to the French sector of the front line, north of the River Somme. George and his battalion formed part of the 149th Brigade, a section of the 50th (Northumbrian) Division (TF). The conditions were grim: 500,000 men were living in tents amongst the mud, and mass graves were being dug.

The Battle of the Somme lasted from 1 July to 18 November 1916. Heavy Allied shelling had had little effect on the German lines there, and during the first day alone, the British forces suffered 57,540 casualties. Over a million men from the British Empire and the French and German armies were killed, wounded or captured. For this cost, the Allies gained six miles of ground.

On 15 September, George and his battalion were involved in the Battle of Flers-Courcelette, supporting the 4th and 7th Battalions who had been sent forward. On 17 September – a hot, muggy day – the 50th Division went on patrol during the Battle of Thiepral Ridge. It was George's last major battle. He returned home, his hearing badly damaged. He was duly awarded the CMG (Companion of St Michael and St George) 'in recognition of his military services on the western front'.[19]

The experiences of war had changed him a good deal. According to his daughter, Liz, he never talked about the war, and, as Nancy observed, 'when my father came back from the war he closed his mind to the world and its intrusions'.[20] He would only reopen his mind to the horrors of those years at the battalion's annual reunion dinners held every April to honour their fallen comrades.

Norah was one of the lucky women whose husbands returned from the war, mostly sound in limb, if not in spirit. But she and her family had suffered their losses: her brother, Alan Smiles, was killed on the Somme in 1916, followed by brother Sam who perished at Ypres in 1917. George remained officially in service, but would retire from military duty before the end of the war. He was awarded the Efficiency (Territorial) Decoration (TD) and returned to the relative peace of attending to the Northbourne estate, his antiquaries, his Roman coins, his poetry and his books – and a new baby.

George and Norah's second daughter was born at a private maternity home, Rose Villa, 1 Archbold Terrace, on 13 September 1917. They named her Nancy Brooker Spain – Brooker, for her father, and Nancy, 'A gipsy name', according to the writer Charles Williams.[21] It couldn't have proved more appropriate.

★ ★ ★

The new baby was baptized at Jesmond Parish Church on 26 October 1917, by the Reverend G.D. Oakley. Not long after, the family moved from Haldane Terrace to 7 Tankerville Place. Tilda Powell helped Norah with the new child for the first six months before leaving the family's service. 'She was a dear little girl – she was so pretty', remembers her sister. 'When she was born, she was a rather dark-red child with a lot of hair sticking up. She was absolutely lovely – tiny, with little pink cheeks and brown curls and eyes'. Nancy thought she looked like 'a little Japanese doll'. Big sister Liz 'loved having a baby sister. I used to look after her. She was in my charge, really. We got on very well, but we were completely different. She was very masculine and I was very feminine'. A photograph taken of four-year-old Nancy showed her 'with beautifully brushed hair, and a row of coral beads, already fighting to escape my fate in the shape of my blue sash and dainty white lace party dress'.[22]

Nancy remembered her girlhood at 7 Tankerville Place (tel. Jesmond 275), a large red-bricked terraced house, as 'a happy, safe childhood in a safe, warm brick attached terrace house like about nine million others'.[23] Their neighbours at number 9 were the family of Mr Woolf, a Jewish art dealer.

Compared to some of the families in Jesmond, the Spain family 'wasn't exactly poor, but, on the other hand, it wasn't exactly aristocratic'.[24] 'I always had enough to eat, I always had lovely toys',[25] remembered Nancy.

George continued to administer the Northbourne estate from the office in Mosley Street in the heart of the city. But it also became, apparently, 'a regular clearing-house for archaeological intelligence, available to all ... who had a concern for the antiquities of Northumberland and Durham'.[26] At home, he had a vast collection of tokens and medals, stamp albums, topographical prints of Northumberland and Newcastle, and notes and sketches of accessions and discoveries of the Society of Antiquaries. He became the first, and only, honorary secretary of the North of England Excavation Committee, formed in 1924, and produced a number of important, meticulous and ground-breaking reports on the region's Roman excavations. His society colleagues admired 'his eagerness, his accuracy, and the lucidity of his style'.[27] This was best demonstrated in his piece 'Thoughts in the Street',[28] a humorous description of Newcastle's archaeological features. Discussing the head of the river god, Tyne, at Akenside Buildings, he mused, 'One wonders why the beard of the god should be so carefully plaited. Is this a usual method in a river deity?'

In 1928, he wrote a radio play, *Bridge of Tyne – A Fantasy with Five Episodes*, in which he portrayed Tyne as an old man. It was broadcast by BBC Newcastle in October that year, on the eve of King George V's visit to the city to open the new Tyne Bridge. Set in AD 123, the play had a narrator and a large cast; the music was written by Tyneside composer Oliver Tomlinson and performed by the BBC Orchestra. It told the story of the River Tyne and the various bridges built across it, starting with the Emperor Hadrian's prayers for his new Pons Aelius and his hope 'that the future may bring prosperity and trade to this new port'.[29] Nancy recalled how writing this play

> must for him have been the supreme escape. He hid himself in his bedroom and locked the door against all comers, surrounding himself with sweet smelling fragrant pipe smoke (Lambert and Butlers Log Cabin) billowing from beneath the door. I can well remember that I was vexed because the 'sacred work' obviously came before me. Emotional my father obviously was. And he tried to be disciplined. This I have inherited from him, together with the occasional efforts at controlling the magic gush of feelings in pieces shaped as verse.[30]

Earlier that year, George had also arranged a number of monthly broadcasts, under the title *Glimpses of the Past*, which dealt with phases of Newcastle's earliest recorded history.

The Spain girls adored both their parents, but it was George who retained a special place in everyone's affections. 'He was very well known in Newcastle', recalls Liz. 'He wrote lovely poetry. He was marvellous – very clever and very quiet'.

Nancy recalled that

> 'worm-eaten' was a favourite expression of my father's, which he used with great affection, slapping us hard between the shoulder blades, remarking 'worm-eaten snail' or 'rorty pets' as he did so. Even now I hear the echo of his voice in my sister's personality and my own.[31]

One of his friends from the Society of Antiquaries, John Cowen, called him

> the gayest of companions. Wherever he went gusts of laughter would fill the room. His *joie-de-vivre* seemed unquenchable. He combined an entirely boyish sense of fun with a whimsical turn of humour, often directed against himself, of the most sophisticated quality. Above all he revelled in the ridiculous, which he could find in any personality or any situation, however unpromising. He ... led with verve and gusto a life of uncommon achievement.[32]

Half-named after her father, it seemed that George's youngest daughter was destined, in more ways than could be coincidental, to be the son he never had – something that suited both their personalities. It is a theory his eldest daughter subscribed to: 'Oh yes, I think so. I think they wanted a boy, anyway. She was very masculine in her outlook on everything'. Nancy would share George's mischievous sense of humour, his love of poetry, his strong sense of duty when the call to arms came, an encyclopaedic knowledge of literary references and, of course, an excellent command of English. Even their handwriting was similar. 'How lucky I am ... to have been the daughter of such a man, to have known him, had his friendship, enjoyed his company, taken pride in his bravery', said Nancy. 'If all women (and men, too) had a father like mine the world would be a very different place'.[33]

Norah, for her part, seemed content for her husband to have a busy, fulfilling life outside of the home. Her primary concern – like her parents before her – was to ensure that her children grew into physically robust young women, in the Smiles tradition, and had the best education that could be afforded by a middle-class family of modest means. Nancy believed her mother was keen for her and Liz to 'Get On In Life' – as befitted the more industrious, ambitious, Smiles side of the family – and that she was disappointed by her clever, gentle husband's lack of ambition. Nancy thought 'she spent most of her life with our father in a state of violent frustration'.[34]

Norah's friends were mainly from the nearby Portland Park tennis club, where the sport was of rather less importance than the social life that came with it. Women members held weekly tea parties, taking it in turn to provide the dainty, crustless sandwiches and the crispy gossip. George was unimpressed with the Portland Park set: 'I'm beastly deaf and don't care for social meetings' was his opt-out clause.[35] Nancy always attributed this antisocial nature to his wartime experiences. 'He withdrew from life almost to the same degree as I now run to meet it', she observed. 'I embrace where he turned from all its horrors, betrayals, triumphs, disloyalties, delights and revelations of affection'.[36]

Apart from a periodical row, Nancy remembered that life at home was pleasant and comfortable: 'the only very occasional unpleasantness were a few skirmishing quarrels between my mother and my sister. . . . They both had big personalities. It was quite impossible to take sides or to know what they were quarrelling about'.[37]

Number 7 Tankerville Place was, as you might expect, crammed full of books: everything from children's classics such as *Treasure Island* and *Robinson Crusoe*, *The Wind in the Willows* and *Huckleberry Finn*, to Shakespeare and Greek and Roman mythology – ample fuel with which to stoke any child's vivid imagination, and Nancy was no exception: 'In my mind's eye it was seldom "nowadays". Usually I was a charioteer, 400 years BC, forearms ringed with heavy gold bracelets . . . or else I was a powder monkey in the Victory at Trafalgar'.[38] The family's library, together with her father's passion for literature, also engendered the beginnings of her own lifelong love affair with books: 'My father was the literary influence in our life'.[39] Kipling was his favourite and he would spend hours reading his short stories and poems aloud. Together, he and Nancy would read Wilde's poem, 'The Sphinx', carefully learning it by heart. George also taught his children respect for books, uncharacteristically meting out punishment if they scrawled in any of the precious volumes: 'My father would take his evening slippers and he would lam into us for spoiling a book', said Nancy.[40]

While George's youngest daughter was nurturing a love of literature, his eldest was already showing a flair for a different art: sketching. 'I always used to draw clothes', Liz remembers. 'I would get hold of the envelopes when the post arrived and draw clothes on the inside of them'. Her baby sister, however, was fascinated by less genteel objects: 'The funny thing about it was that this pretty little girl, all she used to do when she was growing up was draw motorcycles. I was absolutely horrified – I didn't like anything like that'.

★ ★ ★

Then, as now, Jesmond was memorable for two things – 'lots of schools and churches', according to Liz. And she and Nancy got plenty of opportunities to become acquainted with all the local landmarks:

'My mother was determined that we wouldn't grow up to be little townies, so we had riding lessons. I remember Nancy was run away with – she was on a little Shetland pony and it galloped all through Jesmond to get to the stables. And we used to have to go for a walk every afternoon – it was rather dreary. There was a cemetery near the house; we would walk through that and then over the Town Moor'.

According to Nancy, on some of these walks, she and Liz 'would play a game called Weddings. I hated it. "Describe your Wedding Dress", my sister Liz would say. And away she'd go'.[41] Nancy's idea of a good game, apparently, was St George and the Dragon: George played the dragon, Nancy was St George, on a wooden horse, and sister Liz 'was lashed to the bottom of the stairs with skipping rope and scarves'.[42] 'I was considered a sickly brat', Nancy explained, 'and my mother used to hurl me across country with the Newcastle and District Beagles, hoping that five mile bursts . . . would put colour in my cheeks and blow the wheezes from my chest. Beagling is a cruel sport. This never occurred to me at eight years old'.[43]

There were other, more pleasant outings, however. Long, leisurely walks through Jesmond Dene; days spent at the seaside on the spread of beaches at Cullercoats and Tynemouth, where the enormous statue of local hero Admiral Collingwood towered over the Black Middens bay; and trips to the funfair at Whitley Bay. When Nancy was nine, her parents bought her a miniature golf bag and set of clubs, though she didn't become a fan of the sport until some thirty years later. Several summer holidays were spent at Hesleyside, where George and Norah had first met. There were visits to nearby Tarset Castle and, for Nancy, the more primitive delights of looking for skins shed by adders and grass snakes, and swims in a pond called the Wynd Burn Lynn.

Once Nancy was old enough for the journey, the children would spend the holidays in Belfast at their grandmother's house. It was a long trip that involved travelling to Stranraer to catch the Larne ferry, the *Princess Victoria*, where Nancy would first experience the seasickness that would plague her throughout her life. She said she found the visits to Westbank 'terrifying, what with the gardener who had fits and was often found unconscious beside his hoe: and the strange tales "of shootings in the bad times at the bottom of the garden" '.[44] But she did spend happier times with the multitude of Smiles cousins, including uncle Walter's only child, Patricia (later Lady Patsy Fisher), who was three and a half years younger than Nancy. In her young cousin, Nancy found an instant audience for her attention-grabbing antics, including demonstrating her precocious knowledge of literature. 'I was always impressed with her', Patsy remembered. 'She was so clever and bright. I just sat and gazed at her with admiration'.

When Liz was sent away to boarding school, Norah and Nancy would take their walks alone. Occasionally, there would be some – unexpected – light relief: when Nancy was about six years old, she and Norah were walking through the park when they heard someone shout 'bugger'. 'What's that?', Nancy asked her obliging mother. 'It's where one man puts his thing up another man's bum and jigs up and down', she told her daughter. 'I laughed so much I had to hold on to the railings', Nancy later told a friend.[45]

Nancy's slightly more conventional education began in the first of a series of *crème de la crème* educational establishments. The private school in Windsor Terrace – one of many in Jesmond – was run by the Misses Thompson and Potts. The pupils wore little white panama hats trimmed with a purple and white band. Lessons, Nancy remembered, seemed to be taught primarily by chanting: French, geography, even religious knowledge. This, she was convinced, helped foster her impressive capacity for memorizing facts, names, even entire conversations. Apart from this, the best aspect of attending Miss Thompson's school was that she could stay at home. The worst thing about her next school was that she couldn't.

Sister Liz, for her part, had already been dispatched, aged eleven, to Roedean, where she was expected to live up to the standards set by her mother and aunts. After all, if an aunt loves the school enough to write its anthem, what could possibly be wrong with it? According to Liz Hulse, almost everything.

> 'It was a ghastly school. Terrible. I hated it. It was very tough and revolved around playing games, and I'm very bad at playing games. I didn't learn a thing, because the classes were too big. It was a very big school, a prep thing for the younger children and then four houses'.

In what appears to have been a decision reached 'by mutual consent', Liz left Roedean in 1925, after just three years. According to Nancy, the headmistress, Emmeline Tanner, wrote admonishingly on her last report 'Will do well, when she learns discipline'.[46]

Miss Tanner would have been horrified by Liz's next school, Mayortorne Manor, a farm school run by Marjorie Fry, Roger Fry's sister, where there was no emphasis on games at all. 'You looked after the animals, which was much better', remembers Liz. 'I passed all my exams at that school'. Armed with a School Certificate with Honours, she returned to Newcastle. 'I just got on with drawing and went to art school', winning first a scholarship to study at Durham University's King Edward VII Art School, and then, aged sixteen, for the Royal College of Art (RCA), when, as her sister observed, she 'went plunging off to the great wicked Metropolis'.[47]

After a few years' chanting at Miss Thompson's, Norah's next choice for Nancy was a boarding school. Runton Hill (subsequently Runton and Sutherland) was situated at West Runton, a village that lies between the north Norfolk seaside towns of Cromer and Sheringham. It was hardly a convenient place to get to from Newcastle, involving several changes of train, and was certainly a long way for a nine-year-old to be sent. The school itself had three houses: North, South and Bryntirion, known as 'Bryn'. This villa-type building was situated almost a mile away from the other two houses and was ruled over by a Mrs Lipscombe.

Nancy shared a small dorm, 'Blue', with a girl called Frances Sherwood, the niece of the poet James Elroy Flecker. Next door to them, in the larger 'Pink' dorm, was Sally Horrock, the head of Bryn; Pamela Schiele, the niece of Runton Hill's headmistress, Miss Janet Vernon Harcourt; and a musically gifted girl called Viola Tunnard. Nancy admired her 'fine Byronic profile and a lock of hair worn in one real tortoiseshell hair-slide . . . '.[48] Viola could apparently play piano better than Mrs Lipscombe and often accompanied the girls' hymn-singing sessions. She would become better known as accompanist to Joyce Grenfell on her concert tours of the 1940s and 1950s.

On Sunday mornings, the pupils would troop to church in Sheringham and then go for long walks through the woods at Runton where lay the site of a Roman camp. Here, Miss Vernon Harcourt would make them play a game she had invented called 'valley netball' – a rather rough sport that pitched one house against another, and usually resulted in an impressive array of injuries. 'Turning ankles, scratched faces, bruised torsos. That was the very least of it',[49] Nancy recalled. There were less dangerous, local excursions to Blakeney, where the girls took boat trips to look at the bird sanctuary and, if they were lucky, the seals.

Records of Nancy's time at Runton Hill no longer exist, but her own recollections of the school don't give the impression that it offered much to harness her well-developed imagination to productive work. She was more interested in the Apollo-worshipping cult she devised with Frances Sherwood, which seemed to consist of frequent bouts of illicit fire-lighting in the gardens of Bryn.

When Nancy was about eleven, Norah learned to drive and the family acquired a navy blue tourer. The famous walks became less frequent as day trips out in the car took their place. Occasionally, there would be attractions closer to home, particularly in the summer of 1929. Newcastle was hosting the North-East Coast Exhibition of Industry, Science and Art, designed to demonstrate that the region, though already beginning to show signs of the depression and industrial decline that would devastate it during the next decade, had much to shout about.

The exhibition architects assembled a dazzling array of futuristic buildings on part of the Town Moor, including the Palace of Engineering, the Palace of Industry, the Palace of Arts, a 1,400-seat Festival Hall, a Garden Club and a stadium that would seat 20,000 as well as housing the Women's and Artisans' Pavilions. These proved to be two of the most popular sections of the Exhibition. The Women's Pavilion contained continuous displays of arts and crafts, including pottery and enamelling. In the Palace of Industry, visitors could enjoy the working displays of carpet-making and the manufacture of tin cans. The Bull Park was renamed Exhibition Park and its lake was the site for a model boat competition.

The Palace of Engineering housed the region's heavyweights: Vickers Armstrong, Parsons and Swan Hunter. The local press joined in the fun: the *Evening World* provided a pavilion which showed off Malcolm Campbell's Bluebird and the Supermarine S6 seaplane, which could reach speeds of over 350 m.p.h. The Amusement Park boasted a Great Water Chute and a mile-long Himalayan Railway, constructed 80 feet above the ground. The most dubious exhibition was the African Village, where native people from Senegal put on an 'exhibit' of their daily lives, complete with mud huts. The exhibition was opened on 14 May 1929 by Edward, Prince of Wales, and closed on 26 October, by which time nearly four and a half million people had visited it.

There were other outings that summer. Norah took her to Stratford to see *Othello*, which prompted the question, 'Please, Mummy, what is a strumpet?'[50]

Meanwhile, the 'sickly brat' was turning into a slightly more robust adolescent: 'I was all hips and thighs, and where would I put those large red hands?', she wondered.[51]

For two years, hips, thighs, hands and all attended the Central Newcastle High School for Girls in Eskdale Terrace, a Girls' Public Day School Trust establishment set up in 1895, and situated a few minutes' walk from Tankerville Place. Its prospectus stated: 'Stress is laid on the formation of character by moral and religious training and on fitting girls for the practical business of life'. There was plenty of emphasis on physical activities: as well as gym and fencing lessons, 'Each girl in the School is drilled three times weekly'. One former Central pupil who attended with Nancy, Shirley Roberts, remembers it as 'quite a special sort of school, with all the same type of girls'. Or, almost the same. 'Each form had four scholarship girls who, poor things, stuck out like sore thumbs'. But overall it was, apparently, 'a very happy school ... the teachers stayed there for donkey's years ... we wore brown tunics and cream blouses, brown stockings, shoes, hats and blazers'.

The daughters of many well-known local families attended the school: Esther Armstrong who, as Esther McCracken, would become one of Tyneside's most popular writers and actresses; Lucy Pumphrie, of the famous Pumphrie quality grocery business family; the elder sister of young Billy Hardcastle who, as William Hardcastle, would also make a name for himself as a broadcaster; and the daughters of the Mowbray-Thompsons, a Quaker family who lived in Lindisfarne Road. One of them, now Mrs Helen Cottee, remembers Nancy as 'flamboyant, even then. She was tall and dark, and good at games. She was a very dynamic character – my sisters were rather frightened of her'.

The tall, dark and frightening Nancy also made quite an impression on Shirley Roberts. 'There was something about her, right from the beginning. She had a certain aura about her, even when she was a youngster. When I saw her [on TV] in her white turn-up collar and cravat, she had even more'. Shirley Roberts's mother and Norah also got to know each other while their daughters were at Central: 'Her mother was an absolute character. She said to my mother once "The only way now I can be with my friends is to go and sit on a tombstone in Jesmond Cemetery"'.

Meanwhile, in 'the Metropolis', sister Liz was making great strides at the RCA and forming a lifelong friendship with a young man who would also become entwined in Nancy's life.

Geoffrey Wright was a gifted young musician, composer and designer. Educated at Stowe, he was due to go up to Cambridge in 1931. However, he decided first to spend three months in Munich, 'ostensibly to learn German but, needless to say, one got into a set of young American and English people'. One of the young women he met there was Eileen Diver, whose brother had also been at Stowe; one of her friends was Liz Spain, now studying dress design at the RCA. Wright recalled how his relationship with Liz developed:

'I was – always have been – passionate about two things: my music and my theatre designing. When I was at Cambridge I designed every undergraduate production I could get my hands on. Liz would come up from London and see the shows. She became my unofficial girlfriend for a time. At that time I wasn't sure which way my sexual interests lay and was, slightly, trying to be conventional and thinking "Well, I really must make an effort". I was lucky enough to meet Liz, who didn't mind one way or the other; we became very firm friends and I saw rather a lot of her. She was great fun. I used to go to Christmas dances at the RCA as her partner. We used to go to the Chelsea Arts Ball, dressed up to the nines in costumes'.

On one occasion, their outfits had a circus theme: 'Lizzie had a black trapeze artist's costume, which in those days was quite daring. She had a friend called Joan, who went as a white mouse or something . . . '

Liz and Geoffrey got a chance to show off their respective skills in the Footlights Revue of 1934, which had an all-male cast. 'It was rather spectacular', he remembers. 'I wrote a lot of the music and Lizzie did a lot of the costumes. . . . She was an awfully skilful designer – she could have turned her hand to almost anything'. This would not be stage design, however; instead, after graduating from the RCA, Liz became a top designer at Dorville's, an upmarket wholesale clothes company based in London. 'Lizzie had escaped', was how Geoffrey Wright saw it. Back home in Newcastle, however, her younger sister's immediate future had been decided – and there was no 'escape' for her just yet.

'School of Love and School of Might'

from 'Wimbledonia', Roedean School song

Inevitably, the heavy weight of the female family tradition fell on Nancy and, in September 1931, she headed for the school with which she would forever be associated. It was an association that neither school nor pupil would ever be entirely happy about. 'Dear me. How I disliked that anonymous school in Sussex',[1] was how Nancy put it.

The 'anonymous school in Sussex' that became a byword for the education of 'gels' from affluent middle- and upper-middle-class families had, indeed, started life as a fairly anonymous school in South West London. Fearegg House, in the Wimbledon Park area, was home to Dorothy, Penelope and Millicent Lawrence, three sisters in a family of fourteen children. Their father, a barrister, had built the new house to accommodate his burgeoning brood. The children were educated by private tutors and at private schools and, unusually for that time, all the girls were given the opportunity to go to college. Penelope Lawrence, the eldest, was one of the first women students at Cambridge and later became Principal of Froebel College, while Millicent Lawrence was an active suffragette.

In 1881, Mr Lawrence had an accident which put an end to his career and the family was faced with running an enormous house and family on no income. And so the three elder Lawrence sisters decided to turn their home into a school, taking day girls and boarders. By 1885, it was well established and they decided to move to Brighton, which had become a popular centre for private education. The sisters pooled their resources and talents, even borrowing money from the parents of pupils and former pupils, and opened the Wimbledon House School in a rented house in Lewes Crescent, Brighton. Eventually, the school expanded to include two more houses in Sussex Square. A fourth sister, Sylvia, became one of the art teachers.

In the school's prospectus, the Lawrences said that 'The leisure of the pupils is very carefully organized'. They weren't joking: the girls seldom saw life beyond the school grounds and any 'outside hours' contact between pupils and staff was also forbidden.[2] The prospectus emphasized this disciplined approach:

> We wish in the first place to give to physical education and outdoor exercise their due place in every girl's life. Secondly, to train each girl to independence

and self-reliance, and with that view to give as much liberty as can be granted with safety. And thirdly, to supply a sound and careful intellectual training to each girl.[3]

The curriculum comprised divinity, English, foreign languages, arithmetic and mathematics, science, art and craft, music, domestic subjects and physical education; this remained unchanged for seventy years. It proved to be a winning formula: within ten years, the school had gained a reputation that put it at the top of the shopping list of all affluent middle-class parents who wanted their daughters to have the best education money could buy.

Wimbledon House School was bursting at the seams and the Lawrences decided they needed to relocate to new, purpose-built premises. To the east of Brighton, perched up on the chalky cliffs overlooking the English Channel, lay acres of land in a small valley called Roedean Bottom, home mainly to grazing sheep. This, they decided, would be an ideal site for their new building, especially as it would provide plenty of spacious playing fields for the energetic games by which they set such store. Funds were begged and borrowed, and architect John Simpson (later Sir) was commissioned to design the new building; it was to be completed in readiness for the autumn term in 1898. It was the Lawrences' wish that the spirit of the school – the attainment of the highest standards in all things – was reflected in its architecture. So Simpson gave it ornamental towers, cloisters and quad-rangles, while the gym had arched wooden beams and the school chapel was resplendent with white marble and gold inlays.

The Lawrences decided that their grand new school should have its own coat of arms and badge, which was duly granted. The result shows a young deer standing on a hilltop against a background of silver and blue, represent-ing the sky and the sea which it overlooked. The deer wears a collar – the collar of 'wholesome rule' – and it is bound to the Book of Learning by a golden Chain of Kindness. On its shoulder rests the golden Gridiron of Saint Lawrence, patron saint of its founders, which would give each girl a lifelong mark of teaching. The motto reads: 'Honneur aux Dignes' (say it out loud!) a line also included in the school song, composed, of course, by Lily Smiles in 1895:

> Honour the worthy
> And honour the keen
> Honour her daughters
> And honneur aux dignes.

There were four houses in the new school, all identical, and each with its own carved panel bearing the name of the Lawrence sister who was its housemistress. In addition, there were two prefects per house and a matron. When Norah was a pupil, the Misses Lawrence were still in charge. Norah was in House 1, where Dorothy Lawrence was housemistress, from 1902 to 1904. Her elder sisters, Aileen and the unfortunate Lily, had been pupils at the old Lewes Crescent building.

The Old Roedeanians Association was set up in 1900. In 1924, the Lawrence sisters retired; by then, however, a fifth, Theresa, had opened up a second Roedean establishment, in Johannesburg, and Dame Emmeline Tanner took over as headmistress in Brighton. After the First World War there was a large influx of new pupils to the school and, in 1920, a new storey had to be built on each of the four residential houses. Miss Tanner inherited a number of long-serving teachers, some of whom would stay there for thirty or forty years: Miss Macswiney; Mrs Jeffries, the medical officer; Miss Florrie Hill, a laboratory assistant; and Miss Mellanby, house-mistress of House 2 for twelve years, a jodhpur-wearing English teacher who was a particular favourite with her girls over the years.

Despite her mother's wish that she follow the Smiles tradition and go to Roedean, Nancy was always surprised at the decision, as it had not been cheap to send one daughter there, let alone two. Annual fees totalled £200 per girl, and there were extra charges for individual music and fencing lessons, laundry, school books and stationery. By virtue of Norah and her sisters having attended the school, the Spain daughters were granted bursaries of around £70 a year, but this did not help a great deal. However, some savings were made by Norah making Nancy's djibbahs herself. These curious garments had been discovered by the Misses Lawrences while on holiday in the Middle East. Nancy described a djibbah as 'a becoming garment on the lean (or English) type of girl, [which] has short sleeves and hangs, ungathered, like a tabard, from the shoulders. Fat girls, however, did not look their best in them . . . '.[4] Families more affluent than the Spains had their Roedean girls' djibbahs made specially by Debenham and Freebody's or Liberty's, at 10 guineas each.

Approached from behind, Roedean is virtually hidden. But when you do finally see it, you wonder how this could have been possible. The sheer enormity of the place is startling: it looks less like a school and more like an entire city – an Eastern European principality, perhaps – that has been transported from another age, and set down in the little valley on the clifftop. There it stands, a pink and beige empire unto itself. Which is, of course, precisely what it was supposed to be.

Nancy started her four years at Roedean in the autumn of 1931, just before her thirteenth birthday. 'I'm sure both my mother and father thought they were doing their best for me',[5] she said. Her first impression of her new school, she later recalled, 'was the smell of polish on the floors'.[6] She found it

an extraordinary real, narrow, intensified world. . . . The place is part of the most private self, where roots were set to grow for five long years. The years between twelve and seventeen are very long. Roedean is the place where I decided upon a certain outlook, discovered where I might go for pure knowledge, and first tried to settle down in a world that was not my own cosy home. At school there is no kind mother with a motto 'My children, right or wrong' . . . there is no proud father to sustain his daughter who is 'so clever' or 'so good at games'.[7]

The Roedean day began at 7 a.m., with breakfast at 8 a.m. Before this, the girls had to make their beds and tidy their rooms. Sporty types would also leave themselves enough time for some cricket or lacrosse practice. Prayers were at 9.10 a.m., followed by the first 'forty' (each lesson lasted 40 minutes). Games – mainly cricket in the summer, lacrosse in the winter – took place in the afternoon. After tea, there would be prep in the Senior or Junior rooms, supper at 7.30 p.m., in bed by 8.40 p.m. before Matron did her 'lights-out' tour. There was a misapprehension amongst the townsfolk of Brighton that the girls at 'the College', as it was known, all had their own horses and were waited on by teachers summoned by the ring of a bell.

Each year was divided into three forms, A, B and C; Nancy was in class A and in House 1. The separate houses didn't mix much, except in classes. However, Nancy still managed to make an impression on girls outside House 1. Beryl Lucey had more contact with her later on as an 'Old Girl', as they had been in different houses, but she remembers the Spain sisters well: 'Liz was a friend of my sister, Anne – I think she was a very naughty girl. Nancy was very bright – she was in the "A" class – but a bit OTT. Even then she had an eye for the main chance'. The actress Noel Dyson (most famous as Ken Barlow's mum, Ida, in *Coronation Street*) also retained not-so-fond memories of Nancy: 'I didn't like her; I thought she was incredibly pushy'.

Another Roedean contemporary was Pamela Howley (now Clatworthy), Gertrude Lawrence's daughter by her brief and early marriage to Francis Howley, a talent scout from Blackpool who was twenty years her senior. Nancy and Pamela were in different houses, and Pamela cannot remember exactly how their paths crossed. But, given Nancy's lifelong attraction to celebrity, it wouldn't be surprising if she had deliberately sought out the daughter of the most celebrated female star to grace the West End and Broadway during the 1920s and 1930s. As she admitted, 'my love of Celebrities was basely pandered to at Roedean'.[8] As well as Lawrence and her various escorts, including Douglas Fairbanks and Leslie Henson, some of the 'gels' were related to other famous faces: pupils included crime writer Edgar Wallace's daughter, Penelope, and the niece of band leader Henry Hall.

Pamela Clatworthy remembers Nancy as a fascinating person, even in those early years:

'I have her to thank for introducing me to what then seemed rather modern music . . . Debussy, Ravel, Satie . . . and to poets of whom I had never heard. There was, even then, something exotic and un-English about her. And as I was a "fringe intellectual", I was drawn to her as she was so much brainier than I!'.

Gertrude Lawrence's visits to Roedean during term time were, according to Nancy, 'infrequent, but spectacular. . . . She gave one of the best performances as a "mother" that I have ever seen'.[9] Many years later, in a radio tribute to her mother, Pamela Clatworthy observed:

'She was a very good mother in that she saw I had the best of everything – marvellous clothes, holidays, governesses and good schools. When I saw her she was very devoted, very loving. I absolutely adored her passionately. She was great fun and there was a great deal of glamour, especially at boarding school, having a beautiful, glamorous mother coming to visit you at weekends'.

One year, the girls staged *The Trojan Women* as the Colour Play (chosen and performed by pupils who had won 'colours' at sports). Lawrence came down to Brighton to watch Pamela perform in the play, during which the Cricket First XI, doubling up as members of the Greek army, over-enthusiastically stormed the stage and fell into the school orchestra.

Pamela also recalled a more serious incident involving Nancy:

'I once was nearly expelled because of a piece of poetry I wrote to Nancy. It seemed a perfectly innocent work. How it fell into the hands of Miss Tanner, the headmistress, I shall never know – but it certainly upset her! I seem to remember that with theatrical melodramatic "faked" remorse I tore it up before her eyes'.

Nancy took note of Miss Tanner's reaction to Pamela's entirely innocent jottings and kept her own odes well hidden, from staff and schoolmates alike. As she would later observe, 'The private life of a schoolgirl is an extraordinary and secretive thing'.[10] 'As I grew healthy and put on weight and escaped inwards, daydreaming, my subconscious and unconscious mind was driven underground'.[11] So much so, that she decided to keep a poetic diary of her moods, thoughts and affections.

From one of the Roedean stationery cupboards she procured several stiff-backed exercise books and, on the inside cover of each one, wrote the title, 'To Please Myself'. 'This meant, of course, get out, keep off, this pleases me but it might not please you. And it was definitely not intended for publication'.[12] Indeed, apart from a few carefully chosen couplets included in one of her *Woman's Hour* broadcasts in 1956, nothing was published during Nancy's lifetime. But, by a curious quirk of fate, one of these battered blue books, containing the neatly written, imaginative and revealing poetic thoughts of the teenage Nancy, survived. In a radio broadcast, she dismissed the book as 'truculent' in attitude and the poems themselves as 'turgid'. But she did not reveal to her listeners what precious and painful memories the book contained, especially about her post-Roedean years, or the reasons why, despite her publicly avowed embarrassment, she kept them until her death.

She described how during the years at Roedean, 'I longed with all my heart for someone to hero-worship: a hero, a heroine upon whom to model my personality, my character'.[13] Her wish wasn't to be granted, but she still found some subjects which inspired her to put pen to paper. Sometimes they would be verses bereft of any teenage soul-searching, merely rather dry responses to everyday events of school life. One, undated and untitled, was prompted by a school outing:

We started off it seemed at crack of dawn
We staggered round the flats, and patient stood

Beneath a lashing wind not to be borne –
Yet one thought cheered us – that of picnic food
To be enjoyed within a sheltered – verdant wood –
Perhaps some lucky ones might even feel quite fat –
But then Miss Batho said (not meaning to be rude)
Miss Batho said she did not like my hat.

We ate our lunch – sung all we had not sung
We spoiled the countryside and danced around it nude
Ruined her picnic and upset the young
Took useless photographs and lettuce chewed –
Yet we maintain that we were never crude,
And no exception could be held to that –
But dear Miss Batho coldly us reviewed –
And she confirmed she did not like my hat.

In 'The Last Forty' (June 1934), she bemoans the tediousness of sitting through the day's final lesson during the summer term:

The dusty sun in patches on the floor – and the interminable and bee-like drone
Of some old mistress talking more and more – I wish she'd leave this glorious air alone.
A vagrant breeze, heavy with vague sweet smells, stirs in my hair and turns the atlas page
And then the chanting of unnumbered bells turns into happiness my seething rage.

Doubtless, the disrespect shown by calling a member of staff 'some old mistress' would have been enough to incur the wrath of Miss Tanner. But it was Nancy's poems to a mystery woman – possibly a visiting French teacher – known only as 'T.C.C.' which would have sent a quiver through the quads. Most were written during her final spring term in 1935:

Dear lovely lady in whose changing eyes
I once saw captured all I thought was mine
My love of life – my conquest of the wise –
In a strange pagan flame three fourths divine
Could I once more behold that haunting light,
I would give life itself to set it where
The holy lamp might burn by day and night
And I, in exstacy [sic] might stand and stare.

(27 March 1935)

And, again just to 'T.C.C.':

I was so far removed from you, dear queen,
In those drab weeks since last you smiled at me
Miles of drear ocean and gray land lay in between
I was alone – not in tranquillity –

Only at night when darkness covered all
I felt, perhaps, a little nearer you –
Night is omnipotent, an all embracing hall
And large enough, lady, to contain us two –

(8 April 1935)

One of the final poems to T.C.C. was written on 6 July 1935 just before
Nancy left:

Perhaps the very last thing I shall write
Will be a song for you to sing
of the queer places where you found delight
and how you sought them to the world to bring –
And how a few who looked into your eyes
Saw there a hundred things they never dreamed
When the quiet morning smiled upon the skies.

But there were some who never shall forget
the beauty of the golden things you brought:
Ronsard, Du Bellay, Cervantes, and yet
was it for love of them their art you taught?
Was it to place in a dim lock an opal key
and by its turning send us in the quiet groves
like children to explore their fadeless dignity?

Other forbidden items, apart from love poems, were kept skilfully
concealed by the Roedean girls: food, radios, even gramophones. One of
these belonged to Phillippa Crosby, daughter of a South African millionaire,
later to marry the author Nicholas Monsarrat. Crosby, according to Nancy,
was 'the only truly whacky character I encountered all the time I was there
. . . girls and staff at Roedean were without exception high-minded, pure-
souled conformists. Most of the time they couldn't make out what I was
laughing at'.[14] Apparently, Crosby would play Fred Astaire records in her
bedroom after 'lights out', using a pin instead of the gramophone needle to
evade the detection of an ever-alert Matron. Nancy and Crosby were once
sent out of the classroom for giggling during a scripture lesson, presided over
by headmistress Emmeline Tanner. Generally, however, life at 'that strictly
anonymous exclusive dump in Sussex'[15] was no laughing matter for
Nancy.

She was not impressed by the readiness with which pupils informed on
each other to the teachers. She did, however, acquire the famous 'Roedean'
accent – expressed and exploited to its fullest advantage in her radio career
– losing the last vestiges of any Northumberland lilt. She also threw herself
into Roedean's traditional pursuit of games, excelling at cricket and lacrosse,
and competing at tennis with slightly less skill but great enthusiasm. But, like
Liz, she felt it was teaching her little. 'I learned very little at my schools', she
said. 'Because I have a fast mind and an unusual memory I fooled the

examiners. I knew all the time, and I bet they did too, that it was all a trick'.[16]

Nancy consoled herself by retreating into the works of her favourite poets – her beloved Verlaine, Wilde and Gautier – and filling the pages of 'To Please Myself'.

> The instinct to turn inwards and take refuge in my own became, at this school, an instinct of self-preservation ... I was in heart and mind almost constantly elsewhere ... I very seldom, at that time, gave my own future a thought. ... How unfortunate for my poor mother and father who sent me there, so hopefully and making such sacrifices to pay the fees, that I should have been so grim in my rejection of it and all (as they say) it stood for.[17]

She developed something of an adolescent's morbid fascination for the odd murder and suicide that took place near the school. The chalky cliffs, she maintained, were nearly as popular as Beachy Head for dramatic endings. She also remembered – almost fondly – a notorious 'trunk murder' on the Downs, when the police were unable to find the head that belonged to the remains concealed in a large case.

Occasionally, Liz, now working as a designer for Dorville in London, would come and take her sister out to tea. During the holidays, Nancy would return to Jesmond, happy and relieved to be home. And there were other annual events which broke the endless cycle of fifty 'forties' a week, games, games and more games. One Saturday every June, the school held its speech and prizegiving day, to which an establishment luminary was invited to preside over the ceremonies. In 1932, it was Lord Gobell, President of the Royal Society of Teachers, who gave a speech on the 'increased freedom of women'. The following year, the Lord Chancellor, Lord Sankey, and his daughter gave out the prizes.

In his speech, Sankey congratulated Roedean on playing 'a remarkable part in the great movement for the higher education of women'. However, he also added that 'in spite of the many attractive avenues which were now open to girls', he hoped that 'the majority of them would not desert the path of simple duties and home life'.[18] Unfortunately, Nancy's response to Sankey's hopes is not recorded anywhere.

In 1934, most of the speech day proceedings were dominated by thoughts of the next year – Roedean's Jubilee. Miss Tanner announced plans for the forthcoming celebrations and fundraising: it was hoped, she said, that a cheque would be presented to the School Council which would pay off the £40,000 debt still outstanding on the newer school buildings. £8,000 had already been raised. That November, the Roedean Jubilee Ball, a fundraiser held at London's swanky Dorchester Hotel, marked the beginning of the festivities.

1935 was also special for Nancy: it was her final year, and she surprised everyone (but mostly herself) when, for the first time, she actually won aschool prize. It was for a poem – carefully chosen from 'To Please Myself' – called 'Waking (A Picture from Edmund Dulac)', written in the previous November.

Beautiful Ming, daughter of Woo, solemnly smiled at the sun,
Opened her eyes and blinked at the cherry, and felt for her satin toed shoe;
Beautiful Ming, with eyes like black almonds, felt that her life had begun
When a filagree petal, exquisite and white, brushed on her eyelids and
  vanished from sight, curving and fluttering it sailed with the wind, and
  dipped to the dust in the light.

Beautiful Ming, daughter of Woo, curled in luxurious ease,
  raised one frail hand like the filigree petal, and approved of a world that was
  new;
Beautiful Ming saw indefinite flowers, dropping like snow from the trees,
  smiled once again at the yellow cheeked sky, heard with dim pleasure
  the bird music die,
Slid to oblivion with dew on her cheeks and a sensuous exstacy [*sic*].

This ode to 'Beautiful Ming' impressed the Roedean judges and, as Nancy
duly noted in her exercise book, it won her a guinea. She later reflected,
'This must have given me the idea, untrue, that poems get printed and do
make money'.[19]

On Jubilee Day itself (25 July) the guest of honour was Princess Alice,
Countess of Athlone. Old Roedeanians came from all over the world, and
crowded into the enormous marquee erected on the south side of the school.
Newnham College sent a message, wishing 'long life and prosperity to
Roedean'.[20] Eight members of the Lawrence family were also present,
including Theresa, founder of the South African Roedean, and her brother Sir
Paul Lawrence. He told the audience about the days before the school moved
to its current site, and the ensuing scandal when his sisters hired a field in
Kemp Town for the girls to play their hockey, cricket and lacrosse. 'That girls
should play these games and be visible to people passing along the road was
considered wholly improper',[21] he recalled. Princess Alice declared that the
Misses Lawrence and their school had 'transformed the education of girls in
the country ... had made its influence felt throughout the whole of the
Empire'.[22] The head girl, Margaret Woodward, thanked her and presented her
with a souvenir of the day – a piece of pottery made and fired at the school.

The celebrations continued throughout the weekend: the Saturday was
largely devoted to sporting events and, in the evening, 800 guests attended
a private dinner at Brighton's Grand Hotel and were addressed by speakers
including Miss Gaskell (a former pupil, then in her nineties) and Theresa
Lawrence. Sunday's events included a thanksgiving service in the school
chapel in the morning, attended by 1,000 pupils, Old Roedeanians, teachers
and parents, and – a rare treat – a display of Greek dancing by some of the
girls. Furthermore, it was announced that over £15,000 had been raised
towards paying off the Roedean debt.

Old Roedeanians, it seems, either love or loathe their old school. Apart
from Nancy, other notable ORs include the actress Sarah Miles, who was
firmly of the 'loathed it' persuasion; Baroness Lynda Chalker (then Bates),
who was head girl when Miles was there and on whom, apparently, Miles
had a crush; *Guardian* TV critic Nancy Banks-Smith; Ursula Betts who, in

1942, led a guerrilla force of Nagas in India against the Japanese; Margery Fry, who became Principal of Somerville College, Oxford and a leading advocate of penal reform in the 1920s and 1930s; and actress Jill Balcon, mother of Daniel Day-Lewis.

Noel Dyson 'loved it and learned nothing. But I started acting while I was there, though I always played old men. It was very strict; we weren't allowed within ten yards of the fence and we weren't allowed to go into Brighton without our parents'. Jill Balcon remembered that the only men they saw were the groundsmen and the boot boy. Nancy Banks-Smith later recalled that it was the misfits of her era who seemed to do well for themselves: 'It was as though kicking violently against the regime sent you into some kind of eccentric orbit'.[23] And though Nancy's kicking may have been rather less than violent, in later life she certainly got a lot of mileage out of being a 'Roedean rebel'. Even in her forties, she still publicly ridiculed the school whenever she got the opportunity. In February 1959, she took part in a debate at the Oxford Union on the middle classes. She proceeded to treat the gathered throng to a hearty rendition of the Roedean school song, declaring, 'That's why I'm against the middle classes. Can you imagine my parents paying fees for me to learn that stuff?'[24]

After Roedean, Pamela Howley (Clatworthy) was sent to Brillantmont, an exclusive finishing school in Switzerland where, by a curious coincidence, Maria Seiber (later Riva), Marlene Dietrich's daughter, was also a pupil.

There was a final, ironic coda to Nancy's Roedean years: the ever-popular Miss Mellanby created headline news – not to mention a few sniggers from the more rebellious Roedean elements – when she left Roedean the same year to become the governor of Aylesbury Borstal. The sniggers increased when, in the 1950s, she became an Inspector of HM Prisons.

So Nancy left Sussex and returned to Jesmond, to her attic bedroom with its collection of china dogs and horses. That August, she wrote the morose poem 'An Apology':

> If any remnant of my verse should live
> and please a few as much as it please me –
> they will not find that I had truth to give
> Except when that lay in frivolity
> They might find there a little joy,
> a little aimless trapping of a mood –
> some vagrant tune, some fragile useless toy,
> but there will be nothing holy; nothing good.
>
> But all I ask is that some day my song
> May find a resting place in someone's hand,
> who might perhaps not think it wholly wrong
> to write of little things, and understand.

After leaving Roedean, Pamela Clatworthy (then Howley) was briefly at RADA. On one occasion she invited Nancy to dinner at the rented house near Smith Square she shared with her mother. The other guest was Douglas Fairbanks Jnr – no doubt a thrill for the celebrity-adoring young Nancy. But it was her appearance that made the day memorable, as Pamela recalled: 'We were taken aback when Nancy appeared in mannish clothes. She wore a skirt – her jacket, shirt, tie and shoes were all those a man would wear'. Taken aback they may have been, but Pamela was still, at that time, oblivious to what Nancy's attire represented to the outside world. Only much later did she realize:

> 'This will make clear that even then I had no true concept of what a totally lesbian relationship could be. Our knowledge, in my youth, was entirely based on a reading of *The Well of Loneliness*. Our affections were simply schoolgirl "crushes". Later on, I had occasion to realize that there was a physical component involved which I found totally unacceptable'.

Nancy kept minimal contact with her other former classmates and their Alma Mater, and she was a long way from being what could be termed a wholehearted 'Old Roedeanian'. She maintained an almost begrudging contact with her old school, turning out for several OR events. One, remembered vividly by Beryl Lucey, was a cricket match between a team of ORs and a side of current pupils: 'She arrived after the match had started and walked rather pompously across the pitch, with her bat under her arm.' It was a clear statement of intent both to her former school and to the world: she batted on her own wicket, and she batted – unorthodox style – to win.

According to Nancy, Norah was still determined that she become a games or domestic science teacher – a respectable occupation for the unmarried daughters of middle-class Jesmond families. Mother and daughter did the rounds of domestic science colleges and visited Dartford Physical Training College, to no avail. George, it seems, was 'much better able to deal with his embryo Spains'.[25] He told Nancy she could live at home for free, and would have an allowance of £50 a year for 'clothes and amusements'.[26]

Nancy harboured a short-lived ambition to be an actress – an idea which prompted her mother to take drastic action in an effort to dissuade her. According to Nancy, Norah took her on

> a swift and ruthless tour of the theatrical lodging houses in Newcastle-on-Tyne ... 'That's what the theatre really means,' she told me, 'grind, grind, grind and terrible food. You'd have to be as strong as an ox. Anyway you look like an ox. You have to look better than you do, and move better than you to go on the stage. If it was your sister I'd understand it. And the Spains have never been lucky with the theatre. Look at your Aunt Katie'.[27]

Nancy surreptitiously enrolled at Durham University's King Edward VII Art School and started attending life classes (Mondays) and anatomy classes (Thursdays), apparently without either of her parents finding out for some time. She also started going to dances with a young man, remembered by her only as 'Paddy Something or Other'. 'It was all very innocent and rather dull',[28] she later remarked.

She had also joined a local swimming club, where she learned of the existence of a women's lacrosse and hockey club in Sunderland. Deciding to investigate further, she was subsequently accepted into the Northumberland and Durham teams for both sports. Her original intention had been merely to get some fresh air and run after a ball. Instead, she had unwittingly embarked on a new life which would bring her an opportunity to pursue the journalism career she had secretly coveted, some new role models to imitate – and her first, forbidden love.

Miss Sargeant Appeared in a Class of Her Own

Like many of Nancy's new team-mates, 23-year-old Winifred Emily Sargeant (known as 'Bin' to her friends) came from a well-to-do West Hartlepool family. She was the only daughter of Harry and Hattie Sargeant and, by the time Nancy met her, was already a well-established county sportswoman, especially in tennis. She had played in the Durham Open County and Ashbrooke tournaments, captained Durham Ladies' Reserves and been a first-team player. Winifred, according to a smitten Nancy, 'was the height of glamour ... she had a streak of golden hair and blue eyes with a yellow ring round the pupil and she could run faster than any girl I have ever seen'.[1] She had her own green sports car and drank gin and tonic, was also 'terribly clever and very funny', possessing 'a wonderful showing-off flair'.[2] Her best friend – and lacrosse team-mate – was another West Hartlepool girl, Nora Sanderson. Nancy was suitably impressed by her new friends and their comparative wealth: 'They lived in big, prosperous houses with a full quota of maids cavorting in the back premises ... I was mad about them all'.[3] But the one she was maddest about was the glamorous Winifred Sargeant.

It was suggested by Harry Barker, the sports editor of the *Newcastle Journal*, that someone should write reports for the paper about the myriad exploits of the Northumberland and Durham women's teams, primarily to get them some free publicity. By luck or stealth, Nancy was chosen to do the job. Initially, she received no payment for her short articles, but it afforded her invaluable hands-on experience in journalism. Barker gave her a few simple rules to follow: 'Write clearly ... on one side of the paper only, number each page and always get your story here by 2.30 at the latest'.[4] She gave him no cause for complaint, and it wasn't too long before Barker decided that she could cover other women's sports, starting with hockey. From now on, he told her, she would be paid $1\frac{1}{2}$ d. a line for her copy. As spectator/reporter, Nancy shivered on the touchlines, huddled in her special overcoat, an enormous garment which became known as 'Reporter'.

This was to become a familiar pattern throughout her life and career: she would use opportunities, either given or created for herself, not only to further her own career and enhance her reputation but to do the same for those she considered worthy of her love and loyalty. Therefore the opportunity given her by Harry Barker was shamelessly seized upon and milked for all it was worth: she was learning her trade while simultaneously giving fulsome praise to her team-mates and their efforts – and especially to her beloved 'Bin'.

Her first hockey reports appeared in November 1935, when Northumberland Ladies were beaten by Edinburgh University 3–2, a game in which, apparently, the 'teams staged an intensely interesting display of spectacular athletic features', and where 'both teams were closely matched in physique and pace ... '.[5] When Northumberland Ladies were defeated by the East of Scotland, she observed that 'The County gave a good display but their chances were nullified by a slight weakness in finishing'.[6]

That same month, a new arrival at BBC Radio Newcastle caused ripples of excitement. Cecil McGivern, a former Newcastle schoolmaster, and director of the Newcastle People's Theatre, was producing a Tyneside sketch, *The Willing Spirit*, written by and starring local celebrity – and former Old Central High School pupil – Esther McCracken. McGivern had made his own, somewhat inauspicious, radio debut when, with some fellow students from Armstrong College, he raided the New Bridge Street studios during their 1926 'rag' week. The announcement of his latest radio work aroused speculation that this was the first move towards the selection of a 'home' producer for drama in the North-East region. The speculation proved correct: less than two months later, McGivern and his new Newcastle Radio Players produced *Fleeaway Peter's Flat*, a play set in a North Durham pit, billed as McGivern's 'first big broadcast'.[7]

Esther McCracken was to be one of the rocks upon which McGivern built his, and the station's, reputation for quality regional drama. Her loyalty and contribution to Newcastle did not go unappreciated or unnoticed by local pundits over the years: 'If she went elsewhere, there would be a gap that would be hard to fill. As writer, producer, singer, speaker of monologues and actress, she is a very real asset'.[8] Her plays, produced at Stagshaw, included *The Old Watch*, *The Willing Spirit*, *Behind the Lace Curtains* and *Quiet Wedding*, which received a theatrical production in April 1938 at London's Richmond Theatre. This development of regional radio drama in the North-East would eventually provide Nancy with golden opportunities to add more strings to her bow.

In the meantime, the New Year provided a busy line-up of sports fixtures to keep her and 'Reporter' occupied. The Northumberland Women's Festival hockey championship started on 3 January 1936. Newcastle Ladies beat Central Newcastle High School Old Girls 12–1 and then the Midlands beat Northumberland Ladies. Nancy knew why: 'Overhitting spoiled many promising movements'.[9] Before she had time to catch her breath, there was the Inter-County Badminton tournament to cover, beginning on 18 February.

What was really taking her breath away, however, was the dazzling Miss Sargeant. In the privacy of her bedroom, Nancy would open the covers of 'To Please Myself' and pour her heart out in verses to her adored 'WS', who was still oblivious to her passion.

What could I ever say of you?
when all of you I ever saw
was something bright and swift and fair
unheld by time, unchecked by law
who found first principles untrue
and tossed at them your glinting hair –

Was it the wind that called so gay?
and left my heart like aspens stirred
and made my senses keen and bright
to sieze [*sic*] some laughing, maddening word
that half remembered in the day
might come like music in the night –

(6 March 1936)

Unfortunately, as much as Nancy was enjoying her secret ardour and sporting exploits, her personal finances were – as they would be for most of her young adult life – in disarray. The allowance given to her by her parents, and her small fees from the *Newcastle Journal*, never seemed enough to keep her in the style to which she was becoming accustomed, as enjoyed by West Hartlepool's finest.

She decided to apply for an audition with the BBC Newcastle drama department and was duly summoned. For the audition, she took a copy of *The Importance of Being Earnest*, plus a list of sentences in all the dialects she could muster. She was asked to read a column of copy from *The Times* in her normal voice and the audition report noted that, 'for an amateur actress', she had done well. Shortly after, she was called back to audition for a role in a play being produced by Cecil McGivern in a Broadcast Play Festival, taking place from 6 to 10 April. The play was called *The Lang Pack*, a thriller written by Norman Veitch and based on an eighteenth-century North Tyne murder. It was broadcast on Tuesday 7 April, at 6.50 p.m., and marked Nancy's radio debut. She later recalled that her part consisted of screaming '765 times' and saying things like 'Nowt ivor happens oop t'valley. Nowt tae dae but watch the hills torn frae broon to green to white and back ower agin'.[10] Cecil McGivern would later tell her, 'As an amateur actress, you were a remarkably good professional screamer'.[11]

Once the 1936 lacrosse and hockey season was over, Harry Barker asked Nancy to start covering the local tennis tournaments. Her payment was increased to 2d a line and, more importantly, other northern papers asked Barker if his tennis reporter could also cover the events for them. Very quickly, Nancy's little stories of the triumphs and failures of local heroines – including, naturally, the Misses Spain, Sargeant and Sanderson – were syndicated to the North's leading papers: *The Scotsman, the Yorkshire Post, the Doncaster Northern Echo, the Sunderland Echo* and the *West Hartlepool Northern Daily Mail*. In the *Newcastle Evening Chronicle*, her columns appeared under the byline, 'Baseline'. This was in keeping with the paper's tradition of corny monikers: pigeon-racing was covered by 'Loft', athletics by 'Whipper-In', table tennis by 'Flick' and angling by 'Dry Fly'.

In July, Nora and Winifred both took part in the Durham County championships at Ashbrooke, Sunderland. Winifred made it to the women's singles final, where she was beaten by Doris Davison. Soon after, Nancy teamed up with Nora to play in the doubles in both the open and the handicap competitions of the Tynemouth Open Tennis tournament at Prior's Park, Tynemouth. In the singles, Nora fared better than Nancy, eventually losing in the semifinals of the handicap. Nancy got no further than round two. In the doubles, they went out of the open in round two but won the handicap doubles title in straight sets.

The Northumberland tournament, a prestigious annual event, began at the Country Ground, Jesmond, on 27 July. Nancy entered herself both for the women's single handicap and the doubles. The main focus of attention, however, was the defending women's singles champion, the Chilean player, Anita Lizana, with her 'delightfully appealing little lisp . . . the dynamic little woman who is a perfect whirlwind on the court'.[12] Nora was drawn against Lizana in the doubles; she and her partner duly lost. Nancy fared no better than her friend; she received a drubbing in her singles, beaten 6–0, 6–0 by C. Burr and her humiliation was completed when she and partner, Miss Coates, were beaten in the doubles, 6–1, 6–0. Lizana subsequently went on to clinch the title for the second year running.

Nancy, meanwhile, was privately singing the praises of her own, worthy champion:

> My father has been struck by lightning
> My mother's lost her fountain pen –
> Our cook is tight – the housemaid frightening
> My toothbrush is in Harpenden –
> And England are all out for ten –
> A deep depression's on the way
> But something cheers the hearts of men
> For Winifred was born today.
> Then raise your voice in throaty song –
> Waiter, the '28 champagne!
> Who cares if overdraughts [sic] are long
> If there is civil war in Spain
> Away with misery and pain
> If there is sun we must make hay
> A chance like this won't come again –
> For Winifred was born today!

> ('For August 26', 2 August 1936)

And, within a few weeks, it appeared that Nancy discovered her feelings were entirely reciprocated:

> Within my heart an orchestra is playing
> a golden song of loveliness undying
> undying and immortal, yet unborn.
> If I could sieze [sic] one phrase that violin is saying

translate the ecstacy that it is crying
of love at last requited ... once forlorn –

I'd teach the little errand boys to hum it
and dance along the roads on joyous feet,
the friendly hurdygurdy men will strum it –
that you may hear its echo in the street;
And all the whining traffic wheels will bring it you
the song of dreams that must be yours alone
and you in time perhaps will learn to sing it too
and make its golden cadence all your own,
Know that its queer perfection must belong to you
recall its madness laughing soon or late
and you will understand who wrote the song for you
but was too shy with words to dedicate ...

(17 September 1936)

Several years later, Nancy went back over the poems she'd written to
Winifred, and altered some lines to reflect her changed emotional state. This
particular poem was amongst them: 'the song of dreams' became 'the idiot
song that still is yours alone' and the 'golden cadence' became, rather
cynically, 'silly gaiety'.

First love is heady stuff for anyone, both to feel and deal with. For two
young women in the North-East in the 1930s, living with their families and
being groomed for a 'respectable' life, it must have seemed little short of a
miracle to discover that someone else also had the unspoken fears, the
unidentified longings, the feeling of being, somehow, 'different' – yet not
daring to put a name to it. Especially the name that was whispered only
when bedroom doors were closed and children's ears safely covered, the
name that had made its way to a million middle-class breakfast tables in 1928
when 'that' book by 'that' woman was published. When Radclyffe Hall
sprang her *Well*, it wasn't only the horses that were frightened. So Nancy
kept the truth about Winifred and her secret love confined to the pages of
'To Please Myself'.

The start of the lacrosse season provided Nancy and Winifred with a
heaven-sent opportunity to spend time together, on and off the field. The
West Hartlepool team embarked on a short tour of Ireland, from 30 November to 4 December. They would return home via Liverpool in time for the
North trials on 5 December. Winifred was the tour captain, Nora the club
secretary, responsible for making all the travel arrangements. 'West Hartlepool
are looking forward to it keenly',[13] reported Nancy. She would be filing
regular bulletins on the team's progress back to the *Newcastle Journal*. They
warmed up by defeating Durham School and Nancy could say encouragingly
that they were 'at last beginning to fulfil their early promise'.[14]

The Ireland tour began with a convincing win against Richmond Lodge
at the Bladon Rugby ground, Belfast, where 'The defence played steadily
throughout and outstanding among them was Winifred Sargeant ... Nora
Sanderson, at second home, shot with great force and accuracy'.[15] She and

Nancy top-scored, with five goals each. The early euphoria evaporated, however, when they were thumped 15–0 by Belfast Ladies. Searching for something positive to salvage, Nancy told readers back home, 'The game, though one-sided, was fast and keen, but the catching was fast and accurate'.[16] This was followed by another defeat, against the Dublin Pioneers at Trinity Hall, but Nancy, a double goal-scorer, considered it 'the best match of their tour' and picked out Winifred as one of two players who played 'a persevering and at times brilliant game on the left wing'.[17]

Back in England, the team watched the North trials at Liverpool Training College and played against Liverpool Ladies, only to be defeated 21–1. Once home, they promptly lost again, this time to Newcastle Ladies, in a match in which, complained Nancy, 'the ball was too often on the ground and many players appeared rough'.[18] She summed up their Ireland tour thus: 'They played 5 matches, won 2, lost three . . . and their secretary, Miss Nora Sanderson, is to be congratulated on the efficient manner in which the tour was handled'.[19]

Illness and poor weather conditions at the end of 1936 meant that many of the team's matches had to be cancelled. But it meant Nancy and Winifred could spend more time together without having their team-mates playing gooseberry as well as lacrosse. And Nancy could pen more poems to her beloved, instead of scribbling 2d.-a-line reports on the speed and accuracy of shots.

> Dearest – your laughter stirred my heart
> for everything I love was there –
> Oh set its gaiety apart
> that I may feel it everywhere!
> But someone more talented than I
> might steal the motif that it tells,
> beat its carillon to the sky
> on silver tongued cathedral bells –
>
> Though all the world would be impressed
> to hear its glad cacophony –
> I am content to let it rest
> where it belongs – with you, and me.

(9 January 1937)

Once the illnesses and weather conditions had improved, Nancy and her team-mates took up their crosses again. The County team were due to play Yorkshire on 12 January at West Hartlepool, with a line-up which included Winifred in left defence, Nancy on left attack and Nora on second home. A week before they met Yorkshire the West Hartlepool Ladies played against their male counterparts. 'Miss Sanderson and Miss Spain played an enterprising game . . . an amusing and enjoyable encounter'[20] – which the men won.

At this time, an opportunity dropped into Nancy's lap which, for once, she appeared reluctant to pursue. BBC Newcastle's Outside Broadcast director, Victor Smythe, announced that he was looking for local sports commentators. Her experience as a player in several sports, and as a reporter on the touchline and at courtside, would surely have made Nancy an ideal candidate. But the opportunity was not taken. It could only have been that increasing her reporting work – especially in the stricter discipline of radio – would have meant reducing, or even stopping, her own participation as a player. And this, of course, would have meant less time to spend with Winifred. So she continued as a team-player, hurtling across fields up and down the country. In February, she took particular delight in an inter-Territory match – the North versus the South – in the grounds of Roedean, which the North won 7–2. 'They were superior from the first', Nancy gloated, 'the 2 defence wings played particularly well . . . the lacrosse was of a very high standard and the ball was seldom on the ground'.[21]

The season finished with the three Miss S's – Spain, Sargeant and Sanderson – making a clutch of appearances for the Northumberland and Durham team, and for West Hartlepool. Nancy was also trying her hand at squash rackets, playing in the Newcastle Ladies' Club championship – where she lost in the first round – and the North England Women's championship. At the same time, the lacrosse team heard that Roedean would be sending a team up to Northumberland to play several matches throughout the county next season.

Nancy, meanwhile, was pouring out poem after poem, charting not only the depth of her feelings for Winifred, but her anxieties about their future together – or lack of it:

> Perhaps the last thing I shall write
> will be a song for you to sing –
> for as God filled your eyes with light
> you found a joy in everything
> For as some day I know I must awake
> and lose the lovely thing that seems so true,
> I know before I go I have something to make,
> is it too much that it should be for you?

(March 1937)

> In the far distant years when you and I
> and the fair tinkle of my words are dead,
> there will be birds beneath the changing sky
> that say, without effort, all that I once said.
> Even though people, poor unimportant things
> forget that we once lived, that our eyes knew
> you will be in the song the blackbird sings,
> and through the falling rain they may see you.
> And all the blackbirds' effervescent songs
> will light again a flame that *cannot* die –
> and though they know not where the fire belongs –
> they will give thanks . . . to you . . . and so do I.

(29 March 1937)

She was in a lighter mood, though, when she wrote her own interpretation of the lacrosse team's triumphs:

> 'Tis a tale that they tell in Hartlepool
> at the sign of the 'Blue Bloused Bitches',
> where an aged crone still points with pride
> to pair of tattered breeches.
> 'There', she says, 'are all that remain',
> and her voice is far from merry,
> 'of little Prue Prosser and Sophie Spain
> who siezed the Sacred Beret.'
>
> Then to her feet rose Sophie Spain
> and an 'orrible oath she swore –
> that she would not smoke or drink again
> till she'd nailed above the door
> THE BERET OF THE PARKINSON –
> Nay, she would stop at nowt
> to lay the pride of Yorkshire low,
> and stamp the insult out.

('The Ballad of the Sacred Beret', March 1937)

On 24 April, Newcastle Ladies played their last match of the season, losing to Harrogate. Nancy made sure, however, that her season ended on a high note: 'Newcastle's 3 [goals] were secured by individual effort, for N. Spain ran through twice to score'.[22]

Nancy and Winifred were both entered for the Northumberland Lawn Tennis Association County tournament held at Osborne Road, Jesmond, from 15 to 18 May. There was a gala atmosphere to the event: three days previously, the country had celebrated the Coronation of its new King. However, Nancy didn't have much to celebrate at Osborne Road; although Winifred reached the semifinal, Nancy received another first-round thrashing – 6–0, 6–1 – and completed a miserable tournament by losing in the doubles, and then the mixed doubles. But she was undeterred, and the next month entered the singles, doubles and mixed doubles (handicap) of the South Northumberland tournament at Gosforth. However, she could only manage one paltry victory – in the singles. Winifred took part in the Northumberland qualifying tournament for Wimbledon at Leeds, but failed to get through, and instead, in the first week of July, played in the Durham County tournament. Speculation about her chances against her first opponent featured in Nancy's reports: 'Will Anderson's control and accuracy or Sargeant's cool play and courtcraft prevail?'[23] But on the opening day, there was a shock when Winifred withdrew from all events. Her biggest fan reported that she had 'been suffering from lumbago . . . active tennis is out of the question with her for a few days'.[24] To complete the all-round misery, Nancy lost in the second round of both the main tournament and the handicap section.

The last week of July saw the start of the 51st Northumberland Open County tournament at Osbourne Road. 'Chile's cheery Anita Lizana is returning to defend her title in the singles championship',[25] Nancy told her readers. 'Reports to hand give promise of an exceptionally large handicap entry'. Lizana successfully defended her title, beating Mary Heeley by hitting 'shots down the sidelines that left even a grand retriever like Miss Heeley standing'.[26]

The ladies' lacrosse season started on 22 September, with Newcastle Ladies holding their first general meeting and practice game. There was an air of optimism, and more praise for Winifred from Nancy – and for herself, 'for she [Winifred], Nora Sanderson and Nancy Spain showed signs of first-class combination at the end of last season'.[27] Their first fixture was against Harrogate, beating them 12–1. 'This is a promising beginning to the season', enthused Nancy.[28] Later that month, all three were selected for the Northumberland and Durham County team. 'The defence is good and very evenly balanced',[29] she observed. But her attention would soon switch from the upcoming fixtures, and even from her beloved Winifred, to a bigger date in her diary.

It had been announced that, from 19 October, the North-East was to have a new transmitter for its BBC studio – Stagshaw – by which name the station would also be known. The Duchess of Northumberland would officiate at the opening. Cecil McGivern told the local press, 'When the Stagshaw transmitter opens there will undoubtedly be a greater use of North East material . . . '.[30] He had already held auditions for regional talent at the Newcastle studios with David Porter, the regional variety director, and promised that there would be a strong emphasis on drama, written and performed by local talent, with genuine regional accents and dialects.

Station director, E.L. Guilford, Cecil McGivern and his assistant, E.S. Williams, were 'working as a team on ideas for features, plays and broadcasts of all kinds', it was reported. 'An important feature is Thursday's full-length production of "Fell Top"'. The play, broadcast on 28 October, was a dramatized version of a Winifred Watson novel about Weardale, adapted by Patrick Campbell, including Nancy as one of the 'well-known Newcastle broadcasters in the cast . . . '.[31] She played the young heroine, Anne Mary, and her performance was singled out for praise by the local press: 'Nancy Spain as Anne Mary . . . was particularly good. . . . The versatility of the players was most noticeable'.[32] As Stagshaw's first dialect play, *Fell Top* also caught the attention of the national press, including Joyce Grenfell, then radio reviewer for the *Observer*:

> The play was a curious combination of genuine characterisation and a highly coloured background of melodramatic situations . . . the piece was well acted. Nancy Spain and Renee Bruce were excellent as the sisters. The quiet dignity of Anne Mary contrasted well with the simple and friendly Jane Ellen.[33]

Stagshaw, encouraged by the positive response to *Fell Top*, immediately announced plans for another radio production with local interest, to be performed in 1938. *Eight Heroes and a Heroine*, written by Constance

Smedley, concerned local heroine Grace Darling. However, the *Newcastle Journal*'s radio correspondent had a sneak preview of the script and declared it to be a huge disappointment: 'the dialogue is almost unrelievedly trite dreariness . . . narrators are employed to speak incredibly long-winded stage directions . . . '.[34]

Back on the lacrosse field, Nancy's various teams continued to prosper, as she was able to tell her readers: 'With better weather conditions generally the standard of lacrosse appears to have improved in proportion and county prospects appear much more encouraging than is usual at this time of year'.[35] A 13–2 defeat of Scarborough hammered home the point. 'Miss Sargeant . . . whose fast and accurate shooting was the feature of the match . . . appeared in a class of her own',[36] exclaimed her most ardent admirer.

There was more cause for celebration when they played for Northumberland and Durham and defeated the St Ethelburga's First XII at Harrogate. It was the county's first win for three years, and apparently featured an unusual goal from Nancy:

> Miss Spain . . . scored for the County three times in the first half, one of the goals being a strange one: a shot more often seen on the billiard table than the lacrosse field! However, the real credit of the match goes unquestionably to the defence.[37]

The month ended with the North trials at Harrogate where, Nancy complained behind the anonymity of her absent byline, 'Miss Spain, the County third home, has only been selected as a further reserve for the North . . . '.[38]

But this was hardly of great importance, compared to the happiness she was experiencing with Winifred:

> I knew the world was wonderful
> before I even thought you cared
> but now a thousand lovely things
> are lovelier for being shared.
> Dearest, this world magnificent
> that made me feel so frail and small,
> by virtue of the love we know,
> I have inherited it all.

By now, Nancy had managed to save up enough from her reporting and her fees from Stagshaw to buy her first car – a second-hand, fabric Baby Austin, costing £20. It wasn't in quite the same league as the cars driven by her West Hartlepool friends but, at least, it provided her with some welcome independence.

Her New Year began with a memorable encounter between the Northumberland women's hockey team and the Frankfurter Sports Club during the Northumberland Women's Hockey Association festival at Scarborough. Nancy was there to witness the bemusement of the English players who 'were a little disconcerted to start with when the Germans walked on to the pitch, raised their arms in the Fascist salute and cried "Heil, Hitler!"'. Later, one of the German players told her, 'We find playing in England great fun but it is not easy'.[39]

There were other unsettling reminders that, beyond the sports field, awaited the possibility of more brutal encounters between English and German 'teams'. One of Newcastle's local military dignitaries, Lieutenant Colonel T.A. Lowe, appealed to the War Office to immediately establish a women's Territorial Army and reform the WAACs, WRNS and Land Girls. 'Physically women are relatively far in advance of men', he told the *Journal*, 'Why wait for war to break out? Women will have to help then and it will take months to organize them'.[40]

For the time being, his call went unheeded but, in March, volunteers started to be accepted for the ARP (Air-Raid Precautions). Women over twenty-one were eligible and, in the Newcastle and West Hartlepool areas, nearly 400 duly volunteered.

Nancy's attention was, however, still firmly fixed on the lacrosse field and the prospects of the Northumberland and Durham team, who were 'not at full strength', she said, but saw 'no reason why unselfish team spirit and keenness should not prevail'.[41] It did: they scored a narrow win over Leeds and then had 'a busy week in front of them'[42] in early February – though not too busy for Nancy to be able to pen more lines in praise of Winifred:

> I cannot forget the quiet places –
> the distant silence of the hills
> the chasing shadows on the calm spaces
> a singing river that the sunlight fills –
> Here all day I cannot stay or linger
> for the great manmade town propels me on
> urging with subtle threats, pointing a warning finger
> dragging my straining hands from all that's gone –
> [last four lines crossed out at a later date]
>
> Dearest I made you queen a while ago
> of the strange world to which you hold the key
> and if it was only that I loved you so
> you will remember – & you'll come with me.

There was also plenty of praise for Winifred's endeavours on the lacrosse field. When Northumberland and Durham trounced St Ethelberga's, Nancy wrote 'Most of the credit for Northumberland's goals is due to Miss Sargeant, at left attack'.[43]

Meanwhile, there were changes afoot at Stagshaw: it was announced that Cyril Conner would take over from E.L. Guilford as station director at Easter (in fact, he didn't take up the post until August). The BBC also promised a series of radio mystery stories for the autumn and winter.

At the end of the month, the West Hartlepool team went off on another tour, this time to southern England: Winifred, Nancy and Nora were all selected. They set off on 24 February, and played their first match two days later. Their opponents were the Seagulls Club at Littlehampton, who suffered a heavy defeat, with Nancy and Winifred contributing nine goals between them. Two days later, they comprehensively beat Southsea. Then it was on to Bournemouth, where they routed the New Forest team. A day later, they played Berkshire and Reading University in the same day, winning both matches. 'They will return home after a most enjoyable trip',[44] announced a smug Nancy. On the way home, they stopped off at Harrogate and methodically crushed Ethelberga's Third XII 25–0. Nancy was ecstatic: 'Miss Sargeant was always the most dangerous player – she scored 14 goals herself'.[45]

With the season drawing to a close, she and Winifred were soon back in action for Northumberland and Durham when they defeated the Cheshire team. It was, she wrote, 'The best season in the history of the association. The captain of this fast improving and hard-working team, Miss Sargeant, is probably the best example of "team spirit" in the side'.[46] The proud team were duly photographed for the paper.

Winifred again tried to qualify for Wimbledon, this time in the doubles. To warm up, she played for the Durham team who defeated the East of Scotland 7–2, then Jesmond 7–0. But, despite her best efforts and some earnest support, she still failed to get through the qualifying rounds.

Privately, Nancy welcomed her back after their brief separation:

> Dearest – I had forgotten in my heart
> that such sharp things as Fear and Hate could be
> it was so long since we had been apart
> we walked in a fool's heaven you and me –
> Yet for two days I have been at your side
> and you were there, and yet it was not you
> the understanding that a world could not divide
> all overgrown with Fears and Cruelties now grew.
>
> Frantic I searched all day amongst the crowd
> I knew that when I found you I'd be strong
> Lost, in a dream, I called to you out loud
> and waited for your singing all night long –
> I prayed that through the tumult you had not passed by
> and swore that should I wait a thousand years
> I could endure them if that melody
> could whisper once more softly in my ears.

(June 1938)

Publicly, she chronicled Winifred's achievements at other tournaments. In the first week of July she played in the Tyneside Open and then reached the final of the Westoe tournament, winning in straight sets. The ever-attentive Nancy described how 'Miss Sargeant's courtcraft and fine control of length, speed and spin, gave her a well-deserved victory'.[47] She then travelled down to Eastbourne, to play for Durham in the Inter-County tournament, lost in the second round of the Northumberland County tournament and then reached the quarter-finals of the Ilkley Open and, by the middle of August, had risen to Number 2 in the county rankings.

In between all this, Nancy had a family funeral to attend. Her Aunt Mary died suddenly at home, 110 St George's Terrace, Newcastle, on 7 July. She was cremated and her ashes taken to the family grave at Horsley. In her will, she had left all her personal effects to George and the annual income from her investments to her sister, Katherine. But she stipulated that, after Katherine's death, the money should go to her nieces, Liz and Nancy. Since Aunty Katy was very much alive and well in New York, they thought no more about it – for the time being.

In September, it was again time to prepare for the new lacrosse season; in addition, Nancy also became involved in the formation of the Northumberland and Durham Women's Cricket Association.

Stagshaw, meanwhile, was heavily promoting its special Grace Darling Centenary feature, scheduled for Monday 5 September. 'This is Stagshaw's reply to the hopeless mess London made of a broadcast about the heroine some time ago',[48] trumpeted the *Journal*. The feature would include a contribution from Major C.M. Forster, the honorary curator of the Grace Darling National Memorial Museum at Bamburgh and a 45-minute play, *Longstone Light*, by Mary Sheridan, 'wife of a Manchester doctor'.[49] The station had, in fact, been looking for a suitable script about Darling for some time. But, curiously, none had been submitted from the North-East, natural Darling country. The *Journal*'s radio correspondent was amused to learn that the cast's speech 'will be Northumbrian in colour'.[50] The *Daily Chronicle* observed approvingly that the play 'has been written with extreme attention to authenticity. Fourteen Northern radio artists will take part in the broadcast, a notable feature of which will be the sound effects of storm and sea, and the noises associated with the rescue'.[51]

Nancy was cast as the daring Darling, and so naturally became the focus of local press attention; it was her first proper taste of the limelight. A publicity photograph was taken of her – dressed in V-neck sports shirt and with typically wild hair – and duly published in the *Journal* and the *Daily Chronicle*. She was interviewed for the first time by Sally Lane in her 'Gossip' column in the *Chronicle*. 'Miss Spain is one of the most vital people I have ever seen: she is tall and athletic, with crisp chestnut hair that looks as though it tingled with electricity', said Lane. 'She says she is quite terrified by the responsibility of playing the girl who has come to be looked upon as Bamburgh's patron saint'.[52] Nancy told her how she had diligently researched the part, visiting Bamburgh and reading all the books about the Darling family. 'I left her there, shaking in her shoes in case she should do anything to offend the sensibilities of Bamburgh next Monday',[53] concluded Lane.

Nancy was not the only one shaking in their shoes at that time. Prime Minister Neville Chamberlain was attempting to appease Hitler and, though war was still nearly a year away, Newcastle could already boast that it had 'become the most elaborately prepared city in the country for any outcome of the international situation'.[54] Overnight, the ARP brought 278,000 assembled and functional gas masks into the city. Within weeks, women from the city began to volunteer for the hastily assembled Women's Auxiliary Territorial Service (ATS), the formation of which had been announced by the BBC on 3 September, despite being told 'Peace Assured After Munich Talks'.[55] At this stage, the ATS women would only be used as cooks, clerks, drivers, orderlies and storewomen. By the second week of the New Year, twelve ATS companies had been formed in Northumberland, under Chief Commandant Laura Ainsworth.

For the moment, Nancy's cosy world remained untouched by the encircling gloom that was enveloping the city like a Tyne fog. She was deeply in love, and the only imminent battle on her mind was West Hartlepool's first fixture of the new lacrosse season – against Newcastle Ladies – on 8 October. Winifred was made team captain again, Nora was vice-captain and the team got their season off to a winning start. A week later they played Leeds, swiftly followed by the County trials at West Hartlepool. Nancy, Winifred and Nora were selected for the 'Whites' team, and for the Northumberland and Durham team, who played Cheshire, where they narrowly lost. She attributed the defeat to the 'soft ground [which] affected some players' speed ... shooting on the whole was difficult'.[56] She still didn't like losing.

The next match pitched them against arch-rivals, Yorkshire, at Harrogate. When Winifred sprained her ankle in the first half, it didn't bode well for the result. Yorkshire won, but Nancy did not take this particular defeat lying down: 'Mrs Doggart, at left attack, passed beautifully to Miss Spain, often free in the centre, but Miss Spain was unable to convert, several times being "brought down" by the Yorkshire defences'.[57]

But, as she wrote in 'To Please Myself', 'the major attractions stay the same':

> I think a gallop would do you good –
> so come my love as I call your name,
> the Northwind whinneys behind the wood –
> As every turn in the Zoo's a cloud
> where you can lie in my arms and rest
> and at last perhaps I may be allowed
> to tell you the things I love the best –
> Of your upper lip and its gentle curve
> of your hair that flies as a wild bird flies,
> and that happy love that I don't deserve
> in the golden pools of your cloudless eyes –

(November 1938)

The lacrosse team dusted themselves off and prepared for another busy week at the beginning of December, including a match against Harrogate College and the North trials. Not all of the regular faces would be there. 'It is unfortunate but unavoidable ... Miss Spain and Miss Sargeant are not in the trials team. Miss Spain cannot travel owing to business ties and Miss Sargeant, fulfilling the duties of selector, cannot play'.[58] Nancy's 'business ties' was a strange euphemism: she was, in fact, performing in another radio play, *The*

Tindal Rogues. Written by James L. Scott and produced by Cecil McGivern, it was a reconstruction of 'some stirring incidents in the Northumbrian Border country between the times of Henry VIII and James I'.[59]

The West Hartlepool ladies' team went on their annual tour in January 1939, this time to Scotland. They played five teams: Edinburgh Ladies, Edinburgh University, Satellites, Glasgow Ladies and St Andrews, but won only two of their five matches. And in the final contest, against St Andrews, 'both sides were inclined towards roughness',[60] scolded Nancy. Nonetheless, she was able to report that 'all the games were hard-fought and very enjoyable'.[61]

On her return to Newcastle, she was asked to appear as a guest on Stagshaw's *Sports Column* programme, to be interviewed by presenter Andrew Davies. Listeners were reminded of her other main claim to fame: her performance as Grace Darling in *Longstone Light*. 'She will not be keeping to the Grace Darling type in this talk, for she is speaking about lacrosse – a game which would probably have been a little too lusty even for the Bamburgh heroine'.[62]

Cecil McGivern continued his pioneering work at the station. On 18 January 1939, listeners heard the first edition of a new local monthly programme for women, *The North Country-Woman*, and, shortly after, McGivern and Terence Horsley, managing editor of the *Newcastle Journal*, devised a new fortnightly 'behind-the-headlines' commentary programme, *Topics in the Air*, providing the region with its own insight into national issues. Horsley, who was to feature in Nancy's postwar career, was a multi-talented man. A keen amateur aviator, he wrote novels and non-fiction books, such as *Fishing and Flying*.

Northumberland and Durham, meanwhile, continued their successful run of games right to the end of the season. On 4 April, Nancy listed their progress: played fifteen; won nine; lost four; drew two. Goals for: 147, against: 88. Despite the worsening international situation, none of them could have guessed that it would be their last season and, by the end of the year, the war would already have claimed one of their star players. But as war drew closer, other belles of the county began to see the writing on the wall and were joining Northumberland's embryo ATS companies. However, it was still business – and love – as usual for Nancy and Winifred:

> Only the dark, you say, dear heart can cover
> The sweet mad things that spring puts in my heart
> the dreams, desires and fancies of a lover
> who from the loved thing seems eternally apart.
> In the gold joy of spring's returning light,
> by the hard brilliance of a chandelier
> then, you would say, my eyes seem far too bright,
> and they would know me for your lover anywhere.
>
> Dearest, this may be so – I wouldn't doubt you
> I only know I find therein such joy
> I find such happiness in all there is about you

that I can fancy the whole world my toy –
And since the world is here but for my pleasure
and all belongs to me, because you smile
You'd be the last to blame if at my treasure
I showed appreciation for a while.

(2 March 1939)

On 15 April, a new production of *Fell Top* was broadcast and Nancy was again in the cast. Winifred, encouraged by Nancy's self-supporting endeavours, landed a job as northern agent for T.H. Prosser, manufacturers of sporting goods. She would cover Yorkshire, Durham and Northumberland – but not alone. Armed with her trusty Baby Austin, Nancy became her partner in this latest enterprise. Ever the sharp-shooter, Winifred won a lucrative contract to supply shuttlecocks to the North-Eastern Badminton League.

In late May, Nancy put down her crosse and took up a cricket bat for her club, the Wanderers; she was selected for the Northumberland team to play Durham, and the Northumberland and Durham team to play against Lancashire. At the same time, it was announced that there would be no South Northumberland tennis tournament that year, as too many of the players were now involved in territorial and national training. Reported by 'N.B.S.', Nancy still hadn't quite managed her first full byline in the *Journal* yet, but she wouldn't have to wait much longer.

On 19 June Nancy captained her own cricket XI against Miss May Gardner's XI at Chester-le-Street, a charity game in aid of the Royal Voluntary Institution (RVI). The day before, she played for Northumberland against Durham and duly reported that 'despite a good partnership by Mrs Malcolm and Miss Spain, Northumberland were beaten . . . the pair put on 38 of the 78 runs scored in the 25 overs . . . '. Nancy was 25 not out and had bowling figures of 0–8.[63] She then captained the side in a women's county match, again against Durham, and in aid of the RVI.

On Friday 30 June, the first feature bearing her byline was published in the *Journal*:

'Colourful Crowd at Wimbledon' by Nancy Spain

We spectators, who visit Wimbledon in the first week, offer to a student of psychology, or racial characteristics, or even of fashions, a fascinating study. Where do we all come from? Why do we come? And why do we dress in our best to come?

We come from all ends of the earth. In two minutes, under the big frames in front of the centre court, where the names of the players go up match by match, you may hear the whine of our visitors from 'Down Under', the more attractive drawl of our American enthusiasts, quickly spoken French and slower German, and a hundred and one indistinguishable Central European tongues.

. . . to date the crowd might well serve as a fashion guide for the summer. There are ladies' hats that defy coherent description – bird cages, fruit baskets, 'speckled beauties', 'clouded blues', and occasionally horrifying feather clad mountains, the despair of spectators sitting directly behind the imposing quills.[64]

On 6 July, Winefride O'Reilly, National Organizer of the Women's Team Games Board, visited Newcastle and spoke at two functions: an informal tea party at Scout House, Victoria Square, for people involved in girls' organizations, followed by a public meeting for girls and women at Bainbridge Hall, Percy Street. O'Reilly talked about the difficulties faced by women's sport: little money, restricted access to grounds and the lack of 'leaders', which in turn led to difficulties in recruiting players. It was decided that an area games board should be established, 'with the intention of bringing joy and health through outdoor recreation into thousands of North-Country homes'.[65] Nancy (lacrosse and cricket) and tennis player Mrs Brooks were appointed joint secretaries of the new Women's Team Games Board of Northumberland and Durham. In the evening, a programme of films about fitness and games was shown. One of them, a 40-minute profile of women's cricket, was given 'an admirable running commentary'[66] by Nancy. The Board decided that their first priority should be to appoint two paid instructor leaders, 'to teach and organize games of every kind in the villages of the North-East'.[67] The cost, they estimated, would be about £400 a year.

A week later, the committee, comprising some twenty representatives of various organizations – with Nancy serving as the rep for the Northumberland and Durham Lacrosse Association – met and passed a resolution inviting the Duchess of Northumberland to be the association's president. The National Fitness Council offered to pay for 75 per cent of the instructors' salaries, if the Board could provide a timetable of twenty hours a week. Various suggestions were put forward for ways to meet the rest of the expenses, including exhibition tennis and lacrosse matches.

But they were fiddling while Europe was already burning: as the Board worried about raising money to promote regional sport, the first thousand women from the North were assembling at the new ATS camp at Strensall, 120 of them from Northumberland. The women – aged from eighteen to forty-three – were to be trained under 'strict military discipline', receiving instruction from officers of the King's Own Yorkshire Light Infantry in cooking and orderly work, tent-pitching (they would live under canvas for the duration), map-reading and gas-mask drill. Reveille was at 7 a.m., lights out at 10.30 p.m. The YWCA arranged entertainment and leisure activities, and ran a camp shop. The trainees were visited by the Princess Royal and Princess Alice. 'Next year', reported the *Journal*, 'they may train even more thoroughly, for it is hoped to send them to camp along with the regiments to which they are attached and with which they would work in case of war'.[68]

Life in Jesmond continued, after a fashion: it hosted the fiftieth club tennis championships, with Winifred playing for Durham Archery Club, followed, in August, by the Northumberland Lawn Tennis tournament. Nancy continued playing cricket for the Wanderers, who topped their league, and she was also in the Northumberland and Durham team which faced Yorkshire at Jesmond.

Having, perhaps, a greater awareness of the dramatic events that were to come, Winifred decided it was time that she and Nancy took a holiday. From her profitable shuttlecock deal, she bought a second-hand Ford 10 for £75 and planned a touring holiday in the South of France. An excited Nancy sent off for her first passport, collected her currency and maps and arranged her AA membership. Nora was not happy about the trip, but Nancy was determined that not even impending war would prevent it. Before they headed off, 'N.B.S.' wrote what was to be her last sports column, on 16 August, about the Inter-Club tennis league. 'A follower of tennis who shall remain nameless asked me an astonishing question the other day. . . . "Why, since Jesmond Ladies won the league with comparative ease this year, were Newcastle Ladies not equally successful at Brixton, at least in play against Durham, for 5 of the 7 ladies to travel were Jesmond players?" This shows ignorance of personnel . . . '.[69]

With that, Nancy and Winifred left behind the tennis league, the lacrosse fields, the badminton courts and disapproving parents and headed south for the ferry to France.

Once in France, they drove first to Paris, then took the road south, passing through the Loire Valley and Avignon, and on to the Alpes Maritimes. Near a small coastal village between St Raphael and St Tropez they camped in a field belonging to the local butcher, where they had the nearby beach virtually to themselves. Pine trees grew almost to the edge of the water, and flowering in the sand were purple wild orchids. For Nancy, these weeks were 'days of perfection, of sun, and sleep under the stars, and swimming to keep cool, and wine kept in the shade without ice, and hot rolls bought in the village and wolfed in the cool of the morning before the weather went mad'.[70] She enjoyed lobster for the first time one night when a terrifying electrical storm drove them off their beach and into a small hotel. Later on, Nancy came to regard the havoc wreaked by the storm as symbolic of what was about to happen throughout Europe. Indeed, while they were enjoying their idyllic holiday, the 'storm' was gathering momentum daily and even interfering with their beloved tennis. 'The crisis affected the North of England lawn tennis championships at Scarborough yesterday',[71] reported the *Journal*. Hotel bookings at the Yorkshire resort were suddenly cancelled and exiting trains were packed to bursting point.

Winifred and Nancy arrived home shortly before Prime Minister Neville Chamberlain sat down in front of a BBC microphone on Monday 3 September, at 11.15 a.m., to declare that the country was now at war with Germany. Two days before Chamberlain's announcement, schools were closed and vast numbers of children were evacuated from Newcastle. Less than a week later, the evacuation of Tynemouth and Wallsend began. Tynemouth Pier was closed to the public and parts of King Edward Bay were designated out of bounds. Thus, observed Nancy, 'a way of life I had only glimpsed, a way of "no responsibility", of carefree pagan joy, something I had always supposed just to be the "dream" life, was to be forbidden to me for the duration of the hostilities'.[72] She penned some gloomy verses in 'To Please Myself', at once pessimistic and yet curiously convinced that the war would only last three years:

> So, there is time for wasting, and I am free to think
> waiting through three long years of grey industrial war.
> Can I find in this bored and static world one ancient
> that will chain me to the careless past that cannot be any more?
> Perhaps in a flute or a violin, in a tune that once was gay
> I may remember 'Sylphides' – or laughter in the dance –
> the lights may fade in the theatre – could I hear George Gershwin play,
> Or with a Van Gogh postcard will my heart return to France.

> ('Time for a dreamer', September 1939)

And, as an afterthought, she added:

> Out of an Autumn fog, from a peasant damp and cold
> it was ever a lengthy step to the sun and sea of the past
> Yet now with a dull despair I shall see my face grow old
> and my legs and arms may waste e'er I join the sun at last.

Now, women volunteers were reported to be 'pouring in' to the ATS headquarters in Newcastle's Ellison Place. One of these was Winifred, who wasted no time in joining up. Nancy, for her part, volunteered for the ARP as a driver and was duly issued with her uniform dark-blue coat, bearing an ARP badge, and peaked cap. Curiously, the Newcastle ARP became the subject of one of the war's earliest rumours. It was reported in the local press that volunteer ARP workers were being paid 'huge salaries', allegations that were emphatically denied by the ARP top brass.

Nancy and Winifred were not alone in rapidly heeding the call of duty in an area so steeped in naval and military traditions – the North-East was to record the lowest number of conscientious objectors in the country. Within weeks of Chamberlain's announcement, the city's schools were reopened and some were quick to play their part in the war effort. The Central Newcastle High School Old Girls' Dramatic Club 'adopted' the twelve-man Searchlight Detachment of a local regiment, sending them regular issues of books, games, sweets and knitted goods. The *Newcastle Journal* announced that, as from 19 September, it was to merge with the *Northern Mail* 'to save on resources'. Almost immediately the paper began running a 'Women in Wartime' column, aimed less at the many women donning uniform, and more at the patriotic housewife, keen to wage war from the confines of her kitchen. The column contained recipes for cheap, thrifty dishes; what to put in 'treasure bags' for the troops; how to save gas; and the exhortation to 'Make Your Xmas Puddings Now'.

Meanwhile, Nancy was adjusting to life as an ARP driver, adopting a distinctly tongue-in-cheek attitude to describe her new situation:

> Now, since the War, I have a round tin hat
> A suit of oilskins, though they don't fit me –

My uncle's cousin's sister is an AT
and she looks down upon the ARP –
nevertheless I now have more than she;
to items, see above, add 2; shields, eye
A pair of gumboots, and a mask, CD*
and I shall keep the thing until I die.

Then, oh Saint Peter, if with Semite Piety
you turn me away, I'll have another try
I'm sure you'll be impressed by
ARP
PRIORITY
and so I'll keep the thing until I die.

('Ballade of Things Transient and Intransient', September 1939)

* although I have been frequently assured that it is Govt. Property

While she was still in the ARP, there was a welcome visitor to Tanker-ville Place. At the outbreak of war, Geoffrey Wright had joined the Navy and had been assigned to an aircraft carrier stationed on Tyneside. Liz had given him the family's home address and encouraged him to visit her parents and Nancy. In the three months he was stationed there, he would visit the Spain household quite often. For Geoffrey, George remains a vague figure while Norah made more of an impression. 'She was a handsome and very warm woman, and was extremely kind to me when I used to drop in. She just seemed to be a jolly nice person; I never got the feeling there was any friction between her and Nancy'.

Proper Navy

Despite the months of build-up before war was finally declared, it still seems to have come as something of a surprise to Nancy. The war, she said, 'struck my little life a smart blow. It disappeared without a trace'.[1] This was not entirely the case, of course. It was certainly true that Winifred's abrupt enlistment into the ATS left a yawning gap in her life, though they still continued to see each other when they could. But though the war may well have meant the end of her participation in sports and subsequently most of her reporting work, it was entirely her own decision to quit both at that time, and there appears to be no reason to suppose that Stagshaw would have dispensed with her services entirely. It was, quite simply, time to move on to a new challenge: the war, conveniently but dramatically, provided it.

A few years later, Nancy was open about the desire for change and the niggling dissatisfaction she felt with her way of life at that time. It was, she admitted, 'eccentric, colourful, and a little artificial, and . . . lacked responsibility either to a higher or a lower authority. Now, total warfare demanded a responsibility from me'.[2] Her response to this 'demand' was to become a full-time ARP driver. It was an obvious choice: she had, after all, been driving since the age of eighteen. But, after only two months, she decided that this wasn't quite enough to satisfy her need for 'responsibility': 'total warfare demanded a further responsibility of me. I wanted to work really hard. So I joined the WRNS'.[3]

The service she was about to enter had been formed during the First World War, in 1917, and disbanded just two years later. It was originally to have been called the 'Women's Auxiliary Naval Corps', until somebody in the Admiralty observed that, perhaps, *esprit de corps* would be hard to engender in a women's service whose initials spelled 'WANC'. So it was that the entirely more genteel name, the Women's Royal Naval Service – the Wrens – was chosen.

In the early days of the war, the recruitment and utilization of the WRNS was fairly disorganized. As early as 14 April 1939, King George VI had given his permission for the WRNS to be re-formed, specifically to replace male officers and ratings at naval shore establishments. Mrs Vera Laughton Mathews was appointed WRNS director. But such was the shambolic state of affairs, the Admiralty neglected even to organize a typist for the new director during her first weeks in the job. To begin with, prospective recruits were asked to postpone their applications until a booklet had been published, which gave information about the conditions of the service and how to join. When the re-formed WRNS finally opened its doors for business, women volunteers applied directly to naval ports and were enlisted without any consultation with the London-based HQ. Volunteers had to provide three references. In the first months of the war, the WRNS quickly swelled to 5,061 officers and 69,574 ratings.

In November 1939, the first WRNS ratings were sent to work as cooks, stewards, writers and messengers at Kirkwall in Orkney. By the end of the war, Wrens would have carried out nearly every job in the Navy, including crucial work at the code-breaking centre at Bletchley Park. Ultimately, some 460,000 women would serve in the armed forces, most of them in the ATS – 198,000 – and the Women's Auxiliary Air Force (WAAF) – 171,000. But, even at its peak, the WRNS only numbered 74,000, and throughout the war, it was always the hardest service to get into, with recruitment being closed several times.

The conventional wisdom of the day decreed that the Wrens was the best – and most glamorous – women's service to join. If a woman was turned down by them, then the WAAF was an acceptable second best. The ATS, however, was considered to be the bottom-of-the-barrel service. Ludicrously, part of the reason seems to have been that the drab khaki ATS uniform was considered a poor alternative to the rather smarter dark-navy or pale-blue uniforms worn – eventually – by the WRNS and WAAFs. This curiously founded 'caste' system was not discouraged by the women who joined the respective services and consequently ATS women had no great fondness for their WRNS and WAAF counterparts, or vice versa.

Though initially all the women's services were the subject of various scandalous rumours and unfounded prejudices – they were frequently referred to as 'officers' groundsheets' or 'pilots' cockpits' – the ATS women got a particularly bad press. It was whispered that, not only were they to be found in the queues outside recruitment offices, but in those outside the surgeries of doctors specializing in unwanted pregnancies and STDs.

Nancy later claimed that she had pulled every string she knew to get into the Wrens. The service gave preference to women who had a naval family connection – Nancy's most obvious link was Captain Taprell Dorling, her distant cousin. Whether this was sufficient on its own is doubtful but, whatever tale she spun, it was enough to convince the recruiting officer at North Shields: she became a Wren rating on 1 November 1939, attached to HMS *Calliope* at HM Trawler Base, North Shields, for motorized transport duties – in other words, a full-time driver. And so, she recalled, 'It was in this strange way . . . that I found emancipation'.[4]

In this respect, she was not alone. The WRNS, along with the other women's services, attracted women of similar age and background. For many, it was their first experience not only of work but of life outside their family homes. Being patriots and acquiring new skills went hand in hand with learning about sex and bad language. Nancy's new colleagues, the

North Shields trawlermen, were eager tutors in at least one of these: 'Their language ... when the first fine careless rapture of Shocking the Wrens was over, became milder. They became used to the Wrens, or else the Wrens became used to the language'.[5] Then there was a new, 'proper Navy', vocabulary to learn. The dining room was the 'mess deck'; the kitchen was referred to as 'the galley'; they didn't have bedrooms any more, but 'cabins'; and going into town was to 'go ashore'. Nancy didn't take long to catch on: 'I knew from now on that anything Proper navy was very much to be copied. Slavishly, if necessary'.[6] Proper Navy people, she discovered, frequently referred to Nelson, citing him as the reason for many naval traditions.

For WRNS drivers like Nancy, their duties also included carrying out minor repairs and the cleaning of vehicles. They had to have a 'good physique' and be at least 5 feet 4 inches tall – no problem for the 5 feet $6\frac{1}{2}$ inch, 11 stone Rating N.B. Spain. After a medical check-up, the women had their hair inspected for bugs followed by a demonstration of the gas-mask drill.

The Wrens did not have equivalent naval ranks to men, on the basis that they could not carry out full duties, unlike their counterparts in the ATS and WAAF, who were also subject to the same military rules and codes of conduct as their male colleagues. Similarly, the Wrens were not subject to the Naval Disciplinary Act, but instead had their own code of conduct, described by Vice-Admiral Sir John Tyrwhitt as 'a compliment to their womanhood'.[7] WRNS disciplinary regulations would eventually stipulate that 'Members of the WRNS in uniform are not to walk arm in arm or indulge in noisy or rowdy behaviour in public. ... Umbrellas ... handbags ... coloured finger nails are forbidden when uniform is worn'. They were not to salute in railway stations, but always had to do so for the national anthem, even when it was played outdoors – except, presumably, at railway stations.

However, in the first few months of war, there wasn't even a uniform for Nancy and her new WRNS comrades. Nor, at North Shields, was there any room for the new ratings to practise drill, so they ended up marching around the table in the galley. One compensation for their discomfort was that the services did enjoy better rations than their civilian counterparts.

Manufacturers of certain products were not slow in recognizing the advantages for them of the new female force. The pages of women's magazines began to fill up with carefully targeted advertisements for goods which, apparently, were as necessary for winning the war as an anti-aircraft gun or a bouncing bomb. V wasn't just for victory, it was for Vinolia, 'the soap that freshens you – Women in uniform should know'. Then there were Wolsey women's underclothes – 'Keep beneath your Dungaree dainty femininity!' (In fact, Wrens were actually allowed to wear their own underwear.) And, equipped with Tampax, 'Women of the services are winning the war of freedom' although, naturally, no one said exactly how. This was paralleled by another product, widely advertised at the time, that warned, 'Women's tasks today have no room for disability – Anti-Kamnia, for periodical indisposition'. Nothing, it seemed – not even periods – could be allowed to hamper the war effort.[8]

Jesmond was an 8-mile drive from the North Shields base, and Nancy chose to make the journey by train, until another rating from Jesmond, a Miss Penny, showed her the cheaper bus route. They subsequently travelled together most mornings, exchanging grumbles and gossip, to their mutual delight: '"A bit of dirt" was Miss Penny's and my idea of real pleasure. Luckily there was always plenty of it'.[9] She was keen to see what the other Wrens were like: 'I looked round with interest. The Chief Wren was a Miss Broadley, the Chief Cook. None of us seemed to me to be the Wren Type. There is no such thing as a type, I said to myself; you must guard against facile, journalistic thinking'.[10] At the end of her first day, she was exhausted, her mind awash with a heady brew of ripe language, scandalous gossip about the area's notoriously rough and ready cafes, and her first lessons in 'proper Navy' behaviour.

But she soon settled into her new routine. Initially, her duties consisted of delivering ships' supplies in an old laundry van, still bearing its 'Family Bag Wash' sign, to base, dock and yard – everything from nuts and bolts to potatoes and bread. Occasionally, her load might be something a little more animated, such as a Lewis gunner, complete with Lewis gun and ammunition. On one occasion, she delivered a group of sailors to a semi-completed aircraft carrier under construction in the shipyard. Subsequently, her route was changed and she became based entirely at the yard.

The yard's buildings were all given over to 'Supply'. The Spirit Room was devoted solely to issuing rum – 'Nelson's Blood' – decanted from large barrels into gallon wicker jars. Another housed the accounts department. In the 'Beef Screen' hung hefty chunks of lamb and beef. The grocery store contained tinned vegetables, fish, coffee and suet; open bins spilled over with pulses, sugar, tea, dried fruit and ship's chocolate. These loose groceries were dispensed to Nancy in large brown paper bags which, she complained, were apt to burst once they were loaded into her lorry. One of the yard's sailors, 'Charlie', supervised the Wrens' work. According to a grateful Nancy, he made the ratings a comfortable little room of their own, equipped with hard and soft furnishings which had once graced luxury ocean liners.

There was no shortage of work for the new female workforce. Apart from the ships permanently moored at North Shields, many large vessels came in for repairs, as did Allied ships. Nancy was particularly fond of the crew of the Norwegian destroyer, *Sleipner*, which was, she said, 'already a legend when I met her. . . . My orders had been to establish contact with someone aboard, receive orders for food and drink, and eventually to deliver them'.[11] That 'someone' was Lieutenant Petersen, who ordered for his crew fresh milk, cheese, caviar, and 'very much bread . . . and perhaps you will join us to lunch from it all?'[12] She didn't need inviting twice, and was subsequently a frequent guest at the Captain's table. The relatively exotic Norwegian lunches included distinctly unproper Navy delicacies such as herrings in various sauces and salmon. As often as possible, she contrived to ensure that her lunchtimes coincided with the Norwegians' and, occasionally, those of the French crews, who enjoyed four-course lunches of veal washed down with Châteauneuf du Pape 1934 and desserts accompanied by champagne, even brandy. Offering less in the way of gastronomic delights were the small motorboats and yachts donated by patriotic private owners for whatever use the Admiralty might choose to put them to.

On one occasion, when the destroyer HMS *Wordsworth* was accidentally rammed by a merchant ship, killing and injuring sailors on the mess deck, and towed into North Shields, Nancy and Leading Wren Broadley took meals to the shocked crew. They were told not to discuss the incident when they went ashore. Later, Nancy discovered, the rumour going around was that the ship had been torpedoed.

Sometimes her routine would be thwarted by one of the yard's hidden perils: on one occasion, a dockyard crane hook managed to attach itself to Nancy's van, throwing her forward, so that she hit her head on the windscreen and rammed her chest against the steering wheel, and leaving driver and van suspended in mid-air. She felt, she said, 'as though I had been hanged before my time'.[13] Nancy and her van were near-casualties of war on several occasions: she was once caught mid-route during an air raid and shrapnel tore a hole in the van's roof. The ever-resourceful rating tied a sail across the hole. She witnessed another air raid, this time on Newcastle itself, which hit the old Spillers dog-biscuit factory, narrowly missing the bridges across the Tyne and – probably of equal concern to the locals – the brewery.

December 1939 brought its usual bitter North frost and snow, heralding the start of a four-month winter that would turn out to be the coldest since 1894. Still the Wrens had no uniform and were forced to wear what Nancy described as 'Sensible Clothes of peace time'.[14] One of the trawlermen took pity on her and donated a fisherman's jersey, which, made for a much taller sailor, hung past Nancy's knees, and a white balaclava helmet which, she was told, was knitted by Princess Mary. But two pairs of sea-boot socks, two pairs of mittens, a pair of gloves and her trusty 'Reporter' still couldn't keep out the cold and snow. Another trawlerman, innocently prophetic, told her, 'For real smartness, you can't beat a woman dressed in men's clothes'.[15] Eventually she was given permission to wear jodhpurs on duty.

But the cold weather wasn't the only thing starting to bite: on 13 December, magnetic mines destroyed eight trawlers: they included the *William Hallett*, sunk with the loss of eight men, most from North Shields; the *James Cudford*, which lost all seventeen crewmen; and the *Wigmore*, which was torpedoed and went down with all hands. The *Newton Beech*, reported overdue in the middle of November, was declared lost with its crew of nearly forty Tynesiders. Five days before Christmas a total of thirty-seven trawlers came under attack from Nazi planes around Britain's coasts. Two months later, Chamberlain, in a statement to the House of Commons, declared that 'The killing of fishermen, merchant seamen and lightship crews . . . is not war but murder'.[16] As a result, some trawlers were fitted with machine-guns. However, by then, the Luftwaffe's attention was focused on targets further south, as the British Expeditionary Force (BEF) started its abortive campaign in northern France. It proved to be a turning-point for Nancy and the other Wrens, as they realized that men who had irritated them days before with their joshing and pranks, who had given them crash courses in coarse language and 'proper Navy', wouldn't be coming back.

One day, Nancy received orders to 'Proceed to New Quay and there receive verbal instructions from CPO Woods' [17] The Quay was a naval graveyard, littered with wreckage from mined ships. Once there, an unsuspecting Nancy was asked if she had come for 'the meat'. Thinking it would be an ordinary delivery, she said she had. Did she know where to take the meat? Why, the ice-house, probably. No – to the mortuary. Her delivery this day comprised half-frozen sacks containing the unidentified remains of the crew of one of the mined trawlers, the *Harry Perkins*. Nancy drove her van slowly, to avoid skidding and sending the sacks shooting out of the back. At the mortuary, she and an old woman responsible for laying out corpses unloaded the sacks. Making her apologies, Nancy walked across the yard and was violently sick. She was never asked to do this kind of delivery again – she later suspected that her male colleagues had taken pity on her, quietly arranging that this particular rating be spared such a distressing duty. In future, an ambulance was sent to collect the sacks of 'meat'.

It was little wonder, then, that Dame Vera Laughton Mathews would say, after the war, 'The Wren motor transport drivers in the Tyneside Docks in the early days did an extremely tough job and did it extremely well'.[18]

Nancy spent the first Christmas of the war on duty, taking six Lewis gunners to Blyth, negotiating blizzards and closed roads. The crew on a small patrol boat, celebrating Christmas in the traditional naval manner, passed round the hat for her when she came to collect some blankets from them; the master of a merchant ship gave her 200 Players. She handed her 15 shillings 'Christmas Box' to the paymaster-lieutenant, Royal Naval Volunteer Reserve (RNVR), for the Hurricane fund before going to a party in Newcastle where RNVR captains and Wren officers played musical chairs.

But that Christmas, she had little to celebrate. 'I felt withdrawn from all this and was forced to view the preparations with the eyes of an alien',[19] she remembered. On 15 November, Norah's mother, Lucy Dorling Smiles, had died in Belfast, aged ninety-one. Then, on 26 December, George's brother, Walter Spain, also passed away, aged sixty-seven. Three days later, attention switched to a happier event – 'Miss Elizabeth Spain's London Wedding'.[20] Liz married 41-year-old company director Richard Ewart James at Westminster Register Office on 30 December. Typically, she was described by the local papers as the 'sister of Miss Nancy Spain, of broadcasting, dramatic and sporting fame'.[21] Despite the family's recent bereavements, Liz cut a stunning figure, wearing 'a three-quarter coat, of red fox with orchids in the front, a black dress and a black hat'. The couple honeymooned in Ireland where Liz, according to her sister, 'got bored and ran up a collection'.[22] The *Newcastle Journal* observed, 'The wedding was very quiet owing to a bereavement in the bride's family'. Of this emotionally turbulent time, Nancy ruefully reflected, 'Our family have never done things by half '.[23]

However, it was another bereavement that was to strike a terrible blow at her 'little life'.

That month, Winifred Sargeant had become seriously ill with inflammation of the brain – encephalitis lethargica, a viral infection commonly known as 'sleepy sickness'. She was taken to Kentdale Nursing Home in Kendal, Westmorland, and died there on 22 December, aged just twenty-seven.

The *Northern Daily Mail* said the news of

> one of West Hartlepool's outstanding sports girls . . . will be received with great regret. . . . At lacrosse she filled every position in the Northern team, which travelled widely and gained renown for itself. She represented Durham County at tennis for a number of seasons and three years ago played at Wimbledon. She had a great name in badminton circles and played for her county.[24]

Winifred's funeral took place on Tuesday 26 December at Wesley Church, West Hartlepool, with a service conducted by the Reverend J. Parlow. Her coffin was borne by members of the County Durham ATS. The mourners included representatives from the Durham County Tennis Club, Park Road Badminton Club, Durham Lawn Tennis Association and the Durham ATS. But one mourner was conspicuous by her absence – Nancy.

In September 1955, while she was writing *Why I'm Not a Millionaire*, Nancy explained how she 'couldn't even bear to go to the funeral':

> I now realize what a terrible shock Bin's death . . . must have been to me. . . . Quite often I still think I see her, laughing in a crowd; and once I am sure I saw her come into a restaurant. . . . But when I leapt up to say hello she seemed to vanish, leaving a hard clear line for a second, as a piece of paper does when it burns in the fire.[25]

Winifred's death must have been unbearably painful for Nancy; her memories, as recorded in *Millionaire*, showed as much, even in their veiled manner. They also hinted at certain feelings of guilt for failing to be at Wesley Church sixteen years earlier. Shortly before her own death, the obvious pain and guilt she felt over these events were dealt with rather more ruthlessly. Recalling the holiday in France in *A Funny Thing Happened on the Way*, she wrote about it as though she had gone on the trip alone. It is she who makes £75 selling shuttlecocks for the North-Eastern Badminton League; she who buys a second-hand Ford; and whose only travelling companions, apparently, were 'a huge hunk of French bread and a slopping bottle of warm wine'.[26] By then, it seems, Winifred had been laid to rest – in public, at least.

After all the weeks of trauma and upheaval, the New Year brought with it some welcome light relief: the issue of the long-awaited Wrens uniform. For days after their arrival, the packages became the focus of gossip and speculation, particularly concerning the hats. They were in for a major disappointment, however, when they were finally kitted out: 'What we saw did not please us',[27] recalled a disgruntled Nancy. She went home to show her parents the new uniform, but their laughter confirmed her own worst suspicions. Defiantly, she embellished her new uniform with her sew-on ratings badge – a blue star with the letters MT (Motor Transport). At least now she looked 'proper Navy'. It also inspired another poem, steeped in solemnity about what being a member of the armed forces meant for many of her generation:

> As there are some of us you shall not see again
> for you we still shall be the brightest of the brave
> the beauty of our youth shall in your hearts remain
> when all our frailty is buried in the grave
> Wealth and truth and art . . . these you burned in the fire
> or, in a different sort, you sank them in the wave
> But Love, and Laughter and Strength – these and our desire
> these may be remembered as the things that Youth once gave.

('To the Old', Friday 22 March 1940)

She was also learning to follow in one of the finest of naval traditions – namely drowning her sorrows with a drink or two, to temporarily escape the realities of war. It was a tradition which she stoutly defended to some unspecified critic in 'In Defence of Drinking', as she outlined the particular sorrows she was trying to drown:

> And you who drink so deeply with the little God of Love
> I was once like you my friend – the clouds that sweep above
> the thunderstorm that howls and roars – neither cloaked my sun
> I thought the world was in my hands when I was twenty-one.
> And so the time may come perhaps when Love has gone away
> and terror stalk your footsteps that once were light and gay
> then alcohol will warm your heart – so bless the swinging sign
> and think on Future Sorrows friend, e'er you condemn our wine.

(April 1940)

★ ★ ★

That spring, she was astonished to find two destroyers lying in a meadow. It wasn't until several years after this peculiar occurrence that the full details of what the *Newcastle Journal* called 'one of those hush-hush affairs' could be made public. The destroyers had, apparently, been trying to negotiate a bend in the river at high tide, doing an incredible 20 knots. In those circumstances, it was no great surprise that they ended up like a couple of beached tin whales. According to the *Journal*, 'The incident shook a lot of gold braid as we in the newspaper world knew at the time', and a severely embarrassed Admiralty ensured that, for the sake of naval and public morale, it was hushed up.

Nancy turned her attention to her own vehicles: she sold her Austin Seven and took to borrowing a car from some acquaintances, esconced on a paddle-steamer called *The Lily of Laguna*, where she would often play poker of an evening. Then she decided to spruce up her battered van by painting it in camouflage colours. It became known in the yard as 'Nancy Spain's Tombstone'. This was taken in good humour, but clearly tensions were beginning to mount. Nancy's explanation was that 'It is no odd or new thing to observe of women, living or working in a confined space, that they often grow upon one another's nerves'.[28]

The yard's Wren supply assistants had chosen, as the scapegoat for their irritation, a poor wretch known as 'the Timid Wren'. Most of the grumbling concerned the weekly cooking rota, which Nancy managed to exempt herself from on the basis that she was tired from being out on the road all day. When the Timid Wren's turn came, she apparently either burned the food or managed not to cook it at all. Her popularity did not increase when she announced to her vexed 'shipmates' that she was going to write a book called 'The Yard', in which they would all feature prominently.

Though Nancy was certainly disturbed by the culinary failures of the Timid Wren, it was just another factor on a growing list of grumbles. She longed to be in 'civvies' again, and yearned wistfully for summer tennis tournaments – just a year before, she had been at Wimbledon, earning her first full byline. She started murmuring about a transfer. It was, she wrote later, 'Dunkirk that caused my nostalgia and the fact that someone else's war was more important and more dangerous than mine. . . . Our war had suddenly ceased to satisfy us'.[29]

In early June 1940, the focus of the war had turned to Dunkirk and a number of North Shields small craft joined the flotilla to bring back the retreating BEF. When the Battle of Britain began on 8 August, Nancy and her colleagues felt even more separated from the 'real' war effort. And an increasingly dissatisfied Nancy found herself undertaking even less 'warlike' tasks. As the Ministry of Food exhorted people to 'Dig for Victory' and eat more fresh vegetables, one of the men at the yard discovered an overgrown cabbage field. Nancy and two riggers were promptly dispatched for several days to collect as many cabbages as could be found amongst the thistles and nettles. They spent four days hacking away at edible and inedible green matter but, moaned Nancy, 'still there were cabbages in that awful field'.[30]

Another awful field of cabbages would also, one day, bring more misery.

The last straw nearly came in early September. She was delivering a supply of fire extinguishers when one fell over and started filling up the van with white foam. She climbed into the back and stemmed the flow, emerging whiter-than-white, just hours before she had to attend a Wrens drill. It was a most opportune moment for her to be granted her first leave.

After spending nearly a year driving between all points north, she had seen enough, and on 7 September 1940, arrived at King's Cross Station. Her mother was not best pleased at her decision to head south: she was, warned

Norah, 'courting disaster'.[31] Nancy stayed in a hotel near Hyde Park Corner and found herself invited to a party, where she linked up with two brothers, trainee pilots, who persuaded her to share a taxi with them to the East End. Mid-route, they were caught in an air raid, the main target of which was their destination. Understandably, the taxi driver at first refused to take them beyond Holborn. When he eventually agreed to drop the pilots off at their lodgings in Lambeth, Nancy, having arranged to meet them for lunch at the Criterion Hotel the next day, hopped out and began the long walk back to her hotel.

The following day, she bought the Sunday papers and walked around Hyde Park until it was time for her to meet the two airmen. During lunch they discussed the terrors of the previous night and the heroics of the capital's firefighters. In the evening she went, alone, to the pictures in Leicester Square. As she was walking back to her hotel, she realized that, as dull as her job might be, it was still *her* job and she decided to return to Newcastle the next day. A bomb which fell near the hotel, blowing out half the windows on her side of the building and flinging her out of bed, more or less sealed the decision for her. Back at Tankerville Place, she told her mother, 'I was frightened stiff, that's why I've come home'.[32]

Not long after her return, the WRNS suffered their first casualties: on 14 September, ten ratings were killed when a hostel in Lee-on-Solent took a direct hit. For once, being posted in the north-east, and not on the more vulnerable south coast, right in the thick of the 'real' war, no longer seemed so boring.

Before *ennui* could set in again, Nancy was presented with a new challenge: the base commander asked if she would like her name to go forward for a promotion as cypher officer. She wasn't keen, nor were her pals in the yard, who advised her, 'Don't be an officer. You go on being a bloody pirate'.[33] It was advice she was keen to take, but the pressure not to do so was real enough. As well as being the most socially select of the three women's services, the WRNS also divided women into jobs that mirrored their social divisions. Working-class women usually ended up as cooks or carrying out more menial manual tasks; lower-middle-class women were usually appointed as clerks; whereas middle-class women worked in administration or as radio operators. Therefore it would have been considered unsuitable for the Roedean-educated younger daughter of a lieutenant colonel, decorated for his services in two wars, to spend the war driving a laundry van around a naval base. And this, despite the idealistic hopes of the authors of a 1942 report on *Amenities and Welfare Conditions in the Three Women's Services*, which declared that 'The mingling of all classes in the present national effort is a situation full of promise for the future'.[34]

It wasn't too long, however, before Nancy was ordered to appear before a selection board for cypher officers, carefully rehearsing her answers to their interview questions. Yes, she was interested in administration. Yes, she could type, but not at the prescribed entrance speed of thirty-five words per minute. No, she didn't feel she had exhausted the scope of her current job.

Despite this, the reluctant applicant was indeed passed by the board as suitable officer material and in January 1941 left the yard, the base, the 'meat' and the laundry van for the OTC (Officer's Training Course), travelling down on the sleeper to King's Cross, and from there to the Royal Naval College, Greenwich. She had breakfast at a servicemen's and women's canteen and – with amusingly uncharacteristic fastidiousness – went for a manicure, had her hair done and got her shoes cleaned. Suitably spruced up, she reported for her two weeks' training.

During her fortnight's training, the Blitz was raging around Greenwich. When the raids came at night, the cadets slept in the basement of the building, where there were only two mattresses for every three women. Another cadet who put up with the hardships alongside Nancy was 'Miggs' Ackroyd. 'She was great fun, she really made our OTC', remembers Ackroyd, 'She was unforgettable and lit up the whole course'. At the end of their training, Director Vera Laughton Mathews visited the cadet officers, who put on a show for her. 'Of course, Nancy *had* to produce it', recalls Miggs Ackroyd. She was also putting her mischievous pen to paper again, writing what Ackroyd called 'rather unacceptable (to the High Ups, very funny to us) rhymes about various members of the gathering'. She also penned a verse to one of her fellow cadets who, Nancy observed, had become the target of the affections of one of their officers:

> Dear little Kitty
> We are forming a committee
> So that we may guard you
> From the wanton wiles of Cardew.

'I've never forgotten it, all these years', says Ackroyd, adding, 'Of course, we didn't really know about these things in those days'.

With the utmost reluctance, on 7 January 1941 Nancy became Third Officer Spain WRNS, and on 21 January was posted to HMS *Condor*, where she served at the Fleet Air Arm Station, Arbroath, in eastern Scotland, a training base for administrative duties – but not, as she had feared, as a cypher officer. She telegrammed the news to her parents. Just before setting off for Scotland, she learned that one of the young trainee airmen from Lambeth had been killed in an accident on an aircraft carrier. Also that month came more bad news for the WRNS, as twenty-two cypher officers and telegraphists were lost when the SS *Aguila* was sunk on its way to Gibraltar.

But there was a happy reunion in store once she arrived in Arbroath: one of the squadron leaders charged with teaching the young flyers at the base happened to be Terence Horsley, formerly managing editor of the *Newcastle Journal*. Also waiting for the new Third Officer was First Officer Beatrice Jewell, 'a dear, kind girl',[35] who was in overall charge of the (eventual) 400 Wrens who serviced the planes at the base. Jewell remembers Nancy arriving at Arbroath from Greenwich 'full of flu!'

The Wrens at Arbroath were responsible for servicing the planes at the base and Nancy, together with another administrative officer and two cypherers, was responsible for looking after them and administering their varied needs. This could entail anything from organizing tennis tournaments to cycling round the base's 15-mile perimeter to check the drains.

Nancy didn't like Arbroath: it was too big, it was overcrowded and, since it was a training base, she felt it was too removed from the 'real' war. Conditions were certainly rather grim. 'The camp was hardly finished,' recalls Beatrice Jewell. 'Mud and building work everywhere. [Nancy] arranged quarters and all sorts of entertainment for the Wrens, of whom in the early days there were only 60–65'. In 'Greenwich Palace 1941', Nancy reflected nostalgically on the stately splendour of life on the OTC:

> Although at night the heavens blaze
> the immortal river seems to burn
> in our most placid Winter days
> we see the Peace we love return
>
> *L'Envoi*
> The waves with little boats will dance
> where drifts of seagulls white are laid
> and still the setting sun will glance
> on dreaming dome and colonnade.

The WRNS officers at Arbroath shared a brick hut with two naval sisters. 'We all endured lack of heat and hot water for several months', Jewell remembers, 'but Nancy always rose to the occasion'. This included 'making pencil sketches which kept us all amused!' The sisters also amused themselves – and irritated everyone else – by repeatedly playing their favourite records: Marlene Dietrich's 'I've Been in Love Before' and 'The Boys in the Back Room' – a number which would return to haunt Nancy a decade later, when she became one of Lord Beaverbrook's regular dinner guests who were treated to repeated screenings of his favourite film, *Destry Rides Again*.

Not so amusing were the various germs which spread like wildfire throughout the base, along with a distressing infestation of head lice. Equally unamusing was an incident, remembered by Beatrice Jewell, when a landmine was parachuted into the woods between the Wrens' and officers' quarters; it failed to explode and dangled dangerously in the trees. The slumbering Wrens were ordered to vacate their beds and 'proceed to the Main Galley', clad only in their nighties. 'We spent the night on hard wooden benches, to be frequently woken by sailors coming in for cocoa at odd times,' recalls Jewell, 'and at 3 a.m., by the Wren cooks cooking kippers by the hundred over coal-fired ranges by candlelight.' Nancy 'remained good-humoured all the time!'

When Arbroath became unbearably overcrowded, various nearby country houses were requisitioned for military use. Nancy found herself put in charge of The Guynd, a Georgian mansion. This required her to live at the house and commute, by bicycle, to and from the base each morning and evening.

For entertainment, there were tennis tournaments, whist drives, country-dancing sessions and a dramatic society called the Garrison Theatre, in which Nancy seemed to make her best impression. One of the new ratings at Arbroath was Alice Sewell, who still remembers Nancy being 'very popular as an entertainer at the camp concerts'.

Despite Nancy's misgivings about her reluctant but steady rise up the ranks, Beatrice Jewell considered her to be 'a fine and capable officer'. In April 1942, Jewell was drafted to Rosyth and was replaced by Monica Hudson, a cousin of the Bishop of Newcastle.

Apart from the intermittent indignities of head lice, the cold, drab climate of Arbroath left Nancy with a perpetual cold, which eventually became pneumonia. In October 1941, she was sent home to Newcastle to recover and then to the Lake District for a proper convalescence, where she spent most of her time rowing and reading. Coincidentally, the staff and pupils of Roedean had been evacuated to a hotel in nearby Keswick.

When she returned to Tankerville Place, there was a telegram waiting for her: 'Report immediately to DWRNS London for duties as Assistant to Press Officer'.[36]

This apparently innocuous telegram was regarded by Nancy as marking a major triumph. 'It is the dream of every would-be journalist's life to get to London, at least that little bit of it that surrounds Fleet Street',[37] she declared, blithely ignoring the fact that she was still some way, geographically and metaphorically, from the hallowed street.

On 29 October 1941, she arrived at WRNS HQ (otherwise known as HMS *President I*), then situated in Great Smith Street. (In late 1942, the WRNS HQ would be moved into the Admiralty buildings, in Queen Anne's Mansions, where they occupied the whole of the first floor.) She learned she was to be assistant to the formidable press officer, First Officer Esta Eldod. Eldod had been appointed the WRNS press officer in autumn 1940 and remained in this post throughout the war; she was ultimately awarded the MBE in 1945. Prior to joining the service on 1 August 1940, she had been press officer for Radiation Ltd., manufacturers of gas appliances, a job she returned to when she left the Wrens. Eldod's efforts on behalf of the service were unparalleled: during her five and a half years, she travelled over 10,000 miles each year and was in Holland on VJ Day. Almost single-handedly, she was responsible for the service's high profile, particularly in the daily press and women's magazines.

Eldod lived with her friend, Nan Robinson, whom she affectionately called 'Nannybell', in a bungalow in Woldingham and a flat in Great Smith Street. Robinson was then catering officer for Sainsbury's, eventually taking up the same post for the BBC. Eldod was madly keen on dogs and at that time had the first of what would be a succession of dachshunds: Humperdinck (after the war, Humperdinck's successor was a Lord Nelson).

There was no shortage of expertise in the public relations department:

WRNS Director Vera Laughton Mathews had herself once worked as a journalist and edited *The Wren*. Another recruit was a young Wren called Violet Fulford, a trained commercial artist who had been working at Gas Industries House on publications for and about the gas industry. As well as the impressively efficient Miss Eldod, WRNS HQ boasted the presence of Lady Cholmondeley, the former Sybil Sassoon, a society beauty. Occasionally, she would invite Nancy and other Wrens for a grand tea at her house in Kensington Palace Gardens.

Nancy was living in a flat at Penn Court, in Collingham Road, just off the Cromwell Road (the WRNS quarters in Hampstead were full). She had to manage on a monthly salary of £19, plus an allowance of £10 for rent, food and uniform replacement. But her new home alone cost $4\frac{1}{2}$ guineas a week.

One of her first tasks was to help preside over the launch of a film about the WRNS, directed by Commander Tony Kimmins and co-written by Clemence Dane. Noel Coward was amongst the throng of dignitaries and journalists representing the likes of *Vogue, Harper's Bazaar* and *Picture Post*.

Mostly, however, the press office would be occupied with writing features about WRNS activities and planting them in the national press. Occasionally, they would have to deal with embarrassing stories about the WRNS, limiting any possible damage they might pose to the image of the service. Sometimes the press office would find themselves given work that was not strictly 'proper Navy'. Canine-devotee Esta Eldod once penned a short story about the adored Humperdinck which was published in *The Ditty Box*, the Navy's magazine – so called after the small box which sailors kept their possessions in on board ship. Eldod asked Violet Fulford to provide an illustration to accompany her story and summoned her to the flat one morning to sketch Humperdinck. This proved almost impossible, as the diminutive dog kept trying to take chunks out of Fulford.

Sometimes the hand of royalty dictated what work Nancy undertook. In March 1942, the Queen (later the Queen Mother) decided that what were referred to as the Wrens' 'po-hats' had to go and a new design be selected. A group of hats were chosen and, with Wren Doris Chambers chosen to model them for Her Majesty, they were dispatched to Buckingham Palace for royal approval. Later that month Wren Joan Reed (née Rust) was summoned to the WRNS press office. There, she was told by Eldod and Nancy that the Queen had given her approval for a new WRNS hat and that, she, Joan, was to be the model for the press photographs. The shoot took place on the roof of Sanctuary Buildings, Great Smith Street where Nancy coached Reed on which way to stand to show off the latest WRNS fashion accessory to its fullest advantage. The photographs duly appeared in all the papers the following day. However, Reed soon found herself summoned to the press office yet again, where, to everyone's embarrassment, she was tersely informed that she had been wearing the hat the wrong way round and the whole thing would have to be done again.

One of the most famous projects produced by Esta Eldod's press office was *Wrens in Camera*, a book of photographs by Lee Miller that showed

Wrens carrying out the full range of their wartime duties. Many of the trades represented in Miller's photographs showed the Wrens in unexpected roles – as mechanics and signallers, and their involvement in the build-up to D-Day. Violet Fulford designed the layout and lettering and helped select the photographs; the book was eventually published in 1945.

Another former Wren, Eileen Chadwick, remembers being recruited by Eldod and Nancy to accompany a number of other Wrens on a picnic with a group of GIs. It was part of a publicity shoot for an American magazine designed to show the folks back home how well 'the boys' were getting on in England. After meeting up in London, the Wrens and GIs were put in a lorry and taken to a large house somewhere near Cobham in Surrey. Once there, they were snapped square dancing and eating large quantities of good food. Upon her return to London, Chadwick was to report back to Eldod on the day's events. She was also commandeered into representing her service by appearing in a film made by the Rank Organization for Australian audiences, called – rather unimaginatively – *Life of WRNS*.

Chadwick remembers the First Officer and her assistant with affection: 'They were great guns, those two . . . '. Eldod 'was a scream', while Nancy struck her as 'fearless . . . and very handsome'. Once she knocked at her office door and went in, to find Nancy on the phone arguing with an anonymous adversary about a lost document. The conversation finished abruptly when Nancy told her caller, 'Come any time and look, Sherlock bloody Holmes!'

In the deep-voiced, sharp-witted, confident Esta Eldod, Nancy seemed to have found a role model. She even imitated the way Eldod would summon visitors into her office, booming 'Come!' But they did have their clashes as Violet Fulford recalls, 'I guess sparks flew because they were both very strong characters and both very amusing'.

While she was settling into her new post, Nancy received an unexpected invitation to a wedding. The call came from her second cousin, Rosemary Keyes, whose mother, Edith Keyes, was one of Norah's many cousins. Nancy and Rosemary had never met, but Rosemary was determined to gather as many of her numerous relatives as possible when she married David Fellowes on 10 January 1942. Like Nancy, Rosemary Keyes had joined the Wrens at the beginning of the war, at the suggestion of her uncle, Admiral Lord Keyes. 'I was actually interviewed by one of his girlfriends', she recalls. 'She told me, "you must be an officer"'. Rosemary began her service in Dover in October 1939 and became a cypher officer. Like cousin Nancy, she too felt that being an administrative officer meant you were 'not really involved' in the war. Although Nancy couldn't make it to the wedding, the two cousins had a long chat on the telephone, and Rosemary remembers how 'her sense of humour certainly came across'.

There were also regular opportunities for the animosity between the rival women's services to be aired – in sporting fashion, naturally. On the Light Service, members from the WRNS, ATS and WAAF battled it out in a quiz, presided over by Janet Quigley, later to feature prominently in Nancy's life as producer of *Woman's Hour*. The quiz was part of *Women at*

War, a weekly magazine show for women in the armed forces. Pamela Frankau was the programme's 'agony aunt', dealing with servicewomen's more personal problems, such as falling in love with married men. Other items on the programme included the 'Wartime Confessions' of the stars; tips on 'Beauty in Battledress'; a radio 'strip', called *Jill of All Trades*, written by Arthur Ferrier and played by Kay Hammond; news and gossip; and music from Carroll Gibbons and his band. Contributors included Audrey Lucas, Jenny Nichols and Robert MacDermot, all held together by compere Elizabeth Cowell. Wrens were sometimes commandeered into guesting on the show to answer questions about life in the service. One asked to do so was Betty Harboard (now Hodges), who would eventually become Chief Officer Wren of North-West Europe. However, Harboard revealed that her slot was rather restricted by wartime rules: 'As "careless talk cost lives", it was rather difficult to talk about anything we were doing!'

Though Nancy enjoyed doing *Women at War*, she took a rather cynical view of the importance of the broadcasts, and was rather circumspect about its contribution to the 'war effort'. For her, it was (as were her deskbound duties) worlds away from where the 'real' war was taking place, as her 'Ballade of Achievement' reflects:

> My uncle has said that he knows
> of a girl who made thousands in tin,
> while another invented a rose,
> and saw, from a tram, Errol Flynn.
> A record for living in sin
> has been trapped by a Nun in Cawnpore –
> my record is certain to win,
> I have listened to 'Women at War'.
>
> There are men who have rowed round Cape Horn
> in the teeth of a Nor'Eastern gale,
> and some who have even been born
> in a 'bus passing through Maida Vale –
> Galahad, on the march, in chain mail
> had not task quite so tough, or so sore . . .
> he only discovered the Grail.
> I have listened to 'Women at War'.
>
> *The Envoy*
> Yes, Princess, I've a good deal to learn
> and you say that you've found me a bore?
> Well, I have been bored in my turn,
> I have listened to 'Women at War'.

(January 1942)

Nancy also took part in transatlantic broadcasts, including *Answering You*, featuring guests from America and Britain swapping news and views. The respective MCs were Alistair Cooke and Mary Adams. On the show's eighty-ninth edition, Nancy herself was in the London studio with Adams, who gushed to Cooke, 'I can't begin to describe her beautiful trim uniform'.[38] Cooke gushed back to Nancy, 'Aren't you cute?', before asking her a series of undemanding questions such as 'What does WRNS really mean?' Nancy told the transatlantic audience about the Wrens' probationary period, their training and how their make-up should be 'inconspicuous'. And what, asked Cooke, were the delicately made-up Wrens allowed to do on their free time?

> We're allowed to do whatever we please and go wherever we want to go, as long as we don't bring discredit on the King's uniform, so that rather bars sports like standing on the hands in Piccadilly and mounting Nelson's column with a long streamer about 'England Expects'.[39]

The broadcast took an increasingly eccentric turn when Nancy proceeded to inform listeners that her father envied the Wrens their training. George, she said, was 'very anxious to join a Correspondence Course in order to be taught how to do these things. From cooking steak to making beds – he wants to know – he doesn't feel that he's come into his own yet.'[40]

During another edition of the programme, made after she had stopped working in the press office, she informed listeners that although 'In the Navy, you're not allowed to keep a diary', she had just written a book (*Nelson*). She hoped, she said, 'to emerge from the war big with experience'.[41] Indeed, she was already taking steps to capitalize on her experiences. In January, she sent Cecil McGivern a short story, 'School for Heroes', asking that it be considered for broadcast.

In March, McGivern sent a memo to producer Janet Quigley at the BBC. Nancy, he told Quigley, was 'anxious to do broadcasting. Has asked me if I could circulate some info. She has got ideas and writes scripts – of the lighter type!'[42] He summed up Nancy's suitable qualities for broadcasting thus:

> Voice – mid pitch to deep. Soft. Attractive.
> Diction – very clear
> Accent – Roedean
> Manner – pleasant, straightforward
> Voice age – 25–28 (is much younger)[43]

Joining Nancy on many of the *Women at War* broadcasts was her friend Beatrice Jewell. In late 1942, she was posted to WRNS HQ and shared Nancy's Penn Court flat for about six months. The two women would hold small parties at their home, where the guests included Pamela Frankau, Cecil McGivern, her current boss Esta Eldod and Nan Robinson and, most significantly, broadcaster and writer Naomi 'Mickie' Jacob.

Yorkshire-born and of Jewish extraction, the crop-haired, well-tailored 58-year-old Mickie Jacob was a remarkable character. She had been fending for herself since the age of fifteen, when her mother had emigrated to America. She worked as a teacher and then became secretary/companion to the music-hall star, Marguerite Broadfoote. After Marguerite's untimely death, Mickie married briefly, before meeting and falling in love with Henrietta Simone, a barmaid at the local pub in Willesden where Mickie was working in a munitions factory during the First World War. After the war, she decided to try and make a career on the London stage and managed to land a string of small roles in various successful West End plays.

But after contracting TB and spending many months in a sanatorium, she decided to become a writer – and a prolific one at that. Her first novel, *Jacob Ussher*, was published in 1926. Specializing in populist fiction, often romantic in nature but usually set against a broad historical background and drawing on her own experiences of anti-Semitism, her Gollancz trilogy followed the fortunes of the son of a Jewish businessman who emigrates from Vienna to London. Mickie was to turn down the American Eichelburger Prize in 1935 for her book *Honour Come Back* when she discovered that the recipient male author that year was Hitler.

In 1930, following doctors' advice, she bought a small house in Sirmione, Italy, where she spent the winter months of each year. From here, she continued to produce at least two books a year; as well as novels, she wrote books about her life, her friends, her animals and her food, together with a biography of Marie Lloyd. Visitors to 'Casa Mickie' included Radclyffe Hall, who thought Mickie 'a really remarkable mimic [who] tells very coarse stories',[44] and Mickie's lover, Sadie Robinson, who divided her time between her husband and child in England and Mickie. When the Second World War began, Mickie returned to England, appeared in several plays and then worked for ENSA as a welfare officer. She had already begun to work in radio and – like Nancy – was to become one of the BBC's most popular postwar 'personality' broadcasters, establishing herself as a particular favourite on *Woman's Hour*.

In Mickie Jacob, Nancy saw that the personal and professional ambitions she was nurturing could actually be realized: here was another Northern woman who, despite modest means and ill-health, had carved out a successful career as a writer, actress and broadcaster; had had several long-term relationships with other women; and whose image and personality were accepted, without compromise. The impact was enormous: now, she could hardly wait for the war to be over so she could pursue the sort of life she had always dreamed of, as personified by Mickie Jacob.

She expressed her admiration for Mickie in an ode penned as a tribute to 'North-Country Humour':

> There is a mist
> on Merseyside
> that will persist
> when I have died.
>
> Others, no less
> than I today
> some foolishness
> will send away;
> for with the smokes
> that stain these skies

North country jokes
will always rise –

(March 1942)

And, prompted by an innocent enquiry from Mickie, Nancy retorted with
'A Ballade of Earnest Enquiry for Mr Peince of the Liverpool Echo':

I can sing, I can box, I can knit
I can tell when it's going to rain
(although I must softly admit
that I haven't seen 'Citizen Kane')
If you asked me the time of a train
or the date of the Spanish Armada
I don't think you'd ask me in vain,
but – which of you two works the harder?

Sit still just a minute and dream
of the Heavens to which you will go
an Island, surrounded by steam
where Telegraph forms fall like snow –
well, into the idyll will blow
a question, from Lago di Garda –
Miss Jacob is anxious to know
which one of you two works the harder?

(25 March 1942)

And, in 'A rude Ballade of relinquishment and assessment', in bidding
farewell to a friend who was joining a rival service:

Just think of the things you will miss,
you've that Monday night party to thank
for Miss Settle, Miss Jacob, the Quiz
(and your privilege, dear, to be frank)
those things that you ate, and you drank,
I admit most of these were ersatz –
You will miss those gay talks with your Bank
but think of the gain to the ATs.

(January 1942)

She may have found an inspiring role model, but, as usual, her financial
situation undermined everything. It was proving increasingly difficult to
survive in London on WRNS pay. She was not allowed to supplement her
salary by doing journalism work during wartime and the broadcasts she did
for the BBC were unpaid, as it fell within the remit of her post as assistant
press officer. Matters came to a head in June 1943, when Beatrice Jewell was
posted to Lowestoft and Nancy could no longer afford the Penn Court flat.
Eventually, she was given a room at WRNS quarters in England's Lane, off
Haverstock Hill, NW3, sharing with Angela Sanderson.

Lack of money wasn't her only frustration, however: working in the press office, coming into contact more with journalists than other comrades in the services, she again began to feel that she was playing no part in the 'real' war effort. Eventually, a row blew up between First Officer Eldod and her fidgety assistant, who told her she was 'sick and tired of tarting around with journalists'.[45] She was soon posted to HMS *Pembroke III*, initially working at the recruiting department's offices near Green Park. Then, to her surprise and horror, she was summoned by Lady Cholmondeley and told she would be replacing Second Officer Vivien Akerman as travelling recruiting officer (TRO), covering the north of England.

More Wrens were needed to replace the men who were required for sea duty and to ensure there were enough women in the service to carry out the Admiralty's edict that the Wrens would now carry out all Fleet Air Arm maintenance. The service launched a bid to recruit 12,000 more women and Nancy, the new TRO, was sent out on the road as part of this campaign – 'real' war work again. Her new position was, she considered, 'one of the toughest jobs of my life. . . . I travelled round and round the country like a mad mouse in a wheel'.[46] Applicants were referred either by the Labour Exchange or the National Service Bureau. Recruiting officers were told, 'Find out all you can about the girl – her home life, her previous work, if any. Impress upon her the importance of secrecy and see that she fully realizes the slowness of promotion'.

To begin with, she interviewed prospective Wrens in West and South London – at least twenty a day. Once on the road, her travels took her to Manchester, Leeds, Bradford, Sheffield, Derby and Birmingham. She stayed one night a week in each city, interviewing prospective recruits, sometimes in football grounds. In addition, she visited youth hostels, YWCAs and Girl Guide troupes – even the dreaded Roedean – extolling the virtues of the WRNS.

On top of this exhausting schedule, TRO Spain was often short of money to amuse herself in her few spare hours. The Admiralty, apparently, lost her application to change from 'Pay and living in the WRNS quarters' to 'Pay plus travelling plus hard-lying money' – a mistake that went unnoticed until a cheque she paid to the Great Northern Hotel in Leeds bounced. It took nearly a month for the administration department to sort out the error, during which time Nancy had to eschew the comforts of proper hotels for YWCAs and cheap bed and breakfasts. She couldn't even afford to take herself to the pictures. But, bereft of most forms of entertainment, she did start to tap out the beginnings of a book about her earlier duties as a Wren in North Shields. Once solvent again, and in London, she was able to enjoy frequent forays to the theatre. A particular favourite was the revue, *Rise Above It*, starring the two Hermiones, Baddeley and Gingold: she claimed to have seen it eight times.

She had returned to London complete with a finished manuscript and a heavy chest cold that turned out to be a streptococcus infection. Yet again, the WRNS quarters were full, and another officer, Betty Gidden, let her camp down at her bedsitter at 4 Randolph Gardens, Kilburn. Second

Officer Gidden was in charge of WRNS recruitment in the London area. While staying there, Nancy showed her the first draft of *Thank You – Nelson*; Gidden retyped the manuscript, suggesting cuts. Out went most of the swearing, but in stayed one of Nancy's poems, inspired by her days amongst the shipyards of North Shields and the London Blitz.

Nancy decided to start hawking her treasured manuscript around, after first getting permission from the Admiralty to publish it. Unusually for a first-time author, it was no dog-eared, scrawled script; thanks to Betty Gidden's efforts, her 65,000 word debut was typed in double spacing and neatly contained in a cardboard jacket. During the next three months, she took *Nelson* to seven publishers, delivering the manuscript in person and, after seven rejections, collecting it again. Nancy later told *Woman's Hour* listeners that seven wasn't really very many: 'There are at least two hundred London publishers, and I was prepared to go on and be thrown out of all of them'. She put the book's eventual success down to a fluke that was, she considered, 'Heaven's reward for all that plodding'.[47] Those who turned her down included Collins, Hodder and Stoughton, Cresset Press, Robert Hale and Co. and Harrap's. Eventually, she took it to Jarrolds, part of the Hutchinson group, where it came to the attention of Walter Hutchinson himself. One of his editors, a Mrs Beatrice Webb, was impressed by her reader's report on the manuscript and summoned Nancy to the Hutchinson offices in Princes Gate.

Webb asked her if she was writing anything else. Only a detective story, said Nancy. Webb promptly signed her up for that as well, with an option to buy her next two fiction books. They would give her an advance of £50 each for *Nelson* and for her first detective novel. Her royalties would be 10 per cent on a print-run of 5,000. Nancy left Hutchinson's in a state of disbelief, and, from a call-box near the Albert Hall, called Betty Gidden to tell her the good news.

There were two other people she called from that box: one was a young Guardsman called David Fenwick, with whom she was having 'a sentimental friendship';[48] the other was First Officer Kay Jones, who was in charge of recruitment and applications. Along with Betty Gidden, Jones had become Nancy's closest friend, looking after her when she was ill and arranging easier work for her in the recruiting department. Moreover, Gidden and Jones were, said Nancy, 'the first people I had met since my own family who knew that I couldn't really help behaving like a sort of Mickey Mouse in uniform'.[49] The three friends would spend most of their lunchtimes at the National Gallery canteen, enjoying the recitals given by the pianist Myra Hess.

Back at the recruitment department, Nancy had been given the less onerous task of reorganizing the HQ's filing and posting system when, ironically, she was made a Second Officer WRNS on 11 November 1943, a rank equal to a Royal Navy lieutenant. With her new promotion, she was finally given a room in the WRNS officers' quarters in Queen's Grove, St John's Wood. But the legacy of her days in Arbroath was starting to catch up with her and her respiratory infections became more frequent. She was soon spending more and more time in the WRNS sick bay in England's Lane, Hampstead. Working there was Third Officer Kathleen Wyatt-Browning (now Davey), secretary to the medical officer of health. She remembers the ailing Nancy as 'fun-loving and good company although she was ill. She came into our sick bay several times for a short stay'. Despite her illnesses, even in bed 'she always had a portable typewriter on her knees', remembers Davey – and often the sick bay cat, which had been given to Davey by the MO Surgeon Lieutenant Margot Dixon. 'The sick bay's twelve beds were usually full, but there was no air-raid shelter there and, when the sirens sounded, the patients – whatever their condition – were assembled in the corridor and given tin hats to wear. It was the safest place'. Despite their farcical elements, the flying-bomb raids were terrifying and brutal. London suffered 92 per cent of the casualties resulting from attacks during an eighteen-month period that lasted throughout 1943–4. In August 1944 alone, on average a hundred flying bombs a day fell on London, killing 1,103 and injuring 2,292, and destroying 17,000 buildings in the capital and the south-east of England.

Nancy was not oblivious to their terrors: 'I never knew if I left someone at Admiralty Arch, say, and walked across St James's Park to my office, that there might not come a chuffing noise, a gliding silence: and a crash. And I might never see or speak to my friend again',[50] she remembered more than a decade later. On one occasion, her worst fears were nearly realized.

On Sunday 9 July 1944, a V-2 landed on the Guards Chapel, Wellington Barracks, in Birdcage Walk while a congregation of 200 attended morning parade service. Amongst the dead were several Wrens. Nancy was at work that morning and could hear the hymn-singing from the chapel. Then she heard the bomb cut out. Within seconds, her office had turned to rubble: there was broken glass everywhere, the walls began to crack and furniture from the upper floor fell through the ceiling. Nancy was severely shocked but otherwise unhurt; several other Wrens, though, had been cut by flying glass. Applying first aid was difficult, because the kits were locked up and the officer with the appropriate keys was at church in Kensington. The incident left her with one peculiar wish regarding her own death: 'I hope I, too, die singing hymns'.[51] But she later admitted, 'I didn't confide in anyone how much this had shocked me'.[52] Soon, however, she was in for another – though less violent – shock.

Nancy, possibly one of the most reluctant officers to be found in the Wrens, was informed that, as of Monday 28 August 1944, she was to take charge of training officer cadets at Framewood Manor, Stoke Poges, Buckinghamshire. Quite apart from the new, unwanted responsibilities, there was another reason for Nancy's abject horror: she had planned to spend the Bank Holiday Monday finishing off a detective novel which she had begun writing while pretending to give her fullest attention to the filing systems at Queen Anne's Mansions. Instead, she was to be uprooted again and sent to inspire leadership qualities in hundreds of young women, far more eager to hear about 'The Admiralty and What It Means to Me' than she was to tell them.

Cadets on the OTC were usually put through their paces at Royal Naval HQ, Greenwich, but the base, and in particular the Nurses' Home, which also doubled up as Wren accommodation, had been badly bomb-damaged in April 1944. Officer training was switched to Stoke Poges; then, in December 1944, to the New College, Hampstead. It returned to Greenwich just before the end of the war, in June 1945.

Framewood Manor itself was a large red-brick mansion, with expansive lawns that gave the cadets ample room to do their drill. Lectures were conducted in Nissen huts. There were about fifteen divisions on each course. During their month's training, cadets had to learn, amongst other things, how to deal with giving personal advice to lower ranks, and how to apply for courses. They were also lectured on naval history, security, administrative procedures, service writing and the Disciplinary Code. Delivering these lectures now constituted Nancy's new duties: her first was on 'Communications throughout the Fleet'. She lived in a tiny 'cabin' on the ground floor of the manor, from where her by now frequent bouts of coughing could be clearly heard.

In overall charge was the Superintendent, Miss French, who ran the OTC throughout the war. Cadets remembered her for her fondness for making patchwork quilts in her spare time and telling them they should salute 'just like a butterfly'. On the administrative staff was Betty Harboard, by now an officer herself. She would sit on selection panels each week with Vera Laughton Mathews, Lady Cholmondeley and, occasionally, Superintendent French. 'They were sending cadets through at a rate of knots', she remembers.

When Nancy arrived at Framewood, she and Betty Harboard would often play tennis together:

> 'A friend of mine, Pat Lawrence, who was by then in the army, and his wife, Molly, lived quite near and said that any time I wanted to have a game, to come over. Nancy, having been at Roedean, and me at Queen Ethelberga's in Harrogate, were both keen types, so we used to bike over and play together. But she wasn't really a friend – I wouldn't confide anything to her. She was amusing, rather cynical in a way. She had an acid tongue, but she was shrewd, clever. I realized she was pushy – a manoeuvrer. When I read her book [*Millionaire*] it was just like her. And it just irritated me when I saw things she'd written in the *Express* – she was trying to be funny all the time. I thought it was rather a waste of time'.

But while Betty may have felt that Nancy could not be trusted with her secrets, Nancy believed that hers were safe with Betty. Once, she told her that she couldn't have children, and on another occasion talked about her sexuality:

> 'One day she was talking about wanting to become a lesbian. She asked me if I'd heard of them. I said I know one or two people who were, by repute. She said, "I'd like to be one". She would talk about a woman writer who she said she knew was one. I don't know if she was saying it to try and shock me. It did

rather, because I'd never heard anybody speaking to me like that before. She didn't say, "don't tell anyone", it was more like, "oh, by the way ... "'.

For Nancy to make such bold revelations to another officer was either brave or foolhardy, or both. When Betty Harboard was transferred to Belfast, she was told by a petty officer there that the first officer was a lesbian. Words were exchanged in high places and the hapless FO was transferred to the naval base at Cardiff, which had possibly the lowest number of Wrens stationed there. Betty Harboard was promoted to second officer and took over from her in Belfast. Naturally, nothing of this was mentioned by the time Nancy came to write her book about the war years, *Why I'm Not a Millionaire*. According to her, her romantic interests had been directed exclusively at men. At Arbroath, it was a pilot called Arthur who was killed in a raid over Germany. Then, there was her 'sentimental friendship' with David. These followed the 'Paddys' and 'Michaels' of her prewar years, all of whom appeared to have got married soon after Nancy 'fell in love' with them.

In between games of tennis and shocking fellow officers with revelations about her sexuality, Nancy was in charge of her own division of cadets, 'Anson'. One of them was Joan Cockburn who, coincidentally, had been at Queen Elizabeth College with another distant relative of Nancy's, Lavender Keyes, Admiral Lord Keyes's daughter. Of Nancy, she says, 'I was probably the person who knew her best there'. There was, she recalls,

'a suspicion that Nancy had been got rid of a bit [from Queen Anne's Mansion] – whether she'd been giving trouble or what ... Miss French wasn't really Nancy's sort, with her quilts and what have you. Nancy used to come into our rooms after Miss French had said goodnight to us, put her head round the door and take her off, saying, "just like a butterfly"'.

Betty Harboard also remembers that she was 'frightfully good' at mimicking Lady Cholmondeley and sending up her comments about her connections with the Royal Family.

Cadets were encouraged to take part in extracurricular activities such as choir singing, amateur dramatics and sports, particularly table tennis, a personal favourite of Vera Laughton Mathews, who always insisted on a game when she visited. On Sundays, they would go to church up the road from the manor. Each month, there would be the ritual 'passing out' concert, where outgoing cadets would do their comic and musical turns, followed by 'passing out' drinks with their respective officer at a pub in Gerrards Cross. There were also weekly shows every Monday evening, where each division was expected to provide some entertainment. Nancy's 'Anson' cadets, to their horror, found there was no one amongst them who could sing, play piano or boast any stage talent whatsoever. Desperate, they decided to perform a skit on a popular radio programme of the time, *Monday Night at Eight*. Part of it consisted of calling up a surprise guest to do a turn: the 'Anson' cadets decided that, unbeknownst to her, their Second Officer Spain would be that guest. Joan Cockburn recalled the scene:

'She was sitting in the front row, with the Superintendent. And then we called her up. I can still remember the horrified look on her face. So she sat for a moment, then got up, came on to the stage and then proceeded to give the most wonderful display of pantomime characters – the Fairy Queen, the Demon King – it was absolutely marvellous. And, of course, no one believed that we hadn't tipped her off '.

But Nancy did not really enjoy her time as a cadet instructor. Joan Cockburn admits, 'I don't think she taught us very much', while Betty Hodges says, 'She joked all the time and, if you were an officer, you had to have some discipline. Of course, in lectures you did make the odd joke, because some of it was jolly boring stuff '. Nancy herself said, 'I never could get over the basic home-truth that the cadets knew so very much more about Life in the WRNS than I did'.[53] Although this was certainly true, it does not tell the whole story. With *Thank You – Nelson* about to be published, and with what was to become *Poison in Play* in progress, Nancy already had one eye firmly fixed on her postwar career. Lecturing young officers on the finer points of engendering a long, illustrious career in the Wrens was not what she had enlisted for and, with the war entering its final stages, her original reason no longer existed. Her war was ending on an unsatisfactory note.

At their end of their course, the cadet divisions would have group photographs taken with their officers. Betty Harboard's show a rather sullen-looking Nancy surrounded by her fresh-faced cadets. In one, Nancy is actually the only person not looking directly at the camera. Already looking to the future, she appears distracted, her mind clearly on something else beyond Framewood Manor. It is a picture of a woman already set apart.

Symbolically, by early December 1944, Nancy's health problems began to recur – another chest cold, followed by asthma attacks for which the cause could not be pinpointed. Such illnesses were not, it transpired, unusual for women of the WRNS. Official figures released decades later revealed that, during the war, Wrens suffered more than their male counterparts from mental illnesses, including depression, and the number of cases of non-pulmonary tuberculosis were 'significantly higher'.

After just three months' instructing fledgling Wren officers, Nancy was sent to the Hospital for Women in Vincent Square, near Vauxhall Bridge Road, which was full of ailing Wrens, including a certain Rating Werner Laurie who had had appendicitis. Nancy continued to write during her convalescence, including what she called 'silly clerihews' about some of her fellow officers, such as Betty Harboard, who visited her there several times:

> First Officer Harboard
> Doesn't know port from starboard
> She's old enough. She ought
> To know starboard from port.[54]

Kay Jones was also a visitor, bearing packets of asthma remedies for her ailing friend. Doctors tested Nancy for allergies, but found that most of her problems were attributable to a bad tooth and the ever-present streptococcus. She enjoyed the rest, the attention and being able just to lie in bed instead of giving lectures in damp Nissen huts. Significantly, she later said her stay in hospital was 'easily the best bit of my war service as an officer'.[55]

As she had done in Hampstead, she perched her typewriter on her knees and continued working on *Poison in Play*. There was also good news about *Thank You – Nelson*: Vera Laughton Mathews had agreed to write a glowing preface for it. It said, 'Second Officer Spain has turned the hard light of reality on the first faltering steps of the WRNS ... *Thank You – Nelson* is a page of life, and the momentous issues behind its lively story make it a page of history'. While in hospital, Nancy also wrote a poem about her time in service. It was published in *The Ditty Box* and she was paid 10s. 6d.

> The ship's clock of serene and polished face
> Has marked a year or two of service time
> Five years' since I reported at the Base
> And found companionways were hard to climb.
> That clock avoids things not inside its powers
> And so it only marks the happy hours'.
>
> Reason assures me that there was despair
> Bewilderment, hurt, vanity and pain:
> That five years ticking unrecorded there.
> And so, in spite of reason, once again,
> Somehow I hear the bugle in my heart
> As the sun sinks, and as the ensign dips.
> After today I shall not make a part
> Of the intolerable loveliness of ships.[56]

This also appears to have been the time when she decided that the writing career which, she hoped, now lay ahead of her would not be too highbrow in tone and ambition, a determination that is clearly articulated on the final page of 'To Please Myself', in her last surviving poem:

> Preserve, Dear God, the writer from the intellect.
> Tell him he is an entertainer, not a bore.
> Tell him it is more laudable to seek effect
> After the work of Art is finished. Not before.
> Something bewitching in the dark will reach us
> Across the footlights in each, studied measure
> If he remembers that he need not teach us
> But only please himself and so give pleasure.
> For should we find, by some most happy chance
> The passing wind of magic in the dance
> Do you suppose we shall not thank and bless you
> Dancers who did not let your brains repress you?

(1944)

Nancy's war was coming to a welcome, if perhaps undistinguished end. But, with the imminent publication of her first book, it was timely that she should shed the apparel of Second Officer Spain – an unconvincing, uncomfortable character – and prepare herself for a new career as 'N. Spain – Author'.

In January she left Vincent Square and returned to Tankerville Place, awaiting her official discharge from the Wrens. As was customary, she was now on two months' paid leave. While in Newcastle, to her delight, she opened *The Times* on Friday 5 and discovered an advertisement that Hutchinson had taken out announcing the publication of her 'vigorous and witty' first book. Shortly after, a package containing her six author's copies arrived at Tankerville Place. Also that week, her first post-WRNS piece of journalism appeared in the *Sunday Chronicle*, 'Nazis Haunted by Ghost Ship',[57] about the *Sleipner* and her old friends, Captain Ullring and his Norwegian crew.

For Nancy, her war was over and she had to start all over again. Gone were the familiar routines and roles and her place in the world was still uncertain. However, she was certain of one thing: she did not want to settle back in Newcastle.

'I knew I could never go back to life on the old, prewar terms, changing library books, playing a little tennis, helping mother about the house',[58] she said later. She returned to London a few weeks later; home would now be the bedsitter in Randolph Gardens. On 16 February 1945, Second Officer Nancy Spain became naval pensioner Nancy Spain. Six days earlier, she had presented a signed first edition of *Thank You – Nelson* to the Imperial War Museum. It is still in their reference library.

The Admiralty agreed that her respiratory complaints had been 'aggravated' by her war service and duly granted her an 80 per cent disability pension of £2 a week, plus a one-off gratuity of £75 (based on length of service). She was also given a clothing grant and coupons, a civilian ration book and identity card, plus a discharge certificate which could be used as a reference when seeking work or accommodation.

Accommodation she had; work was another matter. She began racking her brains for another idea to take to Beatrice Webb at Hutchinson's and toyed with the idea of writing something about her great-aunt Isabella. To this end, on her way back to London, she visited Amy Dorling, Isabella's last surviving half-sister, who lived in Colchester. Amy regaled Nancy with many interesting stories about Isabella, but the wintry conditions, inside and outside Amy's small house, gave her flu on top of the bronchitis she was still recovering from. She returned home to Kilburn, noticing copies of *Thank You – Nelson* on sale (8s. 6d.) at Liverpool Street station.

She had a raging temperature when she received a telephone call on Saturday 27 January telling her that a James Wedgwood Drawbell, then editor of the *Sunday Chronicle*, wanted to see her. Dragging herself off to the *Chronicle* offices in Gray's Inn Road, she was asked by Drawbell if she would be interested in some feature work for the paper. He explained to a bemused, feverish Nancy that, on the basis of her 'very good review', he

1. Four-year-old Nancy, the 'little Japanese doll'.
Copyright: Nick Werner Laurie

2. The West Hartlepool Ladies' lacrosse team with, in the back row, the Misses Spain (third from right), Sargeant (third from left) and Sanderson (second from left).
Copyright: Nick Werner Laurie

3. The 'anonymous school in Sussex'. *Author collection*

4. 'Proper Navy'. Second Officer Spain surrounded by some of her cadets at
Framewood Manor, Stoke Poges.
Copyright: Nick Werner Laurie

5. Enjoying the post-war London literary life, at a Foyle's luncheon.
Christina Foyle collection

6. Joan Werner Laurie, 'very good-looking with a rather long nose. . .'
Dick Laurie collection

7. Paul Seyler.
Dick Laurie collection

8. Nancy and Dick Laurie at Granny's in Loxwood.
Dick Laurie collection

9. Joan and Gilbert Harding on the good ship *Matina*.
Roger Storey collection

10. Wedlock was not their line.
Roger Storey collection

thought she would be ideal for what he had in mind. He had on his desk an early edition of the next day's *Sunday Times* which, it appeared, contained the said 'very good review'. Drawbell strongly recommended that she get herself a copy.

The next day, braving the steady snowfall, she caught a bus down to Marble Arch, bought a *Sunday Times* and went to the Cumberland Hotel for breakfast. In the top corner of the books page was a review, the like of which every first-time author dreams of – 'the sort . . . that really ought to be set to music',[59] she thought. It was headlined 'A Wren's-Eye View of the "Proper Navy"' and was written by A.A. Milne.

> There have been many such books written; perhaps the best known in this country has been 'What, No Morning Tea' by Anthony Cotterell, and, in America, 'See Here, Private Hargrove' by Private Hargrove. The latter sold a million copies in the States; I read it and thought it good. I think that Miss Spain's book is ten times better, and that she will be lucky if her publishers can find paper for 10,000 copies.
>
> From the first page to the last she does not put a foot wrong. She has written a book all about herself, of which she is neither the heroine nor the stooge . . . the author has told a story of absorbing interest in a delightfully humorous way. This is partly because it is only herself whom she insists on veiling in mask and domino.
>
> She will, I hope, write many others, including those novels for which she has all the equipment. She may even write a better book than 'Thank You – Nelson'. But I beg her . . . not to try to; by which I mean not to roll up the sleeves, spit on the hands and say, 'Now then!' Meanwhile, we have this: for which I shall say, as the Proper Navy must have said to her so often, 'Thank You – Nancy'.[60]

This review reduced Nancy to tears and, she later claimed, ensured that the first two editions of *Thank You – Nelson* were sold out. The occasion would have been even more emotional if she had known of Milne's initial extreme reluctance to review the book. Leonard Russell, literary editor of the *Sunday Times* and second husband of film critic Dilys Powell, for whom Milne reviewed books infrequently, had sent it to him and promptly been declared 'mad' for doing so. It was Daphne Milne who had first perused *Nelson* and persuaded her husband it was, after all, worth a look.

The *Newcastle Journal* and *North Mail* praised the first effort of 'a Newcastle woman with a sense of humour, befitting the daughter of a contributor to "Punch" . . . ' and enjoyed her

> series of adventures, some very gay and some grim and macabre, which she relates with infectious high spirits where they are amusing and with an illuminating restraint where they touch upon the horrific. The war's writings have produced little that is more poignant and eloquent of the ghastly toll exacted by the hazards of the war at sea than her description of her acceptance and delivery of the remains of the crew of the mined trawler, Harry Perkins . . . while her vivid writing makes gorgeous fun for the reader it also makes apparent her admiration for the men who man H.M. ships . . . [61]

Angela Milne in the *Observer* warned that the book

> will be approached warily by anyone allergic to those little chains of dots which usually link up the bits of some Beautiful Thought too deep for composition. But it does not take long to find that the sentences here are remarkably well-turned and the dots do not hinder a rattling good story. It is doubtful if Nelson himself could have commanded a laundry van with more resource and gallantry.[62]

Monica Dickens in the *Sunday Chronicle* pronounced:

> She is no mean journalist and this talent has stood her in good stead. . . . Her keen eye for the 'human story' means her a bit too fond of the ' . . . ' indicating poignancy, but her sense of humour is colossal and her pictures of the 'types' with whom she worked are a joy.[63]

Apart from being considered by many who knew her well as the most honest book she ever wrote, *Thank You – Nelson* remains one of Nancy's most complete, vivid and memorable books. There are some glorious images: one December, she was sitting watching some seagulls and rooks screeching at each other. 'They were like a Manchester mourning party who have eaten and drunk to the departed spirit, who have heard the Will read and who are not pleased',[64] she observed.

Eventually, she wrote to A.A. Milne, thanking him for the *Sunday Times* review, and he invited her to have lunch at the Milne home, Cotchford Farm in Sussex, warning her that

> You will have to work up an enthusiasm for gardens first. Nothing annoys my wife (and me too) so much as seeing a visitor step heavily back onto a clump of aubretia behind her, ignore the tulips in front of her, and ask if we have been to many theatres lately.[65]

It was summer when she made the trip from Victoria to Sussex and was treated, despite postwar rationing, to a sumptuous lunch she could still recall ten years later: 'hot boiled salmon, peas, new potatoes, asparagus, strawberries and cream. A real cricketer's lunch'.[66]

By the time she met Milne, she had finished the next book: the first of her ten detective novels, *Poison in Play*, which was dedicated to Kay Jones, begun during her stint in the WRNS press office. The story was inspired by Nancy's sporting exploits on the tennis courts and in regional journalism, set against the glamorous backdrop of Wimbledon. Serge Ghent – formerly known as Sylvia Salmond – is a deep-voiced, hard-drinking former tennis player 'of peculiar tendencies'. She is married to Piers Ghent, a dress designer who sports painted fingernails. The complexities of the Ghents' personal life is discussed by two sports reporters on *The Banner*, Jack Priestman and Jerry McAlpine. At a tournament, Jerry meets Frances Olsen, a young sports journalist whose mother is a famous Fleet Street editor. Jerry arranges for her to cover Wimbledon. They are interested in the progress of Linda Traynor, the great white hope of British women's tennis, who had been expelled from Roedean. 'All celebrities are expelled sooner or later from Roedean',[67] notes Frances.

Into the fray comes Laurie Speed, head of a sportswear and equipment firm. In London, just before the start of Wimbledon, Frances is introduced to Serge and Piers Ghent. At the tournament, she discovers Jerry dead in the press box. Jack encourages her to write a story about it for *The Banner* and so she arranges to interview the Ghents, who had known Jerry well. She also talks to Gregory Pratov, a Russian ballet dancer turned tennis player. She then learns from Jack that Jerry died from hyoscin hydro-bromide poisoning – a substance Piers gives to his cats. Jack and Frances have dinner at The Bag of Tricks, a club frequented by Jerry and owned by Johnny DuVivien, an Australian wrestler – and now Nancy's sleuth. Jack and Frances make lists of possible suspects and their motives. We learn that Piers is also a qualified doctor and that Johnny has a wife, Natasha. While in pursuit of Jerry's killer, they stumble upon the body of Gregory Pratov. Linda Traynor is seen making a fast getaway from the scene of the crime. They decide to trap her at Wimbledon, where she is due to play on Centre Court the next day.

Though Nancy had already started to settle into her new literary life, she was not unaffected by the official end of the war on 8 May. She did not join the crowds outside Buckingham Palace, or in central London, which had been transformed into the venue for an enormous, impromptu street party, but went instead to Kew Gardens. When she returned to Kilburn that evening, revellers were still dancing in the streets.

In her new 'HQ', from where she could hear the noise outside Buckingham Palace, she took one last look backwards. Flicking through the pages of her first 'To Please Myself', she turned to 'Time for a dreamer', written at the beginning of the war, before Winifred died. She picked up her pen again and made a number of alterations to the poem, as an epitaph to her dead love and all that she had known and lost:

> You are dead. There is time for wasting, and I am free to think
> waiting through six sad years of irrevocable war –
> Is there inside this static world an ancient rusty link
> recalling fun and ecstacy that isn't any more?
> In a flute in a tune in a violin, in a number we thought gay
> I may remember 'Stardust' – your laughter when we danced –
> the lights go down in the theatre – we could hear George Gershwin play,
> On a coloured Van Gogh postcard can my heart go back to France.

The postwar period had officially begun. Now Nancy had to find her place in it.

CHAPTER   FIVE

To Please Myself

Nancy spent her first summer as a naval pensioner cum full-time writer basking in the glowing reviews for *Thank You – Nelson* and working on ideas for another detective novel. She would rise early each day and spend the morning writing – a thousand words a day was her target. Afternoons were taken up with bus rides, mulling over her morning's work or visiting one of the ubiquitous Lyons Corner Houses. She also had an 'A' subscription to Boots' library and would go to the cinema to watch the newsreel screenings. As a civilian, she was, of course, having to manage on civilian rations – this wasn't easy for the average citizen but, for a spendthrift like Nancy, living in a bedsit which had a stove but no oven, it was a nightmare. She lived as frugally as she knew how, waiting for 'the call' from Fleet Street.

Apart from impressing notable critics like A.A. Milne, *Thank You – Nelson* had also caught the attention of Nancy's distant cousin, Sir Mayson Beeton, Isabella and Sam's surviving son. During a visit to his home in Walton-on-Thames, he told her that many writers had approached him to ask if they might write the first biography of his late mother. It was a project which he had planned to do himself but, at eighty, felt it was now too late. Impressed by her first offering as an author, and in view of their family connection, Mayson authorized Nancy to write the first Beeton biography.

The idea may have been planted earlier. In January 1934, Lawrence du Garde Peach's radio comedy, *Meet Mrs Beeton* – 'a culinary comedy for every wife'[1] – was broadcast on BBC Newcastle. It starred Joyce Carey as Isabella, 'a charming Victorian girl of about twenty' and George Sanders as Sam, 'rather shy in manner. ... He and Mrs Beeton are hopelessly in love with one another'.[2] The Beetons are having dinner with their friends Mr and Mrs Jennings, to whom Isabella has shown the manuscript of a novel she has written. Mrs Jennings, it transpires, is a singularly incompetent hostess. She starts the meal by serving some bad soup and Sam tactfully boasts to his hosts, 'The way in which Mrs Beeton can make a soup out of nothing is a wonder'.[3] At the end of the disastrous meal, during which Isabella has dished up all sorts of tasty tips to the unfortunate Mrs Jennings, Mr Jennings declares, 'Dear Mrs Beeton, you are indeed a walking cookery book.[4] ... I salute the mother of English cooking'.[5]

Mayson Beeton had made life much easier for Nancy than she would for her own prospective biographers. He had collected all the letters Samuel had written about Isabella after her death and had carried out extensive research, accompanied by copious notes, on nineteenth-century publishing. Nancy also had access to his library, which contained first editions of all the Beeton books. Isabella's love-letters, written in formal Victorian language and script, had been translated by Mayson's daughter, Belle. Isabella's diaries, written in smudged pencil, had also survived. After looking at all the material, Nancy felt she was up to the task and, despite having no contract or advance, she determined to 'go in search of my great aunt. I couldn't sleep a wink'.[6]

Her enthusiasm was to pall relatively quickly, however. Over ten years later, when the Beeton biography was about to go into a revised third edition, Nancy sent out a warning in her book *Why I'm Not a Millionaire*: 'Writing biographies is an expensive business and should not be lightly undertaken'.[7] In this, at least, she was following her great-aunt's tradition: in the preface to the first edition of *Household Management*, Isabella moaned, 'I must frankly own up, that if I had known beforehand, that this book would have cost me the labour which it has, I should never have been courageous enough to commence it'.[8]

Nancy's research would take her to Epsom, where William Dorling had opened his stationery shop and where his son, Henry, would build the first grandstand for the racecourse. She also went to Paris, to see the racecourse at Auteuil where Isabella had worked as a racing correspondent for *Sporting Life*. She painstakingly – and thriftily – transcribed lengthy portions of Isabella's detailed diaries on the back of old WRNS standard letters. She also travelled to Ireland, staying at the Great Southern Hotel, Killarney, County Kerry, retracing the visit Isabella and Sam had made there in 1860, and which was chronicled in her diaries. Then it was on to France where Isabella had met three Frenchmen in the Hotel de la Gare who, apparently, 'had a grand *désir de fumer*, but very politely restrained their desire till we had finished our dinner'.[9]

But Nancy felt that merely visiting places was not enough. 'I do prefer a biography to be a biography and not a mixture of Zaza's Dream Book and a personal guide to Suffolk',[10] she would say. However, members of the Beeton–Dorling family who had known Isabella were thin on the ground: by the time she came to write the biography, Aunt Amy was dead, and so, of course, was Lucy Dorling Smiles. To help with the finances of the book, she did sell a 'biographical sketch' of the Beetons, based on her initial research, to Leonard Russell for inclusion in the 1945 edition of the *Saturday Book*, an annual miscellany of words and images, with contributors as diverse as Laurence Olivier, Stephen Spender and Stella Gibbons, which had first appeared in 1940.

Background research about Mrs Beeton which could not be obtained from Mayson Beeton was unearthed at the British Library Reading Room. During this time, she saw a lot of Geoffrey Wright, then living in a flat at 28 Great Ormond Street. Geoffrey had had an eventful war: after being stationed on Tyneside, he was transferred to Naval Intelligence and, after

Japan entered the war, was assigned to decoding Japanese messages. In 1941, he had composed the score for the Ealing-produced *Ships with Wings*, a morale-boosting propaganda film about aircraft carriers preparing for battle, starring Ann Todd, Hugh Williams and Michael Wilding. After the war, he had begun to compose music for a number of hit West End revues, including *Big Top*, *Charlot's Char-a-Bang* and *Let's Go Gay*. 'She had decided that I was a good thing towards starting her London life', he recalls. 'She came to all the parties I gave and would also come to lunch quite often'.

It was Geoffrey who introduced her to a new circle of friends – the 'British Museum' set, which included Angus Wilson and his friend Bentley Bridgewater. Wilson was then deputy superintendent of the British Library Reading Room. At the end of the war (during which he had worked for the Ministry of Information and suffered a nervous breakdown), Wilson was given the task of replacing 300,000 books which had been destroyed during air raids. He, Bentley Bridgewater, Nancy and others formed the nucleus of a social circle that would often meet for lunch in the Museum Tavern, directly opposite the museum gates. 'She was great fun and very convivial', remembers Bridgewater, with whom she shared a passion for tennis. 'Nancy was very good, because she would go off to Wimbledon and then tell me all about it'.

By then, the public had also been made aware of Nancy's enthusiasm for tennis, as February 1946 saw the publication of *Poison in Play*. It didn't muster much press attention, but this may have been due more to the fact that paper was still strictly rationed, and most newspapers were so squeezed for space that none of them carried many reviews of any sort. Still, *Poison in Play* did get an encouraging notice from Philip Day in the *Sunday Times*: 'with its fresh and lively picture of tennis champions and tennis background, he [the crime addict] will find ingenuity and excitement, though rising to too fancy a pitch of melodrama in the last volleys'.[11]

Nancy, meanwhile, was still dogged by the effects of the illnesses which had been responsible for her early exit from the WRNS and, now aware of the enormity of the task that lay before her with the Beeton biography, in the summer of 1946, she left Randolph Gardens and took herself off to Bexhill-on-Sea to work, rest and play. Kay Jones – now also an ex-Wren – and her husband, Colin, had just taken over the Bolebroke Hotel in what Nancy called 'a wonderfully hideous seaside town'.[12] The Bolebroke was in the process of being completely renovated: when Nancy first arrived, there were no carpets, the kitchen was ill-equipped and Colin Jones was making frequent forays to London for furniture and machinery. There was also the Joneses' infant daughter – and Nancy's goddaughter – Sheilah to take care of. Within weeks, however, the refurbishments were complete and the hotel quickly filled up with guests.

Nancy rented a small room at the hotel, containing a small desk for her typewriter, a bed and a wastebasket, just the right size for crumpled sheets of rejected drafts. When not grappling with her great-aunt's life, she would sunbathe on the shingle beach or visit the novelist Phillipa Vane – aka Phyllis Hambledon or Phyllis MacVean – an old friend of her Aunt Mary 'Maimie'

Spain, then living in Bexhill. Geoffrey Wright, who had just finished touring in a revue, frequently came to stay at the weekends. He and Nancy would make excursions to Pevensey and Battle and even toyed with the idea of sharing a house in Bexhill. In the evenings, Geoffrey would play piano for the guests and would sometimes be asked his opinion of Nancy's efforts at songwriting:

> 'She was rather keen to break into the revue world and write lyrics, but she hadn't really any gift for it. I would be presented with lyrics from time to time and had to be very tactful – "needs a little work", "it's not such a good idea", that sort of thing. But then she was launching out in all directions. She was definitely an ideas girl, even though some of them were terrible. She was, I would say, very unself-critical and I think this sprang from the fact she was terribly insecure. She had always thought – early on, anyway – that Lizzie was the brilliant one and I think that's why she tried so hard'.

While Nancy was at Bexhill, she was also making progress in another area of her developing career: in August, she learned from the North-East Home Service (NEHS) that one of her short stories, 'The Perfect Crime', was to be broadcast in the 'Storytellers' Club' programme on 13 September, for which they would pay the 'established authoress'[13] 10 guineas. The 'established authoress' was also determined to develop her crime-writing talents and had already finished another detective novel, *Death Before Wicket*. In this, we are introduced to Johnny DuVivien's wife (his second), the beautiful, glamorous Russian ex-ballet dancer, Natasha. Nancy based Natasha on sister Liz. 'My sister Liz is an enchanting woman of enormous chic and ability,' she would say. 'She is beautiful . . . and her way of life has made of her a work of art. She has . . . a manner of extreme inconsequence which hides a will of steel'.[14] While it is true that the same could be said of Natasha, Liz questioned the comparison: 'I didn't think she was like me at all'.

Johnny and Natasha visit Johnny's daughter, Pamela, a pupil at St Anne Athaway's, a girls' boarding school in Yorkshire. Johnny is due to take part in the fathers' cricket match. Other parents assembled for the event are the Hon. Frederick Harringon and his wife Katherine, and Admiral Sir Peter and Lady Piper. They are all known to each other through the same horsey circles. Pamela DuVivien is adored by her classmate, Claudia Harrigon, whose sister, Cecilia (known as Cecil), has a crush on the games mistress, Joan Weir. Pamela is also adored by Dennis Wynne, an ex-Army officer. However, all passion is thwarted when Joan becomes the murder victim, and the DuViviens set out to find her killer. Once again, Jack Priestman from *The Banner* also becomes involved and starts to draw up lists of suspects and motives. By now, it seems that this convention was put to use as much for the reader's benefit as the sleuths'.

An integral part of launching Nancy's new literary life was to cultivate friendships with those she admired and whose prestige, she hoped, would enhance her own career. She wanted her new life to be amongst those gifted, exceptional, often eccentric writers and performers, who were also known as 'personalities'. As she later admitted, she adored celebrities:

> I love a big name. . . . I like to go where they go . . . I always hope (don't you?) that some of their lustre will rub off against me . . . I am a sufferer from one of the most ingrowing diseases of modern times. Yes, I think pursuit of celebrity *is* a disease.[15]

She wanted to enter their firmament, watching, learning which qualities worked to her best advantage. 'If you're going to drop names, I always say, they'd better be big ones',[16] she said. And, of course, the names she would eventually be able to drop were bigger than anyone else's. But though Nancy attached herself to fame and celebrity in order to establish her own career, and was admirably suited to the task, she was not averse, once she was well established, to letting others ride on her coat-tails. So, she would cultivate the professional or personal affections of the likes of Margery Allingham, Elizabeth Bowen, Noel Coward and Gilbert Harding early on in her career. But, in turn, she would encourage and help others, such as Sandy Wilson, Tony Warren, Ginette Spanier and – as the wheel turned full circle – Gilbert Harding.

Nancy's devotee days began with an eccentric, gifted comedy actress whose wartime revues she had admired enormously – Hermione Gingold. From Geoffrey Wright, she managed to get Gingold's phone number (her book, *The World is Square*, had recently been published). Geoffrey had written 'Transatlantic Lullaby', the hit song of the 1939 *Gate Revue*, starring Gingold, which had transferred to the Ambassadors Theatre. It was the first of a string of revue shows which played to packed houses throughout the war, featuring many of the sketches for which Gingold would become famous, including the bow-legged 'lady cellist' – 'they don't come to see me play, they come to see me walk away'. From 1943 to 1946, Gingold's shows were London's hot attractions, beginning with *Rise Above It* at the Comedy Theatre, then *Sweet and Low* and its sequels, *Sweeter and Lower* and *Sweetest and Lowest*, all at the Ambassadors. It was the latter that Gingold was rehearsing when Nancy rang her at her home at 85 Kinnerton Street. During the war, Gingold's house had become an unofficial London stop-over for her friends on leave from the services. Indeed, her hospitality, both in England and when she eventually moved to New York, was to become legendary.

Nancy wanted to write an article about her, she told Gingold, and so they arranged to meet for lunch. From then on, Nancy became a frequent visitor at Kinnerton Street and the Gingold dressing room, which was often packed with pretty, adoring young men of varying sexual proclivities. Nancy blended in perfectly.

Actress Anne Clements, now Lady Eyre, a close friend of 'Ging' for many years, agrees that Gingold and Nancy were unlikely bedfellows:

> 'Being so avariciously heterosexual herself, Hermione found Nancy's lesbian-ism hard to fathom, but Hermione's criteria for judging anyone was only by whether they were fun, intelligent and entertaining, and she certainly found Nancy all of these. Hermione was always drawn to originals and eccentrics and to those who admired the same qualities in her. She was also not unaware

of the benefits of having a powerful journalist as a friend and ally, though I know Hermione genuinely respected Nancy's work, found her extremely entertaining and admired her quick and ready wit'.

The admiration was mutual. 'I know nobody who has seemed to me down the years so consistently funny',[17] Nancy said of Gingold. She often found herself the butt of many witticisms from the mouth of the woman critics dubbed 'Queen Wasp' and 'Malice in Wonderland'. Eyeing Nancy's thick, rebellious hair, she once observed, 'I must get a man in to mow your hair'. When Nancy confided in her about her romantic entanglements, Gingold retorted, 'You have buttered your bed and now you must eat it'.[18]

In between her visits to London to see Gingold, more Beeton research and stays in Bexhill, Nancy went to Dublin where, according to *Millionaire*, she became friends with an exceedingly tall man known only as 'the Captain', who returned to London at the same time. She introduced him to Gingold, who appreciated the tall, elegant Old Etonian. He apparently accompanied Nancy and her mother to an Old Roedeanians' reunion, where she informed an inquisitive Norah that he was married. His real identity remains a mystery and, according to Nancy, their friendship ended after he went on a gin-drinking spree with a woman and Nancy deposited him at a Turkish bath in Russell Square.

She returned home to Tankerville Place in late September. On 26 November she had another story, 'Death of a Coloratura', broadcast on the Storytellers' Club, and December saw the publication of *Death Before Wicket*. Maurice Richardson, the *Observer*'s crime reviewer, was becoming increasingly intrigued by Nancy and her output: 'Here comes a superb curiosity: Victim is wicked, exquisite, young games mistress(!), champion lacrosse player . . . and seduces husbands of half Yorkshire. If this be in any way a sign of the times, we are heading for the last round-up!'[19] And, at the *Sunday Times*, Ralph Strauss was also becoming a fan: 'The murder-mystery which is written with wit and humour and shows that its author has an eye for an unusual character is always welcome. Into this category falls "Death Before Wicket" . . . [which] has some deftly drawn and amusingly uncommon portraits'.[20]

But her great-aunt's life – or rather, that of her errant husband – was posing certain problems for Nancy. When Ward Lock published a third edition of the book in 1956, she revealed the doubts she had had at the time of the publication of the first edition. Apparently, Mayson Beeton, had, she explained, been

> most anxious to restore his father, Samuel Beeton, to a proper status. . . . But as the work progressed, I had the oddest feeling about Sam. His was an attractive personality, a weak and fascinating character, a dangerous man to know, to marry, to write about. It wasn't until the first edition was actually published, though, that this feeling became a certainty.[21]

She had received a letter which had set her on the trail of previously undiscovered material about Samuel Beeton, material which she incorporated into the third edition: even though 'the discovery that their grandfather was a bit of a villain may distress Mayson Beeton's children I know I am right to have made the truth known. The truth can be a very uncomfortable thing'.[22]

Just as Nancy was starting to enjoy her postwar life, there was a shock in store for her towards the end of 1946. Summoned to appear before a medical board, she was subsequently declared well enough to no longer be considered a naval pensioner. This meant she would have to leave Bexhill, return to London and find a proper job and a new home.

It was hardly an ideal time to be an unmarried, aspiring female writer, trying to eke out an existence in London. True, women were being encouraged to work, but only in certain limited occupations. The Attlee government had launched a new campaign in February 1946 to attract thousands of women to work in factories. 'The women will be told their help in the production drive is almost as urgently required as was the great work they did in wartime',[23] the press reported. Newspapers were preoccupied with stories of spivs and spies, courtesy of a flourishing black market born of years of rationing and the cooling down of East–West relations. Many people were still living in prefabs and Nissen huts. Thousands of homeless families had squatted in unused forces and government buildings: 700 took over empty luxury homes in Kensington and Marylebone, where sympathetic police brought them tea. Britain was regrouping under its new Labour government, introducing new towns, the National Health Service and a nationalized coal industry, and negotiating the independence of India and Pakistan. And, a year after the war in Europe had ended, there were still thousands of German POWs in camps up and down the country.

Nancy decided to seek work in one of the few places where she was known and sent some pieces on 'Postwar Life' to Terence Horsley, who she assumed had returned to the *Newcastle Journal*. However, he was now editor of the *Sunday Empire News*, based in Manchester, and though Horsley couldn't use what she had sent him, he was able to offer her a job as assistant to the features editor, Ned Barton, in the London office at £12 12s. a week. Flushed with success, she promptly rented an expensive furnished flat at 2 Chesney Court, Shirland Road, W9, which cost more than her weekly net wage. But at least she was now 'on staff' of a national newspaper, as she had always dreamed.

She was sent by new boss Barton on a number of assignments that never actually made it into print; interviewing a vicar who believed unmarried women should have babies if they wanted; finding a family of four who could survive on £5 a week (something the paper's new reporter clearly couldn't do at the time). She also interviewed the newly knighted Laurence Olivier on the set of *Hamlet*. Though this also failed to make it into print, Horsley decided that she should concentrate on writing about films. There was one slight problem, however: the *Empire News* already had a film critic, Elspeth Grant, writing under the pseudonym 'Kay Quinlan', who contributed 'Kay Quinlan's Starred Films' in the 'Entertainment News Reel'. No sooner had Nancy arranged to have tickets sent to her for press screenings than Grant was on the phone, giving her a dressing down of the first order. Rebuked and nursing a rather bruised ego, she returned to her work on the Beeton biography, rewrote the entire manuscript while pretending to be involved in *News* business and was relieved to have the book accepted by Collins.

Meanwhile, Horsley had decided to send her to cover Wimbledon. Unfortunately, he left it so late that there were no Centre Court tickets left, let alone press passes. As a result, she reported on the women's singles final between two Americans – the eventual winner, 'stockily built Californian' Margaret Osborne, and 'Miami University student' Doris Hart – from one of the free standing areas.

She then watched Hart get her revenge in the women's doubles final when, together with partner Pat Todd, she defeated Osborne and Louise Brough, 'a grand match which ended in sensational fashion'.[24] She managed to persuade a *Daily Mail* reporter to let her use his telephone to file copy back to Kemsley House. But on the Finals' days, no telephone was available and she had to phone through her copy from a public telephone outside the All-England Club grounds. In the end, the sports editor decided that it was easier for them to get their copy from an agency. So she still had a job, but no defined work.

She then persuaded the London news editor to let her work on a column called 'John Gay's Showdown', a bits-and-pieces feature, comprising short and snappy paragraphs on movie stars and directors, actors and playwrights. It was, in fact, the inspiration for the style she was to become synonymous with at the *Daily Express*, the *News of the World* and, especially, *She* – namely, creating the illusion that she was on intimate terms with all the celebrities she discussed. As she admitted, it was here she learned the language that she was later to put to such effective use: 'I bumped into XYZ at a party'; 'My spies tell me' and 'It is not generally known'; and in particular, the signature introductory phrase, 'My friend XYZ'. Sometimes this was accurate, but, in a good number of cases, these 'friends' would raise an eyebrow to see themselves so described by someone they might only have met once.

At *Empire News* Nancy learned how to get invited to the right press lunches, cocktail parties and dinners, to finagle her way into film studios, and to have the patience to hang around for hours to pick up snippets of gossip. But outside the gossipy world of 'John Gay', the real world was a gloomier place. In the winter of 1947, a coal supply crisis coincided with a bitterly cold winter and, in January 1948, there were power supply cuts to homes and industry. Television broadcasting was suspended, as were weekly magazines, and streets went unlit.

Amidst the encircling gloom of that winter, Nancy finished *Murder, Bless It*, her third detective novel, which drew on her art school experiences and her first visit to Paris. Set in November 1946, the story revolves around the dirty doings of film costume designer Sadie Dobson. It begins as Sadie nurses bruises sustained after a beating from her lover, Major George Bexhill, with whom she is spending the weekend in Paris. Natasha DuVivien is also in town with her stepdaughter Pamela to see the fashion shows, and is introduced to two brothers from Ireland, Brian and Niall Niall. Niall's wife has recently left him. At a bar, they meet up with one of Pamela's former teachers from art school, Mr Polygon. Sadie turns up at the bar and it transpires that she was also once at the school. They visit an exhibition together, where Brian Niall (described as a 'sissy' by Pamela) is reunited with his friend, the artist Edward Falasse. When Major Bexhill also turns up, Brian enquires, 'Who is this gorgeous old queer?'[25] The motley crew travel back to London and, on the way to Calais, Bexhill is pushed off the train.

In London, there is a brief introduction to a 'Miriam Birdseye, an actress friend' of Brian's. Niall and Sadie return to her home in Chelsea, where she learns about Bexhill. Brian tells them he was given some jewellery by Bexhill to bring to London. The Major's death is declared an accident and life returns to normal. We are introduced to Niall's estranged wife, Rachel, and their children, little Niall and Mopsie who, apparently, 'were difficult children'.[26] Their father, meanwhile, is involved with Sadie who is not keen to be named in his divorce. She also has designs on a young actor, Sean Proud, a protégé of an older man called Tony Walsh.

The scene then switches to Ireland, where Sadie is working on a film. Also assembled there are Johnny, Natasha, Pamela, Brian, Sean and a lesbian couple, Miss Beggs and Miss Novello, a model at the art school. Inevitably, there is another death: Niall Niall falls from the tower of Gormass Castle. Johnny draws up a list of suspects and motives but, before long, finds himself somewhat bewitched by Sadie. Sean, her most recent lover, is found dead, apparently having fallen off a cliff. Meanwhile, on a boat trip, the Misses Beggs and Novello find a man's wrist-watch: it is Niall's. Sadie tells the police she accidentally pushed Sean off the cliff. Polygon confesses to the murders, but Natasha is convinced they are all Sadie's doing. Sadie runs off and a full-scale search for her ensues. But it is Johnny who tracks her down and Natasha's theory is proved correct.

Unfortunately, just as Nancy had found her natural niche on *Empire News*, disaster struck again. In February 1948 Kemsley Newspapers announced across-the-board cuts in its staff in Manchester and London, and Terence Horsley had to give her a month's notice. 'While I am sorry that things didn't work out, I am sure you will admit you have gained some useful experience',[27] he told her. Disillusioned with her first taste of Fleet Street, Nancy toyed with the idea of going back into uniform – this time, the police. She got as far as the medical examination, but her myopic eyesight ensured she progressed no further.

Now, she was struggling to make any sort of living. Through a former WRNS colleague, Kitty Elliston, she got what must have ranked as her most peculiar job: gathering collection boxes for Bart's Hospital from pubs and factories in the City of London. She also turned out her bookcases, selling many of her volumes to Foyle's second-hand department, and her numerous cookery books – collected during her Beeton research – to her former boss, Esta Eldod, and 'Nannybell' Robinson.

But the main problem was her expensive flat. She managed to sublet it and, in March 1948, moved out of Chesney Court and into a £2-a-week room in a flat rented by architect Barbara Cole (née Poushkine) at 12a High Wood House, 148 New Cavendish Street. Then in her late forties, Cole had studied architecture at London University, became an associate of the RIBA in 1926 and divided her life between her London practice and flat and her cottage at Wheeler End, near High Wycombe. Nancy had found her new home advertised on a postcard in a stationer's window near the British Museum. She was delighted to be living on the edges of Soho where 'the scents, sights and glimmer . . . seeped up towards New Cavendish Street'.[28] She would nip across to a Jewish bakery opposite High Wood House for fresh croissants, which at one point virtually constituted her entire diet. Although not officially a tenant, she was responsible for all the domestic bills of the flat – a recipe for more financial disaster. To survive she would ask Mrs Webb at Hutchinson's for small advances – usually £25 – against the royalties of her next book.

She found another way of saving money that also fitted in with her new philosophy for life and work. She vowed that, no matter how impoverished she might be, never again would she work for anyone who would force her to wear incongruous and expensive little suits and jewellery. While living in Barbara Cole's flat, she 'threw off for ever the last rags of conventional dress and behaviour'.[29] She clipped her hair with nail scissors, wore dungarees, brown cord trousers and a duffle coat. The character called 'N. Spain' had found the right trousers.

In June 1948, *Murder, Bless It* was published, and was greeted with some justifiable bemusement by reviewers still unsued to the Spain brand of quirky crime. Maurice Richardson of the *Observer*, in a crime round-up, declared, 'The lunatic fringe is represented by the incomparable Miss Nancy Spain's "Murder, Bless It", partly set in Ireland and featuring Sadie Dobson, paranoid, nymphomaniacal, homicidal dress designer. I can guarantee it is unique'.[30] In the *Sunday Times*, Ralph Strauss wrote that the book contained 'plenty of murders and some little mystery, but depends for its effect almost entirely on the portraits of its eccentrics and on the wit of its author. In a word, a *bonne bouche*, not to be taken seriously'.[31] The newly trousered N. Spain, it seems, was already becoming recognized as a character of eccentricity and unconventional humour.

She had only been established in New Cavendish Street for a few months when sister Liz invited her to come and live with her in Cork, at 8 South Mall, where she now had a thriving dress factory. Short of money as usual, Nancy duly arrived in Ireland, attired in her newly adopted clothing which, she said, Liz thought was 'odd'. Liz's flat was sparsely furnished and Nancy had to sleep on the sofa. When that brought on her asthma, she bedded down on the floor of the factory cutting room. During her stay, she made herself useful by doing a lot of the housekeeping and cooking. While there, at Liz's suggestion, Nancy decided to cultivate another influential friendship, with the Anglo–Irish writer, Elizabeth Bowen. An impressive literary set, including Eudora Welty, Carson McCullers, Philip Toynbee and

Francis Wyndham, often gathered at her home in Ireland, Bowen's Court and her London flat, 2 Clarence Terrace, at the top of Baker Street. Bowen invited Nancy and Liz to tea at Bowen's Court and, when she moved to Baker Street herself, Nancy pursued the friendship.

In August, her professional life took a turn for the better: she returned to Newcastle to do a 10-minute reading of 'The Browns Go North' for the NEHS as part of an *English by Radio* series, commissioned by the lugubriously named Thetis Tombs.[32] She also acquired her first agent, Margaret Stephens of A.D. Peters.

But the most significant development was the publication of *Mrs Beeton and Her Husband*. It was greeted with mostly favourable reviews. Dingle Foot in the *Observer* enthused, 'Miss Nancy Spain has not only compiled a thoroughly readable biography of her great-aunt but she has also done her an act of belated justice'.[33]

Her earliest fan, A.A. Milne, was similarly impressed: 'It is Miss Nancy Spain who, with a wave of her practised pen, has banished forever the elderly-housekeeper-with-dyspeptic-husband legend which so many imaginations had built up ... Miss Spain brings them expertly to life'.[34]

The *Times Literary Supplement* praised her 'ingenious theory that the alleged extravagance of Isabella's recipes may be due to the fact that as a child she was allowed to watch the preparations for the enormous meals served in Epsom Guard Stand'.[35] Such reviews were enough to ensure that the book had to go into reprint in October – some satisfaction for all the unpaid effort that had gone into the book's making.

Other doors were also beginning to open: Norah Wood at the BBC had seen a preview of *Mrs Beeton* in the July issue of *Vogue* and this, coupled with Nancy's recent radio work, prompted her to write to Helena Malinowska, who was putting together a programme called *Designed for Women*. Nancy, she said, was 'intelligent, unafraid and a good talker'. Malinowska duly invited Nancy to the BBC studios on 30 September to discuss writing sketches for the show 'satirizing some feminine activities'.[36] But the trip was not a success: the next day, Malinowska told Nancy that it would be a 'waste of time and effort' for her to do any work for the programme: 'The little bit of television which you saw yesterday could obviously give you no help in working for the medium'.[37]

So, Nancy and television weren't quite ready for each other yet. She returned to Ireland and, as usual when she had suffered a disappointment, got down to writing another book. From 8 a.m. to noon, and 2.30 p.m. to 6 p.m., she wrote in the cutting room. Here, she produced two more thrillers: *Death Goes on Skis*, in honour of Hermione Gingold, and *Poison for Teacher*, dedicated to Faith Compton Mackenzie.

With *Death Goes on Skis* Nancy introduced a second regular sleuth, revue actress Miriam Birdseye – her fictional tribute to Hermione Gingold. It was a compliment Gingold relished, according to her friend, Anne Clements (Eyre): 'Having herself fictionalized appealed greatly to Hermione's sense of fun and immortality. She was vastly amused at the result'. And Clements testifies to the accuracy of Nancy's characterization of her friend:

'Every single line that the "pale blue eyed" retired actress/detective utters I can hear Hermione's unique deep voice drawl and swoop over. She captures her rhythms and quirks of speech to perfection. Not a line sounds out of character. Although the situations are obviously preposterous Ms Birdseye's character reacts exactly as I feel Hermione would. Nancy actually gets beneath the stereotype comedy actress perception of Ging and shows us her strength of character, interest in things other than theatricals, her sharp penetrating mind, tenacity of purpose, sense of adventure and dislike of outdoor sports!'

Death Goes on Skis is set in the winter sports resort of Schizo-Frenia. Toddy Flaherté and her younger sister Kathleen are travelling there to escape the bitter British winter of 1947. So, too, are Johnny, Natasha and Pamela DuVivien. Completing the line-up is Barny Flaherté, Toddy and Kathleen's cousin, his wife Regan, their daughters Joyce and Margie, their governess Rosalie Leamington – and Barny's mistress, film star Fanny Mayes and her husband Sir Edward Sloper, a famous architect. Joyce and Margie are particularly fond of their aunts Toddy and Kathleen, who herself is in love with Barny. Upon their arrival at Schizo-Frenia, Fanny spots Miriam Birdseye, who is 'a long way from "The Ivy" '.[38] Miriam is a great friend of Natasha, who says of her, 'she was born drunk'.[39] Miriam announces that she and her friends, Roger Partick-Thistle and Morris Watson-Birchwood, are writing a musical version of *Dracula*. 'I'm a Vampire Queen. My mental age is seventeen', runs one of their better lyrics.

The guests are all staying at the hotel run by M. and Mme. Lapatronne. Within days, Regan Flaherté is discovered dead, apparently having fallen from a hotel window. But Natasha decides it is murder. The plot thickens when it transpires that Barny is also interested in Rosalie and discovers that Fanny is pregnant, though the child may not be his. Before long, Fanny is murdered – she is given an overdose of sleeping tablets while drunk. Again, Johnny draws up a list of prime suspects and possible motives. He thinks the culprit is most likely Barny, but Edward Sloper confesses he thought that Fanny was responsible for Regan's murder. However, it is Kathleen who is found with a smoking gun in her hand after Natasha is shot at while out with Barny. But though she admits killing Regan, Kathleen denies murdering Fanny. The killer's identity is revealed back in London, when Barny is murdered . . .

Poison for Teacher begins with a blazing row between Johnny and Natasha DuVivien. She leaves and heads for the home of her friend, the acclaimed comedy-actress-turned-detective, Miriam Birdseye, star of intimate revues including the Ortonesquely titled *Absolutely the End, Positively the Last, Take Me Off* and *Hips and Haws*. When Natasha arrives, Miriam has just dis-covered that her associate, Benjy, has absconded to Portugal with the funds of Birdseye et Cie. They are sorting through a pile of bills when Miss Lipscoomb, head teacher of the famous girls' school, Radcliffe Hall, arrives, claiming someone is trying to kill her and that the reason may lie in the rival school set up by her former partner, Miss bbirch. The three of them head for the school in Brunton-on-Sea and arrive to find that the mother of one of the pupils, Julia Bracewood-Smith, has just killed herself.

Roger Partick-Thistle pops up again, this time as the school's music master. He is also Miss Lipscoomb's nephew. Theresa Devaloys is the French mistress, whose bookshelves are filled with the works of Colette, Gide, Proust and Rimbaud. Most of the school prefects have crushes on Gwylan Fork-Thomas, the chemistry mistress, who is having a 'forbidden friendship' with Miss Puke, the classics mistress. Miss Lesarum, the maths mistress, apparently has a fondness for wearing men's clothes and is described by the bigoted Miss Devaloys as 'a half-caste . . . certainly not white . . . she looks like a West African native. And she's as queer as a coot'.[40]

Miriam and Natasha meet the school doctor, a Jewish man called Philip Lariat, who is only too aware of the anti-Semitic views held by some of those around him. They also discover a letter from Miss Devaloys to Miss bbirch, which shows them to be fellow conspirators, and which also tells her of the arrival of Natasha and Miriam: 'One looks like a tart and the other a witch. Perhaps they are Very Fond of Each Other?'[41] It transpires that Devaloys has been having an affair with Lariat, who's already married. When she reveals to him that she is pregnant, he suggests she gets an abortion, much to her horror. During a rehearsal for the staff play, *Quality Street*, she drops dead after drinking some whisky. Soon after, Mrs Grossbody, the school matron, collapses and has to have her stomach pumped. Natasha and Miriam discover that Miss Devaloys may have been blackmailing a number of people, including Roger, after an unspecified incident when he was leader of a Cub Pack. Soon, another murder takes place: Gwylan Fork-Thomas is discovered by Natasha and Miriam, shot in the head.

In October news reached Nancy and Liz of the death of their aunt, Katherine Stewart, in New York. More welcome news was that she had left them each £400 in her will. They decided to spend it on a winter cruise to Madeira and Tenerife, which gave Nancy an idea for another story. Before they left, she received word that a 10-minute extract from *Mrs Beeton* was to be broadcast on the NEHS on 14 December.

In March 1949, Nancy finally returned to London and set about finding herself a new home. She settled in a top-floor flat at 6 Baker Street, with access to the roof, which she had to herself. The time she spent alone in this flat, she said later, was her 'best loneliness'.[42] This, she decided, was the perfect place from which to relaunch her London literary social life. She bought her first headed notepaper, with a red letterhead that just said 'Nancy Spain' – presumably no explanation would be necessary – and started giving little parties in her new home. She also went to as many of Elizabeth Bowen's literary parties as she could: Bowen's London home was conveniently near, at the other end of Baker Street – quite possibly a determining factor when Nancy was looking for a new home. During her time at Baker Street, Nancy met Ngaio Marsh and Margery Allingham. She had approached Allingham to discuss a proposed article she wanted to write about women crime writers; Allingham subsequently invited Nancy to several of her lavish parties held at her home in the Essex countryside.

While she was rubbing shoulders with the cream of crime writers, Nancy was busy trying to emulate their prolific output. She finished *Poison for Teacher*, sent it off to Hutchinson's and immediately began work on another thriller, *Cinderella Goes to the Morgue*. By now, she had decided to phase out Johnny DuVivien completely and concentrate on the pairing of Natasha and Miriam. As the story opens, it is December: Johnny and Natasha have just been divorced and Natasha and Miriam are in Newchester. They meet up with young Tony Gresham, a PR agent. His mother, Vivienne, is playing Prince Charming in the Theatre Royal production of *Cinderella*, opposite Hampton Court, who is Buttons. Court is jealous, because Vivienne's performance has generated more publicity. Another of the show's stars, Marylyn Franklyn, also hates Vivienne. Brothers Henry (who was once married to Vivienne Gresham) and Banjo DeFreeze play the Ugly Sisters. Henry sends his ex-wife a letter which threatens to 'end it, once and for all'.[43]

Meanwhile, Natasha is roped in to help out with the show's costumes and meets Sir Timothy Shelly, a widower. At the dress rehearsal, Vivienne Gresham falls through the unlocked stage-trap and is killed. In the ensuing investigation, Banjo reveals that he is Tony Gresham's father. Tony, however, hates him. Not surprisingly, Banjo winds up dead in his dressing room half-way through a performance of *Cinderella*: he has been shot. Unfortunately for Shelly, the murder weapon belonged to him, although he had recently lost it. Banjo's will is discovered; he has left everything to Tony Gresham. Then Harry takes an overdose and dies. Newchester's Mayor, Tom Atkins, is by now understandably concerned by the tragedies afflicting the city's pantomime. As the curtain comes down on *Cinderella Goes to the Morgue*, newlyweds Timothy and Natasha drive off.

Nancy would dedicate this book to her new friend, Elizabeth Bowen, but the friendship was soon to go sour. Bowen was certainly no stranger herself to intense emotional relationships with women – in many cases, she positively encouraged the intensity. But she was in the habit of cutting off these relationships quite suddenly and ruthlessly; she also considered fully fledged lesbian relationships to be too sentimental, analytical and 'claggy'. Nonetheless, Bowen attracted some distinguished female admirers. Carson McCullers was infatuated with her for years. May Sarton was another: she met Bowen in June 1936 when she and a mutual friend were invited to dinner at Clarence Terrace. The following spring, their friendship intensified and Sarton subsequently fell deeply in love with her. Bowen confided to her that she had had one affair with another woman in her youth. The emotional intensity that had grown between Bowen and Sarton was consummated that May, when they spent one night together in Rye, where Sarton was staying. It was not to be repeated. As Sarton later said, 'For me that romantic night meant not the beginning of a love affair, but the seal set on a friendship'.[44] Bowen, in fact, left Rye for Boulogne, where she was to meet a man who would subsequently become her lover.

Regarding her relationship with Nancy, the official version, according to Bowen's biographer, Victoria Glendinning, was that Nancy's cultivation of her was 'intense'. Bowen's husband, Alan Cameron, apparently couldn't stand Nancy and was unhappy about the frequency of her visits to Clarence Terrace. When Nancy's visits suddenly stopped, Cameron's friend, Eric Gillett, was told that she had made a pass at Bowen which, as far as Bowen was concerned, signalled the end of her friendship with Nancy. Geoffrey Wright, however, had a different view of what happened: 'I had always presumed that they'd had an affair'. Both women took the truth about what happened between them to their respective graves. But what is certain is that if Nancy was seeking the same sort of committed, all-enveloping relationship she had enjoyed with Winifred, then Elizabeth Bowen was certainly not her woman.

On 24 April came tragic news: Terence Horsley, who had featured in Nancy's life and career for nearly fifteen years, was killed in a gliding accident at Great Hucklow in Derbyshire. He had just finished another novel, *Jamie*, which, it was announced, would be published posthumously in November by a company called T. Werner Laurie. By a strange quirk of fate, Nancy and Horsley appeared on the same page in the June issue of the literary monthly published by the company, *Books of Today*. The magazine included a small photograph of Nancy – in a Hollywood-style bare shouldered pose – and a potted profile, promoting her next book, *Death Goes on Skis*. In the next column was a short obituary of Horsley. The author had once asked him how he managed to combine popular Sunday journalism with his more respectable literary career. 'Schizophrenia,' said Horsley, 'and a very advanced case'. Horsley, it said, 'could combine beautiful writing with enormous physical activity and readiness to tackle anything new'.[45]

In June 1949, *Death Goes on Skis* was published and even the sceptical Maurice Richardson of the *Observer* was warming to Nancy's style, it seemed. 'Miss Spain is rapidly becoming the Ouida of crime-fiction', he declared, and admired the story as 'seen through the prism of Miss Spain's exotic temperament . . . '.[46] In *Tribune*, Julian Symons described the book as 'A native thriller outstanding in its liveliness, humour and over-whelming enthusiasm . . . funny, malicious, sentimental. . . . Mystery lovers should be warned that there isn't any mystery'.[47] And, regardless of what had happened between them, Elizabeth Bowen found the book memorable, if nothing else. 'I cannot find that this racy, continuously absorbing novel conforms in any way to the "thriller" type', she wrote in the *Tatler and Bystander*, 'the mainspring of the excitement is psychological . . . it is for its flavour that one will remember . . . the book'.[48]

Meanwhile, Nancy was still trying to find ways of generating regular income. She scoured the advertisement pages of the *New Statesman*, searching for a job – any sort of job – in publishing. Though she applied for several positions, she only managed to get one – unsuccessful – interview: as publicity manager for the publishers, T. Werner Laurie. In another concerted effort to balance her books, Nancy touted for work as a literary reviewer, and, for the latter half of 1949, this became a source of regular, if tiny, income. The publications she wrote for presented a curious mixture, though: *Time and Tide* and the august left-wing newspaper, *Tribune*, founded in the 1930s by Nye Bevan and other leading figures from the Labour Party. *Tribune* was at that time edited by Michael Foot and its literary editor was T.R. Fyvel, who had succeeded George Orwell at the end of the war.

She started off reviewing general fiction for the paper, including Stella Gibbons's *Conference at Cold Comfort Farm*, a sequel to her highly successful rural comedy, which, according to Nancy, 'does not quite capture the first brilliant delirium of Miss Gibbons' classic satire'.[49] However, she soon progressed to specializing in reviewing thrillers. She tackled the latest offerings by Ellery Queen, Francis Bamford and David Dodge, whose *A Drug on the Market* obviously intrigued her. Set in San Francisco, it concerned a man who supplied dope to 'tea-blowers, reefer-smokers and hayheads (all terms for marijuana addicts)',[50] she informed readers. She also took particular note of Elizabeth Jenkins's *Six Criminal Women*, in which 'true stories of six awful ladies eerily surpasses in rich and fantastic strangeness the criminal fiction of this or any week', including the tale of 'Florence Bravo and her uncomfortable "companion" Miss Cox'.[51]

That August, she returned to Newcastle to do a broadcast for the NEHS, for a series called *Summer Scene*, involving a trip to Coquet Island off the Northumberland coast. But she was anxious to shake off the 'regional' radio label and break through into network radio. She sent a story to Homar Wyatt at the Home Talks department, which he rejected as not being 'really suitable for our audience'.[52]

While reviewing other people's crime fiction, she eagerly awaited the publication and reviews of her most recent offering, *Poison for Teacher*, and continued working on the next, *'R' in the Month*.

When *Poison for Teacher* was published in November, it received some rapturous reviews. In *Tribune*, Henry Fishbank described how it 'starts off as a light detective story and ends almost as a skit on the whole thing . . . more conservative detective fans may find "Poison for Teacher" rather too much of a rag: for the more frivolous devotees, there is extravagant fun on every page'.[53] In the *Tatler*, Elizabeth Bowen said it

> is to be recommended, albeit recklessly, to girls'-school fiction addicts. That here, also, we have a detective story of high distinction, I need hardly state: the signature is enough.
>
> An either intense or sombre approach to crime is to Miss Spain foreign: in her world an inspired craziness rules.
>
> Miss Spain has yet to write a better book than this last one. . . . Her wit, her zest, her outrageousness, and the colloquial stylishness of her writing are quite her own.[54]

And, in *Books of Today*, the anonymous reviewer observed that 'The investigation provides a grand opportunity for Nancy Spain's particular brand of humour and diverting dialogue, without losing any of the excitement of the ingeniously contrived mystery. The story is full of fun . . . with brilliant characterisations in every chapter'.[55]

'R' in the Month had a different structure to its six predecessors: its

narrative was broken up by a frontispiece and subsequent interludes, which consist of Justice Mayhem's summing-up at the trial of the as yet unknown murderer.

This time, Miriam Birdseye heads for Brunton-on-Sea, near Beachy Head, with her friend Frederick Pyke, a poet who stutters, doesn't like crime novels and is besotted with her. Miriam has gone there to write a play and 'break off an undesirable engagement' with 'a Major Bognor'. Bognor lives in the Oranmore Hotel with his wealthy mother. The proprietor, Tony Robinson, a former member of the RNVR, is on the brink of bankruptcy, while his wife Celia, a former chemistry teacher at a girls' public school, is on the brink of a nervous breakdown. Celia is terrified of her two-year-old twin daughters, April and May who, apparently, 'had never shown signs of human intelligence'. She is also nervous of the hotel's cook, muscular, dungaree-clad Connie, who is prone to saying 'You silly bitch' a lot, and 'Tommy' (Mrs Thomson), her 'personal' kitchenmaid. The two women share the basement room and 'a large, uncompromising double bed of singular horror that occupied most of the room'.[56] We learn that Connie and her former partner Mavis ran a guesthouse in Whortleberry Down, in the West Country, which had subsequently gone bust.

Miriam and Pyke are invited to an oyster party given by Mrs Bognor, who subsequently dies in the night. Then Mrs Greeb, Tony Robinson's mother-in-law, dies of typhoid. It is discovered that Major Bognor's aunt and father died at Whortleberry Down in 1946, after Mrs Bognor had ordered some oysters from the Rucksack estate at Brunton.

There are, as usual, a cluster of prime suspects: the Robinsons are preoccupied with their overdrafts and debts: Tony is always borrowing money, and is over-fond of drink. Then there is Rosemary Cathcart, who works at the post office. Somebody had stolen Mrs Greeb's post office book, forged her signature and withdrawn £200 in cash. When poisoning is suspected as the cause of both deaths – possibly involving arsenic and syringes – several people find themselves under suspicion. Celia uses hypodermic needles to give herself liver injections for her anaemia. But needles are also discovered in Connie and Tommy's room – Connie had once been a drug addict. And Major Bognor and Tony Robinson both had access to the store of arsenic at the chemist's. However, when one of Celia's syringes is found to contain traces of dirty drain water, she is arrested.

Nancy declared this heady brew of hokum to be 'Margery Allingham's book. With Love'.

While immersing herself in this surreal atmosphere of post office books, poison and pharmaceuticals, the reality of her financial circumstances could no longer be ignored. The novel she should have been writing at this time was, according to her, to be a modern rewriting of *King Lear*, a proposal mentioned in jest during a chat with Thayer Hobson, president of the American publishers, William Morrow. Hobson told her what others had been stressing – that she was wasting her talent writing crime fiction – and offered her an advance of £100 to write a 'straight novel'.[57] Naturally, no twentieth-century *Lear* emerged; instead, the curious goings-on at the

Oranmore Hotel took her attention and Thayer Hobson's advance evaporated rather rapidly. But her luck was holding, and 1950 would turn out to be the year which brought her the personal and professional breakthroughs that she had sought so avidly.

She received a letter from the publishers, T. Werner Laurie, asking her to become editor of their monthly magazine, *Books of Today*. Nancy later said that this job offer was akin to being reprieved from execution at the last minute – there was no question of her turning it down. So, in February, she duly turned up at the offices of *Books of Today*, housed above Hatchards bookshop at 187 Piccadilly. The magazine, the publishing company and the bookshop were all part of a mini-book-trade empire presided over by Clarence Hatry. In 1944, Hatry had competed with Walter Hutchinson to buy T. Werner Laurie after the death of its founder. The company had certainly been a prize worth fighting for.

Thomas Werner Laurie was born in Edinburgh in 1864, himself the son of a publisher. He worked as general manager for Macmillan in his home town, and then as manager for T. Fisher Unwin, until he left for London in 1904, thus becoming the first of his staunchly Scottish family to move south of the border. Thomas borrowed £800 from his brother, Maxwell (who would become Governor-General of Burma) and set up his own imprint, T. Werner Laurie Ltd. It was an immediate and enormous success: he repaid his brother's loan – worth thousands in those days – in seven months. The T. Werner Laurie imprint would eventually have over 2,000 books to its credit. Werner Laurie's youngest son, Dick, attributed his father's success to one, vital skill: 'He just had a great nose. He had a great ability for earning money, and using his wits as a publisher. He was a *damn* good publisher'.

The company had two main assets: T. Francis Bumpus, who wrote a long-standing series of books entitled *The Cathedrals of . . .* ; and George Riley Scott, who wrote what Dick Laurie describes as 'fairly iffy treatises . . . rather near the knuckle stuff', with titles such as *The Encyclopaedia of Sex* and *The History of Torture through the Ages*. There were other, more *bona fide* scholarly works, including translations of the works of Guy de Maupassant.

As a publisher, Thomas Werner Laurie

> had a feeling for the by-ways and for rescuing works that had been 'missed' or neglected by the undiscerning and were in danger of obscurity. . . . Success in the commercial sense, although a keen man of business, appeared to be of less concern to Laurie than the satisfaction of his own taste and enthusiasm in literature.[58]

After moving to London, Laurie had married one of the daughters of the Kent brewery family, the Neames. From this marriage came two daughters, Jean Marjorie Ellen and Elizabeth, known as Betty. According to Dick Laurie, 'Jean was exposed to by a gentleman when she was about fourteen and never looked at another man again. She ended up living with an absolutely enchanting lady called Ioani Edwards, known as Old Iron, and who had two or three children'. Jean was to die of cancer in the late 1970s.

In the mid 1930s, Betty married a man called Reggie Butterworth who, incredibly, she met in a pub near a hospital where she had been treated for VD.

'He was a remarkable chap', recalls Dick Laurie, 'very handsome and an absolute bounder. He had been at Harrow, the captain of cricket, fives, tennis. He went off to become a Spitfire pilot, lost an arm, came back, learned to shuffle a pack of cards with one hand and then went off again several times and eventually didn't come back at all. We don't actually know what happened to him'.

Far from sitting around pining for years, Betty Butterworth led a colourful life herself. She lived with a married French doctor, in France, for over ten years, after which she returned to England and bred dogs. In the early 1950s, she moved to America, embarking on a new career as a photographic stylist for *Good Housekeeping*. 'She would work with the home economist and accessorize the style photographs – put things in to make them look prettier', explains Dick Laurie.

Meanwhile, her father's roving eye had rested on something pretty: Elizabeth Mary Beatrice Blackshaw. The first Mrs Laurie had succumbed to alcoholism and disappeared into an institution. According to Dick Laurie, 'My father had gone to the cinema one day and got bored with the film. So he went up to the projection room where he found my mother'. Nearly thirty years Laurie's junior, Beatrice 'Granny' Laurie was held in great affection by all those who knew her. 'She was quite a simple soul', explains Dick Laurie. 'She was an East-Ender, from Stepney. Her father was a furniture restorer and craftsman. I don't know whether she tidied her accent up for my father, but she was a Cockney'.

Before long, Thomas Laurie had set her up in a house and she subsequently had at least three children by him, though there is a suspicion within the family that there were more than three pregnancies. So, as Dick Laurie points out, 'All my sisters and brother were born out of wedlock, which in those days was very different to what it is now'. Eventually, Thomas Werner Laurie's first wife died and, on 13 February 1931, aged sixty-five, he married 36-year-old Beatrice, who had already changed her name by deed poll to Laurie.

The second Werner Laurie family – including children Geoffrey, Joan and Sally – settled in Putney, at 9a Lytton Grove. Dick Laurie recalls that Beatrice was given the nickname 'Weasel' or 'Wussy' by her husband: 'He had a piece of stained glass hanging in his dressing-room window of St Thomas and his weasel; so she was "Weasel". She was the most long-suffering woman on God's earth – just unbelievable'. The stern, authoritarian publisher ruled the household with a rod of iron, smoked sixty cigarettes and drank a bottle of whisky a day.

His wife wasn't the only one who suffered: at the age of thirteen, the unfortunate Geoffrey was put into a Shaftesbury Society home. According to Dick Laurie, 'My father couldn't hack handling teenage boys. Geoffrey had a much tougher time than I did. He didn't have any of the advantages;

he wasn't given a proper education'. After leaving the home, he joined the merchant navy, then served in the Royal Navy during the Second World War. 'He ended up as a swimming baths attendant in Finchley and died in 1960 – nobody's quite sure how or of what'.

Eventually, Thomas Laurie's excesses caught up with him: he contracted cancer of the tongue, for which he had to have painful radium treatment. Beatrice's best friend Peggy Pritchard, known to the children as 'Aunty Peggy', and only tolerated by Thomas because she made sure he got a regular supply of cigarettes from the kiosk on Harrow station where she worked, told her, 'Of course, Bea, you realize that radium treatment in a man makes him sterile and impotent, as well'. So, according to Dick Laurie, 'He thought "Sod that", so they upped and had me'. Richard Thomas Laurie was born in 1936. ('He called me Dick, because he said, "That's the last bit of dick I'm going to have"', explains Dick Laurie.)

Up until the last six months of his illness, Laurie continued to work. At that time, he was living mainly at the National Liberal Club, which was near his office. According to Dick Laurie, 'Mum used to drive him from Putney before the war; once there was petrol rationing, he lived at the NLC'. However, Thomas Laurie was at home when he died on 23 July 1944.

Despite his formidable manner and the inexplicable behaviour he exhibited towards some of his own family, Laurie's widow received many affectionate and admiring letters from those who had known or worked with him – an irony that would not have been lost on some of his family. In his will, he left a paltry £50 each to his eldest daughters, Betty and Jean. He stipulated that Beatrice was to be managing director of T. Werner Laurie Ltd., paid a salary of £200 a year, and to hold 2,500 shares in the company. Joan, Sally and Dick were each left two-sevenths of the proceeds from the sale of his investments. Typically, the unfortunate Geoffrey was only given one-seventh.

Beatrice Laurie decided she did not want to be managing director of her husband's company (though she did keep her life directorship) and duly sold out to Clarence Hatry, under whose stewardship the company continued to prosper. The imprint was eventually bought by Max Reinhardt in 1957, along with Bodley Head.

When Nancy took the helm at *Books of Today*, George Greenfield, Managing Director of T. Werner Laurie, explained the financial set-up of the magazine to her. It was a subscription-only publication, aimed at Hatchards customers, priced at 7s. 6d. a year. The cost of producing it was paid for mainly by advertising revenue, from £12 for a full page, downwards. The disadvantage, from an editorial point of view, was that there was no budget to pay contributors. This rather undermined some of Nancy's grandiose plans for the magazine. However, the efforts she had made during the last four years to cultivate friends and acquaintances among the literary great and good were now going to pay off handsomely. She was able to call on favours and build up an impressive roster of contributors who, because it was for her 'baby', were willing to write reviews for no fee. They included Angus

Wilson, Margery Allingham and Esther McCracken; even her father was drafted in to cover the sort of books ideally suited to his interests – coin collecting, archaeology and country sports.

Each month, she would ring round all the main publishing companies to see if they would take out adverts in the magazine. Most of them weren't interested but she did manage to persuade her own publishers, Hutchinson, to place a half-page advertisement for *'R' in the Month* in the October 1950 issue.

The official relaunch of *Books of Today* came with the May 1950 issue. It was now no longer a subscription-only magazine and was on sale in general bookshops for sixpence an issue. Its lead article was by G.B. Stern on Rose Macaulay's *The World My Wilderness*. Nancy's first editorial announced

> we are very, very fond of books ... in Great Britain there are 7,000 of them published yearly. Seventeen per cent of them are reviewed. Therefore eighty-three per cent of struggling authors are never mentioned at all. We are going to try and close this gap. You will say that we have some hope. As it happens, you are perfectly right.[59]

Each month, she promised, *Books of Today* would ' "find" a book that is a contribution to literature'.[60] She would not, however, be drawn into a definition of 'literature'. She introduced 'Aunt Hermione Gingold's Corner', which the contributor herself wanted to call 'Worst Book of the Month', but eventually settled for 'This I Have Loathed'. Every month, Nancy would send Gingold a pile of books, specially selected to suit her distaste. These were subsequently read aloud to various friends and, when Gingold was ready to pronounce sentence, Nancy would take her portable typewriter round to Kinnerton Street and commit her considered opinion to paper.

Other contributors to the first issue included Christianna Brand, Madeleine Henrey, Wolf Mankowitz and Wilfred Pickles – the latter by virtue of being a T. Werner Laurie author. Nancy contributed reviews of works by Virginia Woolf and Elizabeth Bowen. The first 'Find of the Month' was *The Beautiful Visit* by Elizabeth Jane Howard; she returned the favour by subsequently becoming a reviewer for the magazine.

Each issue of *Books of Today* opened with a missive from its new editor, comprising literary news, gossip and highlights of the current issue. The page was decorated with little line drawings of a mouse – a slightly incongruous figure who would reappear, several years later, in another, more apt, publication. As well as illustrations, Nancy also introduced more photographs into what had previously been a text-heavy layout. Inside the pages, the readers would find Christianna Brand reviewing crime fiction rival Agatha Christie, or Faith Compton Mackenzie on flower books. George Spain was a consistent and eclectic reviewer, covering books on championship chess, flags, stamp-collecting, fishing holidays and bird-watching. Nancy herself wrote on everything from Ernest Hemingway to flying saucers. By the end of 1950, she was able to tell readers, with justifiable pride, that the number of possible published books reviewed in the magazine had increased from 10 to 30 per cent. Unfortunately, the year ended with a disappointment too: Hermione Gingold left for America to star in the play *Lily Henry* and thus ended her stint as the most controversial contributor to *Books of Today*.

But, for all the big bylines that appeared in the magazine, the most significant was the woman who signed her work 'JWL'. This shadowy figure had contributed reviews on art books, Puffin titles, even the Duke of Edinburgh. She was the 'Miss Laurie' referred to often by George Green-field: 'go and talk to Miss Laurie', he had told Nancy when she joined the firm. 'Miss Laurie is very clever . . . knows all about printing and she will help cut down the costs'.[61]

Books of Today was professionally important for Nancy: it demonstrated her commitment and enthusiasm for readers and writers alike, and showed any prospective employer that she was not without ideas and talent. But this paled into insignificance compared to the importance of the woman who had now entered her life: the eldest daughter of the formidable Thomas Werner Laurie, and the firm's production manager. Then, as now, the consensus of opinion was that 'Miss Laurie' was something of a chip off the old block.

Years after Nancy first met Joan, she confided to a friend that she had known, from first sight, that 'Jonnie', as she was known by nearly everyone, was 'The One'. And, what's more, she marvelled, it was mutual. But if ever a couple proved that opposites really do attract, it was the pairing of Nancy Spain and Joan Werner Laurie.

Joan Ann Werner Laurie was born at 12 Ashland House, Marylebone, London, on 17 November 1920. Unlike her unfortunate brother Geoffrey, Joan received the best education her father's money could buy, rounded off with a stay at finishing school in Switzerland. However, as she grew up, she still fell foul of her father's forbidding manner and relentless criticism. 'I think I was the only one of his children not to walk out of the house after being given some sort of tongue-lashing', says Dick Laurie. 'Jonnie certainly did – she walked out at dinner one day, and said I'm not putting up with this any more. She was about seventeen or eighteen'. Joan had nurtured aspirations to become a doctor, but nothing came of them, though she subscribed to *The Lancet* all her life and would try to force her medical ambitions on to her own son. What came instead was marriage.

During the war, a man called Clifford Simmonds wanted to marry Joan. She refused, though they remained friends. When Clifford did marry, his wife, Thurza, eventually became a contributor to *Books of Today* when Nancy was editor. Joan's eventual choice of husband was an odd one: Paul Clifford Seyler, then serving in the British Army, was the immensely tall – said to be about 6 feet 8 inches – son of playwright Clifford Seyler. He had a twin brother, Rudolf, and, according to Dick Laurie, the Seylers were 'both as bad as each other. They were borrowers of money, and drinkers, and ravishers of women. My father was quite worried about him'. However, her father's concern would only serve to encourage Joan to marry Seyler. In

Dick Laurie's view, 'It was half defiance of my father, and half for love of Paul'.

Joan Werner Laurie and Paul Seyler were married at St Luke's Church, Chelsea, on 1 May 1942, and had their reception at the Rembrandt Hotel, Knightsbridge. Thomas Werner Laurie had not overcome his dislike of his new son-in-law and refused to attend the wedding, though his wife attended. The couple subsequently lived in Chelsea, at 6 Sydney Street. After his marriage, Paul Seyler went back to war and a rather shadowy military career. It is believed he was seconded to fight with the Finnish army at one point.

At the time of her marriage, Joan had been living at home, and had no regular job but, after Paul had returned to the war, she decided to join the Wrens. She served as a clerk first, learning to touch-type at an astonishing speed, before becoming a transport driver and learning how to fix motors. By the end of 1944, she had become ill with appendicitis and ended up in the Hospital for Women in Vincent Square – at the same time as a certain Second Officer Spain. Though Nancy always said they never actually met, Joan's son, Nick, thinks they did form some sort of attachment during this time. What is certain is that both were nearing the end of their days in active service.

Shortly after leaving the Wrens, with her husband still on duty abroad, Joan got a job at the Marylebone shop of the Society for the Promotion of Christian Knowledge, publishers and sellers of religious texts. The SPCK also sold other church requisites and it was these that the staff, who were on commission, would try to sell more of. Joan never missed an opportunity, according to her brother, Dick: 'She could tell quickly who was coming in to buy candles and who was coming in to buy altar cloths, so she used to grab the person buying the altar cloths. She left the candles to the other assistants'.

When the war ended in Europe, Paul Seyler returned to England and Joan became pregnant. By the time the child was born, Seyler was a captain, serving with the Gurkhas, and Joan was no longer living in London.

Nicholas Laurie Seyler was born on 3 March 1946, at 1 South Park, Sevenoaks, in Kent. Joan had moved into the house of her friend Vivyen Bremner who, by all accounts, was something of a saint. Her home at Brasted – Thatches – was open house for all sorts of waifs and strays, whether they were orphans, children with disabilities or young pregnant women with errant husbands. Thatches was an enormous Victorian house, with a huge garden and lots of slides and tree-houses. Dick Laurie remembers playing there as a child:

> 'Vivyen was a very godly, very nice lady. She had a family that was so huge you couldn't really tell which were hers or anybody else's. I used to worry about going down there, because you were made to do things all the time, races round the garden, that sort of thing. There was no skiving; you were pestered all the time. It was a mighty activity household'.

The kindly Vivyen Bremner supported Joan throughout her pregnancy and in the months following Nick's birth, when she looked after the baby while Joan tried to re-establish herself in London. It was Vivyen who, according to Joan, 'taught me how to grow and how to use my grimmer experiences in that process'.[62] But their relationship became strained when Joan began to grow out of her 'protégée' role; though grateful for all Vivyen had done for her, she resented what she perceived as the obligation to remain grateful. She also felt that, on a personal level, Vivyen spread herself too thinly, leaving no time for her own family. After Joan moved to London, she felt less inclined to spend weekends at the bustling Brasted house: 'a dozen people to tea and fifteen to supper isn't a remotely restful prospect!'[63]

The fate of Paul Seyler at this time remains murky. It is believed that he left England for good in 1948 to become a mercenary soldier in South America and died in Argentina in 1950, where he was said to be a cattle rancher. What is certain is that he was not around, in body or spirit, to play the part that would be officially credited to him in 1952.

By the beginning of 1950, Joan and Nick were living at 35 Carlyle Square, Chelsea, in a flat with huge, draughty rooms that were rather difficult to keep warm. Joan was now working for her father's old firm and, with her regular wages from T. Werner Laurie, had bought herself a natty red 1932 MG J2. Nancy said she had envisaged Thomas Laurie's daughter as 'an elderly spinster, grown etiolated and dry in the service of the firm ... '.[64] What she found instead was 'a girl four years younger than me, very good looking with rather a long nose'.[65]

And one day, Joan and Nick got into the red MG, drove to 6 Baker Street and collected Nancy and all her wordly goods and chattels. Nick thought they had further to go: 'I was absolutely convinced we were going off to Newcastle to fetch her'.

Nancy's feelings for Jonnie were, for the times, expressed publicly and remarkably frankly. 'She is certainly the only person who has ever let me be myself... therefore the only person with whom I can cheerfully live in close disharmony',[66] she wrote. 'Jonnie and Nicky awakened my fondness for humanity, which had lain hidden for so long; hidden away under a sort of barrage of smart attempts at wit and brisk repartee and clever little detective books'.[67]

She went on to explain the basis on which the relationship was formed and how, despite no emotional and physical exclusivity on either side, it worked for so many years – indeed, until death did them part:

I cannot write lightly of her, for she saved my life. By her example and her faith in me she has taught me things I could never have learned in books. Her faith in the fact that I am doing my best is worth a hundred paragraphs of praise from other people. My pen dries and my heart spills over and cannot express itself when I think of everything that Jonnie and Nicky have done for me.[68]

I don't care to make any decision without consulting Jonnie ... Jonnie is rather weak in health but she has lots of mental energy. I have no judgement at all. Jonnie has enough for twelve. But when we work together, we are equal to most things. ... On the day that I began to make judgements with Jonnie's hot beautifully controlled mind assisting me, the whole pattern of my behaviour changed. I began to make a little sense.[69]

And, over a decade later, towards the end of their time together, Nancy still maintained that it was 'Jonnie ... who rescued me from bed-sitting-room life, from years of mismanagement and debts, from unpaid rent ... '.[70]

It was not always thus: Joan had fought to overcome her own demons of despondency and uncertainty. 'I know that I bitterly resent criticism of any sort unless it is heavily sugared and deftly introduced', she once told Vivyen Bremner, 'and that I will fight back wildly and unreasoningly and frequently rudely rather than lose an atom of my very hard-won and still somewhat frail self-confidence'.[71]

This will have surprised anyone who knew the post-1950 Joan Werner Laurie. As Nick Laurie says, 'Joan was a very powerful personality. She was very quick and intelligent and you didn't win an argument with her. She liked to win at everything. Anything she learned to do, she learned to do well'. Seen through Nancy's eyes, however, this meant something rather different:

She is always perpetually, tirelessly, striving, expecting of others the near-impossible standards she set herself. . . . She despises people who don't try. She is the best company in the world and quite the most stimulating companion. To her, boats and companions and islands are delightful, exciting, physical adventures.[72]

Indeed, Joan had inherited what her brother Dick called the

'Laurie can-do philosophy – "let's drive in a rally, fly a plane, edit a magazine, write a book" . . . Jonnie was a jolly difficult person – her tongue was fierce. She was an extraordinary mixture of all sorts of things – like my father, who had a mean old bastard streak in him and was also a very selfish man. She was very much mission control. She would say to Nancy, "I don't think that's a very good idea", or "you shouldn't go on that programme with that person". Nancy very rarely contradicted her. Jonnie spoke very quietly; Nancy would always listen to her and treated her, to some extent, almost as a guru'.

Of course, that's not how everyone saw Joan, or the relationship, according to Dick: 'Liz, I think, was deeply shocked by the whole thing and just didn't want to know. She had little to do with Jonnie'. Liz goes further than that:

'I didn't like her at all. Joan was very clever and very cold and Nancy was the opposite, very warm-hearted. She was just using Nancy for what she could get out of her – definitely. Joan used Nancy to make money, and used all her ideas. I think she got hold of Nancy and she was too nice too escape. I don't know what Nancy thought of her'.

Certainly, money came into it – which was probably no bad thing for the somewhat spendthrift Nancy. But, ultimately, any long-term partnership, running along parallel personal and professional lines, has to have more going for it than a purely financial arrangement if it is to survive. Nick Laurie agrees that Nancy and Joan were devoted to one another, but adding the rider, 'in an odd sort of way':

'They were together fourteen years which, in this day and age, is quite a chunk of marriage. They never discussed their relationship with me – any more than I would discuss mine and Eileen's relationship with our girls. I don't know what it was based on. Part of the glue was a business – they pooled everything. But you don't pool all your worldly goods into joint bank accounts without some sort of love . . . *implied*'.

For others close to them, there were certain aspects of their relationship which intrigued. Dick Laurie recalls that Beatrice initially couldn't understand the sexual side of the relationship:

'She kept saying to me, "What do they *do*?" After they'd been living together for some time, people were starting to make the inevitable remarks about the ambivalence of their sexuality. My mother had one of her birthday parties, got a bit pissed and said, "They do seem to be very happy together, don't they?" I said, yes they did. And she said, "But I don't know what they *do*". I said, "Ask them – Nancy will certainly tell you . . . "'.

Shortly after Nancy moved in with Joan and Nick, *Cinderella Goes to the Morgue* was published. By now, she was beginning to come to the attention of a wider range of reviewers – though not always for the right reasons. Daniel George of the *Daily Express* decided that

Nancy Spain is evidently not going to have it said that her novels are subversive of anything. If murder's here, can merriment be far away? No, it seems: horror is hushed by chirpy humour, crime is cradled in offsmart backchat. . . . I just couldn't stand being twittered at by the author and her playmates.[73]

However, C.P. Snow of the *Sunday Times* decided that the book was one of the best recent examples of crime fiction, 'with much verbal sparkle and bright warm-hearted character drawing a work of considerable distinction'.[74] And Maurice Richardson, tongue-in-cheek, detected a hint of respectability about her work:

The anarchistic Miss Spain, who seemed, at one time, to be on the point of dynamiting the detective story, now insists on being taken seriously . . . she has curbed her clowning and put a lot of hard work into plot and construction. Result: another lively and satisfying whodunit. Bishops, and other serious students of crime fiction, who used to have to hide their Nancy Spains under their pillows, will now be able to read them openly in the Athenaeum.[75]

John Connell of the *Evening News* declared it 'A dazzlingly competent, zestful and entertaining whodunit'. And in *Books of Today*, an anonymous reviewer – almost certainly 'JWL' – said 'Nancy Spain is one of the very few writers who are not content to write a mystery without adding the graces of humour, wit, irony and satire to an otherwise commonplace structure . . . of its kind, quite first-class'.[76]

Her editors at Hutchinson had decided to take full advantage of her increasingly infamous eccentric style and image and commissioned Angus McBean to photograph her for the back cover of *Cinderella*. The impish Welsh-born photographer had became world-famous in the 1930s and 1940s for his portraits of the leading lights of British theatre: Vivien Leigh, Laurence Olivier, Edith Evans, Ralph Richardson, Peggy Ashcroft and Nancy's old pal, Hermione Gingold – all had been given the 'McBean' treatment. His elaborately planned and constructed portraits took days to prepare, using painted backdrops and complex props and garments. Employing montage and multiple exposure, McBean produced surrealistic pictures of the stars which were worlds away from the conventional West End images. Richardson was photographed 'sitting' in a toy theatre; Ivor Novello and Mary Ellis, the stars of the 1939 hit *The Dancing Years*, were portrayed in an embrace in the lower half of an hourglass; and Dorothy Dickson's head appeared to be floating in a lily pond. In the 1950s, McBean was using this surreal style in the treatment of other types of popular personality: the stars of the 'new' medium, television, plus the leading lights of the musical, sporting and literary worlds. Thus personalities like Denis Compton, Gilbert Harding and, hence, Nancy were all 'arranged by Angus McBean'.

For the cover of *Cinderella*, Angus had a proof copy of one of the pages, complete with proofreading marks, blown up. Nancy was photographed lying against this, her head resting on her right hand, surrounded by various instruments of death – a noose, a pistol, a hammer, a bottle of poison and a dagger – and, nestling just under her right elbow, a pair of handcuffs. The teaming of McBean's style with Nancy's oddball appearance and books was an inspired pairing, and would produce memorable cover shots for several of her subsequent detective novels.

In May 1950 Nancy met with BBC television director W.P. Rilla and producer Ian Atkins to discuss a possible 90-minute adaptation of *Cinderella Goes to the Morgue*. Atkins and Rilla were to prepare a treatment of the novel, for which Nancy would then write the dialogue. According to Rilla, it would be 'a new version which will however be based on the original book in that it will make use of the same characters, but not for the most part of the incidents occurring in the book . . . '.[77] 'The adaptation will be in the fullest sense of the word a collaboration between Miss Spain and myself under the guidance of Ian Atkins'.[78] Hutchinson were approached regarding copyright and Nancy was offered a fee of £53 15s. – half in advance – for her work. However, for reasons which remain unclear, the adaptation was never undertaken.

In October she returned briefly to Newcastle to do a live broadcast for the

NEHS on local hero Admiral Lord 'Cuddie' Collingwood ('The Man Who Won the Battle of Trafalgar'), whose gargantuan monument towers over Tynemouth. The 22-minute programme, 'an appreciation by Nancy Spain, with illustrations from Collingwood's letters'[79] read by Guybon Andrew, was duly broadcast.

The next month saw the publication of *'R' in the Month*, to modest reviews. 'Despite the rococo ambience that still surrounds her revue-star-detective Miriam Birdseye, there are signs that Miss Spain is beginning to take death seriously',[80] quipped Maurice Richardson in the *Observer*. In the *Sunday Times*, Christopher Pym said, 'Nancy Spain brings off an impudently satirical story of oyster-fed murder . . . '.[81]

By this time she was already well on the way to completing her next – *Not Wanted on Voyage* – a tale of Hero and heroin, dedicated to Hermione Gingold. Initially inspired by her cruise to Madeira and Tenerife with Liz, Nancy set the story on a ship, the MS *Comet* of the Dutch/English Comet Shipping Line. This time, Natasha has her new husband, Sir Timothy Shelly, in tow. Also on board are Douglass Comett, director of the line, his beautiful wife, Hero, and their young daughter, June Comett, who is treated with indifference by her mother. Just to over-egg the pudding, Hero's lover, 'that odd author of historical novels', Gordon Furbank and his wife, Zitha, are also passengers on the cruise. For twelve years, Hero has been in love with Furbank, a genius 'who required the great release of sex'.[82] Zitha Furbank hates her rival, convinced that he is merely a father figure for her. And, in a further twist, Zitha is the much-adored 'Honorary Aunt' to young June.

Heroin is being smuggled into England and the *Comet* may well be the vessel that is being used to traffic the consignments. Roger Partick-Thistle, the ship's passenger rep, suggests to his boss that a discreet private detective might be able to get to the bottom of things. Comett agrees; what he doesn't know is that Miriam Birdseye is Roger's idea of a 'discreet' private detective. Miriam, accompanied by Frederick Pyke, joins the cruise. Other passengers include Commander and Mrs Fryteful, Mr and Mrs Polyo, Kenneth and Beryl Tennis-Racket, Albert Earole, Mrs Earole, Bert Canteen and Stanley Chew. And, in a stroke of extreme bad taste, the ship's physician is called Dr Belsen. Poking fun at her own predisposition to *mal de mer*, Nancy gets her characters to swap notes on their respective seasickness remedies: Nosix, Quellthatsqueam, Mothersperfectlywells, Kwiksoothes and Soothswells – 'practically neat opium'[83] – the one favoured by Roger Partick-Thistle.

Soon the killings begin. At Waterloo Station, an unidentified man pushes Hero's mother, Mrs Speak, under the 2.55 from Croydon. Then, the *Comet* is only two days out of port when Mrs Comett is found drowned in her bath. It emerges that one of the other passengers is C.F. Bunyip, writer, biographer and editor of the magazine *Now Left, Now Right*. Bunyip had been about to write a book about a famous madam, a certain Marlene Speak of Bradford, who ran a chain of brothels in the north of England. However, Madam Speak's heirs had managed to prevent the project.

Other scandals unfold, including revelations of abortions and secret pregnancies. As the story sails, creakily, to its conclusion, a stash of cash is discovered concealed in a toy panda, a magic show results in yet another killing and the identity of the drug runner is revealed. The book also has a rather sinister ending, as the murderer is discovered in a cabin writing the following confession (the names are excluded here, so as not to spoil the ending for anyone who might read the book):

> She turned sour on me like a cold cup of tea left out on the writing table. That's all that — was. . . . How I hated her. Her physical demands, always denied afterwards. She liked it all the same, damn her. And that 'happy darling' and those pet names for this and that. Since I killed — there has been no woman in my life at all to take my time and my lifeforce from my writing in sex.[84]

1951 didn't begin auspiciously for Nancy. Life with Joan and Nick at Carlyle Square was running smoothly enough, mainly because of the presence of their housekeeper/nanny, Margaret Shaw. Nancy, however, succumbed to her annual winter dose of respiratory illness – this time pneumonia – and after Christmas went to Brighton to convalesce. The illness was partly due to overwork, since, as well as *Books of Today*, she had taken on yet more work. While attempting to persuade publishers to place advertisements in *Books of Today*, she had contacted Olive Bird, the advertising manager of *Good Housekeeping*. She took Nancy out for lunch and, as a result, the National Magazine Company's book division took some space to advertise its cookery books. They were duly sent a complimentary copy, which eventually found its way into the hands of Oliver Robinson, the editor of *Good Housekeeping*. Impressed with what he saw, Robinson wrote to ask Nancy if she would like to become his new book reviewer, replacing Valentine Hall. They met for lunch to discuss it, although she still had every intention of staying with the struggling *Books of Today*. She even harboured a wild notion of buying it outright herself, seeking investors who could come up with enough money to pay for a much-needed circulation manager.

Over lunch, Oliver Robinson made her an offer she couldn't refuse: a position as literary editor, at 20 guineas a month for a book-related feature, with another 20 a month for other features. Robinson warned her that, in view of *Good Housekeeping*'s policy of working four months ahead of publication, she might encounter difficulty in getting books far enough in advance. She assured him that this would be no problem, given the good network of authors and publishers she had established for herself during her time with *Books of Today*. Robinson was satisfied and they agreed that the new books page – to be called 'Title Page' – should make its debut in the January 1951 issue of *Good Housekeeping*. It was flagged as the beginning of 'a feature designed to give news of writers and outstanding publications, for all who love books'.[85] The first books reviewed included the reprints of George du Maurier's novels and Jan Laing's historical novel, *Priscilla* – a T. Werner Laurie book.

One of the first authors Nancy contacted was Mrs Robert Henrey, author of the series of autobiographical *Madeleine* books and mother of child film star, Bobby Henrey. Could Nancy see a proof copy of *The Little Madeleine*, prior to publication in February? Certainly, said Mrs Henrey. The resulting article, 'Focus on Mrs Robert Henrey', was deemed by Oliver Robinson to be good enough to run outside the book page and he suggested that it appear under a pseudonym. Nancy agreed and, again, looked to her ancestors for inspiration: she chose 'Jane Dorling', one of Isabella Beeton's cousins. She used it as her byline for features, she explained, 'whenever a subject seemed too soppy for Nancy Spain'.[86] Oliver Robinson said he imagined this 'Jane Dorling' to be a middle-aged lady, given to wearing a round felt hat and brogue shoes. Subjects considered to be worthy of soppy 'Jane Dorling' included the Italian sculptor Fiori de Henriques; 'A Girl Versus London', a lightweight but practical look at the problems faced by young women from the provinces heading for the capital; 'High Street London', a round-London trip; a poem called 'A Ballade of 1951', expressing the delights of a visit to the Festival of Britain site; and, most ironically, a return visit by its former pupil to 'Roedean', in which 'Jane Dorling' was kinder to the place than Nancy Spain would ever be.

Meanwhile, Nancy was filling 'Title Page' with some interesting material: there was a look at Foyle's bookshop and the Book Society, and an amusing piece about husband-and-wife literary collaborations, focusing on Ronald and Kaye Searle, Compton and Faith Mackenzie, and Margery Allingham and Philip Youngman Carter. Nancy had got herself, and the new section, off to a flying start. The only trouble was, she was now trying to juggle editing one magazine, setting up a major new column in another, working on the next wild crime fantasy and anything else she just couldn't say no to. Something had to give: in the end, it was her health. By the time she returned from Brighton, she had decided that, much as she loved it, *Books of Today* had to go. Or, rather, she would.

The April 1951 issue was the last to be edited by Nancy. In her final editorial, 'Ave Atque Vale', she confessed that she was leaving with a mixture of relief and sadness, and then signed off with some words of farewell, probably not meant unkindly, but still guaranteed to set the teeth on edge: I hope that this last number is the best . . . I always like to think that *Books of Today* steadily improved month by month . . . I may quite easily be wrong. It is always the mongolian idiots who are loved best by their mothers.[87] To celebrate her decision, she and Joan decided to spend the Easter weekend in Paris. But even this was spent mixing business with pleasure: Nancy fixed up interviews with Nancy Mitford and Colette, while Joan picked her way through the selection of glossy French and American women's magazines on offer and noted some fundamental differences between them and their staid English counterparts. From Colette, Nancy got a letter of introduction to interview Christian Dior. A meeting was duly arranged, but it could so nearly have been over before it began. 'I wish you'd seen his face when I turned up at his salon wearing my shabbiest jeans',[88]

Nancy would recall later. But if the legendary couturier's sartorial sensibilities were offended, he was too polite to say so.

When they returned from Paris, Nancy met Oliver Robinson for lunch again to iron out the finer points of her new job. He upped his offer to £40 a month for providing book reviews and book-related features, plus extra for features written as 'Jane Dorling'. However, he explained that there was actually no room for her at the National Magazine Company offices, although she would be expected to attend *Good Housekeeping* 'conference' meetings. At first, she used Nick's bedroom to work in while he was at school (the prestigious Lycée in Queensberry Place, Kensington). But this was hardly satisfactory and, eventually, after a series of small rented offices, she finally settled at 20–21 Took's Court, a four-storey warehouse building off Chancery Lane. This was convenient, as it was close to where Joan was now working: T. Werner Laurie had moved from their Piccadilly home to Doughty Street, off Gray's Inn Road.

The few 'conferences' Nancy attended gave her a chance to meet the magazine's senior members of staff, including Ethne Davis, fashion and beauty editor, assistant editor Gladys Williams and, a tall man with an extravagant handlebar moustache, art editor Michael Griffiths. Though editing *Books of Today* had brought her into contact with some big names, it was her stint as literary editor of *Good Housekeeping* that lifted her several places up the celebrity-interview pecking order. During her first summer working for the magazine, she secured an interview which many journalists would have given a lot more than their right arms for. The exiled Duke of Windsor had written his version of the events which led to his abdication. *A King's Story* was to be published by Cassell and serialized by the *Sunday Express*. Nancy contacted the PR department at Cassell, with an idea for an interview that would compare his current way of life with his previous existence. Given the number of his private secretary, Waddilove, Nancy suggested that the Duke could answer a set of written questions she would send to him. Everyone was happy with this arrangement and Nancy and Oliver Robinson drew up an exhaustive list of questions to send to Waddilove. Then came a typical piece of Spain bravura: informing Waddilove that she would be in Paris next week, she wondered if perhaps the Duke would prefer to answer the questions in person? This outrageous bluff worked, and a meeting was arranged for 3 July, not in Paris but in the south of France.

The interview was to take place at 3.30 p.m., on board the yacht *Sister Anne*, moored at Antibes. However, when Nancy arrived on the appointed day, after a brief stopover in Paris, the boat was nowhere to be seen. Eventually, a car arrived at the harbour to collect her and take her to Cannes, where the Duke was staying at the Carlton Hotel.

In typical fashion, Nancy had not taken sufficient money on the trip to cover her expenses, but she did have enough left to send Joan a cable before she flew back from Paris: 'Got him stony broke please meet'. The red MG and its owner were duly waiting at London Airport to collect the journalist who had pulled off one of the unlikeliest scoops of the year. Naturally, it was not credited to soppy old 'Jane Dorling'.

Given a four-page spread in the October issue of *Good Housekeeping*, and ostensibly dealing with the Duke's book, 'Postscript to a King's Story', it was actually more concerned with relating just how Nancy had managed to get the story. However, at the end of the feature, she did make a comment which, in the light of what has since been revealed about the Duke's pro-Nazi sympathies, was unwittingly profound: 'By his withdrawal, he kept safe the throne of England'.[89]

She encountered some less tarnished icons that summer: allowed on to the set of the studio where the last scenes of *The African Queen* were being shot, she was to interview Humphrey Bogart and Katharine Hepburn for a ghosted piece about 'Glamour', which would be published under Bogart's name. The circumstances could hardly have been less conducive to the subject of the piece. They were in the middle of filming the sequences where Bogart and Hepburn are repairing the boat's broken propeller and have to drag the *Queen* through the reeds. The water was freezing and about 4 feet deep and, before each shot, had to be cleared of debris left by the crew during meal breaks. Nonetheless, both stars made their contributions and Nancy had her story.

While she was busy interviewing disgraced Dukes and Hollywood royalty, her latest book, *Not Wanted on Voyage*, was published. It was, however, one of her least reviewed works. In *Books of Today*, 'JWL' said that it was

> reminiscent of those wicked, sparkling, intimate reviews [*sic*] that used to grace the Ambassadors. ... Unlike them, each new Nancy Spain has more humour (and more heart?) and more naughtiness than the last. Here's wishing her more sparkling poison to her brilliant pen.[90]

Of the mainstream papers, only the *Sunday Times* paid it more than token attention: 'It is in this matter of people that Nancy Spain's rollicking, satirical and very witty farce is a little lacking,' observed Eric Forbes-Boyd. 'The grotesques she gathers for a nightmare cruise are too artificial to be profoundly amusing. ... But I continue to admire the invention, and the neat exchanges of dialogue'.[91]

Interestingly, *Not Wanted on Voyage* would be the first of her books to be published in America. In 1956, Penguin reprinted it, in one of their famous green editions. But Anthony Boucher of the *New York Times* shared his British counterparts' mixed feelings:

> I'm not at all sure what to make of it ... peopled by fugitives from an early Waugh novel; it's very gay and witty and dashing, somewhat self-conscious and callous, and oddly suggestive of decadence. Aside from certain acute flaws in plotting, your reaction will depend on whether Miss Spain's highly mannered style strikes you as delightful or merely affected.[92]

The disappointing reviews were more than made up for, however, by the new friends she was cultivating at this time, including Noel Coward. They were introduced to one another by the theatre critic Pat Wallace, daughter of Edgar Wallace and cousin of Nancy's former Roedean schoolmate, Penelope. During drinks, Nancy told Noel and Pat, a contributor to the *Tatler*, of her latest wheeze: a trip to New York. Flushed with the success of her first celebrity-filled summer at *Good Housekeeping*, she had decided to seize the moment and make some contacts on the other side of the Atlantic, from which possible features might spring. The only person she knew in America was Hermione Gingold, and she didn't even have her current address. Within days of arriving in New York, however, she had met a friend of a friend of 'Ging' who pointed her in the right direction.

For the rest of Nancy's stay, Gingold introduced her to her friends, including a man called Jerry Kilty. He put her in touch with Marlene Dietrich's daughter, Maria Riva, and the two had lunch at Sardi's. Nancy also took herself off to see various magazine editors, including Marie Louise Aswell of *Harper's Bazaar* and Maggie Cousins of the American *Good Housekeeping*. Others, from *Woman's Day* and *Reader's Digest*, were not interested in seeing her. Instead, she went shopping on Fifth Avenue, and loaded up with presents for Joan and Nicky (respectively, nylon underwear and toy space guns and helmets) before returning to London.

Nancy continued to make full use of her arrangement with *Good Housekeeping*: most months, she contributed a feature as well as the book column – though quite a few of them were still attributed to 'Jane Dorling'. It was 'Jane' who profiled a selection of women who had been made Dames of the British Empire, such as Vera Laughton Mathews and Myra Hess. But she was gradually phased out and, in the February 1952 issue, made her journalistic swansong, leaving the limelight to Nancy Spain.

Nancy was keeping busy, making useful contacts, attending book launches and publishers' parties and, as she had with *Books of Today*, covering as many different literary genres in the book column as possible, from crime fiction to biography. Her feature work was at least as diverse: she followed a Court photographer at work at Buckingham Palace; profiled Nancy Mitford; devised a thriller competition called 'Can You Kill the Colonel?' (with a story set in Brunton-on-Sea) and took a behind-the-scenes look at Wimbledon, aimed at encouraging young female players.

In between all this, she was working on her ninth detective novel, *Out, Damned Tot*, which was dedicated to Joan, 'with much love and gratitude' – her first discreet but public acknowledgement of the woman who was now the foundation of her life. It was a dubious compliment, however: the story, as usual, was farcical, but also featured an unusually high percentage of unsavoury characters – most of them children – and situations. It was set in the port town of Plankton, on the island of Manya, home of Evelyn St Leonards, a 'fat, eunuchoid' chap who is the world's most highly paid children's author, with classics such as *Little Winnie Wiskybreath* to his credit. With him are his wife Magda, who is 'stout from lack of sexual expenditure'[93] and her two daughters, Alice (twelve) and Emma (eight), who seem to disturb everyone they encounter, with their 'white pointed faces like stoats'.[94] Magda's sister, Barbara, is also staying with them: an aspiring writer in her late twenties, she is in love with Michael Adayr, St Leonards' literary agent.

It emerges that two men who have murderous intentions towards St Leonards are also in Plankton: Eddie Grimes, a publisher whom the author sued for royalties, and the exceedingly tall Thomas Harryson, Magda's first husband, a bitter and disturbed man obsessed by sex: 'Reality for him meant sex, poor devil'.[95] Harryson is out to win back his ex-wife and daughters who, unlike everyone else, he adores but, like everyone else, he recognizes are possibly as unstable as he is. One of those most disturbed by them is Natasha, who has now left her jealous husband, Sir Timothy Shelly, and is enjoying a holiday with £1,000 in notes that have fallen into her possession. Unbeknownst to her, however, her estranged husband has reported her to the Manyan police for illegally importing foreign currency. Also on the island (of course) are Miriam and Frederick Pyke, whose affections are still divided between the two women.

Evelyn St Leonards gives a dinner party at his villa, to which our heroines (plus Pyke) are invited. Also invited is the outrageous Dymphna, the Bee Woman, 'a stout maiden lady in her fifties', with 'a fine muscular stomach ... apparently knitted into a wrinkled navy-blue fisherman's jersey' and sporting 'a small neat moustache' and hair that was 'bobbed with a bang' that resembled a very bad wig.[96]

At dinner, Evelyn St Leonards proposes a toast – and promptly drops dead. Soon after, Natasha is arrested on currency charges and carted off to the jail. She is subsequently charged with the murder of her host. Meanwhile, at the villa, a teddy bear is found with its head cut off and a trio of drunken journalists turn up in search of a story – the poetic trio of Edgar Poe, Harold Child and, somewhat prophetically, Meriel Juniper, 'the uncrowned human interest queen of Fleet Street', who writes for the papers of empire magnate Lord Cute. They get their story when, mysteriously, Evelyn St Leonards turns up apparently alive and well. He denounces the 'newshounds'.

The incarcerated Natasha (who until now has been taking solace in books such as Samuel Smiles's *Self-Help*) manages to escape from prison. She stumbles into a clothing factory, where she encounters not only the creepy Alice and Emma but a number of other children who, it transpires, are working there as sweated labour, under the management of none other than Dymphna. A fire breaks out at the factory and Alice and Emma perish, but not before disclosing who tried to kill their 'uncle Evelyn' and why.

Nancy had a lot to celebrate that Christmas: she had settled into the sort of relationship she had always craved, with a woman who, even with occasional misgivings, still gave her free rein to be herself; she had polished off her ninth detective novel; and she had started to set up some more exciting and prestigious features for *Good Housekeeping* for the New Year. As a literary editor she received the usual flood of invitations from publishers to attend seasonal drinks parties. Nancy would try to go to as many as possible – after all, people could be notoriously indiscreet at such functions and who knows what literary gossip and snippets of useful information she might pick up. But, as would become apparent in 1952, she returned home from one seasonal function with perhaps a little more than she had bargained for.

There was a royal theme to *Good Housekeeping* in 1952: for the July issue, she took readers to a 'Royal Garden Party' and then profiled Princess Margaret, under the slightly misleading headline, 'When a Princess Gets Engaged'. She also decided to do a piece on her old chum Hermione Gingold, who was back from New York and living in Kinnerton Street. Ging had a book coming out that summer, *My Own Unaided Work* – published by T. Werner Laurie – and Nancy wanted to run a feature to coincide with its release. There was also talk of Nancy ghosting the Gingold autobiography, though Nancy wasn't too keen on the idea. Still, she went round to Kinnerton Street to catch up with all the gossip from 'Mum'. While she was there, a young man called at the house. He had written some songs for one of the Gingold revues of the 1940s and wanted to get her opinion of a new cabaret act he had devised with an Australian singer called John Rose. The two men were broke and decided to perform the act while the young composer finished writing a musical he was keen to get produced – it was called *The Boy Friend*.

Sandy Wilson remembers being 'introduced to a lady in corduroy trousers . . . sort of crouched in the corner. Hermione said, "This is Nancy Spain – do you mind if she stays?"'. He didn't and he and Rose went through their new act, which Hermione praised. Hermione had to leave for the theatre, but Nancy stayed behind. Over drinks, she asked Wilson what else he was working on and he told her about *The Boy Friend* which the Players' Theatre were planning to produce, but had been forced to postpone:

> 'She said, "Can I hear some?", so I played a couple of numbers, and she went absolutely mad. She said it was the most wonderful thing – "It must be done immediately! Now! You must go to the Players' and tell them they've got to do it!"'. That's what I remember about Nancy: her colossal enthusiasm. She was very stimulating, particularly to me at that time. I had done quite a bit, but I wasn't established yet. From then on, we became friends'.

Spurred on by Nancy's vociferous encouragement, Wilson did, of course, persuade the Players' to perform it. Opening on 14 April 1953 at the Players' Club, it transferred to Wyndham's Theatre on 14 January 1954, where it ran for over two thousand performances, making it one of the longest-running musicals in London history. When it transferred to Broadway, it gave Julie Andrews her first leading role.

Wilson's friendship with Nancy would continue into the 1960s: 'She was a very strong personality – I presumed that if one disliked her, one would hate her. I loved her'. But, as many of the friends Nancy made during the next decade would observe, the hand of friendship was extended mostly from only one half of the Spain–Laurie partnership. 'They were almost opposites in personality', remembers Wilson:

> 'Nancy was so forthcoming, and Jonnie wasn't that. She wasn't unpleasant, but she always seemed slightly withdrawn. I think I only met her when I went

to their place. She never came here. I didn't feel she disliked me, but she was not apparently a very lively person, in comparison with Nancy. She'd always be slightly in the background, and a little bit forbidding'.

Joan would display this wary, rather cool, attitude towards many of the people Nancy became friendly with. 'My mother was very reserved about new people', explains Nick Laurie. 'Nancy approached new people completely openly, and immediately fell in love with them, no matter who they were. But she had very little judgement about them'. Dick Laurie agrees: 'With Nancy, what you saw was what you got. She was a very genuine person, very outgoing'. It may simply have been Joan's rather icy way of protecting Nancy from some of her more ill-judged acquaintanceships. 'I can imagine that,' agrees Sandy Wilson, 'because I'm sure Nancy could get herself into quite awkward situations with people who had got on to her, or she had become fascinated with'.

Not long after Nancy met Wilson, she started receiving messages from someone else who was rather keen to get 'on to her'. Some were left at the National Magazine Company offices and then at Carlyle Square, but they all said the same thing: 'Ring Harold Keeble at the *Daily Express*'. At first, she thought the *Express* were interested in the Gingold story. When she finally got around to returning Keeble's calls, however, she got the professional surprise of her life: Keeble wanted her to become the paper's new book reviewer. Fleet Street, as she had always dreamed it would, had 'sent for her'.

She was not slow to heed the call and set up a meeting with Keeble. Her first impressions of the rather pugnacious figure who met her was that he 'looked a little like a bull'. And so did the man – their ultimate boss – for whom she was about to start work.

Nobody Told the Truth in Those Days

Lord Beaverbrook, Nancy's new boss, was one of the twentieth century's most controversial and contradictory figures, revered and reviled in almost equal measure. Volumes have been written about his successes and failures, hypocrisies and loyalties, petty vendettas and grandiose aspirations. (The best of them is the excellent *Beaverbrook: A Life* by Anne Chisholm and Michael Davie.) There is only space here for the briefest resumé of this extraordinary figure.

Like Nancy, William Maxwell Aitken was also raised in Newcastle – though in New Brunswick, Canada. He was born in 1879, in Maple, Ontario, fifth in a family of ten children of the Reverend William Aitken, a Presbyterian clergyman and his wife, Jean Noble.

Young Max started his first commercial enterprise in his early teens, producing and selling his own paper at a cent a copy, though there were only three editions. Having failed his university entrance exams, he got a job in a drugstore, then became a clerk in a law firm. He attended law school for eighteen months then, aged nineteen, bought a bowling alley, and became an insurance agent. He subsequently went from selling bonds to becoming involved in the maritime, mining, lumber and steel industries. By the time he was twenty-eight, Max Aitken had already made his first million. He had also started a family: in 1906, he married Gladys Drury, with whom he had three children, Janet, Max junior and Peter. The Aitken dynasty now includes Jonathan Aitken MP, his sister, the actress Maria Aitken and Timothy Aitken, merchant banker and joint manager of TV-am.

In 1910, Aitken visited England, becoming friends with writers such as Kipling, Arnold Bennett and John Buchan, and buying a country house – Cherkley Court, near Leatherhead, Surrey. He also formed a friendship with Andrew Bonar Law, then leader of the Conservatives, who encouraged him to establish a base in England. Aitken took his advice and, that year, won the seat of Ashton-under-Lyme in a by-election. Knighted in 1911, he remained an MP until 1916, when he was created a baronet. In a rare bout of sentimentality, he took the name 'Beaverbrook' after the stream he had fished in as a boy.

During the First World War, he was the Canadian military representative in England, and in 1917, was made Minister of Information. He was also instrumental in persuading the Liberals and the Conservatives to form a 'national government' during the crisis. When his friend Bonar Law became Prime Minister in 1922, he seemed set for even higher political office, but Bonar Law's own career was cut short by illness and Beaverbrook's ambitions were put on hold. However, by this time, he had already invested in a new business venture: newspapers. In November 1916, Beaverbrook bought controlling shares in the *Daily Express* for £17,500. He proceeded to develop it into the ultimate human-interest paper, steering away from the sordid towards escapism. In 1922 he declared that the *Express*'s creed was 'More life – more hope – more money – more work – more happiness . . . '.[1] But it also meant 'more Beaverbrook'. Before the 1950s, the *Express*, and his other papers, including the *Evening Standard*, were instruments for disseminating his political views, views which were denied a place in legitimate government channels. Beaverbrook also used his newspapers to carry out personal vendettas against those he perceived as enemies. These included Ernest Bevin and Louis Mountbatten, who was pursued with particular zeal.

Beaverbrook was vehemently anti-socialist, against the United Nations and the Common Market. He even launched a brand new title, the *Farming Express*, which emphasized the need for trade within the Commonwealth. Even by the standards of the day, his views on racial issues were hardly enlightened, and he was against the decolonization of Africa and India's independence. However, it was Britain's two major political crises of the late 1930s which best displayed Beaverbrook's contradictions and ambitions.

In 1936, Beaverbrook was on route to America, seeking a remedy for his asthma, when the abdication crisis came to a head. He believed that Edward VIII's intention to marry Wallis Simpson was a mistake, and simply couldn't understand why any man would relinquish the throne of England for the sake of a mere woman. Winston Churchill later told his secretary John Colville that Beaverbrook had taken part in a campaign to frighten Mrs Simpson out of England, which had involved sending poison-pen letters and throwing bricks through her windows. Beaverbrook always denied it, but hinted that somebody connected with the *Express* might have been responsible. Once he became convinced that Edward was determined to marry Wallis, he ensured his newspapers backed the King and campaigned against his possible abdication. Edward also asked Beaverbrook to help him suppress newspaper coverage of Mrs Simpson's divorce case. Beaverbrook did so, using his influence with proprietors and managing directors in England, Scotland and Ireland, and in the French and American press. On 11 December 1936, Beaverbrook listened to the abdication broadcast at Cherkley, in tears. The ex-King rang him afterwards to say goodbye.

But it was not farewell, and soon the Duke of Windsor and Beaverbrook were again on the same, losing, side of a political argument debated at the highest level.

When Ribbentrop was appointed as German ambassador to Britain in October 1936, Beaverbrook afforded him abundant praise. After the Anschluss, he declared, 'There will be no war'. It became his, and the

Express's, oft-repeated slogan. After Chamberlain flew back from Munich, paper in hand, the *Express* predicted, 'Britain will not be involved in a European war this year, or next year either',[2] and the next day's front page assured readers, 'You may sleep quietly. It is peace for our time'.[3]

Beaverbrook was hardly unaware of the realities of Nazi Germany: in March 1938, he had helped Lily Ernst, a Jewish Hungarian-born ballet dancer who was in love with him, to escape from Vienna when Hitler took control. However, he was still in favour of appeasement and his papers maintained that line throughout 1938 and 1939. Both he and the Duke of Windsor thought that Britain should make a peace offer to Germany. Beaverbrook was amongst the misguided group of peers who felt the Duke should return to Britain, and he began mustering support for this idea amongst the City establishment.

Given Beaverbrook's unabashed support for policies of appeasement – and worse – it is astonishing that, once war was declared, he was approached to play an active part in Britain's war effort. However, that is precisely what happened: Leslie Hore-Belisha, Secretary of State for War, unsuccessfully asked Beaverbrook to take over the Ministry of Propaganda, and then Churchill made him Minister of Aircraft Production. In less than five years, the aircraft factory he initiated at Castle Bromwich had produced 11,500 Spitfires. He drafted in women to join the workforce, instilling a sense of urgency in both his male and female workers. In six weeks, the number of aircraft ready for service rose from 45 to 1,040.

His London home, Stornoway House, became his administrative HQ. Here he held meetings, often over dinner, and, on Saturday afternoons, was shown the weekly production charts. Then there was his 'Pots and Pans Appeal', started in July 1940. 'We will turn your pots and pans into Spitfires and Hurricanes',[4] he told Britain's housewives. They contributed not only pots and pans but aluminium parts from cars, gates, etc. What he omitted to tell them, however, was that aluminium was not scarce at all; but it was nevertheless a masterly piece of morale-boosting propaganda that was pure Beaverbrook. His efforts during the war did much to boost his public image and even his bitterest enemies had to concede that this had been his finest hour.

After the war, Beaverbrook had many homes, as many as thirteen at one point. They included Cherkley Court; a penthouse in Arlington House, Arlington Street, overlooking Green Park; a farmhouse in Somerset; a villa, La Capponcina, at Cap d'Ail in the south of France; and four houses in the Caribbean. However, none of his children were allowed to have keys to any of them. His wife had died in December 1927 of heart failure, aged forty-two. Although Beaverbrook was understandably upset, his liaisons with a string of mistresses, begun early into his marriage, continued unabated.

From the mid 1950s until his death in 1964, his life ran to a fixed schedule. From 15 December to the end of February, he was in Nassau. Each March he spent a week in New York. The spring, and half of the summer, he spent in England, dividing his time between Cherkley and Arlington House. During August, he stayed at La Capponcina. In

September, he would visit Canada and then spend another month in New York. An early riser, usually between 5 and 7 a.m., he read a pile of books, magazines and clippings; even his car would be littered with cuttings and memos. He would dictate his missives to his secretary or his Soundscriber after breakfast, standing at a lectern, no matter which country or home he was in. By 10 o'clock, he would begin his round of calls: editors, contacts, secretaries and financial dealers.

At his eighty-fifth birthday party, Lord Beaverbrook told his guests how he defined a good journalist:

> First, he must be true to himself. The man who is not true to himself is no journalist. He must show courage, independence and initiative. He must also, I believe, be a man of optimism. He has no business to be a pedlar of gloom and despondency. He must be a respecter of persons, but able to deal with the highest and the lowest on the same basis, which is regard for the public interest and a determination to get at the facts.[5]

He once told his granddaughter, Jean Campbell, what he considered to be the essential lessons about journalism: 'Emphasise human interest. Write short sentences. Cut, cut, cut. Always interview people face to face. Never rewrite from another newspaper. Keep widening your circle of acquaintances – even if it means accepting the invitations of bores. Use your feet'.[6] If Nancy was never actually given this advice, it hardly mattered: she lived up to the Beaverbrook ideal, to the letter, until the day she died.

The 1950s was to be the *Daily Express*'s last great decade – and Nancy was fortunate enough to be there, in the right place, at the right time. In the year she joined the paper, Lord Beaverbrook (according to a report in *Newsweek*) sold more papers per day – 5 million – than anyone else in the world. By 1960 the *Daily Express* was selling nearly $4\frac{1}{2}$ million copies daily. It was almost matched by the *Sunday Express*, and its stablemate, the *Evening Standard*, had stolen an unbeatable march on the rival *Evening News*. But no matter how influential or gifted the proprietor, a newspaper can only be as good as its journalists. And, since Beaverbrook wanted his papers to be the best, he handpicked editors and writers of the very highest calibre. Paradoxically, for his right-wing papers, he recruited left-wingers, many from the Bevan-founded weekly, *Tribune*: Michael Foot was editor and then chief book reviewer at the *Evening Standard*; Woodrow (later Lord) Wyatt had been a leader writer at *Tribune* before writing for the *Standard*; Robert Pitman and Robert Edwards, later an *Express* editor, also came from *Tribune*.

Hugh Cudlipp, another former Beaverbrook man who became editor of the *Daily Mirror*, observed that, like an impresario, 'Beaverbrook assembled around him a galaxy of writers and cartoonists without equal in the newspaper world . . .[7]

> He was demanding, exacting, tyrannous, vindictive and malicious, yet all or most of the excesses of the master journalist were forgiven by the men and women who worked for him because of the success of his publishing enterprise and his impish sense of fun'.[8]

Another former *Express* man, Geoffrey Bocca, observed, 'It amused him to surround himself with journalistic whizz-kids'.[9] Beaverbrook demanded much from his 'whizz-kids', but would amply reward loyalty and hard work. The wages of his managers and journalists were the highest in Fleet Street. He would send gifts of money – usually around £250 – to women friends and favourite employees on his birthday (not theirs) and at Christmas. One former *Express* man, Tom Hutchinson, was amused by Beaverbrook's attempts to ensure that his showbusiness writers knew their stuff. 'He made it a point to talk to newcoming journalists specialising in it, about their subject – "Did I understand? Now, was so-and-so a homosexual? Was this star sleeping with that star?"'.[10]

But none of what the *Express* became would have been possible without its much-loved and respected editor for over twenty years, Arthur 'Chris' Christiansen. Jokingly described by Beaverbrook as 'the foreigner who edits my chief newspaper',[11] Christiansen was, in fact, born in Wallasey, though of Danish parentage. He had worked his way up in the newspaper business as a sports sub on the *Liverpool Courier* and *Evening Express*, becoming editor of the *Daily Express* in 1933, when he immediately set about changing the style, tone and content of the paper. 'I tried to make news exciting, and on that account I had to change the typography of the British popular newspaper',[12] he explained.

But it was its tone, as well as its style, that set the *Express* apart. It was the paper for the young, 'can-do', conservative people of Britain, who were part of the crumbling Empire that Beaverbrook himself supported so solidly. Enterprising, ambitious, hard-working people from all walks of life would find their aspirations and attitudes reflected, endorsed and encouraged in the *Daily Express*. Hugh Cudlipp described it as 'the "I'm all right Jack" newspaper . . . a distillation of Dale Carnegie and Samuel Smiles'.[13] Arthur Christiansen saw it more romantically: 'The Express should make people reach for the stars'.[14] It did. It also made the people – and the stars – reach for the *Express*. Its famous 'William Hickey' gossip column, presided over for years by Tom Driberg and then, subsequently, by twenty-three other 'Hickeys', including Derek Tangye, Donald Edgar and Simon Wordell, was where the ordinary reader could keep tabs on the rich, famous and educated stars of showbusiness and society they wished to emulate. J.B. Morton contributed the lighthearted, 'all human life is there' column, 'Beachcomber', and one the 'Crown Jewels' of the *Express* was Rene MacColl, the 'Roving Reporter' who, as a global correspondent, clocked up around 25,000 miles each year.

The balance of news was equally fundamental to the paper's success. Beaverbrook advised his editors to run a minimum of twenty-two stories on the front page alone. For every piece of alarming or distressing news, there would be one that was upbeat or humorous. It steered away from the sordid, but embraced respectable sensationalism. It was this cocktail of the good and the bad, the ugly and the beautiful, the controversial and the comforting that gave its readers a sense of the times, the world they were living in – and their place in it.

But, most importantly, the message that Christiansen communicated so successfully to his team of journalists was that, whatever the story – be it the highest of high politics or the lowest reach of common human experience – 'We should never fail to have the COMMON TOUCH'.[15] With this in mind, Chris invented a fictional yardstick 'average' reader: 'the Man from Rhyl', or 'the Man on Rhyl Promenade', inspired by a journey he made from Rhyl to Prestatyn.

There were two other key contributors to the *Express*'s success during this era. One was Harold Keeble, the formidable associate editor; the other was Edward Pickering (later Sir Edward), originally managing editor, who would eventually take over the editor's chair. Their contributions, combined with Christiansen's editorship and the services of some of the best practioners in the business, ensured that the circulation of the *Daily Express* rose from 2 million in 1933, to 4 million by 1957.

Nancy, then, was joining not so much a paper but a Fleet Street phenomenon which, according to Francis Williams, not only 'brought sophistication to the suburbs, but it also brings romance into thousands of rather dull lives'.[16] It earned its enormous popularity by virtue of offering up its readers worlds within the world: success, glamour and the postwar, post-rationing optimism.

Edward Pickering thinks it was Arthur Christiansen and Harold Keeble together who decided to appoint Nancy, but there is no doubt 'The Beaver' himself would have had a considerable say in the decision. Unlike contemporary populist newspapers, he always regarded the book coverage of his papers to be an integral, attractive feature, according to Michael Foot:

> 'He always had a special interest in the book pages. He thought his newspapers should make the fullest use of authors. He would say, "Here are all these writers, producing books all over the world. We should be finding out what they're up to and seeing what they can contribute to our newspapers." So he had a real, genuine interest in books. He had some strange ideas about the book reviewers. He said they should tell the story of the book, as well as giving their opinions, and sometimes he would take that to extremes. But he was a really great editor – absolutely absorbed and fascinated in the news and how you presented it.
>
> I owe a tremendous amount to him. I was pretty keen on journalism before I started but, as with so many, like Nancy, he could teach you things, in order to make his newspapers better. He knew what news was and how it could be treated and followed up, and wanted his papers to be better at it than any of the others. And that applied as much, perhaps even more, to the books pages as anything else'.

Peter Grosvenor, one of Nancy's successors on the *Express* books pages, said that, up to the end of his life, Beaverbrook considered that section of the paper as a vital one, as the *Express* (at that time) had 'the highest AB readership of any newspaper in the land'.[17] Space always had to be found for a regular books page, even at the expense of revenue-rich advertisements.

Foot believes that, though Nancy's sterling efforts at *Books of Today* and

Good Housekeeping brought her to the attention of 'Chris' and Keeble, Beaverbrook may have spotted her even earlier – in the publication where he found so many of his best writers. 'It's likely the first time he heard about Nancy was when she was writing in *Tribune*. He was always on the lookout for new young journalists – he didn't give a damn about their political views'.

Prior to Nancy's appointment, the book coverage of the *Daily Express* had been crying out for some vitality, daring and, even, controversy to be combined with a diversity and depth of literary knowledge. Beaverbrook, according to Michael Foot, had always admired the style of Arnold Bennett's 'Books and Persons' column in the *Evening Standard* and wanted the *Express* to have something similar. But Nancy's role in the *Daily Express*'s development in the 1950s was not an isolated, or accidental, one, as Edward Pickering explains:

> 'She was really part of a great expansion that was taking place. You must remember that in the very early 1950s we were still on paper rations, so we had quite small papers – the *Express* had been eight or even four pages for twelve years. But in the 1950s we suddenly began to expand and consequently, we had to replan a paper and find writers to fill it – and she was one of them. It was a very exciting time; it was the last period when pictures in newspapers were a vital part of the production. Very often we would have full or half pages of *Express* photo news. And it was a period when all the staff were a very enthusiastic lot.
>
> The *Express* dominated the market in the way that the tabloids like the *Sun* do now. Sales of the *Mail*, which was also a broadsheet at that time, were always under 2 million, and the *Mirror* was the only tabloid. The market was different and the opportunity for the *Express* to influence all sorts of ideas was very strong'.

Pickering had the gift of spotting and encouraging talent, particularly when it was contained in lively personalities. And Nancy was the perfect 'lightweight' journalist for the 'perfect' paper of the 1950s.

Her task for the book pages of the *Express* was largely an extension of her work at *Books of Today* – increasing the number of books reviewed and, in a move which made Beaverbrook happy, including more interviews and profile features of interesting or controversial authors. As Pickering explains:

> 'She wasn't a book critic who came in and collected a few books, went away and wrote about them. She used to come in and discuss all manner of things for the feature pages – how to present a particular article – and really took a great part in the whole development of that side of the paper. She reviewed a lot more of the popular books – paperbacks – and then she got into arguments with authors, which, of course, produced good copy'.

The affection, loyalty and respect between Nancy and Beaverbrook was real enough, but she was not, in the strictest sense of the word, his protégée – though that is how some of their respective detractors on Fleet Street regarded the relationship. Edward Pickering takes a different view:

'We were all protégés of Beaverbrook, in one sense, because he was a very dominant personality. I don't think "protégé" is the right word – he was an *enthusiast* for Nancy Spain. There was no sense of him having to promote her in any way; she was immediately accepted as being someone who could really contribute something to the paper. It wasn't Beaverbrook saying to the editors, "I hope you'll give Nancy Spain some space", because they were just as anxious to get her stuff into the paper as anybody'.

Apart from Nancy, Beaverbrook's newspapers boasted a large number of 'name' women columnists during the 1950s. There was Anne Scott-James, once editor of *Harper's Bazaar*, hired by Harold Keeble to write a weekly column for the *Sunday Express* on subjects angled towards women, but also on any subject she saw fit. Anne Edwards wrote something similar, 'The Monday Morning Column' on the *Daily Express*, which could also boast the services of Eve Perrick (who had started at the *Express* in 1939 as a secretary) and her acerbic, witty and much-respected showbusiness column. Many of these prominent women writers left for other papers after Christiansen had gone from the *Express*.

Nancy, of course, had a rather different image to most of her female colleagues. When she appeared in the *Express* office, it was in standard trousers, shirt or jumper. 'I did think her clothes were rather awful by any standard', admits Anne Scott-James. But, as Edward Pickering recalls, she would occasionally confuse the issue with some of her public appearances: 'She would appear in jeans in the office and then appear at a cocktail party or dinner looking absolutely stunning in a Balmain dress. It was like there were two people'.

Harold Keeble took great pains to encourage the *Express*'s women journalists. It was he who, 'possibly alone among his generation, realized that women were no longer prisoners of the nursery, and that newspapers must adapt themselves to providing for readers who had interests other than the kitchen sink'.[18] But this didn't mean that Keeble spared his women journalists. 'He cosseted them, nagged them, encouraged them, sometimes reduced them to tears, but always published their work with the bold and striking typographic displays which were his personal signature'.[19]

Chris maintained that his women journalists were less temperamental than their male counterparts, but complained that those on the *Express* had 'an irritating habit of taking a long time to answer a summons'.[20] However, despite the fact that Chris had originally aimed the *Express* at 'ambitious young men',[21] the importance of the *Express*'s female readership was, with Keeble hammering home the point, never lost on him and he warned his journalists that they ignored this aspect at their peril: 'Never underestimate the interest of women in news which is supposed to be outside their purview',[22] he told them. In deciding what would run on the news pages, he tried, he said, 'to publish serious news alongside news which would attract, say, the woman reader, so that I could lead her eyes to the heavy news of the day'.[23] One of these leading features was Wednesday's women's page, 'She'.

Nancy was as popular with her *Express* colleagues as her bosses, and would join them in the favoured watering hole of *Express* journalists, Poppins in Poppins Court, a tiny road overshadowed by the *Express* building, which was a minute's walk from the front door. 'It was a marvellous office to work in', recalls Edward Pickering. 'Everybody worked extremely hard and tremendous hours. Of course, Nancy enjoyed being in that sort of atmosphere – and she contributed a great deal to it. But she also derived a lot of fun from it herself, and there was a great deal of fun going on all the time when Chris was the editor'. Each day at noon, there was a conference in the editor's room, where he would fire off questions thick and fast. What news is there? Pictures? What books would be good for possible serialization? Did anybody watch television last night? Who was on? What did they do? 'His daily conferences were theatrical performances', recalls Pickering, 'and people were encouraged to make vocal contributions – and there were many lively people on the staff, like Osbert Lancaster, who did the Pocket Cartoons, and Trevor Evans, the labour and industrial correspondent'.

On occasions, Nancy would make her own unique contribution to the fun and frolics in the office, as Edward Pickering recalls:

'It was just before one Christmas. The great toy that was being sold everywhere was a plastic machine-gun which had a drum at the back that you loaded with ping-pong balls and then you pulled the trigger and these things sprayed all over the place. That's what she decided would amuse us all for Christmas, and she suddenly produced this thing and fired – we were all in an open-plan office – and these things went from one end of the office to the other'.

Of course, working for such a hands-on proprietor as Beaverbrook meant that missives from on high were a common occurrence. Mostly, they were targeted at his editors, including Edward Pickering:

'Beaverbrook was a very tough gentleman to work for; he demanded very high standards. But I wouldn't have missed it for the world – he was the best news editor there could possibly be. He was totally different from the other proprietors, because he kept in touch with everything that was going on in politics. He knew all the members of the Cabinet – they all talked to him – he knew people in the arts, in every walk of life, except sport; and was prepared to discuss all that with you. He would give you all the benefit of his experiences and his advice – a marvellous man in that sense and I enjoyed working for him enormously. He could be very difficult, but he didn't interfere.

When I was editing, I produced the paper I wanted. If it wasn't a good paper, I knew about it the next morning. But if it was a good paper, I also knew it. That was a working relationship that I enjoyed. We used to go for long walks in the morning and talk about all sorts of subjects. It was a real education, because he'd been familiar with English politics since about 1909 and there was nobody who could talk in such an engaging way on the subject'.

During the 1950s, Beaverbrook was not in the habit of visiting his papers as frequently as he had done in the 1920s and 1930s, and he rarely attended board meetings. However, he continued to make his views on the content and running of his papers known via his two trusty tools – the telephone and the Soundscriber dictating machine. Armed with these, he would fire off responses to what his journalists had produced in that day's editions, as well as numerous ideas for features, news items, gossip and leaders. He once famously issued 147 directives to his editors in one day. Outside the news editor's room at the *Express*, there was a board in a glass case. On this would be posted Chris's 'Daily Bulletins' – his comments about the previous day's issue. He would dictate them before lunch, have a copy pinned up on the board and copies sent to the *Express's* provincial editors and correspondents.

Nancy decided that the theme of her new column would be similar to the one she had employed at *Books of Today*: waging war on what she called 'the literature of despair'.[24] Her first column in the *Daily Express* was published on 13 March 1952, with the headline, 'Join Me in Fighting the Literary Death Gang'. This meant 'books that glorify Death at the Expense of Life'. ' . . . There are writers who are in love with death and there are those who are determined to make something good from life itself', she declared. 'I also think that those writers who are brave enough to write hopefully should be encouraged'.[25] Of course, this was a bit rich coming from someone who had carved out something of a cult name for herself penning sardonic, occasionally sinister, murder mysteries. And it prompted the first of many letters of complaint – which, naturally, made good copy for the column. 'A letter signed "Disgusted Mother, Wandsworth", lies on my desk', she told her new readers, 'asking me why, if I am on the side of life and light, I enjoy reading those "filthy detective stories"'.[26] This was only the first of several contradictory opinions put forward in her early days.

She also waxed lyrical about the joys of being alive in London in the twentieth century: 'There is no other age or place for me. Above all, there is no doubt that this century is the one for women'.[27] The following week, she appeared to disagree with an author who had said she did not think a woman's place was in the home. 'I'm afraid I do', countered Nancy. 'Certainly there are precious few things we do better than men. Travelling and philosophy are two of them'.[28] But then, this was only the opinion of, as she presented herself, 'a frivolous and insular Old Roedeanian . . . '[29] – yet more bald-faced contradiction.

Something which Nancy conceded that women did at least as well as men was writing books. 'There have never been so many women writers as there are today',[30] she observed. However, she thought they were as obsessed with death as their male counterparts, and took two of them – Carson McCullers and Daphne Du Maurier – to task for it. 'It now appears Miss Du Maurier is as morbidly preoccupied with death as the rest',[31] she complained, in her review of *The Apple Tree*.

For the first year of her tenure at the *Express*, she also remained literary editor of *Good Housekeeping*, though, strictly speaking, Beaverbrook did not look kindly on his journalists 'moonlighting' for other publications – and with some justification. *Express* journalists were the highest paid on Fleet Street: in her first year as book critic, Nancy was paid £30 30s. a week, plus £5 5s. expenses. It's not surprising, then, that she did very little feature work for *Good Housekeeping*, though there would be profiles of Noel Streatfeild and Colette, and pieces on the Coronation preparations and, interestingly, one on the work of district nurses, called 'One Thousand Babies'. She was also working on another book, *'Teach' Tennant*, to be published by T. Werner Laurie. It was a frothy, anecdotal book, telling the story of Eleanor 'Teach' Tennant, the American tennis guru of the rich and famous who went on to coach two world champions, Alice Marble and Maureen 'Little Mo' Connolly. Tennant had been a successful amateur player herself, eventually becoming a professional coach at the Beverly Hills Hotel. Nancy's book was as full of references to the Hollywood stars tutored by 'Teach' as to the coach herself. These included Barbara Stanwyck, David Niven, Joan Crawford, Peter Lorre and Carole Lombard, who gave her the nickname 'Teach'.

In most cases, joining Beaverbrook's chosen few also meant becoming part of his social roster, which boasted infinite variety – and Nancy was no exception. Anne Scott-James observed, 'She was one of the few female staff whom Lord Beaverbrook saw frequently. I believe he was intrigued by her fund of anecdotes and general bohemianism'. 'There was no doubt that Beaverbrook was very fond of her', says Edward Pickering. 'He found her to be great company, and she enjoyed his company'. To begin with, Nancy was invited for private drinks, lunch or dinner. After a couple of years, however, the lunch and dinner invitations were extended to 'Miss Spain and friend', then to 'Miss Spain and Miss Laurie'.

For such a fiercely heterosexual man, Beaverbrook was curiously unfazed by lesbian or gay couples. He called gay men 'bugger-boys', yet seemed tolerant of and fascinated by homosexuals. Many of his male servants were gay or bisexual, including his valet during the 1940s, Nockels. And many gay men were frequent guests at his dinner table: Jean Cocteau and Jean Marais, Somerset Maugham and Alan Searle, Gilbert Harding, Godfrey Winn and, of course, Tom Driberg. In 1935, Beaverbrook had helped suppress the story that his then 'William Hickey' was due to appear in court at the Old Bailey in November charged with indecent assault. Not only did he somehow persuade his rivals to keep the story out of their papers, he even paid for Driberg's defence costs.

Beaverbrook rarely socialized at other people's homes – the Mahomets always went to the mountain; and they might include the likes of former American ambassador and dynastic founder, Joseph P. Kennedy; Elizabeth Taylor and Mike Todd; Randolph Churchill; or employees, such as Robert Edwards and Michael Foot. Guests – never more than a handful at a time – came for lunch or dinner; tea was never served, because Beaverbrook considered it a waste of time. Dinner was the main social event in his daily routine. He sat in the middle, not at the head, of the table. He did not make small talk, but usually jabbed the most noviciate of guests with probing, often highly personal, questions. The food and wine was always exquisite, though Beaverbrook himself was a small eater. Champagne was always served. Before dinner, he would mix cocktails – usually daiquiris – himself in a special, noisy mixer. If the dinner was at Cherkley, once the meal was over, guests would be shown into his private cinema to watch films selected by his film critics and lent by the distributors. Guests were not told in advance what they would be seeing, but more often than not, it would be *Destry Rides Again*. It was his favourite film – he owned his own copy – and 'The Boys in the Back Room', as performed by Marlene Dietrich, was his favourite song.

Beaverbrook had first met Nancy on Thursday 12 June 1952, when she spent an hour with him at Arlington House. In ordinary circumstances, this would have been a nerve-racking moment for any journalist, but for Nancy there was an additional anxiety and, as usual, it concerned what she would wear. Only this time, it was more of a problem than usual; she had to wear something that was appropriate and which would also conceal the fact that she was now six months' pregnant.

★ ★ ★

This rather surprising turn of events had been noticed by some closer to home. Dick Laurie was one of them:

> 'The first I knew about it, I was in the kitchen of their home in Carlyle Square and they had just bought a second-hand Adana printing machine on which they were going to do all their letterheads and Christmas cards and whatever. Jonnie and I were both very interested in this, and she was showing me the machine. She called Nancy in to tell her that I'd arrived at the back door. She didn't hear her, so Jonnie said give her a call. So I went over to the door when she came in – and she had this "little football" in front of her. She squeezed past me and said, "Well, you've probably noticed I'm pregnant". I said, "Who's the father?". She said, "It's none of your business". My mother said to me, "How did it happen?". I said, "Well, you know Nancy – try anything once". But she kept saying to me, "Who's the father? We must find out!". I'm not sure she ever knew, but she was certainly mighty interested. She'd just got her head round two ladies having a relationship and then suddenly one of them's pregnant . . . '.

It would be some time before Dick found out the truth. 'At one stage, she was putting it about that Beaverbrook was the father. Then she said it was her doctor, Norman 'Nelly' Newman. It was a long time before we discovered it was Youngman Carter'. 'Youngman Carter' was Philip 'Pip' Youngman Carter, the distinguished husband of Margery Allingham – neither of whom, of course, were strangers to Nancy.

So how, then, had it come to this? Nancy and the man who fathered her child took the truth of the exact circumstances with them to their respective graves. And so, apparently, did Joan and Sheila van Damm, who was to figure prominently in their later lives.

Born in 1904, Carter had met his future wife when they were students at Regent Street Polytechnic in 1921. They married in 1927 and set up home in

Tolleshunt D'Arcy, in Essex. During the Second World War, he served as a lieutenant colonel in the Royal Army Service Corps, and also co-founded and edited *Soldier* magazine. After being demobbed in 1946, he worked briefly at the *Daily Express* as features editor, before he joined the *Tatler*, first as assistant editor and then, from 1954 to 1957, as editor. Carter was also an expert on wine – he would co-found and edit *The Compleat Imbiber* and wrote a number of books on the subject. In addition, he was an accomplished artist and illustrator, with over two thousand book-jacket designs to his name. He would collaborate with 'Marj' on many projects and was, in fact, the model for her famous sleuth, Albert Campion. After her death, he wrote two novels of his own, *Mr Campion's Farthing* and *Mr Campion's Eagle*. Carter was described by *The Times* as 'a man of fierce hates and unshakeable enthusiasms'.[32] The former included children; the latter, women.

By the 1950s, Margery Allingham was spending most of her time at their Essex home, D'Arcy House. They also had a London flat, at 91 Great Russell Street, where Carter lived during the week. It was a handy central location for his numerous casual affairs which, by 1951, his wife knew all about. According to her biographer, Julia Thorogood, a 'mystery man' visited her in Essex on 10 January 1951. Soon after this visit, Margery Allingham transferred D'Arcy House from her husband's name to her own and informed her accountant that they were leading entirely separate lives. It was believed by her friends that her mysterious visitor may have been the husband of one of Carter's mistresses, who had gone to Allingham for help. Following his visit she had gone to the Great Russell Street flat, to find her husband *in flagrante*, thus prompting the legal action.

Despite these events, Carter spent much of the autumn and winter of 1951 in London helping to promote his wife's work, including selling the serial rights for her new novel, *Tiger in the Smoke*, to the magazine *John Bull*. Naturally, as literary editor of *Good Housekeeping*, and a big fan of thrillers and Margery Allingham in particular, Nancy would have been contacted. And, in the March 1952 issue of the magazine, Nancy ran a piece on crime writers.

No one knows for certain the exact circumstances of how and where she ended up in bed with Philip Youngman Carter, but everything points to a brief, possibly one-off, affair, conducted at 91 Great Russell Street under the influence of some pre-Christmas champagne. Years later, Sheila van Damm told Nick Laurie that 'Marj' 'never knew of their indiscretion'.

However, if Nancy had planned it, she couldn't have chosen a more suitable father for her child than Philip Youngman Carter: witty, erudite, suave, artistic and cultured – and someone who would never want anything to do with the child. 'I think you can be pretty sure that Tom was as unplanned as these things can get', says Nick Laurie. 'In those days, what would often happen was a quick party bonk and babies would come along – you didn't have the Pill in those days, or anything much – and I'm pretty sure that's what happened. I don't think he was planned'. However, once she had discovered she was pregnant, Nancy decided to keep the baby, and, later, explained her reasons to Dick Laurie:

'Nancy told me later that she had always wanted to know what it was like to give birth to a child, and that was why she had done it. But because we didn't know who the father was, and she wouldn't tell us, there was no question of us asking whether she'd been in love with this person or what. It was always put to me as a bit of psychological experimentation: "I wanted to know what it was like, Jonnie's had a baby and I thought I'd like to have a baby and give it to Jonnie" – that sort of thing . . . '.

But there still remained the small problem of how a woman who had just joined one of the biggest newspapers in the world and was beginning to assume a high-profile media image was going to conceal the fact that she was pregnant. Dick Laurie is still mystified as to how she managed it.

'She was hugely visible at that time – she had lots and lots of commitments. I don't know how she concealed it, because she was still wearing dungarees until six or seven months – and she was not the sort of person who could suddenly start wearing maternity clothes without people saying, what the hell's going on?'

Nick Laurie doesn't remember seeing a pregnant-looking Nancy. 'She was a fairly big lady and he was probably a fairly small baby. But you don't really notice these things when you're six'. Someone who did remember, however, was Noel Streatfeild, whom Nancy had interviewed for *Good Housekeeping* and whom she socialized with occasionally. By an odd coincidence, Streatfeild was godmother to Nancy's friend, Tony Warren, and it was she who, many years later, confirmed a story he had heard from Angus McBean. Apparently, during a photo session for the cover of one of Nancy's books, McBean could only shoot her lying flat because she was so obviously pregnant.

But, apart from making the most of her usual baggy jumpers and being able to work mainly from home, as Dick Laurie points out, Nancy would also have been able to rely on the fact that, given what most people knew to be her predominant sexual preference, a pregnancy would have seemed unthinkable:

'You have to remember that those people who knew her would have imagined it so unlikely that she could ever be pregnant that, even if she looked like she was, they would have discounted it. "Nancy going to bed with a man and getting pregnant? No, no, no – it must be too many lunches at the Ivy . . . "'.

A month before the baby was due, Joan decided to make a will – in effect, the nearest thing to a 'marriage' certificate that she and Nancy would have to seal their partnership. On 17 July, she signed a last will and testament, in which she bequeathed her entire estate to Nancy, whose address was given as 20 Took's Court. She also stipulated that

Nancy Brooker Spain should act as the Guardian of my son Nicholas Laurie Seyler until he is nineteen years old. I would be grateful if any sums due to me from my late father's estate could be given to Nancy Brooker Spain to use in any way she thinks fit. Vivyen Bremner and my Mother will both know of my gratitude for all their help in the past and of my love for them, and will understand my reasons for disposing of my estate in this way.

Certainly, they did. But it would be more than a decade before nearly everyone else around them did, and nearly twenty years for those most closely affected by this document.

Six days after Thomas Bartholomew Laurie Seyler was born at the London Clinic, 20 Devonshire Place, on 27 August 1952, Joan put her name to another document. On 2 September, she went to Marylebone Registry Office to register the birth, where the father was recorded as 'Paul Clifford Seyler, Cattle Rancher, c/o British Consul, Buenos Aires, Argentina'. The mother was 'Anne Brooker Seyler, formerly Brooker'. It was this 'Anne Seyler, mother' who was the informant and who, afterwards, returned to Carlyle Square with the illegal birth certificate.

There were, of course, several obvious and substantial reasons for fixing the birth certificate in this manner. Nancy's name and face were already too well known for even the registrar to be told the truth about the baby's natural mother. It also has to be remembered that, in the early 1950s, the stigma and shame attached to unmarried mothers was enormous. The Family Planning Association would only advise on and supply married women with methods of birth control. Moreover, women could still be committed to mental institutions if they became pregnant outside of marriage. A survey carried out in 1950 revealed that, in eleven institutions, this was the fate of a large percentage of the female patients deemed to be 'insane'. But, if the idea was to divert attention away from Nancy to Joan, it is peculiar that, rather than simply naming Joan as the mother, they opted to invent a fictitious character bearing an amalgamation of their names. After all, Joan was still technically married and so in a less questionable position. However, creating a mother who bore half each of their names was the perfect romantic gesture: the baby was, truly, 'theirs'.

At home, the new baby was introduced with minimal fuss, according to Nick Laurie:

> 'It was just . . . "we're getting you a brother" – and suddenly, there it was, and handed over to nannies. From then on, Nancy never . . . did anything publicly that would even hint at the possibility of what had happened. There was never a hint that he was anything other than my brother. A few close friends were aware of it, but the rest of the world wasn't'.

The 'rest of the world' included some of the most prominent people in their lives, such as Beaverbrook and most of Nancy's colleagues at the *Express*. Edward Pickering thinks he was not alone in his ignorance of the situation: 'I don't think it was something that entered into the *Express* knowledge. I'm sure there were some people in the office that knew, but it was never talked or gossiped about'. The truth was also kept from George, Norah and Liz: Nancy's parents never knew that they had a grandson. And, as her and Joan's 'inner circle' of friends grew, there was a curious inconsistency about who was told and who wasn't: for instance, Sheila van Damm was, but Tony Warren, one of Nancy's closest friends in the last few years of her life, wasn't.

Gilbert Harding and his secretary, Roger Storey, were told 'matter of factly', but Denis Norden, for years a co-panellist on *My Word*, was not. For most people who knew and worked with Nancy, the posthumous revelation that she was Tom's mother came as a complete shock – bigger for some than others.

Like most people, Liz Hulse never saw any signs of Nancy's pregnancy and it was some time before she met the baby:

'I remember going to see Nancy, and there was this little baby crawling about on the floor . . . I thought he looked very like my mother's side of the family – the red cheeks and very blue eyes. I remember he kept taking off the gramophone record as it was playing, and I said, "You leave that alone, it's Nancy's". And she said, "How ever can you be so strict with him?"'.

Dick Laurie understands Nancy's reasons for deciding never to tell her sister:

'She would have been mortified, socially, by what was going on anyway – and then to be utterly confused by the arrival of a nephew. . . . Nancy was not the sort of person to have told her out of spite or to see what sort of effect it would have on her'.

The 'official', public version of Tom's parentage was as bogus as his birth certificate, according to Dick Laurie: 'It was put about that Tom had been adopted by them, to cover when people asked where he had come from'. However, Nancy often referred to Tom, as well as Nick, in many of her articles, books and broadcasts, though always as belonging to Joan. To Beaverbrook, Nick and Tom were referred to as 'Laurie's two boys'.[33] To her *Woman's Hour* listeners, Nancy would admit that she had 'a wonderful life. I live in a beautiful mews cottage with a very nice lady publisher and her two sons . . . [the other] is an adopted baby called Tommy . . . '.[34] (Amusingly, one of Nancy's obituaries erroneously reported that she and Joan 'had adopted a little girl'.[35]) She also told them about 'Bodger, otherwise known as Thomas Bartholomew Laurie Seyler, whose mother Joan Werner Laurie quite often lets me look after him for a whole day'.[36] And, in *Why I'm Not a Millionaire*, she referred to Tom as 'the youngest of Jonnie's responsibilities'.[37] Nonetheless, she also said that 'Whether he flies into a rage and kicks me in the stomach . . . or whether he falls over and blacks his eye, screaming like a steam whistle, or whether he coos like an angel and clambers all over me, I have to admit that I love him, desperately, hopelessly, devotedly . . . '.[38] In hindsight, it seems incredible that nobody read between these lines. But then, after all, 'trouser-wearing characters' didn't have babies.

There is no reason to believe that Nancy and Joan ever intended to tell Tom the truth about the identity of his real mother, or that Nancy regretted her decision. As Dick Laurie explains:

'She didn't introduce Tom as her son, because she had, to use an expression, "for love for Jonnie", given Tom to Jonnie so she was mother to both Tom and Nick. She didn't want to rock that boat and she didn't want to upset

Tom. So they had to keep that secret, to some extent. But I don't think for a minute that was a cause of any melancholy for her'.

But though Nancy might have originally fostered some romantic notion of Joan as the mother of two children, while she played the 'father' figure, the domestic reality was rather different, as Dick Laurie reveals:

> 'They shunted the kids off as fast as they could, really. Nick was always being pushed away on holiday. By no stretch of the imagination could one say they "brought them up". They did give them lots of love and affection, and took them on nice holidays, and there were always lots of presents – which is always a bit sus. But they were both getting on with their careers like nobody's business – that's what it was all about'.

And so it would continue.

As if becoming the book critic for the most popular newspaper in Britain and having a baby in secret weren't enough, another door had opened to Nancy. It was to be one of the most important in her career and would play a significant part in establishing her as one of the favourite 'personalities' of the day.

In July she received a letter from Janet Quigley, the editor of *Woman's Hour*. Quigley wanted to meet her for lunch, to discuss ideas for the programme and to see 'whether you are interested in any broadcast possibilities'.[39] It was the start of a working relationship that despite its ups and downs would prove productive, mutually rewarding and remarkably long-lasting.

Nancy, of course, was not an unknown quantity to Quigley: they had met during the *Women at War* broadcasts and had run into each other again when Nancy was in Ireland with Liz. And, while Nancy was appearing on BBC Radio Newcastle in the late 1930s, Quigley had been producing pioneering programmes aimed specifically at women. *Woman's Hour* had made its debut on 7 October 1946, with three pure Reithian aims: 'to entertain, encourage and inform'.[40] Janet Quigley and her deputy editor (and subsequent successor), Joanna Scott-Moncrieff, set the highest of standards for the programme, for which it would become so respected within the industry and beloved of its listeners. The diversity and quality of the women who contributed to *Woman's Hour* would have been the envy of any radio producer. Nancy would prove to be one of the programme's most popular, most requested contributors. Others included Naomi 'Mickie' Jacob, Pamela Frankau and Joyce Grenfell, who recognized what they had in common with each other: 'it was not unusual to find, as an integral part of the contributor's thinking, a personal ethic; a sense of spiritual values'.[41]

Though Nancy's trouser-wearing image is still vividly etched in living memories, it is matched by the echo of her outstanding voice. It was not actually as deep as many people remember, but it did contrast favourably with most of the other women personalities who appeared regularly on radio and television. (Too often, they spoke in a screechy, near-hysterical tone, engendered in part by a bad breathing technique.) Nancy's experience in radio drama, of course, stood her in good stead and all her broadcasts exude a relaxed, measured tone – quietly confident, but not in the least patronizing or lofty. It was warm and inviting, and if a voice could ever be described as having a twinkle in it, it was Nancy's.

However, popular broadcasting was inherently prejudiced against women's voices, even one as luxuriant and attractive as hers. In 1925, a report on that year's Wireless Exhibition concluded that

> Although women are deeply interested in wireless and form the majority of the country's listeners-in, it must be admitted that their contributions to wireless progress have so far been unimportant. Many women are finding careers of one kind or another in wireless . . . the field, however, is somewhat restricted by the fact that women's voices are generally inferior to men's for broadcasting purposes, although, as a broadcasting official pointed out recently, this may be the fault of the microphones, not of women's vocal organs.[42]

Several decades on, there were equally spurious reasons being given for the absence of women in the dominant medium of the times. In January 1951, the BBC announced that all of its eight regular television newsreaders would be men, because 'People do not like momentous events such as war and disaster to be read by the female voice'. Ten years later came an even more ridiculous announcement, from none other than Doris Stevens, head of BBC Television's Women's Programmes. Only male compères would host women's television programmes, she said, because 'Men make better compères and women viewers accept a man much more uncritically than their own sex'.

Nancy made her debut on *Woman's Hour* on 10 September 1952. Her task, for a fee of 10 guineas, was simple: to choose a favourite piece of music and explain why. 'I shall be much obliged if you can play "Black and White Rag" for me as recorded on her other piano by Winifred Atwell, the famous coloured pianist. (No other recording will do!)'[43] Nancy had become a firm fan and, eventually, friend of Atwell, the Trinidadian-born pianist. She shot to fame in the 1950s, with a series of best-selling records and her own television series. In the 1960s, she would fall victim to smear stories published by several British tabloid newspapers, falsely claiming she was a 'slum landlord'. Nancy loved Atwell's famous recording of 'Black and White Rag' and always claimed it was her 'signature tune'. Whenever she played it, she said, 'I feel some of Winifred Atwell's inexhaustible radiance and vitality recharging my batteries'.[44] She subsequently went to as many of Atwell's London performances as possible, and would eventually interview her for *Woman's Hour*.

After Nancy's first *Woman's Hour* broadcast, Janet Quigley was encouraging to her debutante: 'It was your personality rather more than the subject which appealed',[45] she told her. But, to begin with, Nancy was not exactly overflowing with ideas for the programme, as she told Quigley: 'Your kind deputy [Joanna Scott-Moncrieff] said that she had an idea for a series of occasional broadcasts; I must say it is more than I have at the present time'.[46] But by October, she was coming up with more suggestions, though not all of them feasible, as she explained:

I am just off to Paris, to interview Colette for February 'Good Housekeeping' and wonder just about where this fits in. This is one celebrity you could not possibly bring into the studio, as the poor old darling is bedridden in the Palais Royal. I have also started on a terrible round of literary parties and lectures in the industrial North. How do you think Doncaster, Manchester and Derby will strike the listeners?[47]

Quigley said no to the North, but yes to the 'poor old darling' and it was subsequently broadcast in 'Going Places' on 2 December, Nancy's French, which was 'about the standard of Upper IVB',[48] stretched to such questions as 'Que permez vous de atom bomb, madame?'[49]

She and Joan also collaborated on a small radio assignment. Nancy's short crime story, 'The Bewilderment of Snake McCoy', which had been published in Cynthia Asquith's *Second Ghost Book*, was selected for broadcast. It was abridged by Joan, and Nancy told the BBC she was 'most anxious to give credit to Joan Werner Laurie . . . for her work in abridgement on transmission'. Joan's work was duly acknowledged in the *Radio Times* billing.

In December, Nancy arranged to interview Nancy Mitford while she was visiting her father at Redesdale over Christmas, and informed Quigley that a script – 'Lunch in a Cold Climate' – would be ready by New Year's Day. Meanwhile, she was pursuing an idea for a series of slots called *Getting to Know You* and her plans for items for *Woman's Hour* were becoming more grandiose and globe-trotting by the day.

Now I have had invitations from the Elliston Trevors who have taken a house in Barcelona for the next 3 months, Kate O'Brien who as you probably know lives in . . . County Galway and (not so good) Dudley Leslie . . . to Selsey. It would cost £40 to fly to Barcelona, about £10 to go to Galway and nothing at all to go to Selsey. Does the BBC ever pay any expenses for such a trip? Oliver was quite annoyed with me about Colette, but I explained that the script was quite, quite different. 'Ah', he said, 'but will they defray the cost of the expenses?' Certainly not, I said.[50]

Quigley was amused by Nancy's cheek, though not sold on her ideas: 'You really are a one!'[51]

Nancy put forward some more suggestions for the feature, including Bertrand Russell, the Duke of Windsor and Noel Coward. 'I don't think there is anybody I couldn't get to know, given seven days and the opportunity',[52] she confidently told Janet Quigley.

That Christmas, she wrote to Lord Beaverbrook to say she had been asked to write a short biography of him for the 1953 *Saturday Book*; and to seek his approval: 'It would be enormous fun for me to do it, and I admit that I should like to, but I am not going to say yes until I hear that you have no objection'.[53]

Nancy and her now complete family unit spent that Christmas in a new home: 20 William Mews, a cottage in Knightsbridge. They had also acquired two MGs: Joan had bought a second-hand Magnette and Nancy took possession of hers, which was nicknamed 'Babycar'. There were also two cats, Trout and Mackerel, a new daily help called Rita and, briefly, a goldfish called John, given to Nick by Rita. John was put in the best fruit bowl, from where he was plucked by one of the cats.

The New Year was only a few weeks old when another member of Nancy's extensive family made the headlines, though this time in more tragic circumstances. On 31 January her uncle, Sir Walter Smiles, was travelling back to Belfast on the 7.45 a.m. Stranraer–Larne ferry, the *Princess Victoria*. The ship was caught in a sudden gale and, in very heavy seas, foundered off the coast of County Down. One hundred and twenty-eight passengers and crew died. There were only forty-four survivors – Sir Walter Smiles was not among them. The Queen sent messages of sympathy to the families of the dead. An inquiry into the accident in June discovered that the ship had been unseaworthy; its stern doors were found to be very weak, allowing sea water to pour in and sink the ship quickly – eerily pre-dating the Zeebrugge disaster.

Not long after the accident, Sir Walter's daughter – then Patricia Ford – decided to put herself forward for the nomination in her father's seat of North Down, then Britain's largest constituency with 80,000 electors. She succeeded and, barely two months later, was elected unopposed, making history in the process: at thirty-one she was then the youngest member in Parliament, the first woman MP from Northern Ireland to take her seat – and, at almost 6 feet, the tallest woman MP. A few months later, Nancy proudly went to have dinner with her in the House of Commons Strangers' dining room. Her arrival caused something of a stir: 'she turned up in trousers', recalled her cousin.

From 15 January 1953, Nancy's book column was accompanied by her photograph and a bigger byline. Disgruntled authors, who had started to write letters of complaint to the *Express* about her, could now put a face to the name of their tormentor. But it wasn't just the authors whom Nancy berated: she attacked 'the 14 million each week who enjoy their weekend wallow in a fictional blood bath. And as long as this sneaking adult admiration for violence exists, we are bound to see our children grow up in confusion and moral insecurity'.[54]

Though obviously unable to declare her personal interests, she would often return to the theme of children. 'In the children – that is where the hope of Britain lives. And every child is the apple of his mother's eye'.[55] Nor was she reticent about attacking books which featured the sort of gay characters she felt were beyond the pale, such as Patrick Hamilton's *Rope*. 'It is tragic that a novelist should waste his gifts noting the tawdry behaviour of a lot of creatures so repellent and unloveable', she scolded.[56] Her barbs were aimed at everybody, including fellow women authors. 'Whenever I see a book announced as "aware", "sensitive" and Proustian, I reach for my hat. Miss Kay Dick's "An Affair of Love" is the latest depressing work of this sort. . . . To me it is just dull and sordid'.[57] 'Women should write about the things that concern them most deeply', she thumped. 'And the woman's eye view of life is surely not a horrid preoccupation with death, tombs, blood, skulls and Edgar Allen Poes?'[58] Her own favourite author, she revealed, was the romantic novelist Ethel M. Dell, whose career had been launched by Thomas Werner Laurie himself at Fisher Unwin's. 'Ethel M. Dell was always on the side of truth and light', wrote Nancy. 'She was a master story-teller, a genius'.[59]

In May, she headed for Rome in pursuit of Clare Boothe Luce (the writer and wife of Henry Luce, publisher of *Time* and *Life*), who had just been appointed American ambassador to Italy, making her the first woman ever to occupy a diplomatic post in a major European country. Chris had decided it wouldn't make a good story unless Nancy interviewed Mrs Luce *in situ*, so it was decided that she should go by train and write a travelogue-style piece about the journey as well. Once in Rome, the American Embassy patiently but firmly told her an interview was out of the question. Nancy suggested instead that she might talk to one of Mrs Luce's secretaries about Madam Ambassador's daily life and schedule. She was put in touch with Tish Balldrige, Mrs Luce's social secretary (who was to fulfil the same role for Jackie Kennedy). Invited to the Ambassador's villa Nancy was, in fact, introduced to Mrs Luce who, as it turned out, was an old friend of Beaverbrook's. And, as it had done so many times for so many people, that name was enough to get Nancy's foot in the door. She gave Nancy a brisk tour around the mountains of presents that had been sent to her since her appointment, including a wooden gondola bearing the inscription, 'Come to Venice Sometime'. There were also 800 letters of congratulations to answer.

Back at her hotel, Nancy rang back her scoop to the *Express* – at which point, foreign editor Charles Foley suggested that, since she was more or less in the vicinity, she should go to Athens and interview Somerset Maugham. Instead, she went to Naples and Capri, before returning to Rome to attend one of the Pope's public audiences. On her return to England, she joyfully reported to Beaverbrook, 'I am the only British journalist that she [Luce] has received and the others are biting their nails and crying their eyes out – it was all because of you'.[60]

On 2 June, she and Joan were joined by Sandy Wilson and his friend to watch the Coronation of the new Queen at home on their black and white television. 'I remember, it poured with rain, but we went over to watch it and had a hilarious day', recalls Wilson. Nancy was also keen to hear all the news about *The Boy Friend*, which she had seen at the Players' and loved. Wilson told her that, at present, there were no future plans to stage it anywhere. Nancy was appalled and suggested that Wilson write to Noel Coward to enlist his help – which he subsequently did. They met at the Haymarket Theatre, where Coward generously told Wilson, 'Use my name in any way you think fit'.[61]

That summer, Nancy had more reason than usual to take a keen interest in Wimbledon, as *'Teach' Tennant* was published to coincide with the tournament (where Tennant's most successful protégée won the women's singles title for the second time). The book itself did not attract extensive coverage, but the reviews were largely favourable. The *Times Literary Supplement* called it 'a zestful, high speed account',[62] and Susan Noel, the *Sunday Times* tennis correspondent, was equally enthusiastic:

Miss Spain has caught miraculously the extraordinary energy and resolution which envelop her everywhere. This is not a book about tennis but about the character and philosophy which make up 'Teach'. A great deal of this book is in the natural Runyonese language of the central figure.[63]

By now, Nancy had finally parted company with *Good Housekeeping*, handing over the reins of the book column to Joan. Initially entitled 'Book Talk', it then became 'My Kind of Book' and finally, 'People You Hear About'. Well written and conversational in style, it continued in Nancy's tradition, looking at the personalities behind new books. And by the time it had become 'People You Hear About', it was also tackling television and radio personalities, and stars of stage and silver screen, including Isobel Barnett, Marlene Dietrich, Humphrey Lyttleton and Winifred Atwell. It was obvious where some of these ideas and contacts were coming from: 'outspoken *Daily Express* critic Nancy Spain', as Joan called her, one of those 'well-known wildish characters'.[64]

She was about to become even more well known, by linking up with another 'wildish' character.

When Gilbert Met Nancy

In 1953, Ealing Studios made a rather limp stab at satirizing the impact of television. *Meet Mr Lucifer* was a fourth-rate comedy about a fifth-rate pantomime comedian (played by Stanley Holloway) who blames his falling audiences on television: 'Thousands of weak-minded people, staring into a glass box, imagining they can see faces'. An old man in a pub defends the new wonder: 'I never used to believe in spiritualism – but I say to myself, when Gilbert Harding can suddenly appear in my home when all the time I know he's at Ally Pally, why not my old Dad?' 'Gilbert Harding in your home?' snorts Holloway, 'Hypnotism – mass hypnotism'. An accounts clerk, Mr Pedelty (Joseph Tomelty hamming it up as a 'quaint' old Irishman), finds his standing in the community goes up rapidly when he is given a television as a retirement present. Soon, all his neighbours take to dropping in to watch television chef Philip Harben's recipes, country dancing and – most importantly – the panel quiz *What's My Line?*

Meet Mr Lucifer was adapted from *Beggar My Neighbour*, a play by Arnold Ridley, better known as the weak-bladdered Private Godfrey in the classic 1970s comedy series *Dad's Army*.

Though the film failed to live up to its aspirations to be a biting satire on the mass popularity of the new medium, it does have its moments. One of Mr Pedelty's neighbours notices the aerial on the outside of his house: 'Have you got a television set as well?' he asks him. This might seem a ludicrous question but, in the late 1940s and early 1950s, many status-seeking folk, unable to afford a set, stuck an aerial up anyway, so it would make the Joneses keep up with them. But the film was most successful in emphasizing how a former schoolmaster, with more sadness than his burly frame could hold and a razor-sharp mind and a mouth that expelled liberal amounts of wit and scorn, had become a requisite part of people's lives. Gilbert Harding was, quite simply, the most famous male showbusiness personality in Britain in the 1950s. But famous for *what*?

One of his obituaries described him as 'The Rudest Man on Television'. The writer Brian Masters, a friend and admirer of Harding's, called him 'the first household name of the television age'.[1] Both observations were correct. As the decade progressed, postwar audiences began to desert the picture palaces that two hundred million of them had thronged to each week during the 1930s and 1940s, paying homage to the screen idols that they had, in part, created. Instead, they opted to worship in a new temple: their own sitting rooms, furnished with a new-fangled shrine that contained a new breed of more homely gods and goddesses who came right into everyone's homes, like part of the family. Gilbert was everyone's favourite crusty bachelor uncle.

But, of the medium he dominated and decried, Gilbert himself said, 'I think that television is a vital medium. But, like everything else – it's a good thing you can have too much of, if you are not careful'.[2] Indeed, his own mother considered it 'such a silly thing to make him famous!'[3] And, in many ways, it was.

Gilbert Charles Harding was born on 5 June 1907. He was a boy from 'The Grubber', Hereford's Union workhouse where his parents were the master and matron. He went to school at the Wolverhampton Royal Orphanage where, despite its harsh regime of icy dormitories, cold water and 45 minutes' prep before breakfast, he was given a good education. Gilbert's father died while his son was still young and, in 1922, the Hardings (there was a sister, Constance) moved to Bradford. Gilbert went to Queen's College, Cambridge, where he gained a third-class degree. He subsequently became a teacher in various boys' schools all over England, spent some time in the police force in Bradford and briefly studied law. Harding also taught in Cyprus and while there served as correspondent for *The Times*.

In 1940, he joined the BBC Monitoring Service. He eventually became an assistant in the Outside Broadcast department and in 1944 was posted to Toronto to work in the BBC's Canadian Service. His tasks included choosing participants for an hour-long Commonwealth radio link-up, broadcast just before the King's Christmas speech. He returned to England permanently in 1947, and started work for the BBC Light Programme. He became quiz master of the popular *Round Britain Quiz*, *Twenty Questions* and *The Brains Trust*, filling the role of, as he described it, 'intelligent gasbag'. He also became a popular panellist on *We Beg to Differ*, a male-versus-female panel show which made the successful transition from radio to television in 1951. During one edition – in an early demonstration of his soon-to-be-famous bluntness – he told opposing panellist Edith Summerskill to mind her own business.

In the same year, he briefly took over the role of the handyman in *Educating Archie*, the radio show starring ventriloquist Peter Brough. Forced to deliver lines like 'Blimey, Archie lad, and what have you been a-doing of?', it was clearly a mismatch, and it was therefore no great surprise when he was quickly replaced by Max Bygraves. He then found himself cast – for a few weeks – as Tony Hancock's former headmaster, a more suitable role. But his most famous 'role' was just around the corner.

What's My Line? began life in America and was one of a number of popular programmes, including *Twenty Questions* and *The Name's the Same*, for which producer Maurice Winnick acquired the European rights. The British version made its debut on Sunday 16 July 1951. It was a seemingly innocuous game: a panel of minor celebrities had to guess the occupation of a mystery guest by questioning them about the nature of the job – the more obscure the profession, the more entertaining the battle of wits between panel and guests. Over the years, the series' producers managed to unearth a wonderfully eclectic array of occupations: only on *What's My Line?* would you have found a skeleton assembler, doll doctor, banana ripener, confetti cutter, tripe dresser, Jelly Baby varnisher and hog slapper. Other highlights included an artificial eye maker called William Shakespeare. The challengers sometimes received letters from viewers who wished to avail themselves of their skills – the maker and renovator of musical boxes and the bat catcher proved particularly popular. Others were contacted by long-lost relatives who wanted to get in touch again.

Almost immediately, the show grabbed the attention and affections of the British television audience, in a manner which was both bemusing and unequalled for a programme of this kind. Dicky Leeman, producer of *What's My Line?* in 1953–5, decided the secret of its success was 'just plain, human curiosity'[4] – in other words, the basic instinct of wanting to know about other people's lives and jobs. The programme won three consecutive *Daily Mail* awards for 'Most Entertaining Programme' of the year and became the focus of a new form of Sunday worship. A publican in Warley, Essex, complained 'That programme is too popular. It has affected the whole public-house trade'.[5] In its wake came potential successors: *Find the Link, The Name's the Same, One of the Family*, but nothing could ever match the phenomenal success of *What's My Line?* What was particularly unusual about the programme's success was, unlike other popular quiz shows – such as *Double Your Money* – the contestants were not trying to win large cash prizes or expensive luxury goods. It was, essentially, a rather unsophisticated parlour game. What set it apart was Gilbert Harding.

As a panellist, he was an instant critical success: 'Harding is piquant, illuminating, delightful',[6] gushed one. He had originally been picked to be co-chairman with Eamonn Andrews. However, on 25 July 1951, during his first stint, the man responsible for ensuring contestants appeared in the right order sent on John Morgan, a 'Panel Beater', who Gilbert had been informed was a 'Male Nurse'. Unsurprisingly, the panel failed to guess his occupation and, when the error was revealed, Gilbert predicted, 'This is probably the last time I shall appear on TV'.[7] It wasn't, of course, but it did result in Andrews becoming the full-time quiz master. This may have been the source of the tension between the two men that was, on occasion, obvious to viewers. Andrews was often asked if their onscreen rows were staged or rehearsed and, after Gilbert's death, set the record straight: 'so many real rows did blow up that simulation wasn't necessary ... there was no end to the list of things that could make him stammer with rage ... '.[8] Offscreen, Andrews found Gilbert more than a handful: 'I was often terrified out of my life when I met Gilbert glowering along the corridor of Lime Grove, clearly having had a gin or two too many and ready to argue with his own toenail'.[9] Relations between the two men hit an all-time low after Andrews's wife, Grainne, was badly burned when a pressure cooker, bought for the couple by Gilbert, blew up. Andrews was hosting another edition of

What's My Line? and told the assembled panellists about the accident. He was not impressed when Gilbert seemed more concerned about the fact that something he had bought had self-destructed, rather than the injuries it had inflicted on Mrs Andrews. However, Andrews ultimately came to regard Gilbert as 'a kind and religious man. . . . He suffered instant repentance whenever he realized he was in the wrong . . . '.[10]

Eamonn Andrews presided over a panel who, for the twelve years the show lasted, numbered amongst the most popular television personalities of the era, with Gilbert at the top of the list. Fellow panellists, including Lady Isobel Barnett and Barbara Kelly, had their every gesture, fashion accessory and hairstyle avidly scrutinized by the press and viewers alike. The most minor aspects of their lives were often turned into major melodramas, which spawned overblown headlines. The papers were particularly fond of the 'Earring War', developed by the show's producers, whereby each week Barbara Kelly and Isobel Barnett would try to outdo each other with their *outré* or unusual adornments. Kelly swept aside all competition one night by sporting bright green imitation pea pods dangling from her lobes. She was also responsible for generating one of the best ever *What's My Line?* headlines: 'Barbara Kelly Loses Ear-Ring'.

Eamonn Andrews was aware of how constantly being under the public gaze could affect the egos of the new breed of 'personalities', and came to the conclusion that each had to 'decide whether to be a prima donna . . . a *star*, or just assume that one is making new and equal friends at a rate rather faster than normal'.[11] It was the latter view that Nancy subscribed to throughout her career and, though Gilbert did not consider himself to be any sort of star, his behaviour could be (and was) easily misinterpreted as that of a prima donna.

Many television pundits have located the turning-point in the fortunes of Gilbert and the programme as being an edition in 1952. The panel had spent a considerable time trying to guess a contestant's occupation – he was a whisky broker – when a weary Gilbert told the hapless man, 'I'm tired of looking at you'. The BBC was inundated with phone calls and letters of complaint about Gilbert's comments. Unintentionally, he had broken an unwritten rule of 1950s television: always be polite and ingratiating. Everyone knew that was the key to popularity. But Gilbert didn't much care about mass popularity, then or later, and had, characteristically, just been speaking his mind.

The press speculated, 'Will Harding Get the Sack?'[12] But the producers had no intention of losing their best asset, and Gilbert apologized on air to all concerned. But, with typical British hypocrisy, it didn't stop viewers tuning in every week to see how rude Gilbert was going to be; nor did it stop television critics from knocking the programme, in 1953, for being too polite.

Gilbert certainly could have had no conception of the effect this incident would have on *What's My Line?* or his life and career. Suddenly, this large, brusque, keenly intelligent man who, with his dapper moustache and bow tie, still looked like the teacher he had once been, became a national talking-point and, by default, also became the first man on television who, by sheer dint of his personal attributes, became a star of the medium. 'From a minority-audience, slightly egghead radio voice, he suddenly had the nation hopping up and down waiting for his next outburst or pronouncement on some piece of pomposity that might catch his eye',[13] recalled Andrews.

Compton Mackenzie observed later, 'He acquired the reputation of being as remorselessly rude as Dr Johnson used to be two hundred years ago'.[14] Gilbert's rudeness, particularly to hapless members of the public taking part in the shows, shocked some of his friends, who knew that he was as shy and unconfident as those he attacked but hid it behind his articulate, ruthless public persona. When a ghost hunter told him that, yes, he really did believe in ghosts, Gilbert retorted, 'You must be barmy'.[15] When informed that a successful challenger was, in fact, a pomologist, Gilbert huffed, 'It serves him right'.[16] And the infamous hog slapper was asked by a grumpy Gilbert:

'Are you a Slaughterer?'
'No.'
'I wish *I* was'.[17]

The press followed his rise avidly: in 1952, the *Daily Express* observed, 'It Will Be Harding for Christmas'. Between the 21 and 28 December, Gilbert appeared on radio and television six times: editions of *What's My Line?*, *Twenty Questions*, a Home Service programme and a medieval fantasy. In 1955, he presented his own short-lived series, *Harding Finds Out*, where he and his investigators, including one Jacqueline MacKenzie, attempted to answer questions put by viewers.

But this was only the tip of the iceberg. As well as his copious radio and television appearances, he would pop up in a number of British movies in the 1950s, usually as a disapproving figure of authority and mostly in plots involving young pop stars. They included *An Alligator Named Daisy* (1955), in which a young songwriter finds himself the owner of (what else?) a pet alligator; *As Long as They're Happy* (1955), which tells the story of an American singer (allegedly based on Johnnie Ray) who takes over the suburban home of a stockbroker; *Simon and Laura* (1955), about two television actors who are husband and wife both on and off screen; and *Expresso Bongo* (1959), with Cliff Richard taking the part of a raw singer who is transformed into an international star. Gilbert's fame was underlined when Peter Sellers impersonated him in his 1957 television show, *The Idiot Weekly Price 2d. Yes, It's the Cathode Ray Show*, or as it was commonly known, *Idiot's Weekly*.

But he was always contemptuous of this fame, believing that he wasted his intellect on the shows that made him a household name. Eamonn Andrews believed that 'At the back of all his irritability as a panellist was one important factor – the feeling he should be doing something better'.[18] It was a feeling that some of Gilbert's more intellectual friends did not rush to dispel, but which only served to increase his unhappiness and sense of frustration.

Of course, many people who knew Nancy when she was younger –

Pamela Clatworthy at Roedean, Betty Harboard in the Wrens – felt that she too was wasting her intellect on populist, 'personality' journalism, potboiler detective novels and lightweight broadcasting. The difference was that Nancy had made a conscious decision to do this kind of work and loved every minute of it and what it brought her – money, travel, exciting and famous friends and lovers – while Gilbert could never come to terms with the fact that, like Nancy, he too had the 'common touch'.

Harding's celebrity had its hazards: on one occasion, he was in the Turk's Head in Belgravia when a woman attacked him and cut his face with a glass. It was not actually his rudeness she had taken exception to: she had, in fact, mistaken him for racing tipster Raymond Glendinning, who had obviously been on bad form. On another occasion, a Nottingham man – 'he has signed his name, too',[19] observed Gilbert – wrote, threatening to kill him if he appeared on television again. One woman even subjected him to a series of obscene telephone calls. He asked his housekeeper Joan Smith if she would deal with the woman who, apparently, was 'making noises like a recently raped turkey'.[20]

He was well aware of the pressures his unexpected celebrity brought to bear. In a cameo appearance as himself in *Simon and Laura*, he told Peter Finch, 'Start speaking your mind and you're rude and offensive ... stop speaking your mind and you're namby pamby and you're slipping'. By the end of 1954, exhausted by illness, Gilbert was wearying of *What's My Line?* 'I am sick to death of the silly game', he told the *Sunday Graphic*.[21] 'Making me sit on guessing games I don't think the BBC are making the best use of me. I want to start a programme of my own ... '.[22]

But, against the odds, the British public took this gruff bear of a man into their homes and made him part of their lives. Yet it was only shortly before he died that they would have the faintest hint that his unhappy exterior hid an even unhappier man. 'No one can have been blessed with a wider circle of friends than me', he wrote, 'yet I am all too well aware that I am essentially a lonely man ... I find no pleasure in consorting with myself ... I hate to have companionship thrust upon me'.[23]

After the war, Gilbert had lived for a number of years with his mother (widowed at thirty) and sister (who never married) in a flat in Twickenham where, he was to say famously, 'we put up a sort of cloud of sexual frustration that was enough to blot out the sun'. When his mother decided to move back to Hereford, Gilbert took a flat at 18 Cadogan Place, on the corner of Cadogan Place and Pont Street. His last London home was at 6 Weymouth Court, Weymouth Street, just a few minutes' walk from the BBC. He divided his life between London and (from 1956) a house at 20 Montpelier Villas, Brighton. The resort had become a fashionable home for the glitterati – its residents during the 1950s included Laurence Olivier, Douglas Byng, Millicent Martin, Robin Maugham and royal writer Hector Bolitho.

Gilbert's life was organized by Roger 'Podge' Storey, his secretary from 1953 until 1960, and housekeeper Joan Smith (to whom he left his Brighton home in his will). Storey had been an actor and, when he began working for

Gilbert, had been working in administration at a business magazine. Ironically for someone who was working for the biggest television personality of the 1950s, he did not then, nor ever, own a television set.

A Catholic convert, Harding worshipped his mother, collected sixpences in a whisky bottle, loved cooking, had a collection of bow-ties, and never drove, even though eventually he owned a Mercedes and a Morris. 'I am not a Socialist. I am just anti-Tory',[24] he once said. He had a large record collection, which he liked to play loud and late. He suffered from poor health all his life – he was myopic, had chronic bronchitis and asthma, for which he constantly used puffers and, towards the end of his life, always carried with him a portable respirator. In December 1956, doctors found a spot on his lung and, in his final years, he suffered from emphysema and a rare heart condition. This would have been enough to make anyone grumpy and disagreeable, let alone willing and able to continue a busy broadcasting career. He also suffered watching his sister and, in February 1954, his mother, both die slowly from cancer.

After their passing, Gilbert was left alone to deal with his own 'cloud of sexual frustration' – not the easiest thing for a major public personality who was homosexual to do in the 1950s. Brian Masters later explained, 'He liked young men, but it was on a high plane. There was nothing sordid about it'.[25] Roger Storey said Gilbert, who had once described himself as an 'anti-penetrationist', 'was about as good at being a homosexual as he was at being a Catholic'. He did have his moments, though they could end in disaster: while recording an edition of *Round Britain Quiz* in Edinburgh, he took a man back to his hotel, who promptly made off with all his clothes. And, after Gilbert's death, several London papers sent reporters to a number of Brighton pubs to find out if Gilbert had ever been there to 'pick up boys'. But no one had a story to tell, and the hacks went home disappointed.

He once wrote, 'If I were a woman, I'd be a mixture of Mae West (with real diamonds) and Mrs Beeton'.[26] Remembering that Nancy was a Beeton relative, he quipped, 'I suppose I should be a distant aunt of hers. Very distant'.[27]

His unpredictable wit and cantankerousness, his unfettered bluntness, made him both a blessing and a curse for radio and, especially, live television. Harding took great pleasure, just before the vision/sound lights blinked, in telling raucous stories that would take 30 seconds to relate, ending just as viewers saw the programme titles appear on their screen, followed by a calm-looking Harding, slightly more nervous fellow panellists and – off-screen – a sweating producer. Gilbert often sweated himself: he was always nervous before shows and frequently fortified himself – sometimes excessively – with brandy. He was endlessly kind to the backroom crews of the programmes he appeared on. Christmas presents would be sent to electricians and wardrobe mistresses; less seasonal gifts to make-up technicians. This, then, was the strange, contradictory figure whose name and fame were to be linked with an unlikely bedfellow.

When Gilbert met Nancy, it was across the table at a dinner party thrown by Leonard Russell and Dilys Powell in December 1952. Harding regaled the assembled guests with a few choice stories from his vast collection, progressively getting nearer the knuckle. Nancy never forgot one of the more priceless gems:

> He told us about a whore who took a soldier home to Earl's Court and opened the door to reveal a dead horse in the hall. The whore delivered the tag line: 'I said nothing about tidying the place up'. I choked with joy and fell heavily backwards into a procession of tiny china feet that Dilys and Leonard had collected and which occupied a pride of place on their bookcase . . . [28]

Out of the ruins of the Russells' ornaments, a fond friendship was built. Gilbert maintained that he found it difficult to speak to most women: 'I've never been particularly affectionate. I don't attract affection very much and when I do, I repel it'.[29] They would phone each other frequently, exchanging gossip and arranging to meet for drinks, lunch, tea or forays out to musicals. Though he would often answer the phone, it was some time into the friendship before Roger Storey met Nancy, whom he discovered, was 'much younger and very much more attractive than I had expected'.[30] Several months later, another guest was having a drink with Gilbert and Roger when Nancy came up during the conversation. ' "Who is Nancy Spain?", the guest asked me and I said, "London's only famous lady journalist, dressed entirely by the Army Surplus Store" '. Wickedly, Gilbert conveyed Roger's sartorial assessment to her: 'She thought it was wonderful. I cringed . . . '.

Storey recalls how the subject of Nancy's dress became – as with so many who knew her – a running joke between them.

> 'I remember the Dockers invited Gilbert and Nancy to dinner one night, and she felt she ought to do something special, dress-wise. So they went off to Moss Bros and got something. And Nancy always said one of the proudest moments came as they were leaving, when Norah Docker's maid stepped forward and said, "Your sables, Miss Nancy" '.

For his part, Gilbert took up Storey's original pronouncement on Nancy's mode of dress and dusted it off over the years for constant reuse. 'There is no doubt that Miss Spain is a very remarkable woman', he declared. 'In 99 out of 100 public appearances she looks as if she is dressed exclusively by the Army Surplus Stores. No one but Miss Spain would call on Christian Dior dressed in jeans and a fisherman's sweater; no one but she could do that or send Marlene Dietrich a suet pudding . . . '.[31]

'Oh what a winter!'[32] Nancy exclaimed to her readers in March 1954.

The 'winter' had, in fact, begun for her, Joan and the boys the previous April. Early that month, Joan had been in the London Clinic, undergoing an operation to remove a large but benign abdominal tumour. This had precipitated her resignation as production manager at T. Werner Laurie, though she was continuing to write the books column for *Good Housekeeping*. She was still convalescing at home, when they were faced with a new crisis: the prospect of moving out of William Mews. 'Our landlord, a dotty artist called D'Oyly John, has sold our lease over our heads', Nancy told Lord Beaverbrook, 'and we have to rush around looking at new cottages'.[33] Granny Laurie agreed to take the boys for a couple of weeks while Nancy and Joan househunted. 'As this is the first time she has ever invited them we thought it would be tactless to alter the arrangement', Nancy explained. 'I have forbidden Joan to take them on her own because her car inevitably needs cranking at some point and this is not very good for her stitches'.[34] She was soon able to report that they had found 'a perfectly suitable cottage at the back of Gloucester Road'[35] to rent unfurnished – 7 Clareville Grove. Their new neighbours included the mother of Nancy's old friend from her British Museum days, Bentley Bridgewater, who lived two doors down, and Oscar Wilde's surviving son, Vyvyan Holland, his wife Thelma and their young son, Merlin.

'The agent asked me who was my Employer', Nancy told Beaverbrook, 'I said you were and he fell flat on his back. If he writes to you for a reference what on earth will you say?'[36] The agents, Purdue and Greenhill, did indeed ask Beaverbrook for a reference – he told them (with just a hint of irony) that Nancy would be 'a satisfactory tenant in every respect'.[37] Just before they moved, Janet Quigley came to William Mews for a drink with Nancy, to discuss her doing a regular talk for 'Woman's Hour'.

The family moved into Clareville Grove on 20 September and spent most of the autumn doing all the necessary decorating themselves, slapping up ivy-leaf patterned wallpaper in their bedroom.

The cottage was a long stone's throw from Kensington's cluster of famous national museums, in a quiet, attractive, very desirable residential street off the Old Brompton Road. It had a basement, ground and two floors, with a small front courtyard and back garden. Downstairs was the kitchen and the main living room, originally two, now knocked through into one. There were bedrooms for each of the boys and one which Nancy and Joan shared. According to Tony Warren, 'I've never seen anything more like a ship's cabin in my life. It had two of the narrowest beds. The house was dispiritedly tidy, shipshape, it was so tidy'. Nick Laurie remembers things slightly differently: 'The two halves of the room were totally different. One was this sort of tip, and my mother's was all neat and tidy'. Nancy admitted she was slipshod where clothes were concerned: 'I do have to change them every day – they lie about in heaps on the floor; then they get sent to the laundry'.[38]

They set up accounts with local shops: stationery and books came from Wyman & Sons at 50–52 Old Brompton Road; drinks from the branch of the Victoria Wine Co. at number 165; and, from across the road, household repairs were done by Anderson Mason Ltd at number 4. Nancy set up accounts at the two restaurants that were to become her regular West End haunts, Wheeler's and The Ivy. Joan also had her favourite haunts, according to Dick Laurie:

'She was a great creature of habit and tended very much to go to the same restaurants, like the Matelot in Ebury Street, when she was working round the corner from there. She went there frequently, and became known to the management, and always had her own table'.

In November, they christened their new home by holding a Guy Fawkes party. One of the guests was the romantic fiction author, Denise Robins, who shared publishers with Nancy. But it was Joan with whom she became friends: 'Jonnie may look slight and delicate, but the steady observant blue eyes show that amazing strength and driving force which lie behind the apparent fragility',[39] she said.

In December, they relieved themselves of their latest maid, a French woman called Sonia who, according to Nancy, 'seemed to have "hangovers" a lot . . . '.[40] They also had teething problems in their new home: they discovered that Nick had been stuffing newspaper down the bath plughole. Several weeks later, when Nancy was working one night, a pipe burst.

By now, Nancy had begun to do some work for another of Beaverbrook's papers, the *Evening Standard*. On his suggestion, she became its temporary film critic. She started attending the screenings held on Monday and Tuesday mornings in central London, accompanied by Joan who, according to Nancy, 'made all the best jokes in this series and provided all the best criticism'.[41] The reviews appeared throughout September and were more notable for their one-line summaries than anything else: *Laughing Anne*, a drama starring Margaret Lockwood, was deemed to be 'Laughing gas'.[42] *Scandal at Scourie*, a Walter Pidgeon/Greer Garson vehicle, was 'Anon and Old Lace. . . . Some of the dialogue like an old Dutch cheese'.[43] This was, in fact, Joan's riposte to Nancy's comment that 'some of the interiors reminded me of an old Dutch master'.[44] *The Man Between*, a weak imitation of *The Third Man*, was put in its place with a curt 'Wot, no zither?'[45] The Robert Taylor Western *Ride, Vaquero!* was, apparently, 'Not so Rio Grande Oh'.[46]

In the same month, Janet Quigley announced a new series of items for *Woman's Hour*, to be called 'Personality Diary'. 'This has been devised in response to the listeners who say they never hear enough from people they like',[47] she explained. Nancy was to be one of the first four diarists: on 21 September, she talked about an assignment she had been given, to interview the ex-Sultan of Morocco. Also that month *Home for the Day*, the Sunday supplement to *Woman's Hour*, was starting again and, for the first couple of months, Nancy would be alternating with Joan Griffiths as host of the programme. It was, said Quigley, a pre-recorded slot, 'primarily intended for women who are out at work on weekdays'.[48] During Nancy's stint as host, the programme would include a feature called 'Women at Work', in which 'listeners can hear someone unknown but "in the news" being interviewed by Nancy Spain'.[49]

On 23 October, she recorded her first television appearance, on a programme called *Balloon Debate*. Panellists had to discuss which notable personality in history should not be thrown out of a hypothetical balloon, which would surely crash if they didn't lose some weight. In the 'basket' were King Alfred, George Bernard Shaw and Isabella Beeton. For 15 guineas, Nancy had to explain why her great-aunt should not be the one to be ejected.

So, in twelve short months, Nancy had developed the sort of career she had always dreamed of – combining books, the coveted Fleet Street, her beloved radio and now, the medium of the coming decade, television. But the hectic schedule, coupled with a house move and a partner who was still recovering from a major operation, began to tell. After the first *Home for the Day*, Janet Quigley was concerned that Nancy was not happy with her role as compère: 'Is it perhaps something that you enjoy once in a while but find a bore as a regular assignment?'[50] This gentle reproach shook Nancy out of her daze: 'No . . . it is unpardonable of me to let any hint of unenthusiasm show through, I really am sorry, and I'll try harder'.[51] She was, and she did.

By the end of the winter, Joan had begun the groundwork for a major project: a new women's magazine for the National Magazine Company. Meanwhile, in November, Nancy had suffered another bout of flu that developed into pneumonia. Beaverbrook had suggested to his editors at the *Standard* that she would make an ideal guest television critic. She was pencilled in to begin at the end of the year, but decided to postpone it. Apart from her illness, she had enough to be getting on with, starting with one of the first of her 'personality', distinctly non-bookish features for the *Express*. (She also managed to squeeze a 'Personality Diary' recording out of it for *Woman's Hour*). It was hardly heavyweight stuff: visiting Bertram Mills' circus, she was made up as a clown and had to lead a llama into the ring. She was warned not to touch the llama's nose or it would spit. 'Thanks awfully', she replied, 'I can spit back'.[52] Still, recalcitrant llamas aside, enough was enough: she and Joan both needed some sun on their backs and a few days off the treadmill.

The opportunity to get both came when Gilbert Harding, also in need of a holiday, told them of his plans to sail to Jamaica on a banana boat. His mother had just died and he had been ill all over Christmas. His doctors, despairing of his health yet again, had given him a year to live. He told Nancy that, in Jamaica, he would be visiting the Governor, Hugh Foot, whom he had been at Cambridge with. Persuading the *Express* to let her go on the trip, file her books columns from on board ship and write about 'Life in the Sun', Nancy booked passages for her and Joan on the *Matina*. Gilbert had some homework to do on the journey as well: just before he left, John Pudney, a director of Gilbert's publishers, Putnam's, handed him twenty pages of quotations, selected by a researcher, for his *Book of Manners*. Pudney suggested to a reluctant Gilbert that he could put the book together during the voyage. What ensued, if nothing else, provided Gilbert with an excuse for forgetting his 'Manners'.

But before they could set sail, Nancy had a clutch of radio appearances to do: she and Arthur Marshall, amongst others, discussed *The Worst Years or Those Awful Schoolgirls*; she took part in the two editions of the quiz show *What Do You Know*, and one recording of *It's in the Book*. The *Express* also picked her as one of six reporters to attend Billy Graham's evangelical gathering at Harringay Arena on 2 March. Nancy was distinctly underwhelmed: 'I turned up . . . longing to be saved. I wanted to sing some of the good old roaring hymns and have a good cry and go home feeling better. But Billy Graham, revivalist, leaves me cold'.[53] So if Billy Graham couldn't alleviate her fatigue, what could, she wondered? In one of her more obviously provocative statements, she dismissed Aldous Huxley's *The Doors of Perception* as ' . . . dangerous, cranky, rubbishy talk . . . ' while claiming that 'The awful thing is that I should love to take 4/10 of a gramme of mescaline – just once'.[54]

The motley crew aboard the good ship *Matina* left from Garston Docks, Liverpool, in the first week of March. Nancy filed her first column from the boat on 11 March, explaining why she was heading for the tropics; the second, on 18 March, headlined 'The Trouble with Gilbert', focused on her fellow passenger.

Thanks to a force eleven wind, the notoriously seasick Nancy actually spent most of the journey in her bunk, while Joan and Gilbert blithely enjoyed three square meals a day together. Gilbert was not averse to tucking into a breakfast of porridge, cereal, haddock in milk, bacon and eggs, bananas, rolls and toast and marmalade. Poor Nancy endured a daily menu of *mal de mer*, morning, noon and night. And, back in Britain, a storm in a teacup – stirred by the lively imaginations of Fleet Street's gossip columnists – was also brewing.

Mrs Clarke, the wife of the caretaker of 18 Cadogan Place, Gilbert's London home, showed Roger Storey an extract from Simon Ward's column in the *Daily Sketch*, which asked, 'Is Gilbert Harding thinking of marrying? I hear talk of a romance between the irascible 47-year-old TV bachelor and novelist Nancy Spain, who is 37'. The piece continued, 'Before she left London, I'm told, Nancy said to friends: "I am considering marrying Gilbert". It would be a fiery combination – the quick-tempered Gilbert and sharp-witted bohemian Nancy, who even wears slacks to the theatre'.[55] 'How do you fancy Nancy for Mum?' Mrs Clarke asked Storey.

The next day, every national daily began cabling the *Matina* to ask news of the 'happy couple'. Nancy told *Express* readers that, when the first cable was transmitted to the boat, Gilbert's expression was one of 'unconcealed horror'.[56] When she struggled up to breakfast the next morning, Gilbert serenaded her with 'Lady of Spain, I Adore You'. They then composed a joint reply to the *Daily Mirror*:

> Mirror, mirror in the Street,
> What next? You really have us beat.
> The Captain's name is Frederick Inch,
> And though he has a splendid winch
> And lots of hope
> And yards of rope,
> Alas, the law says he may not
> However willing, tie the knot.
> If you did not know that before,
> See Merchant Shipping Act of '94.

Unfortunately, this was rather too subtle and evasive an answer for the hungry hacks. The *Mirror* cabled back with Harding-like bluntness:

> The question was: Are you to wed?
> Not what the heck the skipper said.
> There's land ahoy, and churches, too;
> Where to wed is up to you.
> Please answer either no or yes.
> No matter which, we say 'God bless'.

The prospective 'groom' replied with equal bluffness:

> Alas, in spite of jolly verse
> The answer's short and somewhat terse
> The rumour's heaven, the dream divine
> But wedlock still is not my line.
> So, dear folk, these facts being so.
> The dreary answer's 'No! No! No!'[57]

Back on board, Nancy and Gilbert joked about getting married at the Governor's House in Jamaica, with Nancy in a full white bridal gown attended by Joan as her matron-of-honour.

Not everyone back in Britain was taken in by the rumours: one wag commented, 'A love affair between Nancy Spain and Gilbert Harding? That's getting into the realms of science fiction'.[58] (The press, though, continued their campaign to get Gilbert married off: in September 1957, the *Express*'s 'William Hickey' column reported that he was to marry his housekeeper, Joan Smith.) For the record, Gilbert claimed, 'I was far too fond of Miss Spain to make her life unhappy as Mrs Harding'.[59] 'On the one occasion I did propose to her, a very little colour faded imperceptibly from her ruddy cheeks and she had a fit of the vapours – just like any Victorian Miss except for the trousers and ammunition boots which she happened to be wearing at the time'.[60] And, years later, despite still insisting they had seriously discussed marriage when they had returned to London, Nancy had this to say about their 'romance':

> The truth was this. In the hey-day of our relationship we could scarcely bear to be parted. We saw each other three and four times a week, and fell upon each other's necks when we met. But as the years went by and mutual attraction ripened (and even decayed a little) we drifted apart. But it would be silly to pretend that Gilbert and I were ever in love with each other in the conventional way.[61]

Significantly, it was a photograph taken during this trip of Nancy being embraced by Gilbert that would appear on the cover of *Why I'm Not a Millionaire*. It is a charming picture, certainly, but the benefits of such an image were not lost on Nancy, further underlining her place in the consciousness of the new mass audience, alongside the man who had become its most important male personality.

They arrived in Jamaica on 23 March, where Captain Inch and the crew presented Gilbert with a mock commemorative medal, engraved with 'The

Matina Star 1954'. The next day, Gilbert, Nancy and Joan dined with the Foots at King's House, the Governor's official residence, and Gilbert and Hugh spent most of the evening reminiscing about their Cambridge days. An account of the evening filled one of Nancy's *Express* columns, which Foot called 'a lurid description of wild nights at King's House'.[62] Nancy subsequently interviewed Jamaica's Minister of Housing and Health, Rose Leon, for another *Express* piece. She then visited Monymusk sugar plantation and factory near Kingston and had lunch with the manager, Charlie Michelin, drinking coconut milk and eating limes fresh from the tree. She also took careful note of the small houses rented to plantation workers, of the way they cut the cane from 6 a.m. to 4 p.m. and how it was then processed into either white rum or various forms of sugar. She observed, 'Apparently Jamaica is not immune from snobbery. It is considered low class to eat the bread fruit which grows everywhere at no cost to anyone'.[63] The true aristocracy, she continued, 'is the white BORNYAHS (Born Here)'.[64]

Despite the columns and broadcasts she was able to extract from the trip, it was not a wholehearted success. For a start, an astonishing array of insect life disturbed her: 'Mosquitoes, flying beetles, ants, termites, scorpions – I am a Mosquito's Relish',[65] she complained. Then there were the extravagant prices at their hotel: four drinks cost her 25 shillings, 'a dip in the pool 7/6, 5 shillings for a towel if I wanted to dry myself afterwards'.[66] She and Joan returned to Britain at the beginning of April, on a boat named *Teteela*. As the ship left harbour, a shark tried to attack it.

It was something of a relief, therefore, when they docked at Southampton. Oddly enough, of all the delights they could have brought back from Jamaica, for themselves and the boys, they chose to bring a sack of limes. Meanwhile, the marriage rumours were still circulating. When Gilbert came back to England and *What's My Line?*, he marked his return to the series by appearing under the guise of a challenger – a 'Turtle-Dove Breeder'. Of course, it didn't take long for the panel to rumble the ruse and this gave Eamonn Andrews time to ask him about his health and what he had been up to. 'I've been tearing round Jamaica, doing practically everything', he revealed. 'Getting married too?' asked Barbara Kelly. On this matter, Gilbert feigned temporary deafness and the question went unanswered. A few months later, he and Nancy appeared on *Who Said That?*, a panel show involving the identification of quotations, and why they were said. Commenting on one about marriage, Gilbert happened to say he wished he were married; to which Nancy, right on cue, retorted, 'I wouldn't mind marrying you'.

The 'will they, won't they marry' game was played out for months, mainly because Nancy would insist on proposing to Gilbert in front of millions of people, thus ensuring their names were linked together regularly. In November 1955, Nancy was the guest celebrity on *What's My Line?*, when Eamonn Andrews asked her, 'What is the ambition left to you to be achieved?' 'Marry Gilbert Harding', came the answer. Then she planted a kiss on the cheek of her 'fiancé'.[67] 'The result', she told Lord Beaverbrook, 'is that poor Harding is now in Brompton Hospital. I am going to see [him] on Wednesday when I suppose he will spectacularly relapse'.[68] A month later, she kept the gag running by writing 'Who Killed Nancy Spain: A Christmas Story for Gilbert Harding' in the *Express*. 'Plenty of people have wanted to murder me. Very understandable', began the 'posthumous' story, which then referred back to her appearance on *What's My Line?* – 'I was the best-hated broadcaster in the business', she claimed. The suspects included Hermione Gingold, Terry-Thomas (with a bullet fired from between his trademark gap-teeth), Cyril Lord (wielding an axe) and Eamonn Andrews. In the end, her 'assassin' turned out to be Gilbert, by virtue of a glass of poisoned water. But why, she asked him? 'And then I remembered. Of course. Nineteen fifty-six *is* Leap Year'.[69]

Despite Gilbert's slight irritation at the marriage rumours, he and Nancy remained affectionate friends. 'There was a genuine mutual affection', says Roger Storey, an affection which also extended to him. 'I don't claim to be an intimate friend of hers, but I felt close, because she made sure of that. She was very warm and outgoing and it would have been very difficult to resist her, if one wanted to – and I can't imagine many people wanting to'. Gilbert and Roger numbered amongst the very few to whom Nancy confided that Tom was her son: 'She just came out with it very matter of factly', recalls Storey.

Nancy and Gilbert also shared the same solicitor when she became a client of David Jacobs, the renowned showbusiness lawyer who would later be best known for his association with Brian Epstein and the Beatles. He was also infamous for occasionally wearing full make-up in open court.

Though they resisted joining their names in matrimony, Nancy and Gilbert did end up sharing a name – of sorts. For tax purposes, Gilbert had his own company, called Gilbert Harding (Exploitation) Ltd.; when Nancy and Joan set up a similar company, in December 1955, they called it Spain and Laurie (Exploitations) Ltd., 'which everyone seems to think *very* funny. I can't think why',[70] said Nancy.

I Am NOT a Star. I Am What They Call a Personality

After the Jamaican folly, it was time to get life back to some semblance of 'normality' in their new home. In typical Spain-Laurie fashion, this meant having a boat in the front garden.

The trip to Jamaica had given Joan something of a hankering to have a boat of her own and so, one weekend, they went to Kingston-upon-Thames where, for £75, they bought a 14-foot wooden vessel which they named 'The Tig'. They took out a river licence, but the boat needed a lot of work. So they towed it back to Clareville Grove where it lay in the front garden for several months, much to the consternation of some of their more prissy neighbours. Eventually, having decided that the best place for a boat was, logically, the river, they bought a piece of one of the islands on the Thames near Hampton Wick – with caravan thrown in – for £450. They would occasionally go there for picnics, and Nick would fish, but the island's unruly garden, and the boat's continual needs, defeated them. After less than a year, they would sell island, caravan and boat for £500.

This was not untypical of their 'easy come, easy go' attitude towards money, according to Dick Laurie:

> 'Nancy spent it as fast as she got it. They had a string of people who looked after the kids, each one worse than the last – either loopy or drunk, or whatever. They had cleaners and housekeepers, house-minders and au pairs. They were never rich. Their incomes put together would have been sub-stantial for those days, but Nancy would spend with great gusto. And she was a very soft touch – she would always give money to people, never lend it. She wasn't that interested in money, only in having enough to have a good time. To her, lifestyle was the most important thing. I think, when she first had to go out and fend for herself, that the most important thing was to live with great style – and she did'.

To her credit, she was prepared to work as hard as was necessary to get the money. She was not a nightbird, tending to do most of her socializing during the day. Her day started at 5 a.m., while the rest of the household slumbered on. For the next two hours, she would read books for review, write up reviews or work on her own current book. She would also update her notebooks: over the years, she claimed to have several hundred of these, filled with cuttings, notes on interviews and even lists of people she had met that week. This meant that, no matter who or what she was asked to write about, she would almost certainly have information on them tucked away in the relevant notebook. After breakfast, the rest of the day was spent making countless phone calls, meeting people for lunch, conducting interviews, preparing her broadcasts and, eventually, making television appearances. Her engagement diary was written in red, blue and green ink – a different colour for a different appointment or deadline.

While baby Tom was being looked after by a succession of nannies, Nick was still a pupil at the Lycée and, since it was a French-based school, he enjoyed long, French-style school holidays, including three months in the summer. Consequently, when Nancy was working from home, he would spend more time with her than he did with his own mother:

> 'I hung around with Nancy a lot, and used to go out with her on some of these strange things she used to do. She could make a story out of anything, which is quite a tasty talent to have. She used to latch on to any hint of a strange story or interesting person or situation and then just dive in there head first, chat everybody up, get all their most intimate secrets out of them – and then come back and present them really rather well'.

Nick had a hand in the development of another area of Nancy's career: children's author. Of course, this departure was almost certainly inspired by her unorthodox home life but, according to Nick, commercial considerations were of, at least, equal worth: 'It was a case of "What's selling? Right, kids' books … " '.

The Tiger Who Couldn't Eat Meat (1954) was the first in a series of naive, but charming books about Simpkin the tiger and his friends, not only written but also illustrated by Nancy – hence, her family nickname, 'Tig' or 'Tiggy'. The first Tiger story was about a little boy called Nicky, whose parents live in India. He is sent to stay in England with his 'Globe-Trotting Aunt', who is 'round and fat, with a face like a melon'[1] and lives with his 'South Kensington Aunt', who is tall, smart and beautiful and very musical. Simpkin goes with Nicky to England, where they have a series of adventures.

In *The Tiger Who Went to the Moon* (1956), Nicky makes a rocket, propelled by Simpkin's tail, and they take a trip to the moon. There, they meet strange moon creatures, some of whom are 'quite small and fubsy like kittens'.[2] One of them, Baxy, looks like a cross between a seal and an amoeba, with smooth fur and flippers, and Nicky and Simpkin take him home with them. Baxy subsequently sets up home in the fridge – which, according to Nick Laurie, is where he lived in Clareville Grove: 'Baxy lived in our fridge at home and was responsible for all repulsive noises that happened within range. So, if you farted at the table, or belched, we all turned round and blamed Baxy'.

The 'Tiger' books were not the products of a classic children's author, but they still have a certain naive charm, and are unpretentious and unpatronizing in tone and content. They came in for praise in the few reviews accorded to lightweight children's books. In their 'Children's Book Specials', the

Times Literary Supplement described them as 'lively in style and picture . . . '[3] and 'gay and amusing and wittily illustrated'.[4] However, in *The Tiger Who Couldn't Eat Meat*, they also picked up on something which might have induced a twinge of guilt in someone at Clareville Grove: 'the adults have a regrettable tendency to desert the little boy on any pretext'.[5]

By the time *The Tiger Who Won His Star* was published in 1957, Nicky and his aunts have acquired a brother, Tommy, and the story is set around a visit to a ranch in Arizona. *The Tiger Who Saved the Train* (1960) is set in the south of France, at 'Bon Jour Seaside', served by the train 'Bartholomew and BJ Seaside Railway'. Two villains, Six Gun Pete and No Good Sal, plan to steal the train but are thwarted by Simpkin. In 1961, there were two 'Tiger' books: *The Tiger Who Found the Treasure*, in which Nicky, Tommy, Simpkin and Baxy go sailing in the South Seas; and the *Tiger Annual*. This features some recognizable characters, including 'Vandamski', a bear who wears a crash-helmet and gives lessons on road safety. Vandamski appears in 'Simpkin's Circus', performing 'death-defying motorcycle rides'. The circus also includes a world-famous equestrian act, Mr and Mrs Muir, and a trampoline, high-wire and trapeze act, Mr and Mrs Norden. In 'Baxy's Paris Adventure', the little creature goes to Balmain and gets a 'Big Hallo' from a certain Ginette, then lunch at Maxim's. Other old friends are also drafted in to contribute: the music for 'Simpkin's Song' was written by Geoffrey Wright and the little mouse character from *Books of Today* adorned a number of pages, notably in 'Tommy's Magic Train-Set'.

Though Nancy was notoriously accomplished at latching on to half-ideas and turning them into programmes, articles or even books, occasionally they latched on to her. No sooner had she finished dreaming up Simpkin's first adventure than she was off on another herself. Having endured seasickness on the high seas, she was about to be introduced to the delights of saddle-soreness. Philip Donellan, a BBC radio producer whom Nancy had met briefly just before she left for Jamaica, came up with the idea of getting someone to journey on horseback down the Fosse Way, the 200-mile long Roman road that ran from Lincoln to Seaton in Devon. He approached Nancy to see if she fancied the idea of eight hours daily in the saddle. She accepted the dare and arranged with Harold Keeble not only to file her books column along the way but also to do a series of articles about the ride.

Nancy and Donellan set out from Lincoln on Sunday 15 May 1954. She was riding a slightly nervous horse called Lady Jane, who enjoyed cantering off at a great pace, much to her rider's discomfort. 'By the time I arrived at our first Outside Broadcast spot, two large blisters had risen on my buttocks',[6] complained Nancy. The trip took over two weeks, and involved twelve outside broadcasts.

Not long after this escapade, she was asked to take on another quirky assignment. Sister Liz was getting married again, this time to a 45-year-old, thrice-wed baronet and barrister, Sir Hamilton Westrow Hulse. The ceremony took place at Westminster registry office on 8 July, witnessed by Nancy and Sir Westrow's son from his first marriage, Edward Hulse. Liz had already made the news a few months earlier, courtesy of her sister. In January, Nancy had written a piece for the *Express* about Liz's preparations for her first London show, with models crammed into the kitchen of her Kensington home at 16 Rutland Mews for fittings. Nancy also reeled off a list of things 'My Sister Says . . . ', which, apparently, included, 'One should be able to get in and out of clothes quickly, without scraping one's make-up off' and 'I don't believe in evening dress. . . . It's an anachronism'.[7] The illustrator, Robb, produced a drawing to accompany the piece; it showed a comfortably elegant Liz, at the back of her kitchen, happily watching her latest creations being tried out, while Nancy, in sheepskin jacket and trousers, lurks by the door, making notes about a black and white cotton polo-neck dress called 'Galway Bay'. It was this dress Nancy would wear for her first meeting with Marlene Dietrich a year later, at a press conference held prior to her season at the Café de Paris.

After attending her sister's wedding reception, Nancy had an appointment to keep with Beaverbrook at Arlington House. He had another *Evening Standard* assignment for her: to research and write a series of articles on the life of Gertrude Lawrence.

She arranged to travel to Manchester, on 15 July, with old schoolfriend Pamela Horley to visit Lawrence's first husband, Frank Gordon-Horley. By the end of the month she was able to send 5,000 words to Beaverbrook for approval ('It would be lovely to know if I'm doing all right or not?'[8]) and, shortly after, flew to New York to continue her research, staying with Hermione Gingold in her East 59th Street apartment. There, she met up with Lawrence's agent, the formidable Fanny Holtzmann. She also visited Lawrence's widower, Richard Aldrich at, she claimed, the 'special request of Lord Beaverbrook'. Beaverbrook was not amused and got his secretary, Miss Ince, to fire off a letter to Holtzmann explaining that she 'had no right to represent him as issuing any such request. While Miss Nancy Spain is an excellent writer and Lord Beaverbrook has every confidence in her, he takes no responsibility for anything she writes'.[9] Later, according to Nancy, Fanny Holtzmann 'arrived in London attempting to arrange a seance between herself and her friend Miss Gertrude Lawrence'.[10]

Naturally, she didn't devote all her time in New York to Gertrude Lawrence. She went to several literary salons, where she was introduced to Brian Michie, Marc Connelly and Dorothy Parker, and visited New York's enormous public library. She also attended the 'Mr Universe 1954' contest where one of the vain Adonises on show looked her up and down and said, 'Gee, sister, them jeans are awful slack. Why don't you wear 'em tight like mine?' Before she could answer, he observed: 'Ah, of course, you ain't got such a good figure as I have'.[11]

'Fabulous Lady', the serialized story of Gertrude Lawrence, began in the *Evening Standard* on Monday 27 September 1954 and ran through until 1 October.

By Christmas, Joan had contributed her last 'People You Hear About' column to *Good Housekeeping*, and had a rather bigger fish to fry, as Nancy told Lord Beaverbrook in a letter thanking him for the 'delicious Christmas present of £25' he had sent her.

> We all had flu over Christmas, retiring to bed to hibernate, and Miss Laurie, who is editing the National Magazine Co.'s new womans [*sic*] 1/- monthly SHE is awfully upset and frustrated because the Daily Express won't let her advertise it in its pages. . . . Otherwise she is very well and so are her babies. The young one can now say 'lovely typewriter' so there is hope for him.[12]

Michael Griffiths, the art editor at *Good Housekeeping*, was also the founding father of *She* magazine. 'SHE magazine was the brainchild of Michael Griffiths', explains Richard Deems, former President of The Hearst Corporation, the magazine's parent company:

> 'It was Michael's belief that women's magazines were entirely too serious and completely at odds with women themselves, whom he found to have a great sense of humour.
>   Michael originated and collected material from various sources to prepare a dummy of SHE and submitted the dummy to the then Managing Director of Hearst's UK company, the National Magazine Company, Ben McPeake, who approved the idea and sent it to me in New York as President of Hearst's Magazine Operations. Once it was approved here, Michael set out to find an editor'.

His first choice was Nancy. But, according to Deems, 'She said she was too busy to take on such an assignment, but did recommend her friend Joan Werner Laurie'. Of course, Joan was no stranger to Griffiths, as she was still literary editor of *Good Housekeeping* and, in hindsight, she was a better choice than Nancy. Dick Laurie agrees. 'It would have been far too much of a discipline for her [Nancy], because you've got to be in one place the whole time, especially for the first year or eighteen months'. Professionally and personally, their respective roles on *She* were ideal for them and somewhat symbolic of their relationship: Joan the editor, practical, in control and a steady hand on the helm, while Nancy dashed around the world, providing scoops, celebrities and frivolity.

Joan and Michael Griffiths worked extremely well together and forged ahead with their plans. They were watched over keenly by Marcus Morris, the managing director of the National Magazine Company. The Oxford-educated son of a parson, with a degree in theology himself, Morris was a genius at spotting holes that needed filling in the magazine market (he had been the brains behind the most popular British children's paper, the *Eagle*). 'Jonnie said that one of the skills of being an editor was being able to read a budget or a business plan upside down', Dick Laurie recalls. 'They had gone in to make this presentation and Marcus Morris had got out that day's equivalent of a business plan. She read the bottom line upside down and so knew how much money they'd got for the launch of the magazine and tailored it to that'.

Dick was shown the dummy and Denise Robins was also invited over to Clareville Grove to see it. While she was there, Joan asked her to be the magazine's 'Agony Aunt'. She agreed and, in typically forthright *She* style, decided to call the page 'Straight from the Shoulder'.

Other contributors were gathered. Gilbert Harding was approached to write a column in which he would be free to criticize the contents of the current issue as crustily and nefariously as he wished. He agreed. Nancy was to contribute a two-page spread on 'Gossipers and Gossipees'. Her old 'adversary' from the *Empire News* days, Elspeth Grant, would do film reviews. For the first issue, Joan contributed a feature on 'Godfrey Winn's Home'; Lady Docker wrote about 'How I Manage My Millionaire'. Since there would be no readers until after the first issue, Joan decided to fill the 'Readers' Letters' page with opinions elicited from various personalities about women's magazines. Janet Quigley from *Woman's Hour* echoed some of the *She* ethos: 'Women's magazines have such tremendous influence that I feel they could move mountains if they wished. Instead, they simply move more women to use more make-up'.[13] Wilfred Pickles, of all people, observed that many women never had the time to catch up with the important things going on in the country: 'If only women's magazines could put over some of these more serious facts in an easy-to-read way, they [women] could play a much more important part in the life of the nation'.[14] Joseph McCulloch, the Rector of St Mary's, Warwick, contributed a 'thought for the month'-style column on the letters page.

To keep production costs down, *She* was less glossy than some of its competitors. But Michael Griffiths gave it a brilliantly brash, reader-friendly, vibrant look, eschewing the standard convention of lots of 'white space'. Each page was packed with text, often punny captions, illustrations and photographs – as advertisements for the magazine rightly boasted, 'What a lot of SHE for a shilling!' The first eleven covers featured photographs taken by Keith Ewart, the dynamic South African-born photographer, who would become an acclaimed director of television commercials in the late 1950s and early 1960s. 'He had a great nose for the sort of people who should be on covers', says Dick Laurie.

Nancy was enormously supportive to the *She* team as the deadline for the first issue loomed in December. In the final weeks, most of the staff were stricken by flu. So, when she had fulfilled her own commitments at the *Express*, the BBC or elsewhere, she went to the *She* offices to help out where she could. The staff would work late into the night, and Nancy would go out on mercy missions in search of all-night cafés, from which she would bring back hot soup for the tired and huddled masses at Ebury Street.

The night before the first issue went to press, Nancy was having a nap on the office floor. Suddenly, she got up, put her coat on and disappeared. The next day, when she popped back into the office, someone asked her where she had gone. 'To church, to pray. I couldn't do much in the office last night to ensure *She*'s success, so I thought I'd go to church to pray for it'.[15] 'Britain's gayest, liveliest magazine for women' made its debut at the end of February 1955, with the March issue.

'When *She* came on to the market for the first time, it proved something of a revolution in magazines for women. It was *different*!',[16] enthused Denise

Robins. The Hearst executives were also impressed by their new publication. 'SHE was completely different', explains Richard Deems. 'It was irreverent, it was amusing, it had a sense of humor and it was highly entertaining'. Brian Braithwaite, publisher of *Cosmopolitan* in the 1970s, thought it was 'big, bold and rather brassy'.[17] Perhaps it was no coincidence that *She* was launched in the same year that commercial television began in Britain. They were both aiming to fill tangible holes in their respective markets; while they had to compete, they also had an opportunity to carve out their own identity and attempt to strike out in ways which their competitors either wouldn't or felt they shouldn't do. The importance and impact of *She* cannot be over-stressed, nor fully comprehended by a generation of young women readers who, in the 1980s and 1990s, were spoilt for choice by rackfuls of magazines aimed at 'the woman of today'. Such titles, including the likes of the award-winning *Marie Claire*, were the granddaughters of *She*, the grand old lady of British women's magazines.

As Marcus Morris observed, much of this was down to its founding editor:

> Being so highly intelligent herself, Joan believed that there were many other women in England who wanted something more than the conventional sentimental escapism offered by most women's magazines. She was not one for comfortable unreality; she believed that women, or at any rate, intelligent, young-minded women, wanted to be stimulated, shocked, provoked, given cause to think by word or picture. She believed that they wanted to know what was going on in the world outside their own backyard or comfortable sitting-room, which is why she made her magazine range over the world, lighting on the unusual, the significant, the absurd, wherever it was to be found. Her conviction that even the most controversial subject could be tackled without offending more than a handful of readers was completely justified.[18]

They were both right. By its ninth year of publication, Joan was able to confirm that

> On average not more than about twelve [readers] a month cancel their subscriptions because of their horror at my lack of refinement in choosing the contents.[19] . . .
>
> In November 1962, I published in SHE a major article on abortion. It was a threefold feature and included an article by a woman who had had an illegal abortion and an article by a doctor-member of the Abortion Law Reform Society. In the same issue, SHE had an article by the mother of a thalidomide baby – a subject SHE tackled, with photographs, back in 1961 before anyone else had mentioned the problem.
>
> SHE has dealt in full detail with menstruation, hysterectomy, breast cancer, lung cancer, leprosy, brain tumours. . . . We have even told our readers exactly what a bidet is for.[20]

Other women journalists were not oblivious to the quiet revolution taking place in their midst. 'The subjects that Werner Laurie put into her pages cut across many of the old taboos of women's journalism',[21] observed Margaret Laing of the *Sunday Times*. Nor was the impact lost on the readers who first opened its pages – amongst them the actress and broadcaster Jacqueline Mackenzie, an admirer of Joan and Nancy's work several years before she became friends with them.

' "She" went beyond knitwear and cookery; there was frankness about health situations, periods – all flying off the covers of "She". It really broke down an enormous reticence there. And it was like no other magazine because it was so scrappy, which was intended'. It was, perhaps, the magazine's very 'scrappiness', its diversity, which made it an instant hit with a whole generation of teenage women who found nothing in their mothers' *Woman*, *Woman's Own* or *Woman's Weekly* to attract their attention. ' "She" had a lot of pizzazz and catered for the younger woman, be she married or in her teens', said one. 'It was dynamic compared with the other women's magazines. "She" was everybody's glossy magazine'.[22]

In the second issue, Joan proudly published the first, real reader's letter she received, from Mrs Helene Platman of Southend. 'You are the BIGGEST, BRIGHTEST, BOUNCY, BRILLIANT BEST SIZZLING magazine I have ever read',[23] she enthused. But Mrs Norton of Pontefract voiced dissent: 'In these modern days of print, your dress overall seemed drab at the side of others'.[24] But the eight-year-old Jane Asher – future star of stage, screen and party cakes – meekly asked, 'May we have (us girls) a girls' page? After all, we are SHEs. . . . My mother thinks the cooking is simply lovely. (So do I when it's cooked.)'[25]

> 'I think one of the qualities of *She* was that it was neither good nor bad taste', says Dick Laurie. 'It was so all-embracing: "something for everybody". When the magazine first started – and for several years – it fell somewhere between kitsch and naff. It was a real mish-mash, but it was a mould-breaker of its time. It didn't appear to have any sense of direction at all, but it filled a huge hole, because it was very modern, very topical'.

One of its other outstanding qualities was the attitude conveyed in its features, especially those contributed by Joan and Nancy. They weren't merely women journalists who just wrote about what other people were doing: they were doing – and, significantly, were *seen* to be doing – many of the things themselves. This was, of course, the hallmark of many of Nancy's features for the *Express* and, later, the *News of the World*. But their importance within the context of *She* was that, in a magazine aimed specifically at women, they were helping readers to look beyond the usual, staid, conservative 1950s diet of homecare, cooking and children – *without* making those women readers feel inadequate for still being interested in such matters. This was a breath of fresh air in a decade where women were still discouraged from taking up professions. After the war, many nurseries for working mothers – whose labour had been essential to the wartime economy – were closed. It was acceptable only for young women to have 'jobs' between leaving school – where they were given neither sex education nor careers advice – and getting married. It is no coincidence that the 1950s saw

Young Wives' Clubs mushrooming up and down the country. Many advertisers actively aimed their products at such women.

Given this social climate, it was no surprise that the word throughout the advertising industry was that *She* would not survive long because of its very unconventionality and brashness. Advertisers, it was argued, would be nervous about taking space in a magazine that didn't appear to know exactly who its target audience was. No matter: Joan, Nancy, Michael Griffiths and the rest of the *She* team carried on regardless – pleasing themselves and their readers and confounding the sceptics.

Within its first year, the magazine continued as it had begun. Joan wrote about the London homes of Denise Robins and Noel Coward and Nancy became the magazine's 'Ace Newshound', serving up stories on everyone from Orson Welles to Lena Horne. She also started a series called 'My Millionaire of the Month', including profiles of the textile tycoon Cyril Lord and Raymond Way, second-hand car dealer extraordinaire. This series was the target of one of Gilbert Harding's first gripes: 'I am getting rather sick of these millionaires – And so, I believe, are you, Miss Spain'.[26]

Other members of the family were roped into the act: Joan's sister, Sally, and Tom went off for a behind-the-scenes look at one of Britain's biggest dry-cleaners, Achille Serre, taking with them Sally's husband's cricket flannels, two of her dresses and Tom's teddy bear to be cleaned. As 'Bodge', Tom also featured in a little photo spread on milk and, with Nick, in a survey on children's macs. Elsewhere, Fenton Bresler advised on 'Ladies and the Law', a doctor tackled the taboo subject of piles and Joan Vickers MP gave tips on 'How to use an MP'.

There were also lots of practical, DIY-style features, on subjects usually considered the exclusive domain of men in the 1950s: 'Open-Air Houses', how to clean a spark plug, 'Building Your Own Boat' and simple wood-work. As a result, the magazine started to receive all manner of gadgets and kits to consumer-test. And, as Dick Laurie remembers, the Editor and the Ace Newshound would often put them to the test in their own home:

> 'I went in one day to find Nancy and Jonnie with a big bit of board, and they were mixing up some gunk like Polyfilla. They'd got a coffee table and some rather hideous ceramic tiles which were stuck onto hessian – it was DIY mosaic, done without having to stick them down individually. And once you got your coffee-table top, you cut these things to size, put the gunk down on the table top, slapped them down. If they didn't quite fit, you cut them and grouted them in between. Jonnie thought this was absolutely wonderful – I'd never seen anything so hideous in my life'.

On 13 January, Nancy was one of the *Woman's Hour* 'personality speakers' who were asked 'not only to tell us about the different people they come across in their daily lives, but to bring these friends and acquaintances to the microphone and introduce them to listeners'.[27] This marked the beginning of her regular 'Getting to Know You' slot. She talked about her old friend in North Shields, Percy Mark Cox, and meeting Christian Dior in her jeans. She interviewed Sandy Wilson's mother and – with some nerve –

Margery Allingham. She also included recordings of Tom – or 'Bodgie', as he was nicknamed – learning to count and of Nick performing a recitation. Joanna Scott-Moncrieff was cautious about how the slot would develop. 'I have no very high hopes of the first programme', she told Janet Quigley, 'because I think she needs to discover herself that ad hoc interviews (not thought out in detail in advance) are not necessarily very good listening'.[28]

'Getting to Know You' and, indeed, all of Nancy's personality interviews did improve, both in content and calibre. Her interviewees during this year, for 'GTKY' and *Home for the Day*, would include Orson Welles, Elsa Maxwell and Rebecca West. In turn, she was firmly establishing herself as one of the 'stars' of *Woman's Hour*.

In March, she recorded a series of broadcasts from Askham Grange Prison, and in July, while *Woman's Hour* was taking its summer break, was one of the regular contributors asked to *Reminisce with Records*. In September, in *Home for the Day*, she 'interviewed' herself, and in October, she took part in a round-table discussion, 'Spinsters Talking', with fellow unmarried women Irene Hilton, Marjorie Pollard and Margaret Reekie. 'I shall always go on being a spinster, because I like it', she revealed. 'I like to feel that I'm looking after myself and not to have somebody dubiously looking after me'.[29]

Also that month, she produced and presented her own edition of *Woman's Hour*, 'The Nancy Spain Way'. Her guests included the eternal housewives' favourite, Godfrey Winn, and Rebecca West and Jonty Wilson, the blacksmith who had taken care of the horses on the Fosse Way trip. She and Joan had just returned from Cannes again where, Nancy revealed, 'I actually put on a skirt and went to Monte Carlo and gambled'.[30] She also revealed that, rather astonishingly (though, of course, this was lost on her listeners), they had met up with Margery Allingham and Philip Youngman Carter for dinner at the Hotel de Paris. Nick and Tom also made appearances on the programme, as did Dick Laurie:

> 'She asked me whether I would like to do something for it – it was going to be about what young people do. I was in the Army at the time, an officer cadet in Aldershot. I said I'd love to go to the 100 Club and talk to Humphrey Lyttleton. She spoke to Lyttleton first and set the whole thing up, and I did a little interview with him between sets. It was all tremendously exciting'.

Meanwhile, the ever-loyal Cecil McGivern, now controller of BBC television programmes, was putting out feelers on her behalf. He told the editor of Women's Programmes that Nancy was 'Well worth your seeing. On the surface, flippant, she is underneath serious and intelligent'.[31] He also wrote to the head of Light Entertainment: 'She mentioned she had been auditioned three times by Leslie Jackson for panel games. She was not complaining, and is very anxious to appear on TV'.[32] McGivern's efforts paid off and, that summer, Nancy was chosen by producer Leslie Jackson to take part in the panel game, *Something to Shout About*, chaired by Macdonald Daly. The panel were faced by challengers who had won some trophy or medal, and it was their task to guess what they had done to win them. A typical example featured a man with an all-conquering conker. Sadly, *Something to Shout About* wasn't and disappeared after four editions.

But that same month, Nancy was picked to take part in the pilot of another panel game, *Who Said That?*, alongside Gilbert Harding, Alan Melville, Joanna Kilmartin and John Betjeman. As the title suggested, the panel had to guess who originated a famous quote, and then provide witty explanations as to why they agreed or disagreed with the quote. During the pilot, Nancy was accompanied by a toy tiger cub mascot: Gilbert was not amused and thought it should be removed but Melville insisted it stayed. This programme looked more promising, and the producer Harry Carlisle revealed that the 'morning-after reactions were very encouraging indeed'.[33] *Who Said That?* continued through July and August, but a slight problem was evident, as someone at the BBC pointed out to Janet Quigley: apparently Nancy was recycling material from her *Woman's Hour* appearances and using it in the show. In fact, this was just one instance of her duplicity. Articles based on her assignments for the *Express* were turning up in *She*, as were features about her various radio and television appearances. As they weren't carbon copies of each other, she just about got away with it, but it was indicative of how she would conduct the rest of her working life: fulfilling all her commitments, meeting deadlines, following briefs – but usually putting *She* first.

Meanwhile, working on *Who Said That?*, claimed Nancy,

> showed me up, to myself, once and for all as the same indiscreet, talkative, enthusiastic, apprehensive, Conservative, insular miss who left Roedean. . . . Life, they have promised me, will begin at forty. So perhaps . . . I shall become, by some miracle, discreet, quiet, disillusioned, brave, Liberal, and cosmopolitan.[34]

Though, in some respects, she was right about herself, in others she was indulging in a little self-pity and exaggeration. Certainly, some of those closest to her did not share her rather harsh view of herself. According to Dick Laurie, 'She was a very genuine person. What you saw was what you got'. And in Nick Laurie's opinion, she never harboured any clear sense of her destiny: 'She was just a jolly competent interviewer, journalist and personality, and just got on with doing that. Variety wasn't the spice of life, it was the *stuff* of life for her. She was very, very good with people; she had a very basic liking for people and could get them to talk'.

It was, of course, rather fanciful for her to suggest that she had not progressed since leaving school. But, if this avowed general self-dissatisfaction was genuine, then the next few years were to give her ample opportunities to develop into the sort of person others already perceived her as.

In the early part of 1955, Nancy was finishing – after a gap of three years – what would turn out to be her last published detective novel. Fans of the Spain thrillers, by now used to the usual madcap mayhem and murder, were in for a surprise, though. For this story, she did away with Miriam, Natasha and the usual motley crew of Pynes, Pukes and Partick-Thistles. Moreover, there was no playing for laughs: this was to be an altogether more sinister, cynical effort than the previous eight. For *The Kat Strikes*, Nancy dipped into her pool of memories of postwar London life. The 'Kat' is Lady Katherine Stour, 25-year-old daughter of the Marquis of Stour. Having just left the services, she is trying to set herself up in London when, one night, she rescues James Smith who has tried to kill himself by jumping into the Thames. Smith is an ex-publisher, who has lost his business and his fiancée. He ends up buying, and living on, a boat moored near Hampton Wick.

Katherine is then reacquainted with Terence O'Kelly, an ex-soldier with whom she had seen active service in occupied France. They had been lovers, though it's clear that this had not been an enjoyable experience for her. O'Kelly involves her in a plan to set fire (for money) to the premises of publishers, Datchet Press. When they arrive, they find James Smith shot dead. Katherine ends up living on his boat.

From here on, the story becomes muddled and melodramatic, but without any of the usual wit to rescue it. It includes drug running (again) and yet another unflattering portrait of a gay man, Cyril van Dene, who is described as a 'mother's boy out of his depth'[35] with a 'pansy smile'.[36] There is also a thumbnail sketch of a postwar gay club: below street-level (of course), it is full of 'pathetic waifs in little black bursting dresses; sad lisping boys with volumes of Tennessee Williams ... '.[37] Katherine finds it all 'very sad ... and indicative of some hideous social evil or other'[38] (the only indication that, amongst all the gloom, Nancy still has her tongue in her cheek). There is also another reference to her own image when Frances, eyeing her sister dressed in sweater and jeans, says, 'You look about as feminine as a boxing-glove'.[39] Not surprisingly, the story concludes with the sisters fighting over a gun, which goes off and kills one of them.

Before this, we are introduced to a newspaper baron, Lord Cute, whose motto is 'judgement, industry and health' and who speaks with an unmistakable Canadian accent. He invites Katherine for drinks at his home before she goes off to solve the 'mystery'.

It was not the first time Beaverbrook had appeared as a fictional character, of course. Evelyn Waugh had based his characters 'Lord Monomark' and 'Lord Copper' on him in his novels *Vile Bodies* (1930) and *Scoop* (1938). His Lordship, apparently, was not amused. A more flattering portrait of Beaverbrook was penned by William Gerhardi, with the character Lord Ottercove, who appeared in his books *My Sinful Earth* (1928) and *Doom* (1929). Hugh Kingsmill's fantasy *The Return of William Shakespeare* (1929) had the Bard brought back to life and eager to escape the clutches of rival newspaper proprietors, Lord Westerleigh (Beaverbrook) and Lord Youngbrother (Viscount Rothermere). Rebecca West's relationships with him and H.G. Wells formed the basis of her novel *Sunflower*, with Beaverbrook portrayed as 'Francis Pitt', an Australian tycoon. Not wishing to upset the newspaper baron, Nancy sent Beaverbrook a set of uncorrected galley proofs, for his approval of her portrait of 'a very amiable press Lord. ... I hope there is no harm in it, but should there be, perhaps you can tell me and then I can alter it'.[40]

Beaverbrook had the manuscript read by John Berry Wilson, the *Express*'s news editor. Wilson told him 'Nancy Spain's thriller might pass muster if she had kept it entirely to fiction. As it reads at present Lord Cute, who is identified as Lord Beaverbrook, takes the heroine to his country house and makes her drunk'.[41] And, as Beaverbrook curtly reminded Nancy, 'I never do'.[42] She went to see him a few weeks later at Cherkley, where they smoothed things out over a drink.

Marlene Dietrich's season at the glitzy Café de Paris was due to begin on 7 June and the management decided to enlist a different celebrity to introduce her each evening. Douglas Fairbanks would do it on the Monday, Helen Hayes on the Tuesday and, on the Wednesday – Nancy. For the occasion, Nancy wore a pink silk dress, almost obliterated by its large, loose bow, which Noel Coward had reputedly once decided 'wouldn't deceive a drunken child of two and a half'. (He had a point: A *She* reader wrote in to say that her three-and-a-half-year-old son pointed to the magazine his mother was reading and said, 'Mummy, there's a picture of Davy Crockett in your comic'.[43] It was, of course, the 'Ace newshound' herself.)

She was allowed two guests and took Joan and Michael Griffiths. Luminaries in the audience included Danny Kaye, the Mountbattens and the Sultan of Johore. Nancy and her guests were given ample free food and champagne, but she was too nervous to indulge in either. She had a quick chat with Marlene in her dressing room before the show began, then went back to the stage and, heralded by a fanfare and drum roll, did the honours. In the second half of the show, Dietrich changed into top hat and tails to sing 'All of Me' and then, with the spotlight on them both, handed Nancy her white carnation, to much ooh–ing and ah–ing.

Dietrich's was only one of the big names that Nancy would flagrantly drop in the memoirs she had begun. *Why I'm Not a Millionaire* was prompted, she said later, by Joan's demands to know why, despite all her endeavours, she wasn't one. It is far more likely, however, that the book was born partly out of the soul-searching Nancy claimed was prompted by seeing herself on television, and partly to set the seal on her growing fame.

The book was a highly selective, sometimes sketchy breeze through her life and career thus far. It told of her Jesmond beginnings, her Roedean experiences, her on-field exploits with Winifred *et al.*, life in the Wrens and her steady postwar entry into Fleet Street. It was remarkably, not to say frustratingly, short on dates: she even omitted to mention – of all things – her actual date of birth.

It included many anecdotes about incidents and personalities from her career, such as Joan, the Jamaica trip with Gilbert Harding, and Noel Coward. However, she carefully exaggerated the true importance of certain figures far beyond the actual size of the role they played in her life. For instance, the section on Nancy Mitford gave the impression that she and Nancy were great friends. Though they were not quite enemies, this was hardly a true picture of their relationship. Similarly, she devoted inappropriate amounts of space to Colette, Katharine Hepburn and Humphrey Bogart and, most cheekily, Margery Allingham. The bigger the name, the more pages she devoted to them. After all, although she was a 'name' herself, she was still not big enough to take centre stage without such an impressive supporting cast. And she was canny enough to know that by doing so her fame automatically increased. It was a phenomenon peculiar to the television age of the 1950s and early 1960s, and one observed by the author Daniel J. Boorstin in his book *The Image*. Celebrities, he noticed, became more famous by associating with each other – if you were seen with famous people, the fame would rub off. This was never more true than of Nancy – a true creature of the television age.

In November, *The Kat Strikes* was published. Hutchinson advertised it in the *Sunday Times*, with a quote from Margery Allingham, who declared it 'Terrifying, really exciting . . . like riding a switchback'.[44] Not everyone found it so thrilling, however: the *Times Literary Supplement* reviewer warned,

> At first the reader may be pardoned for wondering whether this is a parody on detective fiction but, alas, it is not: Miss Spain has not directed her humour against the stupidities of the story but expects them to be taken as they are. The style is breathless and dependent on slang, much of which is tired and unamusing. A few of the principal characters seem to have strayed from Miss Mitford's sphere and gone wrong at an early age. The plot, if one of the Kat's unlovely adverbs may be borrowed, is madly dependent on coincidence.[45]

Francis Iles of the *Sunday Times* was equally unimpressed: 'Miss Nancy Spain gives us a rambling disjointed and oddly amateurish strip-cartoon of a thriller, featuring Supergirl with an abrupt ending that leaves half-a-dozen threads still dangling'.[46] And, in the *Observer*, her old pal Maurice Richardson said:

> Those of us, and there are a few, who lose sleep worrying about Miss Spain and the problem of her mental age, will derive little solace from this crazy thriller. . . . There are bright patches and some of the dialogue is good, but there is not enough conviction to convince the simplest simpleton.[47]

As far as the public were concerned, this marked the end of Nancy's crime oeuvre. But this was not, in fact, the case. The 'still-dangling threads' that Iles complained of would be picked up in a sequel that, for reasons unknown, was never published. The jacket of *The Kat Strikes* warned, 'Watch Out! The Kat Will Strike Again' and Nancy did, in fact, complete a sequel called *Kat Dressed to Kill*. In it, Katherine is released from prison, after serving several years for manslaughter. Her brother-in-law is seeking vengeance and so she escapes to France, immersing herself in the glamorous worlds of Parisian fashion and cosmetics. Yet again, the two murders which take place do so against a backdrop of major drug-running. A third 'Kat' adventure was also promised, this time set in New York, but it appears that Nancy never got as far as writing it.

She held firm views about the crime genre:

Crime stories divide themselves neatly into two groups – those which concern themselves with atmosphere and background and the *why* of characterisation and crime. . . . The others are uncomfortable records of violence, well or ill-written, that string out to an endless repetition . . . shocking the reader into stunned acceptance of that peculiar world where detectives seriously say things like 'You're smart. You must have talked yourself out of jail, and that's nice going'.[48]

Obviously, she would have placed her own books firmly in the first category, and her crime novels were excellent in their use of setting. The popularity of *Poison for Teacher*, for instance, can almost certainly be attributed to the fact that it had so many resonances for anyone faintly acquainted with the vagaries of girls' public schools. She also successfully recreated the peculiarly tense and romantic atmosphere of life on an ocean cruise in *Not Wanted on Voyage* and the pretensions of an art school in *Murder, Bless It*. Theatrical life in a provincial town (clearly her own home town) is skilfully evoked in *Cinderella Goes to the Morgue* and in *Poison for Teacher*, the minutiae of life in a small seaside resort are wittily and accurately observed.

However, it was largely the unconventional characters and situations she created that made readers and critics sit up and take notice. News-hungry journalists feature frequently – in *Out, Damned Tot, Poison for Teacher* and, of course, in *Poison in Play*. The latter also drew on her experience of sports, as did *Death Before Wicket*. The subject of drugs is featured time and time again: drug-smuggling in *Not Wanted on Voyage*, addicts like Connie in *'R' in the Month*, and even scenes in chemists' shops pop up frequently.

Nancy's characters also sported some of the most ridiculous names – often verging on puerility – ever to be accorded to fictional folk. Glance through the *dramatis personae* listed at the front of any of the titles and they read like the cast from an episode of *Round the Horne* or a *Carry On* movie, displaying a similarly eccentric and peculiarly English sense of humour: Gregory Pratov, Mr Polygon, Charity Puke, Mrs Buttick, Banjo DeFreeze, Mr and Mrs Polyo, Commander and Mrs Fryteful, Edgar Poe – not to mention Miriam Birdseye.

Then, of course, there were the numerous gay characters, references and in-jokes that Nancy sprinkled throughout almost every book. There was Roger Partick-Thistle, who comes from an artistic family and gets on well with old ladies and foreign sailors, and with whom young ladies are perfectly safe. *Poison for Teacher*, of course, is awash with 'forbidden' friendships, as you would expect in a place called 'Radcliffe Hall'. The book also refers to the resemblance between one of its characters and Stephen Gordon – the central figure of *The Well of Loneliness*. Lesbian characters included the much-adored Gwylan Fork-Thomas and one of her admirers, Charity Puke. *Death Goes on Skis* has the Eton-cropped, brandy-swilling Toddy Flaherté, who even wears a pinkie ring. *Poison in Play* has the try-sexual Serge Ghent, *Out, Damned Tot* Dymphna the Bee Woman, clad in fisherman's jersey and sporting a fine moustache. In *'R' in the Month*, there are Connie and her partners, 'Tommy' and Mavis. 'Wicket' even features a child named in the 'biblical sense': David Jonathan. According to Nancy, her editors were concerned about some of the people depicted in the books. 'My publishers are always actually shattered by them', she said, 'and insists [*sic*] that there are real people in them and that I'm going to be sued for libel'.[49]

Nancy's crime oeuvre has, in many people's minds, remained her most memorable work. Certainly, they were popular sellers – most were reprinted several times during her lifetime and she acquired many devoted, lifelong fans.

One such admirer was a Lancashire schoolboy, Anthony McVay Simpson, later better known as Tony Warren. He remembers how a copy of *Poison for Teacher*, bought by his aunt from Hutchinson's Universal Book Club, came into his hands:

> 'I was much intrigued by the photograph on the back – the Angus McBean shot of a woman lying on a piece of corrected copy. So I started to pick my way through it and I was absolutely riveted. I thought, "this woman is inside my head, she's saying things that I've half-thought". It had an extraordinary effect. I then got hold of as many of the Universal Book Club editions as possible'.

But his devotion to the works of N. Spain got him into trouble at school:

> 'I was caught reading one of the books under cover of the Bible, and I was asked to explain who she was and I got into terrible trouble. This book was held up disdainfully and pages were turned over as though it was a soiled item'.

Eventually, young Tony spent less time at school and more time at Manchester Central Reference Library:

> 'I stopped going to school and set myself to read 1,000 plays and theatrical autobiographies in one year. But I used to have treats – downstairs they had *Spotlight* and the London telephone directory. The idea of the London telephone book was infinitely glamorous. And the very first name I ever looked up was Nancy Spain. It was a Riverside number – this would be about 1948. Then I started to hear her on the radio – this gurgling, laughing voice that always sounded amused. It was so like the voice in the books, which is most unusual – to find an author whose speaking voice is like the tone they convey in print'.

Another admirer of her work was (and still is) John Kennedy Melling, author, lecturer and broadcaster, and an authority on the history of crime and detective fiction. A member of the Crime Writers' Association, he edited a series of reprints of crime classics, published by Chivers Press from 1986 to 1991. One of those selected was *Cinderella Goes to the Morgue*. But Melling's admiration for Nancy's work began many years before this. '*Cinderella Goes to the Morgue* made such an impression on me with its language, humour, action and accuracy of description of life in the pantomime theatre, that I could see how it would adapt as a musical', he explains. Hermione Gingold expressed some interest in Melling's idea and he was given a six-month free option on *Cinderella*:

'I adapted it and Betty Lawrence, formerly Richard Tauber's accompanist, then musical director at the Players' Theatre, wrote the music. I took the book and lyrics, without the music, and they turned it down flat – but at least they couldn't blame the music'.

Despite this disappointment, Melling observed the development of Nancy's detective fiction with admiration and relish. He also detected the emergence of certain trends, as early as *Death Before Wicket*:

'By this second book we can realize Spain has a penchant for woman killers and the beginnings of a dislike for nasty little girls who behave badly, selfishly and can act as a catharsis in the killing fields. *Out, Damned Tot* and *'R' in the Month* continue to develop strongly Spain's versatility, with a greater use of red herrings to baffle the reader, yet more subtle Wodehouse-cum-Dickens nomenclature, ingenious plotting and the establishment of a repertory company of outrageous characters, yet set in a Kabuki-style frame'.

In 1979, Val McDermid (now an accomplished thriller writer herself) reassessed Nancy's crime novels:

Her writing falls into the broad category of the classic English *farceur*, but she never quite manages to sustain the wit or the elegance of style of masters like Michael Innes and Edmund Crispin. And sometimes her endings are too heavy for her lightweight writing. But a lovable and funny Nancy Spain shows through these books . . . .[50]

Like John Kennedy Melling, the writer and editor Alison Hennegan was also responsible for a Spain reprint in the 1990s, after admiring the work for many years:

'I enjoyed the raw energy. I thought they were fairly quaint period pieces. They are curiously anarchic, because you're dealing with terrible murders, mutilations, and it's as though the actual centre of the characters concerned is something quite other. They are quite unsettling. I also find the attitude to children that emerged very intriguing – love-hate doesn't begin to do justice to the passion!'

This is true; the books are crawling with creepy, potentially (and actual) homicidal children: Julia Bracewood-Smith; Alice and Emma, Evelyn St Leonards' stepdaughters; June Comett; Claudia and Cecilia Harrigon; and April and May Robinson. But equally sinister are the books' killers. 'They have very amoral, often male murderers', observes Alison Hennegan. 'The guy in *"R" in the Month* [Anthony Robinson] is quite disturbing under the froth – that smiling, boyish psychopathic indifference to anything. The more that one knows about that sort of character in real life, the more intrigued I am by that particular portrait'.

However, the most fascinating characters were undoubtedly Natasha and Miriam. The pair weren't actually brought together until *Death Goes on Skis*, but the introduction of Miriam heralded the phasing out of Johnny

DuVivien, Nancy's original sleuth. Alison Hennegan still finds the dynamics of the relationship puzzling:

'It's very peculiar. I became intrigued by the personality of Miriam Birdseye because she's curiously sexless. She's like a man in drag, that character. It fascinates me, partly because of the supposed romantic passions which motivate her, but there is something curiously brittle and two-dimensional about the sexual emotions. Gingold's own construction of feminity was very precarious. It's such a travesty – almost femininity in drag. It's no coincidence that the books become quirkier and increasingly farcical once Johnny DuVivien is replaced by Miriam Birdseye, finally going off on a completely, less successful tangent when she abandoned them and Natasha and wrote *The Kat Strikes*. Birdseye et Cie were her anchor characters and she went somewhat adrift when she threw them overboard'.

Throughout the 1980s, Alison Hennegan approached several feminist publishing houses with a proposal to reprint several of Nancy's crime novels, especially *Poison for Teacher*. This was rejected because of the racism and anti-Semitism expressed by several characters, mistakenly perceived as proof that Nancy herself was a raging bigot. 'I tried to mount an argument, which I actually believe in', explains Hennegan, 'that there are very few people who are clean all the way through, judged by the standards of one's own day, and that so much English anti-Semitism is actually [about] class, which then takes an additional colour of which other attributes the person has'. It should go without saying that publishers must exercise such caution. But charges of bigotry against Nancy do not hold water. She was always unabashed about where her political affiliations – such as they were – lay. 'I'm a Conservative', she admitted. 'People are always very surprised about this. I've never voted in any other way and I've never had the slightest inclination to be Labour. I'm sure that it's simply a matter of mad individualism, again. Eccentricity, if you like'.[51] But this was a woman whose friends included Winifred Atwell and Lena Horne and who, on her visit to Jamaica in 1954, wrote in the *Express* (of all places) about the conditions of poor black plantation workers. In 1960, while journeying through America, she compared the attitudes and behaviour of white Americans unfavourably with those of the black Americans she met. Her lawyer and one of her agents were Jewish and her second longest emotional attachment was with a Jewish woman. This is hardly consistent behaviour for a true-blue bigot. Nancy was many things to many people, but she was never a snob. And what is bigotry but a cruder, crueller and more aggressive version of snobbery?

Although the public affection for the Spain crime novels remained strong, they were not actually an intrinsic part of her real fame, which came after *The Kat Strikes*, her last published novel, appeared in 1955. Her increasingly diverse work for the *Express*, the creation of *She* and her prominent profile therein, her numerous radio appearances, running parallel with her emergence as a television personality, were all more important.

In many respects, the books served as calling cards, to gain entrance into certain circles and ensure that her name appeared in the right sort of publications. But although, like all books, her detective novels had a longer shelf-life than her journalism or, to a certain extent, her broadcasting, to suggest they are what she should most be admired for is to lose sight of everything else she achieved in her post-1955 career. For Nancy, they were a means to an end: crime books sold well, were guaranteed press coverage and, given her quirky storylines and characters, virtually ensured her some critical attention, if not respect.

In Geoffrey Wright's opinion, 'The books were not exactly a sideline, but they weren't the important part of her career'. Tony Warren agrees, to a certain extent:

> 'With the books, she was trying to build a public – a sophisticated public, ideally. She was trying to pinch Evelyn Waugh and Nancy Mitford's public, in their more jolly moments. *The Kat Strikes*, I never thought of as belonging to them. It's more cautious; it doesn't say anything and it's a rather bitter book. It's like reading Nancy in drag. I think by then she had the British public well within the palm of her hand, as a result of the TV appearances and so on. I once asked her why she stopped writing the detective stories and she said, "because I got bored with them". But they did have a special place in her affections'.

And he still admires the earlier books: 'They were beautifully written – she had an amazing sense of place. She could take you to a place. I still think of the description of the trip down to Brunton from Victoria with the teaspoons rattling and the rain battering against the window'.

Sister Liz, however is rather less sentimental about them: 'I didn't think those crime novels were very good'.

On 23 March, Nancy took part in the trial recording of what was to become one of the most popular radio programmes in the BBC's history, unpretentiously billed as 'the word game played by people whose business is words'. The show was devised by two men: Tony Shryane and Edward J. Mason, respectively producer and co-writer on *The Archers*, based at the BBC's Birmingham studios. The panel show they created was a pleasant, mild, terribly British sort of quiz, suffused with gentility and charm. Nancy saw it somewhat differently, however, describing *My Word* as 'a literary quiz game of controlled ferocity and semi-controlled eccentricity'.[52]

The game itself consisted of five rounds of questions (set by Mason) on the meaning of words, their origins and the identification of famous literary quotations.

In the final round, it fell to the team captains to provide explanations – the more facetious and fantastic the better – of how a famous saying or quotation came to be created. Thus 'There's many a slip 'twixt cup and the lip' had, according to the official *My Word* version, started life as a quote about a certain French painter: 'there was Manet asleep twixt the carp and the leap'. It was also revealed that 'A new broom sweeps clean' had actually started life as 'A new sweep brooms Coleen'.

The two men who unfailingly – and spontaneously – applied themselves to this task, and who acted as the *My Word* captains from its inception to its conclusion, were the top comedy script-writing team, Frank Muir and Denis Norden. Muir and Norden's record as writers of radio comedy is too easily forgotten: from Tommy Handley's Second World War triumph *It's That Man Again*, to Dick Bentley's *Take it from Here* and many of Peter Sellers's most memorable classics, including *Balham: Gateway to the South*, Muir and Norden had been prominent behind-the-scenes figures. *My Word* gave them a chance to step into the spotlight and display their wit and personalities to unsuspecting radio audiences all over the world. For the programme's first chairman, Shryane and Mason selected John Arlott, the much-loved cricket commentator. They subsequently chose Nancy, whose journalist background they shared, to be Norden's team-mate while, for Muir's partner, they approached Lady Isobel Barnett, by now a popular member of the *What's My Line?* team.

Each edition of *My Word* lasted an hour and would be recorded in front of a studio audience. Shryane and his assistant, Valerie Hodgetts, who made all the arrangements for the show and even kept score, would then edit the tape down to a half-hour programme, removing anything potentially libellous, or material which might be construed as advertising or considered too risqué. The pilot programme was recorded in the Aeolian Hall in Bond Street on a day when Nancy was both preoccupied and overdressed; the recording coincided with the 'Miss SHE' fashion contest finals and she was 'lashed into the fullest evening dress and felt an absolute ass'.[53]

My Word was sharp and – contrary to what a few unbelievers suspected – always unscripted and unrehearsed. But, in particular, it was the final round which, according to Nancy, guaranteed the show's success: 'In this round Frank and Denis (who for many years had blushed unseen, writing brilliant material . . .) suddenly emerged in all their glory as fully-fledged comedians'.[54]

After the trial programme, there was a lengthy gap. Finally, recordings for the first series of *My Word* began on 16 November. However, it was not long before everyone concerned – including the lady herself – realized that Isobel Barnett was out of her depth. She was not a professional wordsmith like her colleagues and, according to her biographer, was rather taken aback by their off-the-cuff quick-wittedness. It was not that she was any less intelligent, simply that her talent lay in reacting to stimuli provided by other people, rather than creating her own. She had experienced similar problems with her first appearances on *What's My Line?*, and was singled out for criticism by the pundits, but gradually learned to relax (aided by a particularly amusing edition when Robert Morley was on the panel) and acclimatize to the programme's atmosphere.

However, after just six appearances on *My Word*, Isobel Barnett graciously told Shryane she thought it would be best for everyone if she left and, by mutual agreement and with no bad feeling on either side, she was replaced by the novelist and critic E. Arnot (Eileen Arbuthnot) Robertson for whom, according to Denis Norden, Nancy had enormous respect. Since the series was still in its infancy, the change was effected with little fuss or publicity.

Editions of *My Word* were recorded across the heartland of England:

Great Yarmouth, Derby, Wellingborough, Malvern, Hereford and – one that was to become a particular favourite of Nancy's – Ashby-de-la-Zouch where, she said, 'we would spend nights of unbelievable glamour'.[55] When the recordings for the first series were over, Nancy sent a card to Tony Shryane in Birmingham, saying how much she had enjoyed doing the show and that 'I only hope that we may all meet again, preferably in thunder, lightning, rain or Ashby de la Zouche [sic]'.[56]

Her wish was granted: three more series were recorded that year and the show settled into its niche of popularity in Britain and around the world. Nancy herself completed nearly thirteen series, sometimes recording four editions a month, and having a grand old time into the bargain. This is particularly evident during the 1961 Christmas edition. The chairman (then Jack Longland) asked her to define 'saturnalia'.

'It's a Roman orgy,' she answered.

'Where did it start?' demanded Longland.

'You give me a bowl of mead and I'll show you ... ', purred Nancy, 'come and see our Christmas sometime ... '

In a section on party games, she had to describe what happened in Snapdragon. Explaining that it involved snatching nuts and raisins from out of some flames, she added 'I'm very good at it because I have asbestos fingernails ... Known as a good hand for pastry, what I have'.

For the *My Word* panellists, their travels up, down and across the Midlands were often as much fun as the show itself – though many of the incidents definitely fell into the 'not suitable for broadcast' category. For the trips, Norden recalls that Nancy would provide hampers from Fortnum and Mason's, which were 'full of the most wonderful goodies that we used to munch and drink all the way up'. He also remembers that the journeys were accompanied by much singing:

'For some reason, Nancy and I shared a freak memory for the lyrics of really rubbishy old popular songs. On the sister programme that came along, *My Music*, I established quite a corner on these. But Nancy was much better than I was and she could remember the verses, which were even more banal and unmemorable – but she was word-perfect on them'.

These included such horrors as 'Toot, Toot, Tootsie, Goodbye' and 'Remember My Forgotten Man'.

Singing on long car journeys was something of a habit for Nancy, according to Dick Laurie:

'I remember coming back once from Bristol, where she'd done a live television broadcast. On the way back, she sang for two hours solid – masses of Noel Coward and Cole Porter – while I drove. She had a phenomenal memory for lyrics of tunes. But I tell you, it was not a pretty voice – it was a boisterous, rather corncrakey singing voice, really'.

Hiring cars for *My Word* proved rather expensive for the longer journeys, so the panellists used to travel by train and stay overnight. Arnot Robertson recalled how Nancy 'would sit, happily munching Bath buns in the buffet, while Denis and Frank and I called for stronger things. She would bring picnic baskets, full of buns, to the shows, often ringing up on the morning to remind me where to be, and to ask did I want tea or coffee in the Thermoses'.[57]

As Denis Norden recalls, the train journeys could be as hilariously eventful as the car trips:

'One thing that sticks in the memory is one of those pauses at one of these wayside stations, which is completely empty and silent and all you can hear is a kind of thrumming noise. . . . In the carriage, we were all reading and Arnot was gazing out of the window, when she suddenly said, very thoughtfully, in this high voice, "Did you know moles have no vagina?" We sort of lived on that, trying to work it into the conversation, for weeks'.

On another occasion, involving a 'sleepover', Nancy and Muir decided to play safe and order dinner at the hotel in advance over the phone. However, when they arrived at the hotel they found the dining room in darkness and no member of staff willing to admit that they had taken the dinner order. Eventually, one of them grudgingly rustled up the hungry panellists some tomato soup – hardly what they had been looking forward to. Then there was the time when Muir – famously unable to pronounce his 'r's – was given a warm spoon: he had actually asked for 'an aspirin'.

Nancy loved every minute, describing these evenings as 'curiously like my war years: uncomfortable, extraordinary and filled with dotty comradeship'.[58] Even when the show became London-based, she still considered that ' "My Word" is a joyous holiday for me. I never think of it as work at all'.[59]

This was hardly surprising, given that there were ample opportunities to mix business with pleasure – of various, occasionally blatant, kinds. Denis Norden explains:

'Frank and I were rather naive, but the whole lesbian thing was introduced to us so naturally and so understandably. But she was also rather rakish. . . . Once, we were doing the show in Cambridge and met for drinks beforehand in what I think was called the Garden Hotel. It was a gorgeous summer evening and we had our drinks on the lawn, which sloped down towards the river. Sitting in a deckchair over a little way to the right of us was a most beautiful young girl. We pointed her out and Nancy sort of said, "Yes".

A little while later, we noticed Nancy was no longer with us – she was talking to the girl. Then we had to go and do the show, and afterwards we came back for another drink at the hotel before we got in the car to go home – and we noticed, again, that Nancy wasn't with us. And when we looked down at the river, we could see her disappearing in a punt, round a bend – with the girl.

Frank and I were sure it was the voice – if she set out to enchant with that voice, it would be no problem at all . . . '

However, as well as observing the 'pirate' side of Nancy's personality, Denis Norden also saw the more responsible side:

'When we went up by train, we sometimes used to stay the night. Nancy used to get the milk-train back in the morning in order to get to the two boys before they went to school and see they had a good breakfast, which we thought was extremely admirable and, in a way, defined her role in that household. She was the kind of father-figure: of the two, if there was a role assigned to either of them, I would have said that Joan was the mother role and Nancy was the father role'.

In 1960, E. Arnot Robertson's participation in *My Word* came to a tragic end, when her husband, Sir Henry Turner, a keen sailor, drowned in a river-boating accident. It came as a dreadful shock to Robertson who, gradually, began to succumb to stress and depression. She died of a sedative overdose which was officially declared 'accidental'. Nancy recalled her with great affection: 'We all loved her very much. She was a gay, inconsequential companion, full of talent and brilliance and she contributed a great deal to our lives'.[60] Not long before this, John Arlott also left the series and was replaced by Jack Longland, former Olympic pole-vaulter and then Director of Education for Derbyshire – a curious combination of credentials. He was also an infectious giggler, not afraid to show his appreciation of the panellists' worst puns; E. Arnot Robertson was replaced by Dilys Powell. Eventually, the hectic rushing up and down the motorways and rail networks also came to an end and the show was recorded at several London venues. Instead of madcap adventures in deserted stations or near-deserted hotels, panellists, producer and question-master would meet in a nearby pub for drinks at 7 p.m., to prepare themselves for the 7.30 start.

My Word was enormously, and unexpectedly, popular. Its special pre-recorded Christmas Day editions became as traditional a 1950s Yuletide ritual as listening to or watching the Queen's Speech. It was heard in Canada, Australia, New Zealand, Hong Kong, Gibraltar, the West Indies, South Africa and even New York. Nancy claimed that, in 1962, while she was lecturing in America, 300 schoolchildren came from Canada to Michigan to see what the 'voice' from *My Word* looked like. Though the actual figures involved might have become embellished over the years, it was certainly true that *My Word* significantly enhanced the popularity that Nancy enjoyed. Denis Norden is still in no doubt as to what lay behind this enormous success, along with her other radio successes:

> 'That unforgettable voice, which must have been one of the best radio voices ever. The number of people all over the world . . . who wrote decades after she died and said they missed the sound of Nancy's voice. Even though the two ladies who took over, Dilys Powell and Anne Scott-James, and various others, were absolutely perfect for it, it was that distinctiveness in Nancy's voice'.

Early in 1956, Nancy became embroiled in the sort of debate, typical of the more frivolous side of the *Daily Express*, which enhanced her reputation for outspokenness. It did not concern an issue of any global importance as such, but one that was quintessentially British: the battle between 'U' (upper-class) and 'non-U' (lower-class) behaviour.

Reviewing Nancy Mitford's *Noblesse Oblige*, she had attacked both author and the 'U' ethos. 'Who wants to be Upper Class?' she asked. 'Not I, for one! I think people should please themselves. . . . Non-U Speakers of the World

Unite!'[61] This would have come as no surprise to Mitford: the year before, she had snobbishly told her friend, James Lees-Milne, that Nancy was 'a rough north-country peasant on the make and anybody who knows her at all knows she is not conversant with upper-class manners . . . '.[62] Nancy would have been the first to agree with the latter half of Mitford's assessment of her, describing herself 'an ill-mannered brute who is in a constant flutter over how to eat asparagus, and where to put my fish fork . . . '.[63]

The *Express* received a mixed mailbag as a result of her denunciation of 'U'. Bob Boothby thought that everyone should become 'U': 'If we must have equality let us have it at the top level. Miss Mitford wants to pull us all up, Miss Spain to drag us down'.[64] Conversely, the painter James Proudfoot asked, 'How can I join your Non-U club? It sounds rather jolly . . . '.[65] Nancy was also invited to take part in a debate held by the Cambridge Union Society on 1 May entitled, 'That this House prefers to be U'. Nancy, naturally, would oppose the motion. Nancy opened her argument by singing the Roedean school song to the astonished audience. 'Now you couldn't have anything more common than that, could you?'[66] she asked rhetorically. She won the debate: the motion was defeated by seventy-eight votes to forty-three.

She would refer to the issue of class and snobbery again in other pieces for the *Express*, and never wavered in her belief. 'I don't believe in the class war at all', she said. 'I believe that our only hope of survival is to admit that we are all Working-Class and the sooner we own up to it the better. The only thing is this: some of us work harder than others'.[67]

The 'U'/'Non-U' pieces marked a new phase in Nancy's work for the *Express*. From now on, she would regularly contribute articles that were lighthearted, rather gossipy 'think' pieces on whatever issues took her fancy. She examined the importance of having the 'right' sort of name, citing Eartha Kitt and Wolf Mankowitz as prime examples. In 'This Wonderful City', she sang the praises of London, and claimed that only adoptive Londoners could fully appreciate it. She responded to an article that had claimed Britain was a nation of hypochondriacs and was proud to admit she was one:

> Every morning before I can face the world I furtively take my pills, powders, tablets and cough mixture. . . . The powder is to prevent asthma. . . . The pill is to clear the powder out of my system. The tablet is for the headache I get from the effect of the pill. And the cough mixture is for the sore throat I get from the tablet.[68]

And, as the year drew to a close, she outlined her 'Money Policy for 1957' and explained why she wasn't a millionaire. 'I am a perfect ass about money',[69] she admitted. Complaining about the sort of things she saw her tax being spent on – atomic research, the armed forces – she compiled a breakdown of her income and expenses for the last year. It surprised no one to learn that her smallest expenditure – £45 – was for clothes.

That summer, she had sent the galley proofs of *Millionaire* to Noel Coward in Paris. He had agreed to write a foreword to the book (Nancy would subsequently dedicate the book to him). He was reading them in the apartment of an old and dear friend who, she admitted to him, had never heard of this 'Nancy Spain'. Once he had finished with the galleys, he gave them to his friend to read – and so Ginette Spanier, directrice of Balmain, to whom dresses were a way of life, learned about the character to whom they were anathema. 'Noel Coward has done many nice things for me in his time,' said Nancy, 'but I have to admit that this introduction to Ginette Spanier comes top of my list'.[70]

On paper, it seemed an unlikely match: Ginette, beauty and elegance personified (Nancy compared her to Nefertiti), head of a major French fashion house, who enjoyed a happy, affectionate relationship with her husband; and Nancy, the rather dashing, pirate-like media personality, with 'wife' and 2.4 children. But, apart from their immediate respective partners, it was to be the deepest, longest-lasting relationship in their lives, forged on a love that would apparently endure beyond death.

In a 1968 radio programme, Ginette Spanier told the interviewer that two things had changed her life: one was meeting Noel Coward, while the other was 'meeting Nancy Spain'.

She was born Jenny Yvonne Spanier in Paris in 1904, into an English/French/Jewish family, headed by Max and Alice Spanier. Max was a jeweller, specializing in pearls. There were two younger sisters: Adrienne, known as 'Didine', who would become a successful interior decorator, and Janine. The family moved to London in 1916, settling in Golders Green, and Ginette attended Frognal School in Hampstead. In 1929, when their father's business slumped in the wake of the Wall Street crash, the Spanier daughters had to go out to work. Ginette did not regard this as the calamity her parents apparently did. They wanted her to become a secretary; instead, she became a sales assistant at Fortnum and Mason, in the gift department. She became a bag buyer for the store, which involved making trips to Paris. There, she was poached by one of the companies she bought from, Bembaron, to become their sales manager. While living with her Aunt Lily in Paris, she met Paul-Emile Seidmann, a tall, handsome, soft-spoken and charming doctor. They married in the spring of 1939.

It is hard to find anyone with a bad word to say about either Ginette or Paul-Emile. 'Paul-Emile was the nicest man – tall, slim, distinguished, but he had kindness written all over him', remembers Tony Warren, who met them both in the early 1960s. The writer, Frances Partridge, was invited to a cocktail party at Avenue Marceau, where she observed 'Our host and hostess had some inner source of overflowing warmth',[71] while Brian Howard, slightly more ambiguously, once remarked to Jean Cocteau that Ginette had 'the sweetness of a dove and the eyes and claws of an eagle'.[72]

When the Second World War broke out, Paul-Emile was attached to a mobile military hospital, and Ginette followed him all over France. After the fall of France and the surrender of the French Army, the couple fled into the Unoccupied Zone. Ginette destroyed anything that identified her as English and Paul-Emile obtained false French papers for her. For a while, they lived in Nice, in one hotel room. There Paul-Emile was able to continue working as a doctor for a while until the French authorities, under the heel of a Nazi decree, informed him that Jewish doctors were forbidden to practise. Ginette found an unusual job as a sales representative for a firm that manufactured sanitary towels. But French Jews were now being arrested in the Unoccupied Zone, and they were forced to leave Nice and head for the mountain villages. In 1943, after Mussolini's fall, the Nazis took over control of the Unoccupied Zone and the danger that Ginette and Paul-Emile would be transported to a concentration camp increased. They moved to a village called Chambéry, where Ginette had some relatives, and called themselves 'Spaniet'. For the rest of the war, they managed to stay a step ahead of the Gestapo and endured cold, hunger and fear, until the Liberation. It was not until September 1944 that Ginette could get word to her family in England that she was safe.

Ginette and Paul-Emile returned to Paris, where she obtained a job with the American Signal Service. In 1947, accompanied by the daughter of a London friend who wished to buy two dresses from a Paris couturier, Ginette visited the collection of Pierre Balmain. Unimpressed by the salesmanship, she berated the Balmain staff for trying to sell wholly unsuitable clothes to her young charge. Pierre Balmain's mother had witnessed the incident and promptly invited Ginette to work for the company. And so Ginette Spanier became directrice of Balmain, a position she was to hold for over thirty years.

She and Paul-Emile set up house at 70 Avenue Marceau, near the Champs Elysées, in a large apartment, from where Paul-Emile ran his practice. Its main feature was the 50-foot-long drawing room, complete with grand piano and even grander fireplace. The lift to the Seidmann apartment was wobbly and tiny and could only take three people at a time. But what people.

During the 1950s, the biggest stars of the showbusiness firmament passed through its doors: Laurence Olivier and Vivien Leigh, Lena Horne, Danny Kaye, Judy Garland, Claudette Colbert, Louis Armstrong, Marlene Dietrich, Maurice Chevalier – and Noel Coward. Ginette had met Coward in the summer of 1946, while holidaying in the south of France, and he, along with his partners Cole Lesley and Graham Payn, became firm and lasting friends. Coward, amused by Paul-Emile's double name, nicknamed him 'Marie Antoinette' and, occasionally, 'Polly Mill', Vivien Leigh's name for him.

Ginette met many of this glittering set through her work at Balmain, and her reputation for hospitality and friendship spread throughout their closely knit coterie. It became known that any luminaries visiting Paris should make it their business to visit Ginette and Paul-Emile – where, inevitably, they were almost certain to meet other luminaries.

As the stars adorned the sitting room at Avenue Marceau, so did they occupy the bathroom: signed photographs of them all hung on every wall, 'like flies in amber',[73] remarked Nancy. In the sitting room, the stars would gossip, fence each other with witticisms, sing, scream and swish while their host and hostess smiled fondly, like kindly, indulgent parents.

The Seidmann marriage was built on genuine and mutual affection, friendship and commitment, but it was far from conventional. By the time she met Nancy, Ginette had been involved with Marlene Dietrich for a number of years. They had met in September 1950, when Marlene went to be fitted for her film costumes at Balmain. Ginette invited her back to Avenue Marceau to have lunch with her and Paul-Emile, whose birthday it was. For many years, the two women had an on-off relationship, conducted discreetly in Paris, New York and London which, as far as Ginette was concerned, ran parallel to her marriage. By all accounts, however, Marlene was jealous of Ginette's commitment to Paul-Emile and looked for ways to cause a permanent split – something, incidentally, which Nancy never attempted or sought. Similarly, while there was never any question of Ginette and Paul-Emile parting, so neither was Nancy's relationship with Ginette ever intended to replace the one she enjoyed with Joan. Ginette, in fact, would become one of the 'immediate' family, visiting them all at Clareville Grove. Tony Warren explains:

> 'It's so hard to explain what those lesbian women were like in those days. They hinted at it. Ginette Spanier would be asked what she was doing in Britain with Marlene Dietrich and she would say, "Because I love her". Yet if you had suggested that they were having an affair, she would have pointed out she was married. If you were accepted in those circles, you were expected to know that the i's were never dotted, the t's never crossed – and, in fact, the veils of mystery were hugely attractive'.

Life with Joan was organized domesticity, with a family unit and a no-nonsense business-like approach to work. Life with Ginette in Paris, America and elsewhere was about glamour, romance, extravagance and, to a certain extent, living and being treated like a celebrity, rather than merely hovering in their shadows. With Ginette, she would play with what had become recognized as her tried-and-tested image. She would also get a rare chance to be someone's literary mentor and groom them for the sort of 'personality' stardom she herself enjoyed.

For Ginette, it may be that Nancy, trousers and all, personified something that she had long dreamed of. Before the First World War, the 'poor children' in France wore uniform black overalls. But when the young Ginette saw them, 'They represented freedom to me', she explained. 'One day, I'd be one of them. Two people in my whole life understood this passionate longing of mine and helped me to get from behind my lace curtain'.[74] One was her governess, Muriel Chapman. The second was Nancy.

Nancy and Ginette met for the first time when Nancy went to interview the Windsors in the early autumn, for the December 1956 issue of *She*. The Windsors told Nancy how they spent their Christmases, showed her round their Paris home and introduced her to their pugs. In the article, Nancy revealed that the Duchess had only one regret: 'I have never known the joy of having children of my own'. Nancy concurred: 'For what is Christmas for unless it is for children to share one's heart?'[75] When she had typed up the article, she took it back to the Windsors, who expressed their approval by signing the manuscript. Mission thus accomplished, she arranged to have lunch with Ginette at Avenue Marceau. Afterwards, Ginette invited her to view the latest Balmain collection.

Their next meeting occurred a few months later in London, when Ginette brought the collection to England. They met for lunch in Wheeler's, where Nancy was adorned with her usual informal lunchtime attire – old sheepskin coat, trousers and lots of books. On her own territory, Nancy was more relaxed, ebullient and boisterous, but Ginette was no less impressed by her. 'Nancy Spain was the person out of all the world who made me laugh most – unexpectedly, from deep down inside me',[76] she revealed later. It was mutual. Nancy was taken by 'Ginette's unique warmth of heart'.[77] 'She has no critical faculty . . . Ginette accepts everyone on precisely the same level, without light or shade, undiscerningly, unhesitatingly . . . '.[78] 'From Ginette I learn something every day. Ginette is worth two hundred of her stars'.[79] Their likes – work, laughter, sun – and dislikes – laziness, amateurs and antiques – were similar. Nancy also saw that Ginette's life, though superficially glamorous and exciting, lacked any real substance: something which Ginette was only too aware of herself. And, according to Tony Warren, Ginette also perceived Nancy rather differently from many of those who saw her only as the brash, gregarious, public clown:

> 'Ginette got one thing right about her – she said the first time she looked at her, she thought "this girl is shy". And she was – but the "pirate" used to roust her out from inside and save her. But there was somebody else living inside. She was hugely complex, multi-layered. The more you peeled off, the simpler it got and the nicer it got'.

From early 1957 until 1964, Nancy, by her own reckoning, spent at least a week each month in Paris. Though she visited Ginette at Avenue Marceau, she usually stayed at the Queen Elizabeth hotel in the Avenue Pierre Premier de Serbie, not far from the Seidmanns' home. Everything was handled with discretion and, naturally, in the best possible taste – at least, most of the time. When Ginette was the guest on *Desert Island Discs*, her luxury item was a silver box 'given to me by my dear friend Nancy Spain'. In July 1957, they recorded two live broadcasts for *Woman's Hour*: a 'Talk of Two Towns', between Ginette in Paris and Nancy in London. Unfortunately, no record exists of what they actually said on the first programme, but, as Nancy herself might have said, 'you can imagine'. Whatever occurred, it was obviously so unruly and undisciplined that it prompted a rare reprimand from Joanna Scott-Moncrieff. 'A number of listeners were as shocked as myself', she wrote to Nancy, 'and I am afraid I find it hard at the moment to encourage you both to go ahead with the revised form of your act'. The BBC had also received some unusually hostile responses from listeners, too: 'I remember that one listener began her letter with the words "and to think I used to like Nancy Spain" '.[80]

They were shocking others too, most notably Ginette's parents and her sister, Didine. Fully aware of the relationship between Nancy and Ginette, according to a family friend they were appalled by it because 'it was so open'. Didine, in particular, heartily disliked Nancy, to such an extent that, nearly forty years after Nancy's death, she could not bring herself to discuss her.

Some of Ginette's loftier friends also decried what they saw as the 'cheapening' of her image. Nancy had decided that the rest of the world should learn about the wonders of Ginette, Paris and its personalities and, early in 1957, wrote a series of articles for the *Express*. Her editors saw how they could capitalize on the irony of the situation. 'They call her Vulgar; they call her Unscrupulous; they have called her the worse-dressed woman in Britain' trumpeted the paper. 'We let her loose in The Snootiest Mile in Europe'[81] (which is how they saw the area of Paris bordered by the Champs Elysées and Avenue Marceau). What a hoot – sending 'Britain's Most Self-Indulgent Writer' to mix amongst the elite of 'The square mile of luxury, wealth, chic and self-indulgence . . . '.[82]

'Are You Pro Nancy Spain?', the readers were asked. The replies were typical of the extreme 'love or loathe' attitude Nancy always seemed to provoke, but were mostly favourable. Jean Rice of Sheffield enthused, 'Nancy Spain takes me away from my kitchen sink to a glamorous world I would so much like to see. I never shall, so herewith, my thanks for her articles'. A Mrs Hancock of Merstham thought, 'Though Nancy Spain's wit is sometimes barbed, it is never mean or vitriolic. Who cares what she wears? She is a colourful personality, and there are few enough about these days'.[83]

It hardly mattered to Nancy what anyone called her: she was in Paris and she was in love.

Before the publication of *Why I'm Not a Millionaire* in September, Nancy and Joan decided to seize the opportunity of a holiday with the boys. They went to Cannes, where they stayed at the rented Villa Lisbeth on the Avenue de la Croix des Gardes from 26 August to 7 September. Fortified by the break, Nancy returned to London and readied herself for the hurly-burly of publicizing *Millionaire*. It began with her chairing a Foyle's luncheon.

The 279th Foyle's Literary Luncheon was held at the Dorchester on Friday 14 September. The theme was 'A Tribute to Achievement' and the guests of honour included Cyril Lord, Billy Butlin, Charles Forte, Sir Allen Lane, the founder of Penguin Books, and Winifred Atwell. In her speech, Nancy bemoaned the absence of Gilbert Harding – 'I suppose he thought I was going to propose to him again' – and pointed out to the assembled throng that, for once, she was wearing a dress. Naturally, she also got in a few plugs for her latest book.

Why I'm Not a Millionaire was published to much fanfare. As if having 5,000 words serialized in her own paper were not enough, Nancy decided to continue the tradition of James Agate, and review her own book. 'As a matter of fact, I don't really believe in this N. SPAIN,' she pronounced. 'Her book column is obviously written by six bald men and an angry midget . . . N. Spain is obviously a figment of Lord Beaverbrook's imagination'.[84] She related the bare bones of her story, dropping as many of the big names mentioned in the book into the review as she could: Coward, Katharine

Hepburn, Orson Welles, *et al.* And, referring to the title, she gave herself some advice: 'If you really want to make some dough in the next 40 years I should stop chasing men and women with highly coloured personalities around. I should stop at home, save your money and keep an account book'.[85]

Gilbert Harding also gave the book a lengthy appraisal in the *Evening Standard*, which he began by outlining why he found some aspects of Nancy highly resistible:

'It annoys me that I do not understand her detective stories – or her publishers' reason for printing them. I'm not drawn to her children's books and, not being a particularly skilful journalist myself, I am prepared to take her writing for the newspapers in the same cheerful spirit as I can leave it alone'.

This said, however, he continued, '[*Millionaire*] is I think the best thing that Miss Spain has written. . . . It's vastly amusing'.[86] He also noticed, with irritation, that he had been misidentified on page 237 as 'Albert Hardy'.

But, with *Millionaire*, some reviewers began to see just what lay beneath the surface. Philip Day in the *Sunday Times* was one:

Miss Spain's detective stories may be an acquired taste but her autobiography, breathless, slap-dash and quick with vitality and humour, is an engaging book for the many. Miss Spain relates, with great good humour and modesty, under a superficial toughness, an agreeable success story.[87]

The *Times Literary Supplement* reviewer felt that the book was

written with an endearing modesty and, generally, an admirable respect for the feelings of those she writes about. As one would expect, the reportage is good. She has an excellent eye for detail and an invigorating style. But it must be confessed that not all the characters she describes will be interesting to the general reader. Her millionaire friends, with the notable exception of Lord Beaverbrook, make dull reading.

Perhaps the strings of 'dear boys' and 'adorables' pall a little towards the end, perhaps there are some private jokes that get missed. But it is an engaging book. Her courage, both on and off the hockey field, is most impressive. Those who admire the muscular heroines of John Betjeman will find the author of this book no less 'strongly adorable'.[88]

But the *Times* reviewer picked up on more nuances than anyone else:

Miss Nancy Spain is a tremendous trier. Having constructed a persona for herself, she fills 250 pages with a determined effort to live down to it; try as she may, however, she never quite succeeds. For the persona is so obdurately unreal that it defeats every manoeuvre to bring it into play as a recognizable human being. . . . tough, ruggedly inept, fancifully silly, roguish through thick and thin. Beneath this artificial surface, however, quite another person is lurking . . . the reader will notice that Miss Spain is kind and funny and spontaneous . . . at the same time she gives evident proofs of a warm heart and an amused intelligence. . . . [The book is] an example of what happens when a 'line' takes control of a personality ... to suffer comparison between the people they really were and the people their public expected them to be. In a world of popular newspapers, radio and television, however, distortions of personal vision become so vast that to recognize oneself, even in silence, has become hard indeed.[89]

This review struck at the heart of her dilemma: how could she really be herself when her career had largely been built on the construction of an image and persona which was ostensibly loud, brash and opportunistic?

Meanwhile, *la fête continue*. During the summer, she had originated and appeared on a weekly radio panel game called *These Foolish Things*. The panel were given odd sounds – cuckoo song, bagpipes, a boxing match – and then had to make up stories based on them. She approached her old friend Cecil McGivern to see if the show could transfer to television. His colleague, Ronald Waldman, reported back to McGivern that the series consisted of 'mildly pleasant anecdotal and story-telling stuff, but no more'.[90] McGivern gave the go-ahead for a dummy recording in October, but *These Foolish Things* stayed where it belonged – on the radio.

At Christmas, came the customary cash gift from Beaverbrook: 'I am going to buy two of those Mushroom heaters that blow warm air through the house. They are electric and whenever I turn them on I shall think of you', she told him.[91]

She was also considering an idea, in time for next Christmas, put to her by Christina Foyle – a *Nancy Spain Christmas Annual* containing illustrations and popular articles. 'I have discussed it mildly with Keeble and he thinks it would "go" too', she told Beaverbrook. 'I'd love the Oldbourne Press to do it: but I am such an ass over finance I couldn't begin to do the costings myself, although I am sure I could collect the material'.[92]

It would prove, however, to be yet another good commercial idea that was destined to come to nothing, because there simply weren't enough hours in the day to squeeze it in. Others went the same way, including some that Nancy originated herself. For example, earlier in the year, she approached BBC Radio's North Region programmes to do a 45-minute programme called 'The Tyne and I'. Presented by Nancy, it was to consist mostly of a written script, with some recorded interviews and music extracts, and was due for broadcast in spring 1957. However, by the end of the year, Maurice Taylor, North Region programme executive, had seen nothing from her. 'I understand ... she has now lost some of her enthusiasm for it',[93] he told a colleague.

Nearly eighteen months later, the proposed programme's producer, Stanley Williamson, replied:

As you will see, the project seems to have foundered on two rocks – the diversion of my attention to television at a critical moment, and the fact that Nancy Spain is a creature of impulse who loses interest in an idea if she cannot work it out right away. ... My own feeling is that even if she could now be dragooned into writing something, it would almost certainly be so unacceptable as to be a positive embarrassment to us.[94]

CHAPTER NINE

The Waugh to End All Wars

Early in the New Year, Nancy visited the ailing Gilbert Harding during one of his increasingly frequent stays in hospital. She decided to approach Lord Beaverbrook about the possibility of Gilbert writing for the *Daily Express*, although with some reservations:

> You see his contracts (£5,000 from BBC per annum, £5,000 from Odham's Press and a promised £5,000 from the Stomach Powder people Maclean's) are of no use unless he appear on Television. And Gilbert has gone in for great extravagance in the shape of a house in Brighton and his flat in London with servants in all of them ... he is an ass.[1]

And in a subsequent letter: 'He ... has in mind (I think) a possibility of becoming a sort of Castlerosse. As you know I am deeply fond of Harding and anxious to help him in any way I can. But whether he is as big a pull with regard to advertising I really don't know'.[2]

It was telling that her loyalty to Gilbert did not supersede her loyalty to Beaverbrook and the commercial considerations of the *Express*, especially as she was about to put that overriding loyalty before her own reputation, credibility and honesty.

Lord Beaverbrook's feuds were infamous, long-lived and relentless. Take, for example, his animosity towards the Astor family, who had owned the *Observer*. In 1949, the paper ran a profile of him to coincide with his seventieth birthday which called him 'a golliwog itching with vitality' and dismissed the leaders in the *Express* as 'political baby talk'.[3] Eternally unforgiving, he took umbrage with the National Trust when the 2nd Viscount Astor handed over his country house, Cliveden, to them. And when the daughter of his ex-mistress, Jean Norton, married the 3rd Viscount Astor, Beaverbrook refused to go to the wedding.

Another target for regular Beaverbrook vilification was Lord Mountbatten. The *Express* poured scorn on Mountbatten's negotiations over the issue of Indian independence and Beaverbrook vehemently opposed Mountbatten becoming First Sea Lord. One reason often cited as a cause for the bad blood is Noel Coward's wartime naval film, *In Which We Serve*, based on Mountbatten's now-proven disastrous Second World War exploits in command of HMS *Kelly*; portrayed by Coward, however, he displays the heroics of a bold and skilful officer. In one of the film's early scenes, a copy of the

Daily Express bearing the headline 'No War This Year' floats in the dirty, debris-ridden water. Beaverbrook took this as a slight against the *Express*'s – and his – support for Chamberlain's policies of appeasement. Mountbatten had also been in charge of the disastrous raid on Dieppe, which resulted in the slaughter of hundreds of Canadian soldiers for no gain. But it's fair to say that Beaverbrook was equally aggrieved to learn that Jean Norton had had an affair with Mountbatten.

Beaverbrook's biographers, Chisholm and Davie, observed that some of the campaigns initiated in his papers damaged their credibility 'particularly when lightweight "Express" writers took on heavyweights such as Evelyn Waugh and Graham Greene'.[4] In this bout, the lightweight in one corner wearing Beaverbrook's colours was Nancy, and the heavyweight out to give both her and her employer a public drubbing was Waugh (who had once been a special correspondent for the *Daily Express*, reporting on the coronation of Haile Selassie, in 1930). This mismatch was the product of a moment of rashness, a rush of blood to the head, that was to prove one of Nancy's biggest professional errors and personal embarrassments.

In the *Spectator* (3 July 1953) Evelyn Waugh wrote a 'review of reviews' of his latest novel, *Love Among the Ruins*. On 29 May, in the *Express*, Nancy had reviewed three books by Catholic authors, including Waugh's. Her considered opinion on *Love Among the Ruins* was that 'I read this in quarter of an hour and yawned and yawned and yawned'. Waugh, possibly deliberately misidentifying the sex of the *Express* book critic, noted that '*he* [author's italics] yawned and yawned and yawned, without indicating the time of day or night when he attempted to read it, or even whether he is adept at reading at all'.[5] Waugh noticed that Milton Shulman in the *Sunday Express* had accused him of snobbery and George Malcolm Thompson of the *Evening Standard* had also reviewed the book unfavourably. 'This unanimity of the Beaverbrook press is striking', he observed. He smelled a conspiracy, but could prove nothing.

Nancy read the *Spectator* piece with glee: 'I don't know which bit I enjoyed more', she told Beaverbrook, 'his doubt about his own height, or the doubt that he spreads about my sex. Is there any way that we could reply? Your adoring book critic . . . '.[6] There would indeed be a reply – but not just then.

Some time after this, on 15 May 1955, Robert Pitman wrote a piece in the *Sunday Express* which did nothing to dispel Waugh's suspicions. To mark the publication of *Officers and Gentlemen*, Pitman had looked up the Waugh crest and declared, 'Mr Waugh's lineage . . . is no longer than yours or mine . . . He paid for his own coat of arms . . . '.[7] The tension was building.

In the summer of 1955, the *Express* ran a series of articles called 'A Cool Look at the Loved Ones – reappraising the famous in the light of their achievements'. It began with a piece on Laurence Olivier and Vivien Leigh. Other subjects to be scrutinized, it announced, would include Sir Malcolm Sargent, J.B. Priestley and Evelyn Waugh. Nancy had been asked to contribute two pieces on writers she admired and chose John Masefield, the Poet Laureate – and Evelyn Waugh.

Nancy decided to have tea with the eighty-year-old poet at his Thames-side home, then drive down to Gloucestershire to visit Waugh at his country home, Piers Court, Stinchcombe. Accompanying Nancy on this particular jaunt – 'for some reason no one ever understood',[8] according to Waugh's friend and neighbour, Lady Frankie Donaldson – was one Lord Noel-Buxton.

Rufus Alexander, the 38-year-old second Lord Noel-Buxton, was, according to Nancy Mitford, 'evidently a candidate for the bin'.[9] He had been invalided out of the Territorial Army at the beginning of the Second World War. In March 1952, to prove that a ford had existed in Roman times, he attempted to walk across the River Thames near Westminster Bridge. A large crowd, several police boats and the speaker of the House of Commons gathered to watch the attempt. Unfortunately, the noble Lord's brisk stroll turned into a quick crawl. 'I am afraid there was much more water than I expected,' he said later, 'It must be all that rain up in the Cotswolds'.[10] Eighteen months later, he tackled the Humber Estuary, this time successfully wading across. A helicopter, appropriately marked 'Pest Control', monitored his progress. This, then, was the rather eccentric personality who was to share Nancy's moment of public ridicule.

Despite Lady Donaldson's bemusement, there was a reason why Noel-Buxton accompanied Nancy on her assignment. He had met her socially on a few occasions and had, in fact, arranged her meeting with Masefield. He was, he said, 'a longstanding friend of John Masefield. One of Miss Spain's ambitions had always been to meet Mr Masefield and I duly arranged this ... '.[11]

On the morning of 21 June 1955, Nancy telephoned Waugh at breakfast time, asking if he would agree to be interviewed at home later that day. According to Nancy, Waugh's wife, Laura, said that he 'was Not at Home to the Daily Express';[12] according to Waugh's lawyers, Laura told Nancy it was no use coming because her husband did not see anyone at home on business. This was perfectly true: Waugh conducted his official business in London, while Piers Court was for family and friends. Waugh was famously known to have an aversion for interviews, a view perhaps partly engendered by his encounter with a young woman journalist during a trip to Sweden in 1947. The writer, representing the Stockholm paper *Dagens Nyheter*, turned up in his hotel room unexpectedly and announced, 'Good night, Mr Wog. Excuse please, I must make a reportage of you'.

Nancy and Noel-Buxton left Masefield and drove on to Stinchcombe. According to Noel-Buxton, they 'went on west because I gather Miss Spain had some business with Evelyn Waugh'.[13] They first stopped off at the village pub, the Yew Tree, where they got chatting to a local man who offered to show them where Waugh's house was. At 7.45 p.m., Nancy and Noel-Buxton swept through the gates of Piers Court, noting but ignoring the 'No Admittance on Business' sign. Nancy rang the doorbell and Laura Waugh answered. No, they could not stay, she told her. Then a voice from inside the house called 'Who is it? What is it?' and Mrs Waugh answered, 'Lord Noel-Buxton and Miss Nancy Spain'. 'Tell them to go away', said the voice, which was getting nearer. Then Waugh appeared at the door and said, 'Go away, go away! You read the notice, didn't you? No admittance on business'. Noel-Buxton insisted, 'I am not on business, I'm a member of the House of Lords'. Waugh was equally insistent: 'Go away'. Realizing she was on a hiding to nothing, Nancy went back to the car and drove off, leaving Waugh to shut and bolt the iron gates after them. 'So much for our literary pilgrimage', commented Noel-Buxton. True enough, Nancy hadn't got the copy she had intended, but she *had* got something she could make a column out of.

Later that evening, Waugh rattled off a letter to Arthur Christiansen, complaining about the incident and saying he hoped 'the delinquents would be punished'.[14] In his diary, he said he was 'tremulous with rage' at the intrusion for the rest of the evening and all the next day.

On 23 June, the story appeared under the headline 'My Pilgrimage to See Mr Waugh'. Waugh, said Nancy, 'used to be a Bright Young Thing who wrote bright young novels . . . then he withdrew into the country and wrote books we didn't enjoy quite so much'. Masefield, she gushed, 'was hospitality itself' and 'a darling man' who apparently told her, 'I have a great fondness for journalists'.[15] She continued the piece with an account of what had taken place during their brief visit to Piers Court – what Nancy called her 'attempt to gate-crash my favourite idol'. The whole piece was a none-too-subtle attempt to punish Waugh for refusing her, making a crude comparison between his behaviour and that of the 'darling' Laureate (whose 'hospitality' would later turn out to be rather less than Nancy had implied at that time).

Waugh was shown the piece over lunch with Jack McDougall at Brooks' club. He then contacted Malcolm Muggeridge at *Punch* to see if he would be interested in publishing the Waugh response. Muggeridge agreed in theory, but eventually decided against printing the piece. Instead, Waugh wrote an entirely different response for the *Spectator*, published on 8 July, called 'Awake My Soul! It is a Lord'. The main object of his ridicule was Noel-Buxton, but he also took an indirect swipe at Nancy ('the fifty or sixty thousand people in this country who alone support the Arts do not go to Lord Beaverbrook's critics for guidance'). Privately, in a letter to Diana Cooper, he sneered at Nancy, saying that she was 'said to practise unnatural vice as well'.[16] An *Express* critic and a lesbian, to boot – the perfect target.

Noel-Buxton attempted to make light of the incident, and sent Waugh a telegram congratulating him on the *Spectator* article. However, he also sent a letter to the magazine's letters page, claiming that Nancy had misquoted him in the *Express* and denied uttering the infamous 'House of Lords' comment. The incident, he said, was 'inflated by Miss Spain into an article . . . which would certainly have angered me if I had been Mr Waugh. I did not trouble to correct Miss Spain's falsifying of the incident – largely because it seemed to me her piece, however irritating, was of no consequence whatever'.[17]

Waugh thought Noel-Buxton's response was 'caddish' but, in a letter to the *Spectator* on 22 July, asked 'if this is how she [Nancy] treats an old and valued friend, what would she have done to me?'[18] Noel-Buxton, of course, could hardly be classified as either an old or valued friend of Nancy's, but Waugh had made his point.

Nancy fought back. Responding to Noel-Buxton's letter in the *Spectator*, she wrote: 'I would like to point out for what it is worth that the day after our visit Lord Noel-Buxton rang me up. I read out to him and actually explained the relevant passage in my piece. Not only did he raise no objection. He actually applauded me'.[19] 'I think I begin to see, Sir, one of the drives and motives of her piece', replied Noel-Buxton, '– which was to produce later the hysterical and ignorant outburst of Waugh'.[20] He also denied that Nancy had read the piece to him.

By now, Joan – clearly irritated and weary of the entire episode – felt compelled to enter the fray, and wrote a letter to the *Spectator*:

> I did happen to be in the room when Nancy Spain read her piece over the telephone to Lord Noel-Buxton and I could not fail to conclude from the mutual cooings that all was harmony. The splendid phrase [Noel-Buxton's 'House of Lords' comment] was heard equally clearly by me on that occasion and must also have been heard by the gentleman Nancy was referring to as 'darling Rufus'.[21]

Thus, as the editor decreed, 'this correspondence is now closed'.

On 31 December 1955, Nancy ended the year with a piece on the brothers Waugh, sarcastically describing Evelyn as 'easily the most arresting personality I met in 1955'.[22] On the strength of this 'meeting', she said (not to mention the fact that his novel *Island in the Sun* was about to be published), she decided she had to meet Alec, too. They met for a drink in the bar at the Ritz, where Nancy noted with approval Alec's apparent friendliness, and jibed, 'My, how different you are from your brother'.[23] Throughout the piece, Nancy implied that Alec was a more interesting, talented man who had been overshadowed by his younger brother. She concluded by saying that 'Brother Evelyn's only amusement at the moment appears to be an esoteric warfare that he is carrying on with his friend Nancy Mitford in the pages of literary magazines. The war is about Proper Upper Class English Usage'.[24]

On 24 February 1956, an edition of the *Spectator* included a piece by Waugh entitled 'Mr Wodehouse and Mr Wain'. It was in reply to an article in the *Observer* called 'A Book Sales Enquiry' and a hostile criticism of P.G. Wodehouse's novel, *French Leave*, by John Wain, which Waugh felt was unwarranted. 'An investigation has lately been made in the book trade to determine which literary critics have most influence on sales', he declared. 'The Beaverbrook press is no longer listed as having any influence at all'. Waugh didn't have to wait long for Nancy's response – unfortunately. It was a reply for which she and her employers would pay, in different ways, a heavy price.

On Saturday 17 March 1956, Nancy's books column consisted of a piece entitled 'Does a Good Word from Me Sell a Good Book?' In it, she declared:

> There is a war between Evelyn Waugh and me. He said, some weeks ago in a literary weekly, that the 'Express' had no influence on the book trade. The 'Express', he complains, sold only 300 of HIS novels. He once had a book chosen by the Book Society so that sold well. But the total first edition sales of all his other titles are dwarfed by brother Alec. 'Island in the Sun' (Cassells 16s) foretold by me as this year's runaway Best Seller has now topped 60,000 copies as a direct result of my 'Daily Express' notice. So the publishers told me yesterday . . . .

The same day, Waugh gleefully wrote to his agents, A.D. Peters, 'I have waited a long time to catch the "Express" in libel. I think they have done it this time'.[25] He told Ian Fleming's wife Ann, 'I, in my modest way, am suing the "Daily Express"',[26] and informed Diana Cooper that the paper had been teasing him for five years 'and they went too far'.[27] His solicitors wrote to the *Express*, demanding an apology, substantial damages, indemnity as to costs and an undertaking not to publish any future libels against him. The *Express*'s lawyers replied that the article was not libellous. A suit was duly filed and Nancy retaliated by filing a counter-claim for damages, on the grounds that Waugh's article in the *Spectator* was defamatory of her. The gauntlets had been thrown down.

Less than a week later, Lord Beaverbrook rang Ann Fleming at home. He had sent her a copy of *Island in the Sun* and she thanked him for it, mentioning that Evelyn had been at her house when it arrived. Beaverbrook guffawed and proceeded to cast doubts over the truth of Fleming's story, declaring that Evelyn was jealous because Alec had made more money out of his books. Fleming refuted his claim, to which Beaverbrook replied by saying he was going to call Nancy and tell her Fleming's 'joke', that Waugh had been at the Flemings' house when the book arrived. Twenty minutes later, he called Fleming back to say he had done just that and that Nancy was also well acquainted with Evelyn's 'jealousy'. Thus were the seeds of Nancy's perjury, and public humiliation, sown.

Waugh, meanwhile, set about his pursuit of Beaverbrook and what he called his 'senile aberration' with relish. He wrote to his brother Alec to see if a representative from his publishers, Cassell, would be willing to go into the witness box and refute Nancy's claim that they had given her the information on which she based her article. Meanwhile, Beaverbrook attempted to soothe Nancy's nerves over dinner on 8 May. Thanking him, she assured him that 'You have cheered me so much about Mr Waugh. I am so grateful',[28] later enquiring, 'I long to do something to show you how grateful I am for your belief in me. But what *can I do*?'[29] (She found 'something' — she bought £320 worth of Beaverbrook Newspaper shares.)

The case of *Waugh* v. *Beaverbrook Newspapers Ltd. and Another* began in the Queen's Bench Division on 19 February 1957, before Mr Justice Stable and a jury. Waugh was represented by Gerald Gardiner QC, Neville Faulkes and I.E. Adams; Sir Hartley Shawcross QC, who had been the chief prosecutor at the Nuremberg trials, and Helenus Milmo represented Beaverbrook and Nancy. Evelyn and Laura Waugh had spent the previous night at the Hyde Park Hotel, drinking champagne, confident of victory.

According to his counsel, Waugh 'did not read the Daily Express and he had not heard of Nancy Spain . . . Since then, counsel understood, she had taken part in panel games on television and was therefore to-day as well known as the Prime Minister'.[30] Every sentence in Nancy's piece, he said, was untrue: 'There was no war between the plaintiff and Miss Spain unless she was still smarting because he would not see a "Daily Express" reporter . . . the article was obviously written recklessly and in a flaming temper'.[31] The article, he claimed, had made it look as if Waugh's books had only sold about 40,000 copies in total and presented in evidence total sales figures of approximately 4,280,125 for Waugh's titles in Britain and America. Waugh then took the stand and gave his brief account of what had happened. Shawcross, cross-examining, quoted from reviews of *Why I'm Not a Millionaire*, which, he said, revealed Nancy as 'a friendly, warm-hearted person'. One of the reviews was from Gilbert Harding in the *Evening Standard*.

> 'Perhaps you do not approve of him?' he asked Waugh.
> Waugh did not reply.
> 'No, I thought you would not,' quipped Shawcross.[32]

Moving on quickly to press home his advantage, he flustered Waugh by asking him if he took himself a bit too seriously, which Waugh, with difficulty, had to answer in the negative without sounding as though he did precisely that. He did testify, however, that he 'was not so much annoyed with Miss Spain as with Lord Noel-Buxton', whose remark about being a member of the House of Lords seemed to show him as 'an extremely ridiculous person'.[33]

Waughs were summoned from far and wide to come to the aid of the cause: Laura Waugh made a brief appearance in the witness box, giving her version of events at Piers Court on the 21st; while Alec Waugh came from Tangier to give what proved to be crucial evidence on the relative importance of first-edition sales of books. Alec's answer implied that a book might go into seven or eight reprints without outselling a book that had fewer editions, since a 'reprint' might not involve the same number of books as the first edition.

The case for the defence was crumbling, and was not helped when Shawcross had to leave the court urgently 'for personal reasons' (his mother-in-law had been involved in a serious car accident). Milmo reassured the court that he would be back the next day, adding that he considered the jury 'would have heard sufficient of the case to feel that they were there about precious little, and that the whole matter was very much a storm in a teacup'.[34]

Milmo then moved on to the matter of Nancy's counter-claim, claiming that Waugh's *Spectator* article 'could only mean that the "Daily Express" critic was a person who had no influence at all'.[35]

Then it was Nancy's turn to take the stand. Lady Frankie Donaldson gleefully noted: 'The afternoon of the first day passed with Miss Spain in the witness box denying hour after hour the undeniable'.[36] She wasn't far wrong.

Nancy began by expressing her admiration for Waugh's books, particularly the early works, which she thought were 'simply brilliant'. She continued that Waugh 'was probably one of the greatest living English writers . . . probably the only one who would be thought of in 40–50 years' time'.[37] She explained that she thought Waugh had been referring to her in his *Spectator* piece and that her subsequent *Express* article was in reply to this, and not a result of any personal dislike of Waugh himself. Things went downhill from there on:

> Gardiner: 'Is it your view that a "Daily Express" reporter can go on anyone else's property whether he has a right to or not?'
> Nancy: 'A reporter's function is to do his best to get a story.'

She then made the mistake of trying to play for the jury's sympathy by explaining, in mitigation, that she had had nothing to eat all day except an oatcake at John Masefield's and that Waugh had not so much as offered them a drink after their long drive. She agreed that there had been 'discrepancies' in the offending article and that she had not 'taken any steps before the article was published to ascertain whether it was true or not'. The cross-examination continued:

> Gardiner: 'Have you ever discussed Mr Evelyn Waugh with Lord Beaverbrook?'
> Nancy: 'No.'
> Gardiner: 'Did not Lord Beaverbrook tell you that Mr Evelyn Waugh was very jealous of his brother?'
> Nancy: 'No, certainly not.'
> Gardiner: 'In your book you say you love Lord Beaverbrook.'
> Nancy: 'Yes.'
> Gardiner: 'He does not like Mr Evelyn Waugh, does he?'
> Nancy: 'I have no idea.'[38]

With this testimony, Nancy had, to use Waugh's words, 'lied sturdily on oath'. It was not one of her finest moments.

The sole witness in support of her counter-claim was the redoubtable Leonard Russell, who appeared at the end of the first day's hearing to say that he believed Waugh's *Spectator* article had indeed referred to Nancy.

The next day, matters were quickly brought to a close. Milmo, in conclusion, said that it was Waugh who had started the 'pen war' with the *Spectator* article and that Nancy was doing no more than defending herself against an allegation that she had no influence as a book critic. 'Mr Waugh has decided to come into this arena and since he has we will meet him here. If he gets a bloody nose in the scrap it is his own fault'.[39] Gardiner summed up:

> I am not making any sort of imputation on Miss Spain as a writer. Her articles are most cleverly written and amusing and it may well be that as a result of this case she will receive a higher post in the Beaverbrook organization. She has certainly followed her master's footsteps.[40]

Justice Stable told the jury they 'were not here to decide whether Miss Spain was ill-mannered or impudent, or whether Mr Waugh was inhospitable or ill-tempered'.[41] They were to decide whether Waugh's article reflected discreditably on her and, if so, she should be compensated accordingly. They then had to decide whether her subsequent article was defamatory of Waugh, and whether 'any intelligent person' reading the relevant paragraph would have formed an adverse opinion of him. If so, he was entitled to appropriate compensation.

After nearly two hours' deliberation, the jury delivered their verdict: it was in favour of Waugh, who was to be awarded £2,000 damages; furthermore, Nancy's counter-claim was dismissed. Despite this, she was able to behave, as Waugh thought, 'in a gentlemanly fashion', shaking his hand and telling him 'the better man won'. He responded in similar fashion by sending her a bottle of champagne. But he hadn't finished yet.

On 4 April, the two legal teams were back in court again, this time in front of Mr Justice Glyn-Jones, to settle Waugh's suit against Beaverbrook Newspapers Ltd. and Anthony Hern, literary editor of the *Daily Express*. On 16 October 1956, an article by Hern had appeared in the paper, headlined 'Rebecca West Attacks Evelyn Waugh'; Graham Greene was also targeted in the piece, which was based around the 1956 reissue of West's *The Meaning of Treason*. Under a photograph of Waugh ran a caption quote from the book: 'They [Waugh and Greene] have created a climate of crash-brained confusion between virtues and vices ... a climate in which the traitor flourishes'. Hern commented that 'This is the most devastating exposure of the essence of treachery yet made. . . . For years, Mr Evelyn Waugh has been implying that the worthless and dissolute are more worthy than people who are in fact worthy and who keep sober'.[42] Waugh took this libel more seriously because he was a Catholic, his counsel said.

Incredibly, before the case had come to court, but after Waugh had filed suit, Nancy reviewed West's book in the *Express*, quoting the very comments over which Waugh was suing for libel. The ease with which some of the *Express* reporters made such embarrassing mistakes was matched only by the slackness of the paper's lawyers in allowing such blunders to slip past them unnoticed.

Thus, Waugh took on Express Newspapers for the second time in six weeks; this time, they did not contest the suit, made a public apology and settled out of court for £3,000 plus legal costs. Waugh received gratuitously unpleasant congratulatory telegrams from Anthony Powell ('Congratulations on Burning Sappho') and Graham Greene ('Congratulations on Singeing Spain's Whiskers').[43]

Singed 'Spain' certainly was and there were some within the *Express* who, after this embarrassing and costly incident, would have happily inflicted worse damage on her, as Sir Edward Pickering reveals:

> 'There were some people, executives, in the organization, who didn't like her and so blamed her for the whole thing. But, these things happen and finally it's the editor's responsibility to say yes or no. Nancy certainly suffered quite a bit during it all – she didn't enjoy the experience or the result. But when it was all over, she got a lot of support from the office and from Lord Beaverbrook as well. Many felt that although he [Waugh] had won, it was a pretty difficult case and might easily have gone the other way'.

Julian Critchley agreed. He told Tom Blackburn, 'Although Nancy Spain's paragraph was full of mistakes our lawyers did not think action would succeed . . . Nancy gave evidence and did extremely well'.[44]

Others, too, were aware that her 'gentlemanly' acceptance of the verdict concealed rather different feelings, as Roger Storey explains:

> 'Everyone thought Nancy was as tough as nails, because she acted like that and she was a courageous, brave woman. Beaverbrook was wholly capable of using anyone, though he was a very good friend and Nancy adored him. But he was utterly ruthless – you don't get where he did if you're not. But I'm damn sure he used Nancy then. Everybody thought, "Oh larky old Spain, she'll come through this; whether she smells of roses or not, she won't give a damn". But she gave a damn about a lot of things . . . '.

Only the year before Nancy had told her *Woman's Hour* audience, 'If I do anything wrong, I'm destroyed. There's a great fault – I am terribly indiscreet . . . but I really don't mean to do any harm. . . . The only thing that matters is telling the truth, isn't it?'[45] There is no reason to believe that she didn't mean the things she said during that broadcast. Indeed, during her dealings with Evelyn Waugh, she had done something wrong, displaying a lack of discretion that harmed herself and the paper and proprietor she loved dearly. But, most importantly, while she was in the witness stand, she had ignored the 'thing that matters' – she had not told the truth. And the pain for Spain was that she had only herself to blame.

Nancy and Joan dined with Beaverbrook towards the end of May, shortly after his birthday. As usual, he had sent her a cash present to mark the occasion; she used it to purchase some more Beaverbrook shares. During the course of the evening, he sought to reassure her regarding her position at the *Express* and of his faith in her and her work. She was not ungrateful:

> You who understand women so well will know how full my heart is this morning and how all my energies will be directed in the future to serve you. I have been a little bewildered lately but this morning I woke for the first time

for a long time feeling complete again. And I know that is something for which I should thank you alone.[46]

She soon had another reason to feel bewildered, courtesy of Miss Tallulah Bankhead. In May, the great actress arrived in London to do a six-week cabaret season at the Café de Paris. Unfortunately, both star and venue were past their best and, for most of the season, Bankhead played to only half-capacity audiences. However, Nancy still knew a real star when she saw one and interviewed Bankhead at the Ritz. It was to be published prior to the first night. 'Although she is as dated as Michael Arlen's "Green Hat" she is about to be the smartest woman in town',[47] declared Nancy. During the interview, Bankhead castigated the press: 'I would like you to know that everything everybody says about me in the newspapers is a lot of mis-quotations'.[48]

Nancy was due to attend Bankhead's press conference held at the Ritz. Gilbert Harding had also been invited, but opted out and suggested Roger Storey go instead. Another of Bankhead's friends, Gerald Hamilton, arrived at the Ritz for the press conference, where he was passed by a flustered Nancy heading for the exit, muttering 'I can't stop!' According to Roger Storey, Nancy had rung Bankhead on the day of the press conference, to arrange to show her the article she had written, before publication. Bank-head agreed and Nancy went up to her room. Roger Storey relates what happened next:

'There was this big arrangement of gladioli, and this came crashing in Nancy's direction. She had to flee to her car. She was so upset she drove it into one of the columns outside the Ritz. Of course, she made wonderful stories out of these things, but it mattered to her. Taking it to Tallulah Bankhead was quite a gesture – she didn't have to do it, but she admired the woman enormously and was upset that she'd upset her, particularly over something which seemed so trivial'.

However, Gerald Hamilton's sympathies lay with Bankhead and, when she told him what had happened, he recited a poem he felt appropriate for the occasion:

Sink me the ship, Master Gunner –
sink her, split her in twain
Fall into the hands of God,
not into the hands of Spain![49]

Nancy bounced back from the Bankhead experience, full of ideas to inject some new life into the books page. Instead of merely filling it with review after review, she interwove them with big-name mini-interviews and gossip. She launched it with stories about Jack Benny, Cole Porter and Maurice Chevalier, to tie in with the publication of the French crooner's latest autobiography. Nancy wrote to Beaverbrook about the new format:

I expect you will have noticed that the 'Daily Mail' is already making an attempt to copy the new-style book column. My own feeling is that they haven't quite understood why I did it. The books in August are really so awful as a rule that one must surround them with gossip to pull them through. Do you think I ought to go back to the old-style column again, though, once the dog days are over? Collecting gossip is rather a different business from straight reviewing and might become rather tiring . . . [50]

Though Beaverbrook approved of the new approach to the books page, he felt 'it should not be a permanency. But there is no reason why you should not revert to it from time to time'.[51] Nonetheless, he continued to express his support for her, making sure that her best efforts did not go unnoticed: 'An excellent article in the *Daily Express* of Saturday August 3. Admirably done. Lively. Picturesque. And with punch'.[52] Nancy's other bosses at the *Express* were also keen to sing her praises very publicly during the post-Waugh months. They flagged her as 'The Writer Who's a Book Critic Plus!'[53] and promoted 'The Nancy Spain touch – into the world of books the inimitable approach . . . '.[54]

Another series of *These Foolish Things* was scheduled for the early summer, but the producers felt that, although it was Nancy's idea, they did not want to be dragooned into including her in every programme. 'In the past we have always included her in the panel as recognition of the fact that the programme was her idea', Pat Dixon told the contracts department. 'This, however, is rather limiting to the selection of the panel but at the same time I do not feel that we can legitimately drop her out of any programmes while still using her idea unless she is compensated'.[55] Thus Nancy was offered – and accepted – a royalty for each programme, supplementary to any appearance fee. Additionally, each broadcast continued to be announced by the chairman, and was billed in the *Radio Times*, as 'Based on an idea by Nancy Spain'.

Shortly after the conclusion of the Waugh case, the books page ran a headline: 'The Fastest Woman I Know'.[56] This referred to a review of a book of memoirs called *No Excuses*, written by the woman who had, almost by accident, become Britain's top racing driver – Sheila van Damm. Neither the paper nor Nancy were unfamiliar with the author: eighteen months earlier, the *Express* had run a series of pre-publication extracts from the book. But what was more important was that Sheila van Damm had become – although no one is sure exactly when – part of the 'immediate family'.

Since the 1930s, the name van Damm had been synonymous with London's famous Windmill Theatre, where the careers of the cream of postwar British comedians had begun. Peter Sellers, Jimmy Edwards, Tony Hancock, Harry Secombe and Michael Bentine all trod the Windmill's boards, providing the jokes between what most of the theatre's punters had come to see: the chorus-lines of 'Windmill girls' and, eventually, its nude tableaux. All this took place under the management of Vivian van Damm. Sheila was the youngest of his three daughters, born in London in 1922. At seventeen, she became the Windmill's publicity manager. In 1942, she was conscripted into the WAAF, working as a driver for senior officers at RAF Stanmore. She was demobbed in June 1946 and returned to work for her father but, within weeks, left after a blazing row. Vivian suggested that, as he wanted to start a private charter airline, she, Sheila, should learn how to fly. After about a hundred hours of private tuition, she joined the RAF Volunteer Reserve and became a pilot officer.

In November 1951, the *Daily Express* was holding a 1,200-mile 48-hour non-stop national car rally and Vivian persuaded her to enter, as a publicity stunt for the Windmill. She drove a Sunbeam Talbot for the Rootes Group, with the words 'Windmill Girl' painted on the side. Her sister, Nona, was co-driver – it was to be the only time she would partner Sheila who, by her own admission, spent most of the forty-eight hours shouting at her. Despite this (or perhaps because of it?) they ended up winning the third prize in the women's section. Sheila also learned the two basic rules for surviving rallies: 'Never overdo the pep pills; and never lend anything to anyone . . . '.[57] In January 1951, she was asked by Mrs Elsie Wisdom to join the all-woman crew, driving a Hillman Minx in the Monte Carlo Rally. Not long after this, she took the women's prize in the RAC Rally, driving her own Hillman. From then on, she regularly drove for Rootes: she won first prize in the women's section of the 1952 MCC Club Rally and, in 1953, she drove with Anne Hall in the Alpine Rally, winning the Coupe des Dames and a coveted Coupe des Alpes for finishing the perilous course without any loss of marks.

Success followed success: she won another Coupe des Dames at Zandvoort in the 1954 Tulip Rally and the ladies' prize at the Viking Rally in Norway, completing a triumphant year by clinching the Ladies' European Touring Championship. The following year, she eclipsed even this achievement by winning the Coupe des Dames in the Monte Carlo Rally and, later that year, won the Women's European Touring Championship, again with Anne Hall. After an unsuccessful attempt to defend her Monte Carlo title in 1956, Sheila gave up rally driving and switched to motor racing. She drove a Sunbeam Rapier in the gruelling Mille Miglia, a 1,000-mile race round twisting, turning Italian roads, and won her class.

On the face of it, the stockily built Sheila van Damm would have seemed the perfect chum for Nancy, whose rich, fruity-accented voice closely resembled her own. 'Good-humoured, self-confident, she gives away her precious vitality to everyone she meets',[58] declared Nancy. In many ways, it could almost have been a self-description. But it was with reserved, wary Joan that Sheila's affections would lie and, by 1957, she was part of the family.

That year, Nancy and Joan joined her in Italy when she made another attempt on the Mille Miglia. Sheila's mother, Natalie, also went along and the trip became the subject of a four-page spread in *She*, penned by Joan. The race was marred by the death of one of the drivers, de Portago, but Joan still came away believing 'that racing, and road-racing in particular, does more to improve our transport than any research laboratory ever can'.[59] Nancy, however, was not enthusiastic: 'The Miglia is not for me. I don't care for death at such close quarters. I like life, lots and lots of it'.[60]

Sheila van Damm was one of a very small group of people who, during the late 1950s and early 1960s, were considered by Nancy and Joan as 'one of the family', as part of their inner circle – 'a little nucleus of about half a dozen people', according to Nick Laurie. They included Ginette Spanier and two men who, unusually, even found favour with Joan: Roy Ruther-ford – also known as 'Rutterford' – and Australian-born DJ, Alan Freeman, who had arrived in England in 1957.

Nancy met Freeman when she started appearing on *Juke Box Jury* and he was subsequently interviewed for *She*. Nick can remember his first visit to Clareville Grove:

'Nancy brought him back for Sunday lunch. My mother went into a sort of rage – she didn't want strange people coming into the house. But they became very, very close and she shared a lot of secrets with him . . . For about four years, I don't think Alan missed a Sunday lunch with us. He was great fun. He and my mother used to call each other "Bro" and "Sis". He was really unaffected by other people's fame and glamour, and my mother was the same'.

Or, as Nancy put it, 'My partner Jonnie . . . is as allergic to celebrity as some people to shellfish'.[61]

Freeman recalls this time fondly:

'I got to know all the family. We had quite a few times together – picnics and things. Nancy was always wonderful company – Joan was quieter and Nancy was more flamboyant. While she was a very superior lady, she had the common touch. There was no side with either of them: it was "what you see is what you get", and the honesty was just something to feel very secure about'.

And, their other relationships notwithstanding, Freeman has no doubts about the security and commitment of Nancy and Joan's partnership:

'I always thought it was a very happy relationship – I never saw them behave in any other manner other than it was a very good solid relationship. Tom and Nick loved Nancy. There was a lot of love flowed between them all and it was nice to share that atmosphere. You felt that the moment you got together with them, you were part of the family. Nancy used to send me up something rotten; I sent her up rotten and we'd laugh and giggle, but it was very much family. I'm a better person for knowing them, even for a short time. All they showed to me was kindness. So I'm very proud and happy to have counted them among my friends'.

By all accounts, Roy Rutherford was a truly colourful character. Accord-ing to Nick Laurie, he was 'a very intimate friend of the family – and an absolute riot to visit'. A former merchant seaman, advertising executive and interior decorator, Rutherford was a friend of Joan and Dick Laurie's half-sister, Betty Butterworth. According to Dick, he had once asked Betty to enter into a marriage of convenience with him because he wanted to open a brothel in Delhi and needed some veneer of 'respectability'. 'He was general manager for J. Walter Thompson in Delhi just after the war', explains Dick Laurie, 'and thought a brothel would be much more profit-able. He sent her a cable that said "Must marry you immediately. Come at once"'. She declined. Eventually, Rutherford opened the Hotel Cecil in Tangier, a gay brothel, and, later still, a small hotel in the South of France, where he also had a house for a time.

Although he knew the Lauries first, it was with Nancy that Roy would have most of his adventures. 'They were very good friends', says Dick Laurie. 'They used to go away together on what I would imagine were probably rather louche holidays'. Rutherford's friend, Frank Ellul, remembers that Roy and Nancy were 'inseparable – they did everything together'.

When Roy opened The Eyebrow in 1962, a bistro-style restaurant off the Fulham Road, Nancy plugged it at every opportunity. (Nick Laurie even worked there for a while as a washer-up.) She also took many of her newer showbusiness friends and acquaintances there, including Dietrich, to give it a classy profile. It worked: the most beautiful of the 1960s people were soon passing through its doors, including the Rolling Stones, Nureyev and David Hockney, who used to sketch on the paper tablecloths. Unfortunately, no one bothered to keep them.

Though Nancy was not estranged from her parents or sister, they did not feature in her London 'family'. Nick Laurie thinks that there was 'a certain kind of tension' between Liz and Nancy. 'Liz married a Sir and people who marry Sirs didn't like Nancy's way of life. She thought Nancy was letting the side down, writing for magazines and being on television. I didn't like her at all'.

The Spain–Laurie extended family functioned efficiently and happily, for the most part. But, according to its youngest member, Tom, its inner and outer warmth was down to Nancy:

> 'I respected Jonnie; I liked her occasionally. Jonnie was the organization person, the brains behind the outfit. If Nancy wanted to do something really spectacular, it would be Jonnie that would argue the pros and cons – do the staff work, so to speak. I liked her, that she would enter into the spirit of the things, but not as totally as Nancy would. Usually, she would hold back a little bit. Whereas Nancy was really the life and soul of the party'.

Dick Laurie agrees:

> 'Jonnie was very good to my mother. She was diabetic and she [Jonnie] would ring her from the office four times a day, to make sure she'd taken her injections. She was very good at that sort of thing – she used to ring Nick up regularly at school and see what he wanted and how he was'.

Nick, however, denies this.

Joan's reputation as an editor, meanwhile, was going from strength to strength, as *She* grew in stature. 'I was very thrilled for her when the American directors congratulated her on the rising sales', Nancy proudly told Beaverbrook. 'Hers is the only magazine in the Group going up'.[62]

The magazine was continuing to set new standards for taboo-breaking, running features on 'Life After Death', 'Unmarried Mothers', 'Epilepsy' and 'Jury Service'. Home and health features covered subjects like yoga and DIY furniture. Kenneth Horne took over from Gilbert Harding as the new man who 'Criticizes SHE'. Nancy weighed in with features on Rock Hudson, Ronnie Hilton and Richard Avedon, who took some photographs of a relaxed, clowning Nancy in the Bois du Boulogne to accompany her feature on 'The £1,000 Charmer'.[63]

In late September, she and Joan went to Cannes for another holiday. She had just turned forty but, she told Beaverbrook, 'I think I am going to stay 39 for quite a long while'.[64] In Cannes, Joan decided she wanted to hire a cutter and sail to some of the other resorts along the Côte d'Azur for a few days. Despite her seasickness, Nancy went along with the idea, though she must have had second thoughts when she saw the name of their boat: the *Evelyn*. Their charter cost them £15 a day, which included food, wine and a two-man crew. On the first day, they sailed to Villefranche-sur-Mer, where they dined at dusk. The next day, they headed for Monte Carlo, where rougher seas sent a suffering Nancy to the bottom of the boat. Joan was luckier: she won a 100-franc jackpot at a local casino. On the way back to Cannes, flushed with success, she told Nancy of a way to cure her seasickness. 'You keep fighting the boat', she announced. 'Wedge yourself somewhere and not move – you are part of the boat and ride it like a horse'.[65] Unfortunately, Nancy's reply to this smug deliberation is not on record.

Shortly after their return, Nancy decided to rent a furnished house in Brighton, at 10 Wentworth Street, so that she could concentrate on a new book she had just begun. This time eschewing the crime genre, it was, apparently, 'a novel about a young woman's infidelities. It is called "O, Rose" ... '.[66] 'I find that writing something of "my own" gives me a little stability of mind. So I do hope you don't disapprove',[67] she told Beaverbrook.

She rounded off her year's work for the *Express* by taking a look back at 'My Cockeyed Year'. 'I spent a lot of the year in Paris',[68] she revealed – without saying why, naturally.

CHAPTER TEN

Ace Newshound

At the turn of the year, Nancy wrote to thank Beaverbrook for his customary Christmas present:

> 1957 was a turbulent year for me, in many ways, as you know, and I look forward to 1958 I hope with courage. I expect you will smile when I confess how much older I feel ... I want to thank you for being my boss. I really cannot imagine what I should do without you. I only wish you were able to live in England more so that the inspiration were more direct.[1]

As life grew busier, she took steps to ensure there was less turbulence in some aspects of her work. Spain and Laurie (Exploitations) Ltd. had been established at the beginning of 1957 and, for tax purposes, all her fees were paid into the company account. Her radio and television appearances were now becoming so numerous and wide-ranging that she needed an agent to handle them all properly. She employed one of the very best: Kavanagh Productions based in Regent Street, the company headed by Ted Kavanagh, creator of *My Word* and *ITMA*. Nancy's agent was April Young, who was married to the comedian Peter Glaze, and who also represented Frank Muir and Denis Norden. Young and Nancy enjoyed a happy professional relationship, which lasted until Nancy's death. Most of their dealings were done by telephone, though Young did attended some of Nancy's recordings and there was also, of course, the odd lunch at Wheeler's. Handling her magazine work was Ernest Hecht, the Czech-born publisher who had founded Souvenir Press and Euro-Features Ltd. – 'sharp, lean, passionate for football and gay with all his success',[2] according to Nancy.

Legal matters, including her later book contracts, were handled by David Jacobs, the outrageous showbusiness lawyer whose list of clientele read like every Hollywood PR's A-list: Judy Garland, Liberace, Laurence Olivier, Marlene Dietrich and Shirley Bassey. He represented some of them in libel suits, including Liberace's infamous case against the *Mirror*. Lord Beaverbrook himself is alleged to have said once that he 'would rather have Jacobs on his side than against him any time'.[3] Jacobs's father was Albert Jacobs, whose family owned Times Furnishing and Willerby's the tailors. Young David had studied law at Cambridge and, in the Second World War, joined the Royal Artillery. After the war, he set up his own law firm, specializing in arts and entertainment. He treated his clients as friends, often inviting them to lavish parties at his homes in Chelsea and Hove. He also entertained at the Caprice, where he had a table on permanent reservation. Tall, elegant and always exquisitely dressed, Jacobs raised eyebrows in the courtrooms he frequented by complementing his Savile Row suits with full make-up. In many ways, he was the perfect lawyer for Nancy who, tongue-in-cheek, profiled him in *She* as the 'Most eligible lawyer'.[4]

Within a few weeks of the New Year, Nancy's profile in the *Express* changed. In February, the paper announced the beginning of a new series of features: 'Week End with Nancy' – 'When Nancy Spain goes off for the weekend, be sure the people she meets will be both stimulating and provocative'.[5] It seemed to be an ideal solution for all parties: the new series gave her a chance to concentrate on people, rather than books; it gave her editors a chance to ease her out of the book critic's chair – a little too small and upright for her in any case – and it offered the readers a voyeuristic peek into the glamorous worlds they longed to be part of. 'It might be a grand country house . . . it might be April in Portugal . . . it might be New York or just at home with The Goons',[6] they learned.

To begin with, though, it was Paris. Nancy wrote about Marlene Dietrich's double role in her new movie, *Witness for the Prosecution*, which had just opened. Also that weekend, she and Ginette went to see the first night of the new Zizi Jeanmaire/Roland Petit ballet at the Alhambra. She borrowed a Balmain dress and panther coat for the occasion and, later, wrote a piece about the evening, sprinkled with snippets of conversation from Jean Cocteau, his partner Jean Marais and Lady Diana Cooper. It was followed by another piece about the weekend, that included a discussion of a book written by Resistance hero Picquet Wicks and a description of her meeting with Yul Brynner and Melina Mercouri.

The next week, she was in Rome, to meet up with Fiore de Henriques, the cigar-smoking, trouser-wearing sculptor she had first profiled in *Good Housekeeping*. It was accompanied by a hilarious photograph of two trouser-wearing women tossing each other a sculpted head of Vivien Leigh. While in Rome, she also went to a party given by Judy Montagu, a friend of Princess Margaret's.

A few weeks later, after a holiday in Tangier with Roy Rutherford, she flew to a snowbound New York to meet Frankie Vaughan, whose career was starting to take off. Nancy also wrote a profile of Richard Avedon who had taken the accompanying photograph of Vaughan. Later, they went to the Forum restaurant and then to a party given by Gloria Vanderbilt.

Occasionally, her weekends were slightly less glamorous. In April, she went on the buses with Bridie Palmer, a bus conductor, learning to be a conductor on the No. 2 route from Golders Green to Crystal Palace. She did not enjoy the experience: 'If Bridie Palmer was going to strike in May for more pay I would understand why',[7] she declared. The following day, she went to Brighton to take part in a special edition of *The Brains Trust* at the Corn Exchange, in aid of the Brighton Girls' Club. Also on the panel were Gilbert Harding, Alan Melville and Godfrey Winn, all residents of Brighton; the chair was Lord Rupert Nevill. Almost inevitably, one of the questions they tackled was whether women should wear trousers or not. According to Nancy, Melville and Winn were rude about her attire. In reply, she said she felt 'more secure in trousers' and then 'stood up on my seat as a sort of revolving model to prove their point. Gilbert suddenly got very cross indeed and sent me a note saying "DO behave"'.[8] After the game finished, everyone went back to David Jacobs's house in Hove where, Nancy observed, Robin Maugham 'and 22 other young men sat about in dinner jackets eating smoked salmon and caviar and truffles and paté de foie gras', adding, for the benefit of those who would know what she meant, '(Yes, this sort of thing goes on in Brighton all the time.)'[9]

By now, Nancy had become so busy with her feature work that she had abandoned trying to write 'O Rose' and given up the rented house in Brighton. Joan's attention, meanwhile, was focused on another typical Laurie dare. 'She is practising hard to be a motor rally driver and hopes to drive in the Tulip Rally next week. I think she may do well in spite of being a beginner', she told Beaverbrook.[10] Sheila van Damm was her co-driver for the first half of the race, and was then replaced by a young trials driver, Daphne Freeman. In their VRW 502 Sunbeam Rapier, Joan and Daphne came eighth in their class of sixteen, and seventy-eighth overall. Only 95 out of the 240 starters finished the rally. Nancy joined Joan and Sheila in Switzerland and wrote about her rallying experience in 'Nancy Goes Round the Bend!' On 'Her Craziest Week-End Yet',[11] she went climbing with Jack Longland on the Windgather Crags in Derbyshire.

This sort of 'stunt' journalism was immensely popular in the British press of the 1950s and 1960s. It was, however, an unusual line of work for British women journalists, although it had been pioneered by a young American female writer. In 1912, Djuna Barnes, then aged twenty, was working as a reporter for the *Brooklyn Eagle*, producing pieces of classic 'stunt' reportage. She got into a female gorilla's cage, was rescued by firefighters from the top of a skyscraper and underwent forced feeding in order to write about the plight of the English suffragettes in prison. Nancy's work for the *Express* – and subsequent similar assignments for the *News of the World* – were generally light in tone. The hard news was left to the boys on the packed front page and special correspondents like Rene MacColl, while Nancy and similar columnists provided the frothy, frivolous fun for the paper's middle pages. She was also using 'stunt'-orientated material for her radio work. For *Woman's Hour*, for instance, she spoke about her experience of launching a crane in Dagenham Docks, where she was made a member of the Crane Drivers' Club, and about a day spent at a gliding club, in 'Moments of Fear'. And the crossover was complete when she started doing similar work in *She*. For the magazine's third birthday, Joan sent her off to Simon's Beauty Salon in Basil Street, where she underwent treatments for bags around the eyes, involving carbonated air and electricity.

But her main work for *She* at this time consisted of a series of articles about the Royal Family, notably the social circle of Princess Margaret, of which she herself was now becoming a peripheral member. 'I think Margaret the greatest of the crown jewels', she gushed. 'And those who enjoy her favour are happy indeed'.[12] She spoke to the Princess's more conventional society friends first, breaking a taboo which said that 'A real friend of Princess Margaret is one who never discusses her'.[13] These friends needed to earn at least £6,000 a year, said Nancy, come from a well-established family, be witty and 'a little bit in love with life itself'.[14] They included Mark Bonham-Carter, Lord Porchester, the Marquess of Blandford, Colin Tennant and Lord Rupert Nevill. 'Princess Margaret's Unusual Playmates' included Danny Kaye, Joyce Grenfell and Nancy's head-throwing chum, Fiore de Henriquez. But Nancy's Royal exposés did not find favour with all *She* readers. One from Tottenham said they were 'so disgusted by Nancy Spain's breaking of the "taboo", finding it such distasteful reading'.[15]

These articles, however, were the perfect foil for the intensely practical, tomboyish features found elsewhere in the magazine: women and motorcycling, women MPs, heart operations, halitosis, marriage breakups, 'How To Be a Police Woman', 'Women Who Get Tattooed', 'Make Your Own Pottery', 'Is a Jewish Wedding Different?', 'Women at the Trigger' and consumer surveys, such as '*She* Tests a Scooter'. For two months, a DMW Bambi scooter was tested by various staff members, including Joan. Outside opinion came from Nancy and Sheila van Damm, who liked it but said she would stick to her 99 m.p.h. Sunbeam Rapier. Nancy was photographed in pain, after she was caught on the ankle by the kickpedal. Joan, naturally, had no such problems and was 'most reluctant to part with Bambi for others to test . . .'.[16]

As well as the lighthearted stories, there was also a discernible political edge creeping into some of the picture spreads. A photograph of an American soldier guarding nuclear warheads was captioned, 'Is this what our peace depends on now we are civilized?'[17] Another showed Ku Klux Klan members with the comment, 'What a picture of 20th-century civilization!'[18] *She* also reported on the opening of Winnie's Salon in Railton Road, Brixton, owned by Winifred Atwell, which was the first beauty salon specifically for black women.

In May, Nancy became the 'Woman of Britain' – at least, for one day. She was also booked to appear as herself, on a fictitious panel game, in a new BBC sitcom called *Trouble for Two*. Starring Jacqueline Mackenzie (also its co-writer) and Lorrae Desmond, it was a 'bachelor girl' comedy series about two women involved in showbusiness who share a flat and employ a cleaner, Humphrey (played by the late Donald Churchill). It was considered to be somewhat ahead of its time and was scrapped after only four weeks. Nancy was its first celebrity guest.

Now better known as Jackie Forster, the then Jacqueline Mackenzie was no stranger to fame herself. She had, of course, done a stint as one of the investigators on *Harding Finds Out*. Then she mimed her way into the limelight in 1955, with her four-minute appearances on the BBC series, *Highlight*. She grimaced, pouted and frowned her way through impressions of rugby and boxing matches, art exhibitions, even the Motor Show. But there were other, more substantial, contributions to *Highlight*, including her award-winning coverage of the wedding of Prince Rainier and Grace Kelly in Monaco in 1956. She also commentated on other, more parochial, events, such as the Ideal Home Exhibition, the Chelsea Flower Show, Chipperfield's Circus and the Henley Regatta. In many ways, her work for the programme mirrored what Nancy was doing in newspapers, magazines and on radio: a personality imparting their subjective views on events, journeys and places. She even branched out into one area that Nancy steered clear of – politics. In March 1958, it was revealed that the 'rubber-faced mimic . . . married two weeks and just back from a Paris honeymoon'[19] was to stand as Liberal parliamentary candidate for Cheltenham.

It was her husband, Peter Forster, who first met Nancy, by way of *Woman's Hour*: like her, he was a frequent and popular contributor to the programme. Jackie Forster also encountered Nancy during her stint on *Gilbert Harding Finds Out*:

> 'He threw this party for Marlene, and there was Nancy, Joan and Marlene, all in this tight little group. A lot of people were saying, "Who's that with Nancy?" "Oh, *that's* Joan Werner Laurie . . . ''. There was an acceptance that they were an item, but they were rarely seen together. Of course, I didn't have a clue what was going on – I was straighter than the Fosse Way at the time! They were just people in their own right. Whenever Nancy was present, there was never any mention of lesbianism, or "nudge-nudge, there's a lesbian" – she was "Nancy Spain". There was a tremendous sensitivity; she was very female despite her, what we'd call now, very butch image'.

The Forsters saw more of Nancy after her appearance on the ill-fated *Trouble for Two*. 'She came to dinner a great deal', recalls Jackie Forster, who has particularly fond memories of the first occasion:

> 'We had James Robertson Justice, Francis Day, Alan Brown and his then girlfriend Nancy Ryan. It was an evening of enchantment – they all mixed wonderfully well. The laughter and the wit and the scandal flying round . . . the next time, she invited Peter and me to a wonderful restaurant on the Fulham Rd. At one point, Nancy suddenly did the most brilliant version of Hetty King – we had been talking about her – and she just stood up and did it. It was the most brilliant performance: you could see this sailor's bag and her walk – and the whole restaurant applauded. And she was quite overwhelmed. All these diners saw this crazy woman and they knew it was Hetty King. And that was so *her*'.

And, despite her increasingly heavy workload, Nancy was enjoying herself with other chums, too. Accompanied by Sandy Wilson, she attended the launch party of Beverley Nichols's new book, *The Sweet and Twenties*, held at the North Audley Street home of Lady Aberconway on 14 May. However, they found the whole affair rather boring and the 'Twenties' atmosphere rather artificial, and went for dinner at the Ivy instead.

Nancy and Wilson shared another dinner that year, during the West End run of his musical *Valmouth*, based on Ronald Firbank's 1919 novel. According to Wilson:

11. Nancy snaps Joan in Jamaica with some local fruits.
Dick Laurie collection

12. 'Lady of Spain, I Adore You': Nancy and Gilbert fuel the rumours.
Roger Storey collection

13. 'The Editor'.
Dick Laurie collection

14. Joan in Clareville Grove
with Nick (right) and Tom.
Dick Laurie collection

15. Alan Freeman joins the family.
Dick Laurie collection

16. Sheila van Damm and Joan doing 'butch boysy stuff' – this time in Llandudno.
Dick Laurie collection

17. Nancy and Madame Directrice, Ginette Spanier.
Copyright: Nick Werner Laurie

18. A trouser-wearing character and her Hillman relax outside
Clareville Grove.
Courtesy of the National Portrait Gallery, London

19. Nancy picks the hits and misses on *Juke Box Jury*.
Courtesy of News International

20. 21 March 1964: 'And still there were cabbages in that awful field'.
Courtesy of News International

'It caused quite a sensation at the time, one way or another. In one scene, there's a dippy country girl who's madly in love with the son and heir of the lady of the manor. He's a naval officer overseas, and she goes down to the river and sings a song, because she thinks the river is going out to sea to join him. And the director said it would be fun if she got into the river, wrung out her skirt and found a fish in it – and sings the number to the fish. So Tony Walton, the designer, made an imitation fish, which was rubbery and wriggled'.

All went well, until Princess Margaret attended a performance. A member of the audience subsequently wrote to the *Daily Express*, outraged that this scene should have taken place in front of the Princess. 'As a result, they sent the Lord Chamberlain back to see the show', remembers Wilson, 'and he said the fish could remain but it mustn't be alive – which I thought was horrible, because now she was doing the song to a dead fish'. Wilson got Nancy tickets for the show and, when he met her for dinner afterwards, had one question on his mind. 'I said to her, "What's the fuss about the fish?" She said, "Don't you realize? A fish is one of the oldest phallic symbols in the world!" And I had no idea – none of us did . . . '.

By now, *Express* readers were no longer being given the opportunity to share a 'Week End With Nancy'. She was spending many of them in Paris, visiting Ginette and gathering gossip for *She*. However, outside of that elite existence, France was in turmoil. 'France is facing civil war',[20] warned the *Express*, in one of the reports about the crisis that was subject to French censorship. A general strike was threatened and Gaullist rebels in Algiers were planning a coup that would start in Nice.

But the closest Nancy got to tackling French current affairs at this time was to review the *Dictionnaire du Snobisme*, edited by Philippe Jullian. It was, of course, a subject she had rather strong feelings about. 'Everyone is a snob', she declared. 'There are all sorts of snobs'.[21] She was promptly asked to list them, in three specially commissioned pieces, 'My ABC of Snobbery', illustrated by Osbert Lancaster. According to Nancy, a snob's preoccupations included braces, caviar, emeralds and gambling. And, Nancy being Nancy, this was turned into a book proposal on the subject, which she and Joan – 'a splendid Scottish snob in her own right',[22] according to Nancy – took to Ian MacLennan at Hutchinson's. They were offered an advance of £150 and 12.5 per cent royalties on a print run of 5,000. 'The book should certainly be a big one rather than one of these slim and select volumes that grace booksellers' shelves but don't seem to be bought with any great frequency', MacLennan told them, ' . . . perhaps about 40,000 words . . . '.[23] Hutchinson would provide illustrations for the book, which was scheduled to be delivered by the end of September.

Work began on 'Snobbery', but it was another bright idea destined not to be completed, despite the fact that Nancy even got *She* readers to write in with ideas for possible inclusion in the book. 'My partner and I have been playing the Game of Snob together for a great many years', she wrote in the unpublished manuscript. 'And we have developed a secret language to define those people who do not quite measure up to our subtle standards. INCY we call them, Incorrect MIFFY – Milk in First, something Nancy Mitford and Evelyn Waugh feel you should not do'.[24] The object of the book, apparently, was 'so that other people might play The Old Snob Game'.[25]

They only got as far as 'D' in their alphabetically arranged 'game' – later categories would have included 'Sex', 'Titles' and 'Women'. They did, however, finish some amusing and, in retrospect, ironic sections:

> BIOGRAPHY. This is not an art but a superior type of journalism. BIRTH CONTROL. Considered very middle-class by such authorities as Evelyn Waugh . . . CARS. Virility is obviously suggested by an open car . . . CLEAN. At gatherings of artists the well-scrubbed stand out like Omosexuals . . . AEROPLANE. To run your own and be able to pilot it yourself is excellent.[26]

While they were working on 'Snobbery' together, they attended a joint interview with Doreen Stephens, the editor of BBC Television's women's programmes. Stephens was trying to assess whether either or both of them might be suitable presenters or interviewers. She was not entirely convinced:

> Nancy can be persuaded out of trousers on occasion and should, I think, be on our list of possible interviewers. She is another one who is only any use to us . . . on the right occasion, but she has a brilliant brain and is a clever interviewer. Past experience of using her in a series of her own which she offered us as a package deal was not successful because she really had not got the time to do enough work for us. I am not so sure about Joan Werner Laurie, who is rather a quieter type of person, more likely to be useful to Beryl and the Family Problems panel'.[27]

Though Nancy was continuing as *Express* book critic, it was clear to all concerned that, compared with the lush life of gay Paris, writing mere reviews was no longer as enthralling to her as it once was. No book coverage appeared through all of August and most of September. Still, every effort was made to inject some new energy into the job. Arthur Christiansen came up with a scheme to get bookshops interested in the *Daily Express* and its literary coverage. 'I suggest I write to a thousand or so principal bookshops in the UK, telling them about Nancy Spain and asking them whether they find that there is an upsurge of sales when books are reviewed',[28] he told Lord Beaverbrook.

But a feeling that Nancy's best efforts were not being directed into her work at the *Express* was beginning to pervade and the tension was growing between her and Harold Keeble. However, not all of her bosses felt that her multiple commitments were a problem, as Sir Edward Pickering emphasizes:

> 'Clearly, there was a conflict, but at that time she was perfectly capable of riding two horses, which she proceeded to do. She wasn't in the normal sense a staff operator, where she had to report to the office every day, though she did come into the office a lot. She was certainly on the payroll, but there were

payments in addition to the payroll when she was doing special assignments'.

Nonetheless, by the end of the summer, Nancy felt her position had become intolerable. On 31 August, she wrote to Beaverbrook:

> This is a very hard letter to write: and one which I have tried to send you many times during the last year. But last week things finally came to a head between Harold Keeble and myself and he accepted my three months' notice of resignation as your 'Daily Express' book critic.
>
> My affection for the paper, the group, most of all, yourself goes unaltered. This is entirely a personal matter between myself and Harold. The decision is not a sudden whim. I have had time to think it over, very deeply, lately. I only hope that you will remember me when you do so with some of your generosity and affection.[29]

Beaverbrook was taken aback: 'This is very bad news. Please write and tell me all about the circumstances'.[30]

During the next few days, Nancy had second thoughts:

> I have tried to think over and write down all the circumstances that brought me to the conclusion that I should have to leave you, but on paper they all seemed quite petty. It would be easy to discuss it with you, I know, at dinner and such things talked out do not then look undignified and childish.
>
> However, Harold and I have talked together and we are determined for these three months to swallow all our incompatibilities of temperament, and (who knows) we may be able to arrive at a relationship together that might mean I could stay with you. At the moment, I do not feel like this. But I promise I am going to give it a try.
>
> So, please God, you may enjoy my pieces once more. Meanwhile, here is my love, as always.[31]

Although Nancy may have exasperated Harold Keeble, Sir Edward Pickering is not convinced the blame lay solely with her:

> 'There were so many crises with Harold it's impossible to remember what that one was about. He was a brilliant chap, but, my God, he was difficult as well. You could never pin him down on anything. He was temperamental and with contributors, he was a bit of a bully. He liked to do things his way and no doubt he wanted to do something with one of Nancy's articles and Nancy said no. And Harold would then try and go ahead and do it, and then there would be a great uproar. I don't remember having to settle that one, but I had to settle so many disputes with Harold and various members of staff . . . '.

In November, George Millar took over stewardship of the *Express* books page permanently and Nancy's talents were utilized elsewhere in the newspaper. It was announced that 'The "Daily Express" has assigned Nancy Spain, in an intriguing new development of her reporting career' to write a series of articles on 'The Wax Idols' – interviewing musical personalities at home, revealing 'the side of their lives not on record'.[32] The 'idols' included

Ted Heath, Alma Cogan and Joan Hammond, the Australian opera singer. But the series itself was merely a stop-gap before her next proper role on the *Express* was determined in the New Year.

The year also brought changes on the home front. There was one terrifying incident involving, as Nancy told Beaverbrook, 'our darling 6 year old falling from a window and cracking his skull in two places . . . '.[33] Despite some moments of real anxiety and fear for all concerned – not least of all Nancy – he pulled through.

On a less traumatic note, the Clareville Grove family household now had a new member: Sheila van Damm. Nick Laurie recalls, 'I seem to remember at the back of my mind that Sheila only came to stay for a few days and ended up moving in'. So now they were five – and it was an arrangement that seemed to suit everyone, as Nick Laurie explains:

> 'She fitted in very well in the nutty world that was that house. She was actually the only sane person in the house. She and Mum would go off and do fairly butch boys' things together; Nancy and my Mum would do fairly glitzy, glamorous things together; and Sheila kind of fitted in with whatever was going on'.

What was 'going on' in that household, in fact, was an example of how postwar, pre-feminism women were attempting – and, in this case, succeeding – to 'have it all'. According to Nick Laurie:

> 'All three of them were essentially emancipated before their time – in a way, precursors of the feminist movement. There were three pretty powerful personalities in the house, but actually getting on in surprising harmony. Sheila ran the Windmill, my mother ran what was the most successful women's magazine of its time and Nancy was among the most successful popular journalists of that time. To me it seemed the most natural thing in the world. But then it was a pretty weird world . . . '.

Sheila had her own room at Clareville Grove. Though the exact arrangements between her, Joan and Nancy were never ascertained by anyone, it was Sheila's deepening friendship with Joan that had brought her into the household. Dick Laurie thinks Joan probably had a completely platonic relationship with Sheila:

> 'I don't think there was any jiggery-pokery, because they were both leaders – both very formidable people. I just think they were very good mates. Certainly, I never saw them in bed together as I would see Jonnie and Nancy, when I would come in the house and they would call me upstairs and I would sit in the bedroom and talk'.

As far as Sheila was concerned, Joan was 'an immense tower of strength, upholding my morale. I valued Jonnie's wisdom greatly; almost more than anyone else's'.[34] Whatever the nuances of their respective relationships, it was a domestic arrangement that worked for all of them, and which they kept intact for longer than a good many, more 'orthodox' partnerships.

Tom, meanwhile, had begun school, though, according to him, his first year was rather unsettled: 'I spent the first term in a Montessori in South

Kensington, the second term in the Lycée and the third term I was somewhere in Kent, in a primary school near Benenden'. It was while she was driving back from visiting Tom in Kent that Nancy had an experience which, if it didn't entirely change her attitude to life, certainly consolidated her view that each day was precious and should be lived to the full.

She had recently splashed out on an enormous white Zephyr and her friend, Raymond Way, offered to customize it for her. First, he painted it chocolate brown, to match its hood, mounted the spare tyre on the back of the car and decorated it with a facsimile signature, 'Nancy Spain', in gold paint. The *pièce de résistance* was to fit it with number plates that spelt 'NSPAIN'.

That October, returning from Kent along the Dartford bypass, exhaustion overcame her for once and she fell asleep at the wheel. The car somersaulted twice, with the hood taking the full impact. Riding her luck, Nancy climbed out of the wreckage with nothing more than a few bruises, though she later said she had no recollection of anything that had happened immediately before the accident. Fortunately, because the car had her name emblazoned all over it, passing drivers were able to call for an ambulance and tell them exactly who their patient would be. In Dartford Hospital, the police told her she was lucky to be alive. No one was more aware of it then Nancy. The next day, she recalled, 'I put my affairs in order assuming that any day could be my last, and I lived in that way ever since'.[35]

Her year ended on a sore note, spending Christmas in some discomfort and in unusual surroundings – the London Clinic. After her accident, 'Nelly' Newman had given her a complete check-up and discovered that, apart from her punishing work schedule, there was a medical reason for her fatigue. 'I am here for three weeks', she told Beaverbrook. '1 week beastliness and two of convalescence as the parts of me that have been operated on are of some importance in maintaining a decent and sober life!'[36] This was no exaggeration.

The two operations – 'both trivial but damned painful'[37] – were for piles and a fistula, an unnatural channel in the bowels, in women sometimes caused by injury sustained during protracted labour. The only treatment is an operation and the healing a rather tedious process, because the wound has to be packed each day after every bowel movement. 'PILES ARE SUCH FUN though indelicate . . . they perform terrible indignities on me daily . . . Hacked to pieces I am no longer in great pain . . . ' she told Beaverbrook; his traditional Christmas cheque 'went a long way towards providing one with a new *derriere* for the new year . . . '.[38]

Friends rallied round to cheer her up. Raymond Way sent her flowers and oysters, Ginette sent caviar from Paris, Noel Coward rang her several times and Sheila van Damm brought champagne, vodka and, to relieve the creeping boredom, an acoustic guitar. Thus fortified, she wished her boss 'a happy Christmas and a better 1959 than we had . . . '.[39]

After Christmas, Tom was sent to prep school in North Wales, at the tender age of six. It was, says Nick Laurie, 'not because he was an embarrassment, more as a convenience. They were very career-minded'.

Shopping for his school uniform and new clothes was turned into a consumer piece for *She*. He and Nick were taken on an expedition to see how other mothers could buy reasonably priced, quality clothing for two boys. Most of their outfits came from Marks and Spencers, as opposed to the 'approved' shops mentioned on the school's clothes list. 'We no longer need high prices and the glory of your name to reassure us',[40] she told them in her article.

During the next five years, Tom would only return home for the holidays. 'And not always then, because I spent a lot of time in North Wales even during the holidays', he explains. Nick Laurie concurs: 'Nancy and Joan would go to Cannes quite a lot, and we'd be packed off to wherever they could think of that summer. So Tom didn't get as much quality contact time'. 'There was a trip to the South of France when I was four', Tom recalls. 'That turned out to be a disaster. I suppose I was fairly insufferable and Nick wasn't all that good either'. According to Nancy:

> Instead of ten days of relaxed charm and inactivity ... we found it could be a long struggle with mosquitoes and sunburn and endless instructions for children on 'How to Live' ... it became increasingly clear that the sun was too strong for our darlings, who moreover did not awfully want to lie quietly there and didn't like wine. And we began to long for the day when we could return them both to base.[41]

'We never went to France again after that', says Tom. 'We tended to go to the south coast – Littlehampton, Angmering, that kind of place – staying with the van Damms'.

It was not only Nancy and Joan's careers, however, that were the dominant factors. Nancy's growing involvement with Ginette had now entered a new phase: that of literary mentor. Years before they had met, Ginette's great friend, the American director Joshua Logan, had encouraged her to write about her wartime experiences. She had done so, but all attempts to get the manuscript published had foundered. In answer to Nancy's constant questioning about what it had been like living under occupation, Ginette showed her the oft-rejected manuscript. Nancy pinpointed what was wrong with it: it failed to hold the reader's attention because it revealed nothing about Ginette's background. Readers needed to know more about *her*, Nancy explained. So Ginette wrote a new section about her childhood and youth. On her behalf, Nancy took the two mini-manuscripts to Collins, who had published *Mrs Beeton and Her Husband*, and arranged a meeting so that Ginette could discuss the book with them. A third section was needed, they told her: about her work for Balmain. If she wrote this, there would be a complete book.

So she and Nancy spent the first few months of 1959 working on this new section together, as well as editing the other two – all fitted in between their respective commitments.

As an editor, Nancy was relentless, according to Ginette:

> ... let it not be imagined that with it all she was an angel of tolerance. I remember remarks like, 'Would it hurt you to write one sentence that will

not make everybody feel physically sick?' and 'The banality of your choice of words is such that it makes "Peg's Paper" look like Marcel Proust'.[42]

But the sarcasm, pressure and encouragement worked and, in March, 'William Hickey' was able to report that Ginette's book, provisionally titled 'Mink – The Hard Way', had been accepted by Collins. It would be published later in the year, by which time it had become *It Isn't All Mink*. Noel Coward agreed to write a foreword.

Unlike many successful journalists and popular authors, Nancy was not averse to helping new writers who she felt merited advice and encouragement. She had done so in her years as a book reviewer, from *Books of Today* to the *Express* and, after she was firmly established in her own right, went out of her way to help in a more hands-on way, particularly regarding members of the 'immediate' family. She had brought Joan to the attention of the National Magazine Company and, thus, brought her the chance to become founding editor of *She*. When Dick Laurie discussed the possibility of becoming a journalist, he recalls that she was a fount of advice.

> ' "Start on a local paper", she told me. "And specialize – be better and learn more about something than anyone else. Go to as many places as you can and get to know all the people you can". She was more of a sister to me than Jonnie, because she wasn't jealous. The Lauries were a jealous family'.

Nancy was not averse to helping even the youngest of budding scribes. At one of Granny Laurie's birthday parties in Sussex, Nancy was introduced to a little boy of about twelve or thirteen called Simon Dring, who was then Dick Laurie's brother-in-law. 'He said, "I want you to introduce me to Nancy Spain, because I want to be a journalist. I thought "that's a bloody cheek", but I introduced them. She was exceptionally kind and helpful to him'. At seventeen, Simon Dring left England. 'He hitchhiked to Antibes for the jazz festival and wasn't seen again for three years', recalls Dick Laurie. By the time he was twenty-one, Dring had covered every major contemporary war, including Vietnam, first for Reuters and then for the *Daily Mail*, winning a 'Journalist of the Year' award. In 1995, he revisited the 1960s 'hippy trail' to India for the BBC's eight-part series, *On the Road Again*.

Nancy's role at the *Express* was under revision yet again. For the first three months of the year, she was the guest film critic, reviewing movies such as the Oscar-winning *Separate Tables*, *Gigi* and *The Horse's Mouth*. She also wrote film-related features for the paper, including a fascinating investigation into the business of how studios acquired 'Established Literary Properties' for adaptation. However, by the end of March, she had switched hats once more: 'Irrepressible reporter, controversial critic, and national personality NANCY SPAIN today begins a new assignment – "Express" guest critic on TV'.[43] In fact, Nancy would fill this 'temporary' position for nearly a year, with James Thomas, the television critic of *She*, deputizing for her when other commitments took her away from Clareville Grove and the new press-button television set she had bought.

It may have been coincidental that this daily column, dealing with a medium that she herself was becoming an increasingly familiar face on, contained some of her punchiest, pertinent and audacious criticism. Yet again, one of her earliest comments sparked off a public row. She criticized *Tonight*, presented by Cliff Michelmore, for being one of those 'so-called magazine programmes [which] lacks urgency'.[44] The next day, she told readers, 'Mr Cliff Michelmore is steamed up about my report on his programme "Tonight". So he wasted a good five minutes of "Tonight"'s valuable half-hour in trying to take the mickey out of me'.[45] The row was still rumbling a few months later: 'One day the "Tonight" team will learn that the best jokes are quick, clean and over before anyone can think about them'.[46]

But her complaints didn't stop there. 'I deeply dislike all TV plays and semi-documentaries that rub my innocent nose in the gloomier aspects of life',[47] she complained. Cowboy series also tested her patience: 'I often lose my temper with Westerns simply because they don't appeal to me', she explained. 'The 8,000,000 women who drift past the sets daily can't be expected to enjoy Westerns, even if their sons and husbands do. You see, there is no one in a Western for a woman to identify herself with'.[48] She was not averse to lavatorial humour, but thought that 'one such joke per evening is enough'.[49] And what was the one thing on television which attracted her unfettered enthusiasm? 'In my opinion, sport is the greatest thing that can be shown on TV',[50] she declared. She particularly enjoyed watching coverage of the international swimming between the Netherlands and Britain, 'when the Dutch girls waded cheerfully about the shallow end of the bath after the race, kissing their deadly rivals'.[51] Though she was generally sniffy about 'commercial' television, she thought that advertisements were the best thing it offered: 'beautifully directed and quite often they entertain'.[52]

Then, she started to get on her soapbox. Britain's passion for television was beginning to pall, she decided. This was based on statistics which showed that in the first quarter of 1959, nearly 2 million radio sets had been bought in Britain. 'The big huddle at the TV is breaking up', she declared. 'It was the teenagers who first rebelled against the nightly misery of that tight little TV group'.[53] She attributed it partly to the popularity of portable transistor radios, partly to too many American imports and, finally, to the apparent discovery by audiences 'that we do not miss it at all ... Yes, the British public are at last sliding away from the mass hypnosis once exercised by the telly ... Programmes and personalities have lost their bite. Even "What's My Line?" has no more tug on the public consciousness'.[54] In this, she was correct; she also observed, rather prophetically, that 'TV is a terrible monster. Like some ghastly carnivore it chews up and spits out talent'.[55] But she did pick out two television personalities who, she felt, were exceptions to the rule: David Attenborough and John Freeman.

If the *Express*'s letters page was to be believed, many of their readers agreed with her views. A shopkeeper from Molesey observed, 'it is surprising how many of my customers say the programmes are not worth watching'. However, another attributed television's decline 'to all those ghastly football, cricket, and racing programmes'.[56]

Though nearly every issue of the *Express* featured Nancy 'Looking In', her flexible arrangement with the paper still gave her enough time to fulfil her other assignments. Some of these were headline-grabbing stunts: she teamed up with Freddie Laker to take part in the Marble Arch–Arc de Triomphe car race. 'We did 2 hrs 35 mins 28 secs',[57] she told Beaverbrook proudly. Then she was a co-driver in the London to Bright Veteran Car Run. In the summer, her name made another, slightly more unusual headline: 'Nancy Spain Raid – Man Jailed'.[58] A few months earlier, one Eugene Moriarty, who lived in nearby Queen's Gate Terrace, had broken into Clareville Grove and stolen 'property worth £460'. He was jailed for twelve months.

She had also written what turned out to be one of her oddest and least successful books: *My Boy Mo*. It was a reworking of the basic 'Romeo and Juliet' story, with illustrations by Pamela Kington, set in what her publishers called 'the teenage-coffee-bar world'. It appears to have been something of a rather crass, ill-conceived attempt to stay in touch with the new, fast-developing 'teenage' culture: much of the action takes place in a supermarket and the Expresso, and there are references to 'Jazz Cellars'.

In the autumn, she made a new friend. Lena Horne was doing a four-week cabaret season at the Savoy and Nancy went to talk to her for *She*. 'Lena is an artist even when she is slouching round in skin-tight pants',[59] she wrote admiringly. The following weekend, she was in Paris and met Horne's two children from her first marriage: Teddy, who was a student at the Sorbonne, and Gail, who worked for *Marie Claire* magazine. 'She taught me lots of new teen-age expressions', recalled Nancy. ' "To drag" is to bore ... "To snow" is to seek to impress by working great names into the conversation'.[60] And, for once, her job as television critic was a total delight when Horne did three shows for ITV:

> If I could have Lena Horne in my drawing room for three weeks, singing and doing her stuff, for half an hour, songs with steam coming off the top, I would cheerfully pay someone £4 [the price of the television licence] a night. And that is what we are getting ... I'll take a wager that Lena Horne would make 'Rule Britannia' the sexiest song ever written.[61]

In September and October, Britain was in the grip of election fever – a political event that even Nancy, as television critic, could not ignore. She reviewed the two main parties' electoral broadcasts, starting with Labour:

> They are superb actors and script-learners, but here and there a little appearance of spontaneity and honest hesitation would help them. And I feel they are very foolish to leave the delightful Woodrow Wyatt suspended in mid air at the end of each of their broadcasts, asking a question.[62]

But, though she admired Labour's style, it was still the Conservative substance that impressed her, despite its stodgy presentation: 'I propped my eyes open with matchsticks in order to catch the Tory party TV circus. The overall impression was one of stolid steadiness and reliability'.[63] In that month's issue of *She*, Joan was more ambiguous about who she was supporting, though she was unequivocal about one thing: 'It's considered very bad form indeed for the Editor of a popular magazine to mention the horrible word POLITICS', she explained in the letters page. 'So may I put it like this: if you don't bother to vote this election, you jolly well deserve all you get from the next Government!'[64]

On 8 October, Harold Macmillan's government were re-elected – the third Conservative electoral victory in a row – with 365 seats and an increased majority. Labour, led by Hugh Gaitskell, trailed a long way behind with 258, while the Liberal Party managed to win only 6 seats. One of their victors was a thirty-year-old barrister called Jeremy Thorpe, who, according to the *Express*, won his North Devon seat 'by a mixture of hard work and clowning'.[65] This election also introduced the world to a new woman MP – 34-year-old Mrs Margaret Thatcher. Perhaps, if Nancy had been more interested in politics, she might have considered the Oxford-educated mother-of-two an ideal interviewee. To have the embryo standard-bearer of 'Victorian values' confronted by the trouser-wearing co-parent of a 'pretend' family would have been an event worth buying tickets for.

My Boy Mo was published just before Christmas, where it was rather lost amongst the seasonal mêlée. What little coverage it did receive was hardly favourable. It was reviewed 'Last, and easily least . . . ' in the *Times Literary Supplement*'s round-up of children's books, and told 'the story of Julie Capulet who runs a supermarket and falls in love with the son of Montague, a rival grocer. Any resemblance to Romeo and Juliet ends there. This dim little piece is not improved by being printed as though it were poetry'.[66] However, the book was serialized for *Woman's Hour*, with Nancy reading the five parts herself, and sold enough to go into reprint.

But at least there was some vicarious pleasure to be had at this time. *It Isn't All Mink* was published in November and was a huge success. It had to be reprinted within a month of publication, and Collins also decided to publish it in America in 1960. Jean Soward of the *News Chronicle* said it gave 'The most revealing glimpses into the French high-fashion world that we are ever likely to get. It is very frank'. In the *Observer*, Alison Settle commented, 'It gives a picture that we have all hoped for'. However, George Millar gave it a very sniffy review in the *Express*. 'Not one flicker of this intelligent woman's undoubted charm gets through to the reader',[67] he complained.

With the book's publication came a glut of personal and media appearances. And, in a reversal of roles, Nancy helped groom Ginette for this new life as a 'personality'. Ginette was accorded a Foyle's Luncheon at the Dorchester, with Paul-Emile and the rest of her family in attendance and Nancy proposing the vote of thanks. In keeping with her 'real' job, two of Balmain's top models, Bronwen Pugh (who later married Viscount Astor, one of the peripheral figures caught up in the Keeler–Profumo–Ward 'affair') and Pat Donald Smith showed off some of the latest formal evening gowns, complete with tiaras. There was also an 'author's tea' at Harrods, a civic reception in Chester, an appearance on *Tonight* and, finally, a series of lectures for ladies' luncheon clubs, organized by the Maurice Frost Agency. By a curious coincidence, the tour started in Newcastle upon Tyne, where

Ginette was given a 'first night' party, at which 'Miss Spain got drunk and sang Geordie songs in dialect. I was launched'.[68]

That winter also saw another 'launch' for Nancy, when she made her first appearance on the programme that not only sealed her firmly in the affections of television audiences but remains one of her best-remembered. However, when she reviewed the first edition of *Juke Box Jury*, it was with some disdain. The programme would be a success, she said, 'if someone on the panel were to stick a neck out . . . '.[69] She wasn't optimistic about its future. By the second edition, she declared

> The BBC's 'Juke Box Jury' seems to be a dismal flop. I actually heard Pete Murray, speaking of a record which sounded to me like the insistent yowling of a tom-cat, say it was a 'prestige record'. If this programme has a value (which I rather doubt) it will lie in the comparisons which we can make between the panel's prophecy and the actual hits.[70]

Within six months, the producers had decided that Nancy would be the perfect person to 'stick a neck out' and speak up against any cat-like yowling. Given her previous criticism of the programme, Nancy had to find a different approach to adopt – but what? Since words had always been her business, why not concentrate on them – it didn't matter that it was a music programme. She would pay special attention to the lyrics and make them the focus of her criticism or praise. 'She brought to it that amusing thing of trying to analyse a lyric that was beyond analysing, in many cases', recalls David Jacobs, the long-serving chairman of *Juke Box Jury*. 'She never looked down her nose at them – but that was her thing, she always talked about the lyrics'.

Juke Box Jury did have a broad audience appeal, with panellists chosen not just from the pop industry but, like Nancy, from Fleet Street and stage and screen. But, for the generation of teenage 'baby boomers' of the early 1960s, *Juke Box Jury* became the television highlight of the week, as *Top of the Pops* would do in its heyday in the early 1970s. Teenagers would huddle round the family television sets at Saturday teatime to hear the latest releases and decide, with the panel, whether they would be a 'Hit' or a 'Miss'. And though the programme had considerable entertainment value, David Jacobs points out that it also took on some importance:

> It was always good fun, but in certain ways it was a very serious programme. We were discussing people's careers and giving them exposure to 20-odd million people – it was enormously popular. Our highest ever figure was 22 million. *Juke Box Jury* was very influential – record producers were queuing up to get their records on. I used to select them all, with the producer, and I would choose some because they were bad, otherwise we'd have nothing but compliments.

Ironically, the once-sceptical Nancy became one of the most popular and regular panellists on *Juke Box Jury*, along with Pete Murray, Alan Freeman and Brian Matthew. David Jacobs remembers her fondness for the programme:

It was a great favourite of hers and she was on it quite a lot. There was an extremely friendly atmosphere. We did two programmes at once: one went out live, then we would move the audience at the front to the back, and the back to the front, and then record the next week's show.

Only two recordings of *Juke Box Jury* have survived and, thankfully, one of them, broadcast on 29 October 1960, captured a typical performance by Nancy. The other panellists that day were jazz singer and musician Carmen McCrae, Pete Murray and American actor Richard Wyler. Resplendent in a striped, monogrammed shirt and eyes a-twinkle, Nancy grimaced at Roy Orbison's 'Blue Angel', while trying to work out the lyrics. Meanwhile, Carmen McCrae, puffing away on a cigarette (unthinkable now, of course), thought the record was 'lousy'. Nancy agreed: 'I think it's a terrible record. He should just let her go on crying'.

Next up was Lloyd Price and 'Just Call Me'. Nancy declared, 'I like it when they're called Lust or Power'. She adds, 'I want a new noise, a wild noise – preferably the hiccups'. Then David Jacobs played Nat King Cole singing 'Just as Much as Ever'. 'He sends me', declared Nancy the hip groover. Connie Francis wailing 'My Heart Has a Mind of Its Own' induced the biggest grimace from Nancy. And for Paul Anka, intoning 'Summer's Gone', she professed some sympathy: 'Poor thing'.

Nancy was one of the personalities who were not afraid to pass honest, if sometimes harsh, judgement on the songs and performers who underwent trial by *Juke Box Jury*. But her impact on the programme and some of its audience went far deeper than a few wisecracks at the expense of hapless musicians. Some of the youngsters who avidly watched her appearances on the programme knew somehow that they weren't tuning in just to hear her words. One of these was the young Alison Hennegan:

'It would be very difficult for a young person now to have any sense of how different, physically, she was, because even though *Juke Box Jury* was informal, none of the women took advantage of that informality to be anything other than femmy-poo. It was just very tilting – things shifted on an axis when you saw her, particularly when you saw her on with Pete Murray, because they were two versions of a similar model, as it were. And he was always a rather less convincing version than she was. The quiff, the Brylcreem, the oozing, easy masculine affable charm, which was completely OTT – and she was doing a much better version of it, which was far more attractive and compelling. If you got the two of them in a frame at the same time, it was very amusing'.

Nancy's general demeanour also made quite an impression:

'I used to be amused by her exchanges, when they would have a guest, a wretch who had actually made one of the records that was being listened to. Usually, Spain would have been the rudest about it and she was always singularly unfazed by this. She wasn't callously indifferent to what the guy was feeling, but she certainly wasn't going to retract her opinions. Watching her not go into any of the feminine dither, any of that submissive, supplicant, conciliatory stuff . . . courtesy of course, but no feminine fluff'.

Nancy's persona and image on *Juke Box Jury* contrasted sharply with her appearances on other popular programmes, such as *What's My Line?*, where she dressed slightly more conventionally. For that, she had to project an image that wasn't quite her; in *Juke Box Jury*, she could really be herself, as Hennegan recalls:

'I was aware of her and Isobel Barnett as an interesting duo. There was such a difference between those two personae. *What's My Line?* was still 1950s television in spirit and so the women were in evening dress. And the contrast between that and *Juke Box Jury* couldn't have been more glorious. That was the tweed jackets, monogrammed shirts and cufflinks. It was a fascinating split image – the evening wear and the casual natty gents' sportswear'.

It was an image which struck not one, but many, chords:

'She made sense of so many things – her appearance and her persona – I remember thinking that, somehow, this woman has something to do with me. Somehow she and I were part of the same thing and that the ways in which she was different from other women were ways which I found very sympathetic and congenial. She remained a presence in my awareness, as a way in which things could be done and the sort of person you could be, the way you could look and dress and . . . and conduct yourself'.

Nancy was having a similar impact on other young people. A secondary school in Cornwall held an essay competition, called 'People I Would Like to Meet'. One of the teachers, Mrs Freda Hicks, wrote to Nancy to tell her about one of the third year pupils, Susan. Mrs Hicks wondered if it was possible for her young charge to meet Nancy or, at least, for her to write her a letter or send her an autograph. Susan, apparently, kept a scrapbook of cuttings about Nancy from magazines and newspapers and had made her the subject of her competition essay. 'Nancy Spain has never married because she has never met anybody who could match her brains',[71] Susan decided. Elsewhere, a young man who spent many hours glued to the television in the early 1960s was learning things about himself by watching the likes of Nancy – the author Keith Howes:

I knew there was something different about Nancy Spain and Sergeant Grace Millard, the unmarried policewoman in 'Dixon of Dock Green': they were intelligent, stylish, outspoken and they were admired for being dashing, which was very attractive in those days. So it was gay women who were a beacon to me.[72]

CHAPTER ELEVEN

The Nine Lives of a Lady of Letters

Nancy's stint as television critic had finished and her decade began with a rather more rigorous assignment: the *Express* sent her down to Cornwall to join Dr Barbara Moore on the last segment of her 1,000-mile walk from John O'Groat's to Land's End. She had just got back from Paris and, as she said, was ill-prepared: 'Sitting up in a nightclub until 3 a.m. drinking champagne with Marlene Dietrich is not really what I should have chosen'.[1] In pouring rain, they set off from a point a few miles outside of Okehampton, and arrived at Land's End late on the evening of 4 February. Nancy filed her front-page report at midnight to make the cover of the next day's issue. 'The Amazon of the A30', she said, had 'established herself as one of the great English eccentrics'.[2]

She recuperated by going with Ginette to spend the weekend with Noel Coward at Les Avants, his home in Switzerland. 'The Master' had been suffering from phlebitis and, though he enjoyed their visit, was less than amused by Nancy's subsequent behaviour, according to his diaries:

> Unfortunately Nancy let down the side rather badly by writing a eulogistic but acutely embarrassing article in the 'Daily Express'. Neither she nor Ginette knows that this was bad taste, but dear God! I do! Nancy is gay, intelligent, affectionate and well read, and yet she is so trapped in her journalistic training that she cannot see or feel how vulgar it is to betray to the world the intimate jokes and fun of a private weekend among friends. There is *no hope!*[3]

The 'vulgar' details included Nancy revealing the colour of his pyjamas – one pair purple, another yellow – and that Coward had said her hair would always look like a mat – 'All you need is welcome on it in golden letters'.[4] She also revealed that the other guests that weekend were George and Benita Sanders, but omitted to mention Ginette's presence.

There were others, however, who didn't mind their weekends with Nancy becoming news items. After she returned from Switzerland, she turned a round of golf with comedian Charlie Drake and cartoonist Roy Ullyett into a photo-feature. The following week, they were joined by Max Bygraves and Eric Sykes, now dubbed 'The eccentric Golf Circle of Nancy Spain'.[5] After a wobbly start, she became addicted to the sport and would grab a game wherever she was, be it Paris, Las Vegas or Lancashire.

The sporty theme of her *Express* features continued when she went to Aintree to interview Mirabelle Topham, chair of Topham Ltd., who owned and ran the Grand National. Mrs Topham told her all about her negotiations with the BBC to televise the National, despite her fears that people would no longer want to watch the race live, preferring the comfort of their own homes. Nancy reassured her: 'There's literally nothing in the whole world to beat a day's racing in the open air'.[6] On the eve of the Boat Race, she interviewed supporters of Oxford, that year's favourites. The Oxford coach, 'Jumbo' Edwards, told her about the strict diet followed by his crew. 'Peas, beans and beetroot are out', he said solemnly, 'All these, and lettuce too, cause terrible indigestion!'[7]

During the next few months, however, Nancy did very little work for the *Express*. She continued to gather gossip for *She* and fulfil her radio and television commitments, including *Juke Box Jury*, *Something to Read*, *My Word*, even an appearance on *The Charlie Drake Show*. But her *Express* features were thin on the ground and usually described one of her social engagements – for instance, the christening of Diana Dors's baby son. For reasons which Nancy couldn't fathom, Dors and her then husband, Dickie Dawson, asked her to be godmother to young Mark Richard Dawson. She agreed, and bought her new godson a Bible and a £20 pair of inscribed silver hairbrushes. And, of course, it made a good picture feature.

She and Joan were trying to buy a rather special present for their boys. 'We are still collecting capital together to buy land and build a seaside house, at Angmering in Sussex for Laurie's two boys, so that one day they can have a happy healthy holiday, on their own premises',[8] she told Beaverbrook.

Meanwhile, she continued to hob with the nobs. On Friday 6 May, the wedding of Princess Margaret and Anthony Armstrong-Jones took place in London. Afterwards, there was an elite lunch party, which both Nancy and Noel Coward attended, along with the likes of the Duchess of Devonshire, James Pope-Hennessy and Lord Bob Boothby. In June she was invited to a 'very strange house party in Wiltshire' that could almost have been scripted by Noel Coward:

> [The guests] all piled into cars and drove to swim in Serena Dunn's swimming pool. There was a gramophone playing Mozart all the time and one of our party dived in with all her clothes on – I think to balance my own exiguous costume – Serena swam in a straw hat like a dear little pony in Italy.[9]

But, if she was enjoying a sultry, relatively frivolous summer, the autumn was to bring another whirl of excitement and activity.

While she was visiting Noel Coward in Switzerland he had read her his new play, *Waiting in the Wings*. 'I enjoyed the play-reading very much, and I am fairly certain that I was not *entirely* influenced by my pleasure in the fact that one of the heroines of the play was a newspaper lady wearing trousers',[10] she said. Indeed she was – a trouser-wearing character, called Zelda Fenwick, but quite clearly based on N. Spain.

Waiting in the Wings, a three-act drama with six specially written musical numbers, is set in The Wings, a small charity home for retired actresses. No actress under sixty is admitted to the home. Miss Archie (Margot Boyd) is the superintendent of The Wings, a former member of ENSA who has a 'gruff and rather masculine manner', wears corduroy trousers and sweaters. The residents include the once-great actresses May Davenport (Marie Lohr) and Lotta Bainbridge (Sybil Thorndike). Graham Payn played Perry Lascoe, a former actor, now secretary of The Wings and it is he who brings Zelda Fenwick (Jessica Dunning) to the home on a September afternoon, at the beginning of Act II. 'Zelda is in her middle thirties. She is nice-looking, trim and wears well-cut trousers and a sports shirt'.[11] She is, of course, in search of a story – her editor has apparently been trying to get the inside story for years – and she tries to reassure a nervous Perry. He has made a deal with her that, in exchange for making an appeal on television for donations for the home's solarium, she will get an exclusive.

> Zelda: 'Don't worry, I'll be discretion itself. It's just possible, though, that one or two of them might recognize me.'
> Perry: 'I doubt it, your photograph never appears in your column.'
> Zelda: 'My name does.'[12]

Perry introduces her as 'Miss Starkey'. 'She drives like a fiend. I think she has a Stirling Moss fixation'.[13] Zelda recognizes a fellow former service-woman in Miss Archie. 'Were you Waafs, Wrens or Ats? I was a Wren. Malta for two years'.[14] When she learns that two of the actresses have fallen out, she sniffs a scoop. 'There's a good story in that, isn't there? Old foes still feuding in the twilight of their lives!'[15] Unfortunately, Lotta Bainbridge recognizes her: 'You're really Zelda Fenwick, aren't you – the one who writes the "People Are News" column in the "Sunday Clarion"? I saw you on television a few weeks ago'.[16] When May Davenport tackles her, she explains, 'I am always in a professional capacity, Miss Davenport. That is an essential part of the job'.[17]

Zelda reappears at the beginning of Act III, on Christmas Eve. Her story has been printed, but no appeal was made on television, upsetting the residents and staff of The Wings. She is dressed for the evening, 'wearing black corduroy trousers, a black velvet jacket, a white shirt and a red scarf. She is carrying a large and obviously heavy package – which she deposits on the piano'.[18] It is a case of champagne. She announces, 'I hasten to add that I am not here in a professional capacity, for once. It's just that I had rather a guilty conscience'.[19]

Her boss, Lord Charkley – obviously based on Beaverbrook – has also given her a cash donation of £2,000 for the home, to make amends:

> He's a barking old tyrant but he is in mortal dread of hell's fire and so he occasionally likes to make a gesture. It may be a form of spiritual insurance or it may even be genuine kindness, with him it's difficult to tell.[20]

Waiting in the Wings was offered to Binkie Beaumont, who turned it down, and Michael Redgrave opted to produce it. Directed by Margaret Webster, the play was premiered at the Olympia Theatre, Dublin, on 8

August 1960. It opened at the Duke of York's Theatre, London, on 7 September, and ran for 188 performances.

In the England of 1960, Noel Coward and his works were considered unfashionable and unexciting and the critics duly lambasted *Waiting in the Wings*. The *Express* dubbed it 'A Play About Nothing At All' and the *Mail* thought it was 'Just Timeless Rootless Prattle'.[21] However, audiences queued round the theatre nightly for tickets and, after performances, waited in the street to cheer and applaud the venerable cast as they came out of the stage door.

And Coward himself, though at first shaken by the hostile critical reception given to the play, defended it proudly:

> Perhaps I was wrong in the first place to have written a play about old age and the imminence of death and contrived at the same time to make it entertaining . . . All these 'perhaps' add up to nothing . . . I recommend this play, more than any I have written for many years, to the reader's most earnest attention.[22]

Zelda Fenwick was not the only Spain-inspired character to appear that year: Nancy Lisbon, sultry-voiced interviewer, was also unleashed on the world. She was actually created by Nancy's *My Word* chums, Frank Muir and Denis Norden, in 'So Little Time', one of the sketches on the album *Songs for Swinging Sellers*. 'We used her name probably because we knew we wouldn't get any hassle from her', explains Norden. They didn't. 'Have you heard Peter Sellers's imitation of my voice . . . on his new record?', Nancy asked *She* readers. 'It's brilliant, sounds more like me than I do myself . . . and it's one of the best compliments I've ever had'.[23] Sellers's wickedly accurate impersonation made Nancy Lisbon as recognizable as her real-life counterpart.

In 'So Little Time', Nancy Lisbon is sent by her editor to interview Major Ralph-Ralph (pronounced Rafe-Ralph), a former horsedealer turned manager of a stable of young male pop stars. They include Lenny Bronze, Clint Thigh and Matt Lust, and groups The Fleshpots and The Muckrakers, who live with him in his luxury flat in Mount Street. She confesses her ignorance of pop stars – 'I'm mostly on book reviewing'. Ralph-Ralph introduces her to one of his young men, Twit Conway, a callow youth who has been trained to trot out answers to her questions by rote. Unfortunately for Ralph-Ralph, they come out in the wrong order. 'Are you fond of Shakespeare?' she asks him. 'We are just good friends', replies Twit.

While everyone was enjoying the joke, Nancy's bosses at the *Express* were less than amused by some of her recent contributions. A rambling piece about trends in the arts had appeared in the *Express* on 22 October, 'Why I'd Rather Be Third Any Time than Second', sparked off by the news that the Irish actor Michael Mac Liammoir would be performing *The Importance of Being Oscar* in the West End. It prompted a puzzled cable from Beaverbrook to Robert Edwards: 'Will you please explain to me the meaning of many passages in Nancy Spain's article . . . and tell me who read it before publication'.[24]

Edward Pickering reported back to Max Aitken:

'she was asked to write an article for Saturday's leader page. She delivered it
after 4 o'clock on Friday afternoon; Mr Keeble read it, was unhappy about it
but decided to use it because of our very early press times and the fact that
Nancy Spain had written very little for the paper over the last few weeks . . .
The point Nancy Spain was making – and it is an interesting point – is that in
many spheres things tend to go in cycles of three, whether it is: Films, Popular
Singers, Fashions, or British Railways . . . Unfortunately, the article is woolly,
ineffectively argued and obscure. It was a mistake to print it and great care will
be taken in future to watch Nancy Spain closely.

At the moment, Nancy Spain is in a very curious emotional state. She asked
me last Friday to send her to America to write the Lena Horne story. I told her
that I was not in favour of the project. She then decided to take some holiday
and is travelling to New York – flying with Jeanette [sic] Spanier'.[25]

Max Aitken then contacted his father:

The article was very poor indeed, but at the present time Nancy Spain is
doing no work as she is off on an emotional flight. It might be a good thing
if you could see her in New York, and explain that she must either work or
be fired. She is getting £100 a week from us at the moment for 50 articles a
year.[26]

To describe Nancy as 'in a very curious emotional state' and 'off on an
emotional flight' was an accurate appraisal of her mood that autumn. Even
as Pickering and Aitken were exchanging their respective views about
suitable reprimands, she was on her way to Paris. In the wake of the success
of *It Isn't All Mink*, Ginette Spanier was about to embark on a lecture tour
of North America and Nancy was to accompany her as her 'secretary',
except for a few days when she would go to Las Vegas to see Lena Horne in
concert and discuss the possibility of writing her ghosted autobiography. Of
course, a trip to America might provide a wealth of juicy gossip for the 'Ace
Newshound' column in *She*, but she was largely putting her own professional commitments on temporary hold to help Ginette. Meanwhile, her
Express work was clearly being neglected and even her devoted Beaverbrook was evidently not amused.

However, this was all far from her thoughts as she headed for Paris in the
last week of October. On Friday 28, she went with Ginette to see Judy
Garland in concert at the Olympia. Ginette provided her with a smart little
blue Balmain dress to wear, which Nancy found almost impossible to
squeeze into:

(Jenny says it's my own fault and I should have come for a fitting with it, but
I think I was just full of wind) because later in the evening it began to fit quite
well. I bought new blue shoes to go with it and they were too tight at the
beginning of the evening, after fitting perfectly in the shop, they too settled
down. Fancy, I wonder if this ever happens to anyone else? Perhaps it is the
change of life.[27]

At the post-concert party, they were joined by Vivien Leigh, then pre-occupied with her impending divorce from Laurence Olivier. Nancy found herself 'intimidated by the strange atmosphere old mother Leigh spreads around her ... '.[28] 'She asks continually about L and files her divorce this Wednesday (or so they tell me) but Larry never even thinks about her. Talks about her sometimes as though she were dead'.[29]

They didn't leave the party until nearly 3 a.m., and it was a tired and slightly apprehensive Nancy who wrote to her 'Darling sweet Mrs Bunny' as she waited to leave for the airport on Saturday:

> It is all very strange and rather frightening, but exciting too and I can't believe any of it at all. Quite a different life it seems from dear familiar Clareville Grove. This is to say I miss you very much my best beloved little cat and hope you will be OK and Sheila look after you nicely and my best love and I will bring you lots of surprise presents and give my love to the bunnies etc.[30]

When Nancy and Ginette arrived in New York later that day, they were met at Idlewild by the chauffeur and Mercedes of Ginette's friends, Joshua Logan and his wife Nedda, and were whisked off to the Logans' luxurious home in Stamford, Connecticut, in time for dinner. Nancy was very impressed: 'the Logans were divine and Jenny and I shared a delicious guest room. The whole house was a dream, Japanese garden, huge studio with sauna bath in the basement and everything linked up by telephone as if it were a hotel'.[31] Nancy, Ginette and Nedda took a sauna together, much to Nancy's amusement.

On Monday, they checked into their New York hotel: the Blackstone, on 50 East 58th Street – 'a funny old hotel, with lots of bits falling down, not very chic at all',[32] she told Joan. 'Floral tributes keep arriving for Madam from all her friends, so the feeling is rather like the London Clinic only more so'.[33]

Once settled, they met up with Laurence Olivier and his new love, Joan Plowright, who were both in Broadway shows at the time: respectively, *Becket*, at the St James Theatre, and *A Taste of Honey*, at the Lyceum. Nancy and Ginette went to see both plays in their first few days in New York. Unfortunately, Nancy was underwhelmed by *Becket*, as she reported to Joan:

> This is the biggest bore I have ever seen. Apart from the fact that L looks 15 years old and the place was packed with bewildered Americans who are mad for a bit of culture there was nothing good to be said at all. Larry obviously wasn't paying the slightest attention to what he was saying, and meandered through the thing in an absent-minded daze, while the supporting cast were really bad, particularly Anthony Quinn who played the king.[34]

While Ginette recorded her first radio appearance and met up with her editor at Random House, Lee Wright, Nancy arranged to have lunch with Maggie Cousins of *McCall* magazine, to see if she would be interested in a feature on Lena Horne: 'I looked very smart because I had bought some very splendid gloves at Bloomingdales, also a splendid beige bag, so all my accessories matched, as the saying goes'.[35]

An air of suppressed hysteria was already beginning to surround the trip. During one of her radio appearances, Ginette was introduced by the host as 'G-I-N-E-T-T-E for Ginette S-P-A-N-I-E-R for Spanier and her book is published by Random House at 3 dollars 90 and now, Madame Ginette Spanier you were telling me of how you were tortured in the German occupation'.[36] Nancy, for her part, was reduced to uncontrollable giggles whenever Nedda Logan rang them at the Blackstone: 'I keep seeing her stark naked in the sauna bath beside me throwing pannikins of water on to the pebbles with broad free actor's gestures and enormous dignity, what time the sweat drips down from her great big pink buttocks'.[37] And, as more flowers poured into the Blackstone for Ginette, she remarked, rather ungratefully, 'They're really horrible, aren't they? Won't it be lovely when they're dead?'[38] 'She is a strange girl and no error',[39] Nancy told Joan.

On the morning of Thursday 3 November, Nancy flew to Las Vegas, and booked into the Sands Hotel, where Lena Horne was performing. 'Lena's divine maid Ireen unpacked me and I was very worried about my knickers you can imagine',[40] she told Joan. As for Vegas itself, Nancy was not impressed: 'Everything you have ever heard about this place is true, that's what's so awful, but I am disregarding the life usually lived'.[41] A faint whiff of homesickness was starting to creep up on Nancy in Vegas: 'Darling, if you were here it would make it all quite perfect because then I'd have someone to giggle with ... I'm not too sure if I can giggle with Lena and Lennie [Hayton, Horne's husband and musical director], perhaps so'.[42] Unfortunately, the proposed 'Lena Horne Story' fell through: Lena was 'very anxious for me to do the life story, but Lennie is quite impossible and won't even discuss it. So I'm afraid that's a chance gone by',[43] she told Joan.

Nancy attended several of Horne's shows at The Sands, some of which were recorded for the *Lena at The Sands* live album – and on which, according to Nancy, 'if you listen carefully, you can hear N Spain's unmaidenly laughter ringing out when Lena sings The Begat'.[44] But she found little to laugh about in Horne's schedule, which involved doing two shows a day, seven days a week. The last show would finish at around 1.30 a.m: 'Then she has supper and winds down, usually in a filthy temper with the drummer or the bass or something. By 4 a.m. she's asleep. She wakes at 4 p.m. when it's already getting dark',[45] observed Nancy. Horne was 'lashed to her terrible life from dressing room to bedroom, only interrupted by the effort of making those bastards cheer her ... '.[46] And there were worse indignities suffered:

> Lena says that she walks through the gambling rooms not looking because so many people say negroes are bad luck at the tables etc. Or that 'God-damned nigger bitch' passed behind my arms when I was throwing dice. They might just as well say women are unlucky, and indeed many of them do.[47]

While in Vegas, Nancy played golf with Dick Pierce, recording manager for RCA, Lena's record company, and his wife Gail. After the game, the conversation turned to a discussion about why America's reputation on the other side of the Atlantic had suffered. The usually non-political Nancy weighed in with an answer that did not best please her fellow golfers:

> I said, 'Well, maybe a country that was founded on the bill of rights that everyone had equal chances and would live in happiness with others no matter of what race or creed shouldn't have allowed such things to happen as they drifted into at Little Rock'.[48]

While Nancy was falling in love with America, with people like the Logans, with the shops and restaurants of New York, she was not unaware of what lay beneath its brash, confident veneer:

> The whole country, so far as one can see, is in a state of wild insecurity and tremble. The negroes all have charming manners and are very intelligent and gentle. The white people desperately insecure and obviously terrified the whole time of everything. Not sure quite what. Atom bombs. Negro supremacy. Not being accepted socially. Not being good in bed. Not being loved. Not being as smart as Mrs Incinerator next door. Not being thought smart, virile, clean, successful, capable of rearing children. Terrified of what people will think, say, terrified the whole thing will collapse.[49]

She flew from Las Vegas to Chicago on the morning of 9 November – the day of the presidential elections – where Ginette was due to address the Women's Athletic Club. 'I swear I'm the first Jewess that's ever spoken there, let alone from Golders Green',[50] she told Nancy. They were staying at the Sheraton-Blackstone, where their eighth-floor suite gave them wonderful views of the city which, according to Nancy, looked 'beautiful after dark ... but in the day-time is just about like Manchester'.[51] Still, anything was better than Las Vegas which, she said, 'really got me down'.[52] She had found the 24-hours-a-day obsession with gambling

> Extraordinary. Weird. Wonderful. Rather horrid ... silver dollars dominate everybody there and nobody takes the slightest interest in anything else – daylight, night, love, marriage, food, drink, everything. You need to be much stronger minded than I am before you don't get rather cross with it or else become a zombie yourself.[53]

On election night, Ginette took Nancy to see Leonard Speigelgas's play *A Majority of One*, starring Cedric Hardwicke. She was delighted to be back with Ginette: 'I have a whale of a time with Jenny, much nicer than hanging round listening to Lena and Lennie quevetching (I gather this really means fart not grumble as I thought it did, very funny) ... '.[54] Ginette was a big hit in Chicago, selling and signing hundreds of copies of *Mink*, despite the fact that, in a wonderful case of mistaken identity, the French Ambassador told a somewhat bemused Nancy that she should be awarded the Legion of Honour for her work in France. Ginette and Nancy were latched on to by 'Mrs Wrigley of the chewing gum who is the 1st lady of Chicago',[55] and were invited to a cocktail party in honour of Ginette at her luxurious Lake Shore Drive home. According to Nancy, Mrs Wrigley 'took a mad fancy to me also and I have promised that Baxy will always chew Wrigley's gum and no other'.[56] During dinner, which was, as Nancy reminded Joan, 'right in the middle of Jew and negro hating republicans on the day following the election', an extraordinary exchange took place between hostess and guest of honour. Mrs Wrigley asked Ginette, 'Why did you spend all the war escaping from the Germans?' To which Ginette replied, 'Because my husband and I are Jews, Mrs Wrigley'.[57]

Before they left Chicago, the society editor of an American Sunday newspaper came to interview them, for which Ginette and Nancy had their photograph taken sipping milk shakes in a drugstore, in mink coats and hats. The PR woman from Random House told Nancy to 'Adjust your cuffs . . . You look too casual, this is for the society page . . . '.[58]

On 10 November, they flew to Cleveland, where Ginette did another lecture and signed copies of *Mink* in Higbeeb's store. In the evening, they flew back to New York and checked into the Blackstone again. They visited Marlene Dietrich who was about to appear in cabaret in Las Vegas at the Riviera Hotel. Nancy's view of the great star was hardly that of a fawning celebrity-chaser:

> I'm sorry to say she looked very very old, but when we left we felt very very old and she looked very young . . . I found her pathetic somehow. Her husband's mistress is in the loony bin, she has to pay 12,000 dollars for her . . . a strange extraordinary splendid dame and no error.[59]

They met up with Laurence Olivier and Joan Plowright again, dining at a restaurant called Gatsby's. According to Nancy, because Olivier was still officially married to Vivien Leigh, and to avoid the attention of the press, the table had been booked under the name 'Mr and Mrs Gage'. All was well, until Olivier found he couldn't pay the bill, which came to $170. He had to tell the management who he really was and, when they didn't believe him, was forced to produce some identification.

Ginette had one more engagement to fulfil: this time in Richmond, Virginia, where she was accompanied by a now reluctant Nancy who, at the Marshall Hotel, was appalled by the sight of the Daughters of the Confederacy, who were holding their annual conference: 'They were all about 93, many of them bearded, many of them with their daddy's medals on their bosoms . . . shoving, pushing and saying "Lulabelle, puuuuunch the eeeelevator"'.[60]

On 17 November, they flew back to New York, where Nancy sent Joan a 'very very loving' cable for her fortieth birthday. In a longer letter, she insisted that

> next time we MUST go to America together and have a giggle. All the ladies clubs say they would be glad for me to lecture, but what on . . . How to write a Book, I say and they all seem pleased at the idea.[61]

But, for the time being, she was most keen to 'be at home in the bosom of my family':[62]

> I got the trots I worried about you so, and finally said to Jenny 'I want to go Home' in a little wailing voice and Jenny said severely 'You are not to want to go home until Monday' so I felt I'd been a bit mean . . . I love you most awfully and miss you too . . . .[63]

On Monday 21 November, her wish was granted and she touched down at London Airport at 9.30 p.m. She had arranged for her hire car driver, Mr Diet, to meet her so that, she told Joan, she wouldn't 'feel guilty at having tired you on top of everything else'.[64]

After her return, she had lunch with Joanna Scott-Moncrieff to discuss the possibility of doing some American-inspired broadcasts for *Woman's Hour*. Scott-Moncrieff commissioned her to do a 6–8-minute broadcast, provisionally entitled 'Las Vegas, Chicago, Virginia and More: Nancy Spain Remembering'. 'Make it a mixed sort of dish', she told Nancy, 'including perhaps . . . a demonstration of how you proved to Americans that there isn't *only one* English accent, the rain and the fruit machines and the extraordinariness of arriving in Las Vegas'.[65] Nancy duly obliged and 'Visit to America' was broadcast on December 20.

It coincided with the release of one of her most unlikely departures – an EP record. *The Worst of Nancy Spain* came out just before Christmas, on the Pye label, and its cover featured a photograph of a barefoot, trouser-wearing Nancy lying on her back with her crossed legs in the air. The record itself consisted of three of her radio pieces: 'And Friend', which sent up her attachments to famous names and included anecdotes about – and impersonations of – Lord Beaverbrook, Noel Coward and Hermione Gingold; 'Susan Grainger's Corkscrew' and 'My Big Chance', about being given a guitar and her encounters with Larry Parnes and Marty Wilde. 'There is a bit too much of Noel Coward and a suspicion of showing off but, on the other hand, some of the quotes are excellent', thought one reviewer. 'The story of going to the Lyceum and introducing Marty Wilde is a most original creation full of submerged social comment . . . as a party piece this disc certainly goes on to the shelf alongside – well, Arthur Marshall, perhaps'.[66]

While in New York, Nancy had received sad news about her former 'fiancé'. Gilbert Harding's future in television and radio had increasingly begun to look uncertain. He was sacked as chair of *Twenty Questions* after turning up drunk for one edition. During the programme he declared the quiz to be 'an idiotic game', said of fellow panellist Joy Adamson that she was a 'Joy by name but not by nature' and carried on questioning after an object had been identified. A BBC television producer explained that 'A time came when we . . . began to wonder how much longer we could go on displaying this drunken homosexual, like a freak at the sideshow'.[67] But television had not quite finished with the 'freak' yet.

John Freeman had built up a formidable reputation as a television interviewer with his series *Face to Face*. Freeman's subjects were not the politicians of the day, but entertainers or one-off 'personalities', like Gilbert Harding. Nonetheless, he asked penetrating questions in an ice-cool, unsettling manner, which usually led to his guests revealing much more about themselves than they had intended. And so it was with Gilbert.

The fact that it was broadcast just two months before he died gave it, in retrospect, greater poignancy. It plunged him into the headlines again, in the saddest possible way. One of Freeman's questions to him was 'Have you ever watched anyone die?' Gilbert struggled to answer 'yes' and then, to everyone's horror, began to cry. According to Leonard Miall, Freeman had intended to broach the subject of Gilbert's sexuality by asking him why he had not served in the armed forces, in the knowledge that men known to be gay were not drafted. But before he could, he asked THAT question, unaware that Gilbert had watched his beloved mother die. Faced with the tears of a distraught man, Freeman immediately changed his line of questioning.

Freeman came under fire when the interview was broadcast, with many viewers and pundits feeling that he had treated Gilbert too harshly. However, it was revealed after Gilbert's death that he had seen the programme before transmission and pronounced himself satisfied for it to be broadcast as it was.

Meanwhile, his column in the *People* had become an outlet for his righteous indignation, blasting forth like a trumpet on subjects dear to his heart. Sometimes they could be petty, such as 'These Health Service spectacles are cruelty to children',[68] or slightly more obscure – 'Give them the money now',[69] on flood victims in Devon. But on many occasions he hit at hard and worthy targets. His last completed column for the paper was entitled 'In Praise of Killing', a response to a book about fox-hunting, *In Praise of Hunting*, and also included an attack on a racist pamphlet, 'A Call to Action' as well as an argument against hanging.[70] His *People* column was, according to the paper's editor, 'where he could really be himself'.[71]

On Wednesday 16 November, at about 5.30 p.m., Gilbert had just finished recording two editions of *Round Britain Quiz* in the BBC overflow studios opposite Broadcasting House, at 5 Portland Place. Throughout the recordings, he complained about the heat of the studio and, before he began work, inhaled oxygen from his portable cylinder and imbibed some whisky. He finished the programmes which, although they betrayed no hint of how ill he was, were subsequently not broadcast.

Gilbert rang his driver, David Watkins, to ask him to collect him. He left the building, chatting to Christopher Saltmarshe, a current affairs producer. They had reached the steps of Portland Place when Gilbert suddenly fell backwards into Saltmarshe's arms and died. Watkins arrived and tried to administer oxygen from the ever-present portable machine. The two men then carried him back into Portland Place. They headed for the ground-floor cafeteria, which was hastily emptied and closed, and Gilbert was laid gently on two tables while his shocked friends waited for an ambulance to arrive.

Gilbert's small, 'no flowers' funeral service was held at St Charles's Roman Catholic Church in Marylebone a few days later, attended by Eamonn Andrews, Roger Storey, Joan Smith, David Watkins, Gilbert's solicitor, his Uncle Charles, sister-in-law and nephew and Mrs Clarke, a cousin. He was buried in Kensal Green Cemetery. Readers of the *People* flooded the paper with enquiries about the fate of his beloved pug dog, Susie, and were reassured with the news that Mrs Smith would keep her.

In the face of overwhelming demand, tickets had to be allocated for his memorial Requiem Mass, held at Westminster Cathedral on 9 December. As well as ensuring that the right people got their tickets, in certain special cases, Roger offered them a little keepsake. He wrote to Nancy, and asked if she and Joan would like the 'Matina Star' medal that had been presented to Gilbert by the crew on their infamous trip to Jamaica. Accepting the offer she replied:

> I didn't write before because I didn't want to add to the volume: but now you have written to me I must honestly say how very glad I am that Gilbert died occupied and successful and that he had no time to be afraid.[72]

When the 'Matina' medal duly arrived at Clareville Grove, Nancy hung it above the door of her study.

A few weeks later, Fanny and Johnnie Cradock came up with the idea of putting together a collection of memoirs written by those who had known or worked with Gilbert; the profits would go to charity. A committee to oversee the project met in January 1961, and included the Cradocks, Eamonn Andrews and Wynford Vaughan Thomas. Andre Deutsch agreed to publish the book. An appeal for donations was made in the *People*, and the Gilbert Harding Memorial Fund eventually totalled £30,000 – no small sum, and a symbol of the affection in which this strange, square-peg of a figure was held. But even Harding's fame and reputation failed to weather the emerging themes of the 1960s – sex and scandal: in 1964, his waxwork in the Brighton Wax Museum was melted down and remade into Christine Keeler.

The meltdown of Harding into Keeler could not have been more symbolic of how different the new decade was going to be. As the 1950s drew to a close, Woodrow Wyatt canvassed some 'expert' predictions on what life in Britain would be like in forty years' time, in 1999. The pundits' predictions veered from the naive to the curiously perceptive. The status of the monarchy would remain unchanged; the middle class would have increased, as would the divisions between the classes. The Tories would remain safely in government and it would be unusual for the Labour Party to win an election. The air in London would be as clean as in the countryside, all fresh food would be irradiated and fridges and freezers would become unnecessary. Telephone calls would be much cheaper and colour television would be available on a 'shilling-in-the-slot' basis. And in Britain, as elsewhere, the emphasis of the 1960s would be on youth culture.

Of course, it had already begun long before the clocks struck midnight on 31 December 1959 – Elvis, rock 'n' roll and Hollywood rebels such as Dean and Brando had seen to that. In one year, juvenile crime rose by 13 per cent and 5 million pop records were bought by British teenagers. In fashion, there was a switch from the dominance of the Paris houses to the young unknowns in London – Mary Quant and Ossie Clark. Carnaby Street was replacing the Champs-Elysées. British teenagers were spending 12s. 3d. a week on clothes; in 1958 alone, £165 million worth of teenage fashions were sold. And the world was opening up. Tourism boomed, with the rise of affordable package holidays for many people, and the beginning of the 'hippy trail' that spanned oceans and continents. Between 1960 and 1970 Britain, France and Belgium would relinquish most of their colonies. The British Commonwealth was formed. The new heroes of the new decade symbolized youth and change: Castro, Che Guevara, the Kennedys, Martin Luther King; in Britain, there were the fresh-faced pop stars – the Beatles, Cliff Richard and Adam Faith. Anne Scott-James warned her staid *Express* readers, 'All through the 1950s we adults have complained and resisted too much. In the sixties we must put things straight'.[73]

Like other adults, Nancy had also tried to resist the prevailing trends in society and entertainment while she remained an *Express* writer. However, once the 1960s were truly under way, she would lower her resistance and make concerted efforts to keep her finger on the pulse. She positively welcomed the earthy, kitchen-sink themes that were starting to dominate British literature, theatre and cinema. She, too, had grown sick of the 'epoch of the writer with private means' – the Sitwells, the Bowens, the Lehmanns, even Virginia Woolf – and welcomed the age of Wesker, Bart, Sillitoe, Delaney and Osborne:

> I'm not saying that they weren't admirable, but with their sensitivities and their beautiful china, and their 'acts of passion' they represented a way of life that simply wasn't true. The literary scene was ripe for outspoken characters from the North to blow it all sky-high . . . And the readers of the 1960s, fresh from university, filled with free education and little respect for romance, seething with ambition, are demanding something a bit more from life on the printed page than that lady tinkling with her lustre.[74]

But if it was possible for her to remain in sync during the first few years of the new era, it would have become increasingly difficult. For if the 1950s was the decade when no one told the truth, then the 1960s would be the decade when the 1950s would go belly-up and give up their secrets. Sixties satire – *Beyond the Fringe*, *Private Eye* and *TW3* – would start to sweep the skeletons out of their closets. And, of course, there was the increasing influence of television. Cosy parlour panel games would make way for earthy drama, like the *Wednesday Play*, and hard-hitting social documentaries and current affairs series, such as *World in Action*. Pop programmes would flood the networks: *Thank Your Lucky Stars*, *Oh Boy!*, *Ready, Steady, Go!* The more demure *Juke Box Jury*, however, maintained its popularity.

As the role of newspapers diminished and altered, they too would struggle to find their place in the decade. To survive, the populist papers would turn away from news and embrace sleaze, sex and scandal. And, after the revelations to come in 1963, anyone was fair game.

Nancy's move away from the *Express* to the *News of the World*, and her increasing popularity as a television personality coincided with the emergence of a new influx of friends in the early 1960s, most of whom were gay men. They included Francis 'Franzie' Goodman, one of London's most popular society photographers during the 1930s. Born in 1913, by the time he was twenty-one Goodman had worked for *Vogue* and *Harper's Bazaar*, and enhanced his reputation with some memorable portraits of the most glamorous actresses of the age, including Gertrude Lawrence, Tallulah Bankhead and Anna May Wong. During the Second World War, he served in the Army, where 'khaki seemed wholly out of place in his bohemian aura, and the intricacies of drill were always beyond him. "Who's that marching like a tart", roared the sergeant major at one parade'.[75] Euphemistically described as 'flamboyant and unconventional . . . '[76] he considered himself unattractive and suffered from bouts of depression.

By the time he met Nancy, Goodman's reputation had waned. During the 1960s and 1970s, he would write travel features for the *Daily Telegraph*. Just before his death in 1989, the National Portrait Gallery bought most of his original prints and he had begun work on his autobiography.

Laon Maybanke was another notable portrait photographer, specializing in stars of the theatre and cinema. Witty and stylish, in the early 1960s Maybanke also ran The Calabash, a gay club behind a cinema in Drayton Gardens, Kensington. The walls were adorned with some of his framed photographs of the great and the good, not entirely complemented by its plush red decor and flock wallpaper.

Maybanke's social set included Dolly and Leon Goodman, a couple who lived a life of extreme opulence and extravagance. Portraits of Dolly Goodman were included in Laon Maybanke's first collection of photographs, *First Faces*. Goodman himself was head of Leon Goodman International (a large advertising firm) and Leon Goodman Displays and was chairman of TV Commercials Ltd. He had 'shot to fame with his eye-catching street decorations for the Coronation'.[77] He collected modern art and Epstein bronzes. His flamboyant wife, Dolly, was born Cato Mishiku; half-Japanese, half-Portuguese, her father had been a diplomat. The couple lived in a luxurious home at 21 South Street, Mayfair. They dined regularly at the Caprice and Claridge's. In 1956, thieves raided the Goodmans' house and made off with jewellery estimated to be worth £25,000.

Michael Barker, who was also a friend of Maybanke and the Goodmans, and was introduced to Nancy by them, remembers that Dolly was

> 'Always in minks – she died in mink – and she always wore diamonds. She wouldn't wear pearls; she thought they were unlucky. She never opened a car or a front door in her life, and she had never been on the bus or the Underground. They lived in a fabulous house, with Italian servants. The drawing room was full of Epsteins'.

Barker first met Nancy when she joined him and the Goodmans for lunch at Claridge's. They warned Luigi, the manager, that Nancy was one of their guests and that she would probably turn up in trousers – would that be all right? He assured them it would be. As Michael Barker recalls, she caught them all off guard by turning up in a dress: 'We didn't recognize her. She looked stunning'.

Subsequently, Barker and Nancy shared various escapades with the Goodmans and Laon Maybanke. 'She was very cutting, caustic but very intelligent. She could be difficult – she didn't suffer fools. We used to collect funny walks – different ones we'd seen – and we would make up silly names from car number plates'. On one occasion, he and Nancy were driving through Piccadilly with Maybanke in his Mayflower convertible. When they got to the corner of Haymarket, a pedestrian suddenly sprang out in front of the car. 'We hooted and screamed at him – and he put his head to the window and shouted "Arseholes!". So that became "Arsehole Corner"'.

Apparently, Nancy took quite a fancy to Dolly, though nobody else, including Dick Laurie, could see the attraction. 'God knows what Nancy thought she was up to with Dolly Goodman – she was a monstrously awful woman. There's that famous story about her sending a martini back at the Dorchester, because she thought the ice was dirty ... '. According to Michael Barker, 'Nancy wooed her but never got her, as far as I know, though Dolly was fascinated'.

But the person who was to become one of her closest male friends during this time was the young man who, years earlier, had got into such trouble for reading her books: Tony Warren.

At one time a child actor and model, he had now turned to scriptwriting. He joined Granada Television in the late 1950s, first in the promotions department, before he signed an exclusive contract for the company which meant they owned everything he wrote. To begin with, he was put to work on adaptations of popular books, such as *Biggles*, but soon asked if could write about something he actually knew about. Producer Harry Elton agreed and Warren wrote the opening episode for an unlikely sounding series, based on everyday life in a small Manchester street, provisionally called 'Florizel Street'. By the time the script reached the screen, on Friday 9 December 1960, the series had been renamed *Coronation Street*. Still in his early twenties, Warren and his creation became the toast of commercial television. Though the pressure of fame and success would eventually overwhelm him, by the time he finally got to meet Nancy, he was a 'name' in his own right.

One day, over lunch with an announcer from Granada Television at a new Italian bistro in London's Old Compton Street, Tony caught the eye of another of the diners: 'I looked across the room and I'm looking at this woman who's looking at me – and I could not believe it'. His companion, Bob Jones, said, 'There's Nancy Spain'. She was sitting with Joan. 'I walked straight across and said, "I've been mad about you since I was twelve – come and have a drink with me, at 6 o'clock at the Salisbury". She said, "Who are you?" So I said, "I invented *Coronation Street*"'. Joan, apparently, was shooting filthy looks at Warren, but Nancy did agree to meet him and 'It was as though we'd known each other for ever. She said, "I've got the feeling we're going to be great, great friends"'.

They were. Nancy would say that the reason they got on so well was because 'We're the same person'. 'He is that most unlikely creature – a completely spontaneous human being',[78] she said, later adding:

I realized, looking at Tony ... that he had something that all the novelists of sensibility in the world would never have. He knew how to *love* . . . It is as though the South wind had been trapped in a grey suit, or a black leather jacket and told to sit still and behave.[79]

They made a promise not to write about each other:

'She was very fair, very loyal and I told her all sorts of things which she could have published but she never did because I trusted her implicitly. I knew a lot of secrets and so did she . . .

She wasn't really a night-time person – lunchtime was her big time. We used to go out to lunch, usually the Ivy, where she always had the same table. In those days, there was a little cocktail bar on the right as you went in and her table was the second down on the left-hand side against the wall. She was very punctual but often she would be there earlier and would always have a book on her. If she was at all late, I would also have a book. The waiters called her Miss Nancy. I said she ought to change her name to Nancy Boy and she said, "That's a joke that's already been made by Miss Hermione Gingold". That was about the level of our conversation – but we would also talk about quite serious things. The one thing we never discussed was *Coronation Street*, because she couldn't stand it. She would say, "It's the only thing I don't love about you".

There was a great deal of champagne. When I think of champagne, I always think of her – a pretty green bottle with gold foil and laughter. We acted like speed on one another – we over-stimulated each other. We would sit howling and clinging to one another like badly behaved children – but she liked that. I remember she was hugely tactile'.

Oddly enough, she did not share her biggest secret with Tony Warren, though apparently she did once come close to it: 'One day we were sitting in the Ivy and she suddenly was very itchy and said, "There's a young man I want you to meet." She was quite giggly about it. She said, "He wants to be a scriptwriter"'. They went back to Clareville Grove, where he met Tom for the first time:

'He was a wonderful little boy – lively and fizzing with energy and exploding like a box of fireworks, and full of clever, original thoughts. He kept cracking jokes – they were jokes he'd made up himself and they were good ones.

I could see her watching me and studying my reaction. I'd never before seen her seek my approval but she made it very obvious she sought approval of this child . . . on another occasion, she was teasing me about something and I said, "You shut up – people say you're those boys' father". And she said, "I wish I was . . . "'.

Though he was impressed with Tom, like many others who were close to Nancy, he and Joan did not warm to each other. This may, he suspects, have had less to do with him than Nancy. Apparently, Nancy was once on the phone to one of her lovers – 'it was full of protests of undying love', says Tony Warren. Unfortunately, Joan walked into the room and overheard Nancy's side of the passionate exchange. Later on, when she asked her who she'd been talking to, Nancy covered herself by saying it was Tony. Warren has reservations about Joan's motives:

'If Joan had an adjective, it was "cold" – with an eye that watched you. I never thought of Nancy having joined the grown-ups. Joan, perhaps, was the grown-up, the stern nanny – but it kept her on the straight and narrow, kept her disciplined. She kept working and had some belonging in her life – and belonging was hugely important to her. They were her belonging, they were her family. And in her very guarded way, it seemed that she was very frank in saying, "This is my extended family and I love them". Except with hindsight, it was a very devious flag she was waving'.

By the end of 1960, Nancy and Joan had managed to buy some land on which to build the boys' seaside home ('our joy and our ambition'[80]) near Rustington on Sea, in Sussex. But another crisis was looming at the *Express*. 'I daren't write to you about the situation at present existing between myself and the *Daily Express*', Nancy told Beaverbrook, 'as I feel my personal feelings have already confused your 3 editors quite unnecessarily. Whatever happens though I shall always love you very deeply, out of all proportion to our relationship of boss and hack'.[81]

The article she had written in October – the subject of memos flying between Beaverbrook, Max Aitken and Edward Pickering – was to be the last piece Nancy wrote for the *Express*. She filed nothing while she was in America, nor after her return in December. Considering the terms under which she wrote for the paper, her bosses appeared to have every right to be vexed. As far as they were concerned, her best efforts were still directed elsewhere – mostly towards *She*. It must have been galling for them to watch her produce countless big-name scoops for her partner's magazine – the Duchess of Windsor, Laurence Olivier, Princess Marina of Kent – while they were receiving articles that consisted of rehashed, mostly Parisian, gossip.

But – possibly with some justification – Nancy was feeling rather taken for granted herself. Reflecting on her years at the *Express*, she wrote:

Ten years went by, of pressures and excitements incorporated, rewards flattering and near fatal, law suits even. And I practised my craft. I did it at such speed that no one recognized the toil and sweat that went into it. They thought it was a 'gift' without discipline.[82]

The more she was being appreciated elsewhere, she felt, the more the *Express* ought to have valued her loyalty to them, even if her work didn't strictly fulfil the terms of her contract. Despite all her other commitments – radio, television, books, lectures, magazine features, plus a rather complex personal life – she was still coming up with the goods for the *Express*. As far as she was concerned, there shouldn't have been a problem. But there was. And there was only one solution.

On 10 February 1961, she brought it all to an end. She wrote to Beaverbrook:

I am distressed to have to write and say that I am leaving you, but I did not want you to find out from anyone but me. As you probably know your Editors and I have been trying to come to an agreement – we have failed. Because I must live I will go on working at popular journalism, but I cannot bear to find myself in competition with the 'Daily Express'. So today I am signing an agreement with the News of the World.

My gratitude to you for the past is something no words can express. Your generosity, kindness and genius still mean a great deal to me in the present. For the future: that our relationship should be harmed would be one of the things I should regret most.

I love you – and I always shall.[83]

It was a sad, rather abrupt ending – but without much bitterness and, perhaps, not altogether untimely. When Tony Warren asked Nancy why she had left the *Express*, she told him simply, 'I had outlived my usefulness there'. She had spent many years reading and writing about other people's work, and

all the while life was catching up on me, and absorbing me to the point where I could no longer stand fictions and only the truth was exciting ... All I wanted, all I still want, is to tell the truth and convey my pleasure in the telling of it. Not easy.[84]

Sir Edward Pickering saw it rather differently:

'She may have felt that, but I don't think the people on the *Express* viewed it quite like that. I think the paper could have made good use of her for several years more. But she was reaching a stage where she wanted the change and it was an agreeable parting'.

Nancy remained on good terms with her former colleagues, often dropping into the *Express* offices. 'She wanted to come in and talk to people. Despite her great air of confidence, she did require, every now and then, some reassurance', explains Sir Edward Pickering. And though her visits to Beaverbrook became less frequent, their mutual affection and admiration endured. She made sure she never forgot his birthday, especially in the year of her 'defection'. She and Joan sent him eighty-two roses – one for each year. 'They make a wonderful display, and Cherkley is glowing with warmth and colour',[85] he told her.

Stafford Somerfield, the brazen, canny editor of the *News of the World* was thrilled with his new acquisition. 'We took her on gladly because she was such a great newspaper woman. A professional',[86] he said.

But, as Nancy jokingly acknowledged by beginning her first *News of the World* column with the words, 'Mother always said I would end up in the "News of the World"', a paper which did its utmost to unearth celebrities' most intimate or sordid secrets was hardly the natural home for her. She was aware of the contradictory nature of the public's taste for such stories – fearing them while feeding on them. 'People are terrified of sex and they are afraid when they see a sexual scandal that something of the sort may happen to them if they don't watch out',[87] she observed. And the *News of the World*

was just the paper to catch them with their pants down. Like J. Edgar
Hoover and his library of personal files, it gave people in the public eye
something to be afraid of: 'live a life of indiscretion and you, too, could "end
up in the *News of the World*"'.

Nevertheless, as Sir Edward Pickering points out, it did have its qualities:

> 'It was a scandal sheet – always has been, but for most of that period it was a
> broadsheet, not a tabloid. It was rather a different sort of paper – it did cover
> everything in a complete fashion. Its sports coverage was way ahead of
> everybody. On the main leader page there was always an article by a minister
> or someone like that. Bob Boothby used to write a regular column – Percy
> Cudlipp used to refer to him as "the fig leaf on the NOTW". It wasn't
> regarded at that time in quite the same way as it is now, because newspapers
> have changed altogether in the last thirty years and TV has very much caused
> that. TV and radio are now the purveyors of news, whereas it used to be
> newspapers, and editors have had to find a new role for the papers. With the
> qualities, it's to provide a great deal of background; the tabloids have gone
> into investigative scandal-mongering, which has attracted more and more
> readers'.

Despite the paper's tawdry reputation, Nancy and her articles were certainly
in step with its motto: 'All Human Life Is Here'. When Stafford Somerfield
became editor in 1960, its circulation was already 6.5 million but he was far
from pleased: ten years earlier, it had been nearly 8.5 million. On his first day
in the job, Somerfield asked his staff, 'What the hell are we going to do about
the circulation?'[88] It was largely rhetorical, for he knew the answer: 'We want
a series of articles that will make their hair curl',[89] he declared. He began with
Diana Dors's 'kiss-and-tell' life story, persuading Christine Keeler to do the
same in 1963, and continued, unabashed, to live up to the paper's Fleet Street
nickname: 'News of the Screws'. Nancy, of course, would largely steer clear of
such shenanigans in her new column, even though she was given *carte blanche*
to write about whatever took her, or Somerfield's, fancy. 'She accepted any
job', he remembered, 'not once to my knowledge saying it wasn't her line or
it was too difficult. Some stars talk like that. But not Nancy. Anything went.
But anything. She was a great reporter'.[90]

Somerfield made a big hue and cry about Nancy's arrival, flagging the
new column, 'Get Around with Nancy Spain', the week before it began.
She made a memorable debut: 'The Shame of Spain Goes Slowly Down the
Drain' was an account of her visit to the Town and Country Health Club.
She put her $34\frac{1}{4}$–$28\frac{1}{2}$–41 figure through some rigorous exercises in an attempt
to firm up her hips and bust. She tried out the vibrator belt, which was
'rather sexy . . . I was asked to sit down upon a revolving drum, which was
sexier still. I absolutely loved it'.[91] 'She's Gay, She's Provocative . . . She's
Going Places', blared her column headline, and it was no idle boast. In the
first few months of her new job, her assignments included conducting the
Joe Loss Band at the Hammersmith Palais; a location report on Deborah
Kerr's *The Innocents*; visiting a plastics factory that made mannequins; being

'sawn in half' by Robert Harbin at the Festival Hall; judging the Mecca National Ballroom Queen Finals; watching wrestling at Welling in Kent; and giving the lowdown on ten-pin bowling after enjoying a game with Charlie Drake in Stamford Hill. It was all unashamedly populist and slightly tacky – and she was loving every minute of it. She told Beaverbrook, 'I greatly enjoy it. I am rather proud of the fact that we are 250,000 a week up on this time last year and that the Editor thinks it has something to do with me'.[92]

It was worlds away from the glamour and sophistication of life lived in Paris, amongst the high society of fashion and showbusiness – but completely in keeping with her thirst for people, places and passions from all walks of life. 'My greatest pleasure . . . has always been meeting people', she said. 'By people I don't necessarily mean celebrities . . . I wish I could fill the eleven enchanting hours of the day with nothing else at all but meeting and talking to new people'.[93] She admitted that this wish had limitations:

> Obviously it would be idle to pretend I would lie down and die for any member of the public who cares to speak to me in the street. But for the talented, particularly those in the middle of the struggle to arrive, I will put up with a very great deal.[94]

And, despite the self-imposed rider, her polygamous need for people drew them to her, and she to them. 'I imagine a day doesn't go by in which I do not start some sort of relationship, or communicate in some way with someone, somewhere',[95] she observed. Unwittingly, she had pinpointed the key to all her successes: rather than being an 'educator', she was, quintessentially, an entertainer and communicator.

And one thing that she was communicating – an attitude rather out of step with the mood of the times – was the celebration of diversity and infinite variety: of class, culture, colour, credo and calling. It was a paradoxical message from a self-professed 'conservative' woman of the time, even though Tony Warren observed one curious flaw in the make-up of her consciousness:

> 'It was odd that she was highly critical of her fellow gay men and women – and very rarely were her gay characters sympathetic. The only time the generation gap showed with Nancy was on the subject of sexuality and my absolute refusal to wrap any veil of mystery around what I was. The idea of gay politics was anathema – it was not to be spoken of. I think she found me much too much out of the closet. She never actually told me not to, but sometimes I could almost feel disapproval when I was so open about it. But there she was, in full drag, as it were, still being hugely closeted'.

Meanwhile, her own life continued to be awash with infinite variety and contradictions. One day, she would be judging the heats of an Old Tyme Dancing competition in Barnsley or the *News of the World* Angling tournament in Hastings; the next, spending weekends in Switzerland or Paris with Ginette. She had now become as much a part of what Noel Coward called 'the 70 Avenue Marceau circus'[96] as any of the glittering names she had once been in awe of. Now, accepted and regarded as one of them, she could be equally as awe-inspiring. One weekend, Coward joined Nancy, Ginette and Paul-Emile in Paris to see *West Side Story*. The next day, he took the young dancer, Grover Dale, to Avenue Marceau: 'he emerged, all things considered, with flying colours. It must have been startling for the poor boy to be faced suddenly with Ginette, Lena Horne, Sue Fonda, Nancy Spain, etc., all shrieking at the tops of their voices in different languages'.[97]

Despite Coward's previous complaints about Nancy turning her social weekends into Friday's fish-and-chip wrapping, she was more judicious about what she revealed in public after she joined the *News of the World*. Most of her star-studded stories would now be reserved for *She*. She might not have minded having her name splashed all over a notorious Sunday scandal sheet, but the luminaries whose circle she had become a part of certainly did. It was also in her own best interests to be more discreet in the company of *News of the World* newshounds, as the paper, with its staunchly anti-censorship stance, was not averse to eating its own if it made a good story. Stafford Somerfield asked only two questions: 'Is it right to publish it and is it within the law to publish it? Even members of the staff did not escape'.[98]

But, even with all her secrets, Nancy felt secure, as Tony Warren recalls:

> 'I remember we discussed sex once. We both said we thought sex was wonderful – and she said no one could accuse her of any activity with any woman in England. And yet, oddly enough, not long afterwards she arrived in a very rosy and giggly state, claiming to have been seized in a bathroom by a very famous American star of, let us say, *irretrievable* heterosexual reputation'.

That summer, Nancy persuaded George and Norah to make the long journey south and have a holiday with her in Brighton. George's deafness had worsened considerably in recent years – he even had to stop going to the meetings of his beloved Society of Antiquaries because of it and was spending more time at home. Nancy decided a holiday would be a welcome break for both him and Norah. By all accounts, they had a wonderful time – Nancy even introduced her father to the delights of champagne cocktails and he marvelled at finding something new to drink at the age of eighty-four.

In August, Nick and Tom also got to spend a holiday with Nancy, although, inevitably, it was linked to an assignment. The *News of the World* were sponsoring a 'Stars of Tomorrow Novice Competition' and Nancy was asked to cover it. The competition was being held at Butlin's in Bognor Regis, so off she trooped to Sussex, with the boys in tow. When Nancy informed her readers that she was being accompanied by two young men, she hastened to add, 'Those who see a romantic link in this may wipe that silly smile off their faces. The boys are nine and 15'.[99] Nancy didn't particularly take to holiday-camp life, though the boys had a whale of a time playing table tennis and riding on all the roundabouts. For her part, Nancy was asked to judge the Knobbly Knees competition and, when she took to the dancefloor one evening, 'A small boy in a green jersey remarked "If that's Nancy Spain, I'm a Chinaman"'.[100] Paris must have seemed a long way away.

During the next few months, she was often called on to be a 'celebrity judge' – and in some unlikely places. In September, she was at the Miss United Kingdom contest in Blackpool. Her fellow judges were footballer Jimmy Armfield, Arthur Askey and Cliff Richard who, according to Nancy, greeted each new contestant with 'Holy mackerel!'[101] The eventual winner was eighteen-year-old Rosemarie Frankland, whose picture was printed in the paper alongside Nancy's boast, 'Well, can I or can I not pick 'em'.[102] The next month, she and Craig Douglas were amongst the celebrities attending the National Hairdressers' Federation festival at St Pancras Town Hall. And a few weeks later, she joined Helen Shapiro in Glasgow to adjudicate another noteworthy event: the South of Scotland Electricity Cooking Competition for children.

In contrast, Joan was continuing to fill the pages of *She* with features on rather more weighty and taboo matters: breast cancer, 'The Curse', mammaplasty, fibroids and women's self-defence. However, that autumn, Nancy would be able to put the tacky summer of knobbly knees and beauty queens behind her and return to the American lecture circuit with Ginette.

On 10 October, George was at home when he suffered a sudden, massive heart attack. He died there on 12 October, aged eighty-four. Nancy, by now already in Jesmond, registered the death, informed the local press and helped arrange the funeral. The will was straightforward: George had left his estate of £16,155 to Norah.

Although, of course, extremely well known in his own right in the North-East, his name was still eclipsed by that of his more famous daughter: 'Father of Nancy Spain Dies',[103] ran the *Newcastle Evening Chronicle* headline. He was cremated on 14 October and then his ashes were interred at the family grave at Holy Trinity, Horsley, on Monday 16 October. Joining his family for the ceremony was the current colonel of the 6th Northumberland Fusiliers, the ex-colonel and George's transport major who had served with him in the First World War. Nancy stayed in Jesmond for a few days more, from where she filed her *News of the World* column: it was her own tribute to 'my darling father', who was 'a gay, brilliant, happy, fascinating creature, who loved his life right up to the week of his death. And I refuse to pull a long face and shed tears'.[104]

Beaverbrook sent Nancy his condolences. 'This is a sad blow for you and I send you my warmest sympathy. Parents are our closest link with the past. Their death is always a tremendous shock however much we may think we have accepted the probability that we will outlive them'.[105] 'He was a wonderful man and I was deeply fond and proud of him',[106] she replied.

For years, Nancy had unsuccessfully tried to persuade her parents to move south. Now, even after George's death, Norah insisted on staying in

Tankerville Place. As a result, Nancy's visits became more frequent, usually once a month.

Sheila van Damm's father had also died by now and this left her facing a professional, as well as a personal loss. In his will, Vivian had stipulated that the Windmill should be closed after his death. Sheila was not convinced, but felt that she should comply with his last wishes. That is, until Joan intervened.

Sheila was lying in her bedroom, stricken with flu, when Joan came in and, for two hours, practically bullied her into changing her mind. She accused Sheila of being 'gutless': 'How had she possibly won the Monte Carlo Rally? Was she really so spineless? And then, clinching the argument, asked "Hasn't it ever struck you that your Father might be wrong?!"'[107] The harsh words struck a chord and Sheila decided to keep the Windmill's doors open, becoming its sole manager. However, this wasn't the end of her problems, since the theatre's shows were now starting to look rather tame and outdated compared with what was on offer in the clubs run by the burgeoning empire of Paul Raymond. In hindsight, she might have been better off ignoring Joan's advice.

A few weeks after George's death, Nancy was getting ready for her trip to America. In Paris, she shopped for some new clothes; to go with the requisite dresses and skirts, she even bought a French girdle. 'The Americans are rather down on ladies in trousers',[108] she explained. Before she left London, she was invited to a dinner party by her doctor, 'Nelly' Newman. The other guests were Denis Magill, a Lloyds underwriter, Peter Hunt, director of *From Russia with Love* and Rena Harper, an Athens-born Greek woman, then married to an Englishman, Kenneth Harper. During the meal, the subject of islands came up in conversation and, casually, Rena Harper said that she could arrange for Nancy to buy some land on a Greek island. Nancy leaped at the idea. She had always longed to have an island she could 'escape' to and Greece would certainly be a more romantic location for this than Hampton Wick, site of her last abortive attempt at island life. Harper told her it would only cost a few hundred pounds for the land, though obviously to build a house on it would require more, assuming she was granted building permission. Without consulting Joan, Nancy told Rena to go ahead with the plan.

Nothing was finalized before she and Ginette flew to New York in early November. They stayed in a twin room at the Westbury before heading off to criss-cross the country. It was a hectic schedule, professionally and socially: there were lectures as far afield as Texas and Ohio, and parties held by Claudette Colbert and Dinah Shore in Los Angeles.

They returned to New York at the beginning of December, from where, exhausted, she wrote to Joan:

Darling angel cat darling

We got in here last night more dead than alive . . . I have collected marvellous material for the SHE column and will write it either before I leave . . . I plan to leave on the 7th, as it is a good number for travelling or living by.

I am well, happy, brown from California and all my pipes are working smoothly (as Dad used to say) and I had an excellent letter from mum written last Sunday, very funny.[109]

As promised, she flew back to England on 7 December, armed with plenty of gossip: 'I saw 2 nuns doing the twist in Santa Barbara'.[110]

Within days, she was involved in more assignments for the *News of the World*: for their Christmas Eve edition, they arranged for her to fly on wires at the Scala Theatre, where *Peter Pan* was playing. To round off the year, she trotted out 'Old Spain's Almanac for 1962', where she predicted:

V is for VIRGINIA, one of the places where Old Spain will not be invited again . . . M is for MONROE who will be late, all through 1962 . . . X is for XENOPHOBIA which will go on and on and on, same as before, particularly in America.[111]

Island of Dreams

Nancy's year began with two *News of the World* assignments that typified her work for the paper: travelling to Switzerland to do a feature on winter sports one week, the next, back to Butlin's at Bognor to judge a Glamorous Granny competition. Not so typical, however, was her support in February for striking ITV performers, then in the thirteenth week of their industrial dispute. She was highly critical of Peter Cadbury, then chairman of Westward TV, and even called for a strike in support of a minimum wage. 'DO SOMETHING!',[1] she implored.

Then she received a call from 'Nelly' Newman: Rena Harper had bought the land in Greece for a mere £100; she had also purchased a plot for James and Gloria Jones. Nancy had met the author of *From Here to Eternity* and his wife in Paris and New York, and had suggested that they also buy a piece of Greece. Nancy discovered, however, that the land Rena had bought for her didn't fit her precise requirements – a south-facing area with a beach. So the obliging Rena bought her another plot, 'an olive grove, washed on three sides by the Aegean Sea',[2] for £450. It was on the island of Skiathos, latterly one of the more upmarket Greek holiday resorts in the Sporades, but then one of the least accessible of the 'Sprinkled Isles'. In 1962, it took four hours by boat to get to Skiathos from Volos on the mainland, two and a half from Pifki and four hours from Orei. The 61 square km island itself was 'green from end to end',[3] enthused Nancy. Skiathos Town, on its south-eastern tip, had only two hotels and one road.

Having got her land, Nancy now had to get permission from the Bank of England to spend £1,000 on building a house. It was duly granted and Rena arranged for a Greek lawyer to register the deeds for the land on the neighbouring island of Skopelos. While she was waiting for the Bank's decision, Nancy spent hours with Rena in London, pouring over maps of Skiathos and the Greek mainland, studying boat timetables, and calculating the cheapest way of getting herself and car to her plot of Paradise.

Then Stafford Somerfield came up with a suggestion that suited her purpose admirably. How about going on a 'round the world' trip with Air France, starting from Paris and taking in the Far East – and, of course, a stop-off in Greece? There was an obstacle, however: she had two recordings of *My Word* coming up, separated by only ten days. Air France said that was no problem and thought the idea would be good publicity for them. Nancy asked if Granny Laurie could join her on the trip; Air France and the *News of the World* agreed. While she was away, Nancy's columns during March would be filled with a four-part series by Mirabelle Topham – 'My Grand National Story'.

Their trip would include stop-offs in Japan and Thailand, so Nancy went off to the respective embassies and organized visas for herself and Granny. Her Japanese visa stated that the 'reason for visit' was 'Public Relations'. They also had to have jabs for smallpox, yellow fever and other assorted diseases. Fortified with antibodies, in the third week of February, they flew to Paris with Air France representative Cyril McGhee, for the start of their trip.

They spent an evening at the lavish Les Assassins restaurant, where they were joined by Ginette. The next day they flew on to Rome and, from there, to Athens where they were met by Rena and Kenneth Harper. They were driven to the island of Euboea, situated between the mainland and Skiathos, towards their eventual destination of Pifki, from where they would catch a caique. Once on the island, Rena took Nancy on a tour of Skiathos Town before setting off along the lone road which passed near her land. At the end of a steep, rough track, only accessible by foot, was Nancy's plot – 'On top of the forty-foot-tall cliff, rough, gloriously overgrown with olive, oak, gorse and scrubby bushes of all sorts'.[4] Rena explained to Nancy how the land would have to be flattened before her house could be built and Kenneth Harper pointed out the path that led to the small private beach. 'I suppose I have had a few moments in my life that compare, emotionally, with this one', Nancy said later. 'And it is no use pretending I don't like the struggle that I recognize at such moments. The "struggle" to me is everything'.[5] If this was true, then the Greek adventure would more than satisfy her hankering for a hard new struggle.

Back in Skiathos Town, Rena introduced her to the builder and engineer who would design her new house. Money changed hands and toasts were drunk to the new venture. Nancy and Granny then headed back to Athens and journeyed on to Bangkok, where things did not go as smoothly as they had in Skiathos. Cables confirming their hotel reservations had not arrived, the temperature was over a hundred and Nancy was suffering from nettle rash, picked up in Greece.

They had a better time in Hong Kong, where the popularity of *My Word* had ensured she was treated like royalty, and where she recorded countless television and radio interviews. Next stop was Tokyo, where there were more interviews and a meeting with a Grand Master of Aikido. 'Your helpless posture reminds me of the giant insect in Kafka's *Metamorphosis*', he told her. Nancy mentioned the incident in her column for *She*, adding 'The Editor, who has been trying for years to think what I reminded her of, was highly delighted by this'.[6] She also visited a bar, where she heard a sixty-strong choir rehearsing. She later discovered that the bar was the local Communist meeting place and the choir were rehearsing for the next rally. After this, there was an even briefer stop in Anchorage, Alaska, before she and Granny flew on to Hamburg and returned to Paris, from where Nancy filed her first copy for the *News of the World*.

On her return to England, she opened a letter which told her she had been awarded the Freedom of the City of London. She had to pay 3 guineas for the privilege; this entitled her to sell matches in the streets of the City and, if sentenced to hang, it had to be done with a silk rope. A few months later, another Freewoman, Mrs Elsie Liley of Chelsea, wrote to inform her of another peculiar prerogative: they could drive cows across London Bridge, if they so wished. Nancy suggested that she and Mrs Liley try it early one morning – 'I feel the City Police would enjoy this addition to the rush hour traffic'.[7]

While her diabetic mother had been tested to the limit by chasing round the world in ten days, Joan had been more deskbound. But she was continuing to stretch the boundaries of what was deemed acceptable in a woman's magazine. Of course, there were always the more conventional subject matters – she roped in Alan Freeman to be one of the judges of that year's 'Miss SHE' competition, held at the Albert Hall. But in 1962, the magazine's readers learned about vegetarianism, abortion, wet-weather driving (courtesy of Sheila), even cremation. She also visited Chailey Heritage, a school in Sussex for limbless children, some of them early victims of thalidomide. The school needed a new swimming pool but were short of funds. Touched by what she had seen, Joan instigated the 'SHE Chailey Pool Fund', to which readers were invited to send donations. Money immediately started to arrive at the *She* offices.

Meanwhile, finances were becoming rather a sore subject at Clareville Grove. 'The villa on Skiathos went on swallowing money like a well-loved, fractious, spoiled child,' wrote Nancy. 'Ironically, because I hadn't got the cash, I couldn't go and see how the building was getting on'.[8] Irritatingly, she was hearing plenty of enthusiastic reports from others who had also built on Skiathos about how wonderful their new houses were looking. James Jones had bought a large piece of land near hers and Denis Magill had bought the next headland along. While visiting his own building, he filmed some home movies of Nancy's house and told her, 'There is a clear picture of a man on your land, digging in the bottom left hand corner. He must be digging your cess pit, surely?'[9] Nancy joked that it was more likely to be her grave. 'By now the island dream had a bad flavour to it', she admitted. 'It had almost become the island nightmare'.[10] Even her dream of it as a place where she could go to 'escape' from the assignments, the deadlines and the ever-ringing telephone was looking rather ragged: she discovered that Harold Keeble, who had just left the *Express*, had also bought a piece of land on Skiathos not too far from her site – 'to our mutual disgust',[11] snapped Nancy.

As if the Greek folly wasn't accounting for substantial sums of her income, Nancy was somehow persuaded to invest some cash into a theatre show. Even more incredibly, she then persuaded Joan and Granny Laurie to do the same. Some of the music reminded her of George, she would later say. Whatever the reason, she could hardly have chosen a worse moment to gamble on such a risky venture. But then, as she admitted, 'Folly is one of the things that I love best'.[12]

Little Mary Sunshine was an American musical, written and composed by Rick Besoyan, a spoof operetta, originally produced in New York in 1959. It ran for over a thousand performances and was one of the longest-running off-Broadway musicals ever. Set in the Colorado Rockies, it concerned the story of the romance between 'Little Mary' Potts and Captain Big Jim Warington of the Forest Rangers. The Captain has a love rival – the Native American Yellow Feather, portrayed, in typical 1950s American style, as a thoroughly 'bad injun'. The Captain finally woos Mary by singing her the 'Colorado Love Call' – clearly an offer no girl could refuse.

It took several years for the show to reach London, but finally it opened on 17 May 1962 at the Comedy Theatre, directed by Paddy Stone and starring Patricia Routledge as Little Mary, dancer Joyce Blair as her friend, Nancy Twinkle, and Bernard Cribbins as Corporal Billy Jester. It was greeted with mixed reviews, though some, like *The Times*, predicted a healthy future for the show: 'The book and lyrics are accurate pastiche ... one would not be surprised to find Little Mary Sunshine becoming something of a cult'.[13]

Nancy took the responsibilities of being an 'angel' very seriously. She plugged the show whenever and wherever possible. She interviewed Patricia Routledge for *Woman's Hour* and dragged friends to see it on more than one occasion – Laon Maybanke endured it three times – in the hope that they would spread the word. Unfortunately, not even Nancy's money or publicity could prolong the life of *Little Mary Sunshine* in London and the curtain came down after a paltry forty-four performances. Nancy attributed its failure to several factors: 'For a start the general public could not make head nor tail of it ... the show was written by an American ... it was somewhat over-lavish in production ... '.[14]

While lobbying on behalf of *Little Mary*, Nancy decided she had to go back to Greece again, and to hell with the expense. She hired a VW Slumberwagon, complete with kitchen and calor-gas lighting, booked passage for it and herself on the *Ionia*, a Greek freighter sailing from Marseilles in late May – and then told Joan. Surprisingly, she thought a few weeks on the island would be good for Nancy, but insisted she take a companion. Tony Warren toyed with the idea of going with her but hated Athens, so decided against it. But there was another candidate. One friend who had been treated to the rare delights of *Little Mary Sunshine* was the writer Alfred Allan Lewis. He was a relatively new chum, made – like many others – during one of her visits to New York, though their first meeting was in London. Lewis's nickname was 'The Waster' and, though it might have been a slightly harsh sobriquet, he had enjoyed something of a wayward life thus far.

In his youth, Lewis had been an actor: Mae West had cast the 6 ft. 3 in. nineteen-year-old as 'Mister Muscles, da Champ' in a touring version of *Diamond Lil*. He then worked in PR before becoming a playwright, but seemed to spend more time moving from continent to continent and always appeared to have plays 'under option' to various film producers. Lewis happened to be in London for the first night of *Little Mary Sunshine* – he had been asked over by Michael Redgrave to do rewrites on one of his plays. When Lewis found out about Nancy's plans to go to Greece, he offered to go along with her for the ride.

They stocked up on provisions for the journey. Lewis announced his intention of buying a revolver and a hunting knife. Joan thought this was ridiculous and said so. Revolver and knife were subsequently scratched from the shopping list.

And so, on 20 May, Nancy and Alfred Allan Lewis set off for Skiathos in the camper van. Once in France, they headed for Paris and had lunch with Ginette, Paul-Emile and Marlene Dietrich. On 23 May, they reached Cassis, a fishing village near Marseilles and spent the next two days there. On the 25th, Nancy remembered to send a cable to Beaverbrook, whose birthday it was. They set sail the same day at about four in the afternoon – first stop, Genoa.

At Piraeus, they were met by Harold Keeble's wife, Sue, and Rena Harper. After that, however, things started to go wrong: they ran out of petrol in the middle of Athens and the engine stalled on the way to Thebes. Struggling on to Lafkardia, where they were to meet up again with Sue and Rena, they caught a boat to Skiathos from Arkitsa, via Euboea. When they arrived in Skiathos, they were told the road that would lead to Nancy's house was not yet finished. Fortunately for Rena, her house was close to Skiathos's solitary road and, on the way to the beach where Nancy and Lewis would set up camp, she insisted they stop and look at her nearly finished residence.

The next day, she drove Nancy to inspect hers. Plumbers, carpenters and builders were all demanding more money and Nancy realized she would have to cut short her holiday, get back to England and seek out some lucrative work – possibly another book. The decision was reinforced with the arrival of three letters. One was from the *News of the World*, who wanted to know when they could expect another column from her; a second was from Granny Laurie, with the news that *Little Mary Sunshine* was in trouble; and, finally, Joan's letter told her that Nick had managed to blow himself up in the school chemistry lab and might lose the use of his hands. So they hauled the VW van out of the sands and, after what amounted to a long weekend in Skiathos, drove wearily back home. While she was on the boat to Marseilles, she began writing what she hoped would be a money-spinning book. It would be, she told Beaverbrook, 'a sort of memoir'.[15] It became known, provisionally, as the 'Escape Book'.

Everyone, it seemed, was becoming involved with Skiathos. Nancy had been asked to do a series of interviews for *Woman* and Sir Basil Spence, the architect, was one of her subjects. Spence and his wife, Joan, subsequently saw Nancy socially on several occasions and, of course, the the Greek house came up in conversation. Spence was alarmed that it was being built without the supervision of an architect. He said he would write to an architect he knew at the Technological Institute in Athens, Constantinos Doxiadis, and ask him to send one of his assistants to Skiathos to visit the site and assess the situation. Naturally, Nancy would have to pay for this.

But at least she had found a new, if rather tiring and time-consuming, way of making more money. During her last visit to America with Ginette, during which she had done a few lectures herself, she had acquired something of a taste for it. 'If I can warm up an ice bound audience in a cinema at 10 a.m. when they haven't got the foggiest idea who I am I think I can do anything',[16] she told Ginette. She took herself off to the Fifth Avenue offices of W. Colston Leigh Inc., who then just happened to be the biggest lecture agency in America. She successfully auditioned for them and a fifteen-date tour was booked for her, to take place during October and November 1963. The agency circulated publicity material that boasted 'Among International Celebrities Everybody who is Anybody Knows Britain's Fabulous Journalist, best selling author, critic and television personality'.[17]

In the meantime, 'Britain's Fabulous Journalist' had to come up with some suitable summery features for the *News of the World* and, as Tony Warren recalls, roped him in to help her:

'She was the most fun to go on an adventure with. She was doing a series about going off to meet *News of the World* readers all over the seaside resorts of Britain. "I need a new angle", she said. So I suggested she went to a deserted town in Wakes week, because, in those days, Northern towns had public holidays and the entire town would close down and move out and people would meet their neighbours by the seaside. Blackpool would become Oldham for one week. With Wakes came a fair. We discovered the following week was Ashton-under-Lyme's Wakes week. I met her in Manchester; we went to Ashton, to the fair, and visited a showman's caravan. Then we went and knocked on people's doors. She was certainly not the great "I am" – she said, "My name's Nancy Spain from the *News of the World*". And in every house, they were doing decorating'.

She followed this up with a story on the Paris Collections, accompanied by a picture of her in a dress and high heels. 'Now You Know Why I Prefer Slacks',[18] she declared. 'I know I'm a rebel. My attitude to women's clothing may well have been conditioned by the fact that my sister was once a famous designer'.[19] But defiant though she was, she was becoming concerned that the significance of her now familiar trouser-wearing image was filtering through to those who were not 'the converted'. According to Tony Warren, she had been rattled after overhearing a remark made by a mother to her little girl. They were in a shoe shop and obviously the child was not keen on the usual assortment of dainty footwear. Her mother played what she must have thought was her trump card: 'Now you don't want to grow up to be a Nancy Spain, do you?'[20]

Whoever that mother may have been, she was not alone in knowing what being 'a Nancy Spain' meant, according to Alison Hennegan:

'What I became more aware of as I got older and people talked about Nancy Spain . . . you could sense that very conventional people were intrigued by her, slightly shocked but not repelled. I became impressed by that sleight of hand: that she'd managed to do and be something that she shouldn't have been allowed to be, that for most people was quite clear but it wasn't spelled out. So they didn't have to take that "L" word and deal with it, though in fact she'd already infiltrated sufficiently far into their awareness of who and what she was, and somehow been accepted. It's a very English trick – you get in under the guard and there you are, in the middle of the room. Also, she played the class card. She was a "class" act and she was an upper-middle-class woman and it gave her, whatever her insecurities may have been, a terrifically quiet, attractive authority'.

For over fifteen years, she had been getting away with 'pleasing herself' and being herself. But, as her fame increased, particularly on television, so did her marked difference to other prominent female media personalities. 'She was one of those very few people who had very feminine and masculine parts to her', explains David Jacobs. 'She had an equal quantity of both'.

In many ways, her openness was remarkable for the times: there were the constant references to 'my partner, Joan Werner Laurie', to Nick and Tom and, self-deprecatingly, to how ill at ease she, a short-haired, trouser-wearing woman, felt in the finest feminine fashions. By the early 1960s, it was already obvious that sex scandals were going to become meat and drink to the downmarket end of Fleet Street. And, as Stafford Somerfield had made clear, no one would be immune from exposure if it made a good story.

Despite Nancy's boast to Tony Warren that no one could have any proof of her affairs with other women, there could be no guarantee of this. Rumours about her relationship with Ginette had been circulating amongst the Fleet Street gossip columnists for years, though, obviously, nothing had appeared in print. After Liberace had successfully sued the *Daily Mirror* for libel for suggesting he was gay, editors were understandably cautious, even if they knew the stories were true. But Nancy was aware that she was too well known and her image too notorious and resonant for the facade to continue unchallenged. Something had to be done to nip the rumours in the bud – or at least diminish their impact – before the situation got out of control.

Increasingly, she had been making strenuous efforts to dress more conventionally for her public appearances. 'Ever since my 40th birthday, when my hips started spreading steadily sideways, I decided that this middle-aged Peter Pan act must stop', she explained. 'Anyway, in public'.[21] She borrowed outfits from sister Liz and Ginette and sought advice from other women on how to behave in certain dresses at certain functions. 'I remember my mother, who liked Nancy, ... giving her lessons in how women behave at a ball', says Tony Warren. However, he didn't entirely approve of such attempts to 'cover up':

'I only ever saw her in those kind of clothes once or twice and the second time I had a big argument with her. It was as odd as seeing a heterosexual male transvestite as a woman – the appearance is at variance with the aura. Believe you me, Nancy dressed as a woman looked a tragedy. Nancy dressed as Nancy looked like a wonderful gutsy pirate'.

Nick Laurie agrees:

'All the photos of her in *Millionaire* and *A Funny Thing* were out and out frauds. She lived in jeans, very old men's tail shirts and big, baggy sweaters. Dresses were for dressing-up occasions only. She hated dressing up. Many, many times, when she was getting ready to go to some "do", I heard her complaining about having to dress like that ... she just didn't look like her'.

But Tony Warren says it was not a simple case of 'butch' dressed up as 'femme':

'It's such a simplification to write her off as a lesbian – it was much more complex than that. She saw herself as a creature. I think in her dreams she was a boy. My relationship with her was like being friends with a very good-looking boy who I didn't remotely fancy but I loved – that was how we played it. Once I saw her dressed as a woman, I felt sorry for her. She'd constructed this image, which was not entirely original. There'd been a literary version with Radclyffe Hall, and there'd been the mass-market version with Naomi Jacob. For some reason, some criticism had rocked her faith in what she'd created'.

It also caused her to consider another course of action – entering a 'lavender' marriage with a like-minded man, one of whom was the distinctly unclo-seted Tony Warren. 'She debated aloud whether we should get married', he recalls. Naturally, he didn't want to. 'There was somebody else and she introduced me to him – Alfred Allan Lewis. She asked me if I thought she should marry him, and I said no I do not'.

There was a third candidate: Roy Rutherford. According to Frank Ellul, Nancy discussed the idea with him and revealed one of the reasons why she thought she should go through with it. 'She'd been chatting to a taxi driver and he had said to her, "You're not what my wife thinks you are – one of those funny people"'. Noel Coward had been right all along: no amount of big-bowed dresses were going to fool anyone, whether they were a three-and-a-half-year-old child or a London cabbie.

However, Nancy continued to make half-hearted stabs at 'bearding' herself. For the *News of the World*, she registered with the Golden Key Marriage Bureau, who agreed to try and find a 'match' for her. She filled in the requisite form:

Age: 44, rising 45.
Religion: Doubtful, baptized and confirmed C. of E. but more like a Buddhist really.
Income: ... Ah. There's the rub.[22]

She requested a man of fiftysomething, in any trade except writing or journalism. She got a 53-year-old designer from Kensington, who had requested an intelligent gay brunette. Which was exactly what he got – but far from what he wanted.

Roy Rutherford, always the man for a dare – if not marriage – offered to drive to Greece and keep an eye on the builders and plumbers. His cables back to Nancy were not encouraging: the builder needed another £500. She sent it. Meanwhile, other aspiring members of the Skiathos circle were also having problems. James Jones wrote to her, anxious that he had not heard from Rena Harper:

> What worries me most is that I still do not have my deeds to my piece of land from her. Until I do, I will be worried that something peculiar might happen and lose me the place. Can you help me in any way with this?'[23]

On Alfred Allan Lewis's suggestion, he planned to write to Roy Rutherford, who was still on Skiathos, to see if he could help. Jones also suggested that he and his wife could rent Nancy's house to live in while their own was being built next to it. Nancy hoped that her house would be finished by 1963, but she was not holding her breath.

In September, she went back to Northumberland and Durham to cover the *News of the World* Leek Shows, being held in Durham Town Hall. She was pictured balancing the winning leek on her head and reported that it had 'already been on television where it gave a fine and slightly unnerving performance'.[24] She also interviewed Patricia Routledge again, who was starring in Granada TV's production of *Hobson's Choice*, and took the opportunity to praise her fellow Northerners, including Tom Courtenay and Albert Finney.

On Thursday 4 October, Nancy set sail for America from Southampton on the *Queen Elizabeth* for her six-week tour of women's luncheon clubs, where she would lecture on 'Why the English Are Such Snobs'.[25] Liz had made her a white tweed outfit to wear at the lectures. The tour would take her to Michigan, Wisconsin, Alabama, West Virginia, Pennsylvania, Tennessee and Kentucky. Her first was a 'Book and Author' luncheon in Charleston on 13 October, where she and fellow speakers Gina Allen and Dr John Anthony Caruso were given a taste of old-style Southern cooking: baked ham, sweet potatoes and apple pie. She also got a chance to browse round Woolworth's; she was fascinated by the pets' section, where turtles could be bought for 50 cents.

Joan and Sheila were in the South of France again when she left England and didn't return to London until 15 October. Sheila went to Angmering, while Joan not only had to pick up the reins again at *She*, now relocated in new offices at 16 Lower Regent Street, but also had a myriad of domestic matters to deal with. The boys were due home for their respective half-terms, and the basement was awash with damp, which would require urgent attention before their lease was renewed. She also complained that her sister, Sally, had rung her in some distress and asked her to arrange for her and Granny to have a holiday in Paris. 'Well, I had nothing else to do but get 51 pages of Christmas issue to the printer in 5 days, so why not',[26] said Joan. Then apparently, Sally decided not to go after all – then changed her mind again. Joan told Nancy she was wondering 'why on earth I didn't come to America with you, then all this could be happening to somebody else'.[27] It wasn't, and nor was that the end of it. In Nancy's absence, Joan rang Norah, to check that all was well:

> She has mice (worse than fleas?) and the Rodent Officer is charging 5/- but she doesn't mind that as long he does the job. Quarrelled with the nurse who baths her and got her day mixed and then said it was Ma who'd got her days mixed. . . . Darling Darling Tig doesn't all this make it seem super to be in the old USA? So peaceful, and so splendidly un-family. I miss you but I'm glad you weren't here for that last lump of laurie [sic] hysteria, you'd have divorced us all.[28]

Nancy had news herself: while she was at the Westbury in New York during the first week of her tour, she was cabling columns back to the *News of the World*, using her cable card. Somehow, the cable messenger boy managed to embezzle $133 from the Westbury's cashier, using Nancy's card.

After Charleston, her next dates were in Bethlehem, Pennsylvania, and Gadsden, Alabama. In Bethlehem, she was chaperoned by Mrs Elma Bratt, who enlisted her to help in canning tomatoes.

Joan and Sheila spent their weekend helping out Vivyen Bremner with various charitable events, during what Joan called 'our Good Works orgy'.[29] On the Saturday, they went to a fête for blind charities, where Sheila gave the opening speech. 'All desperately depressing though,' said Joan, 'full of knitted nasties and no customers'.[30] The next day, they went down to Chailey, where they were told the money from the *She* appeal had now reached £10,000.

Joan's main concern was Nancy's presence in America during the Cuban missile crisis:

> There's a lot of solemn gloom about it all here and I imagine the full hysterics there. Sheila says she'll be bloody annoyed if they bomb the Windmill because she just had all new seats in the stalls. . . . Take care of yourself darling. DON'T get involved in Cuba. Come home safely . . . [31]

If Nancy was anxious about warships confronting each other, she was keeping it to herself. She was more concerned that her lectures were too long and not funny enough. From the Westbury, she wrote to Joanna Scott-Moncrieff, suggesting that the lectures might form the basis of a *Woman's Hour* package. She also told her that the funniest part of her last lecture had been when she was talking about American song titles and 'The Gold Diggers of Broadway' came out as 'The Broad Diggers of Gold Way'. Scott-Moncrieff, however, was not put off and thought it was a good idea.

Nancy clearly wasn't enjoying doing the rounds of the lecture circuit without Ginette. Her letters had a grumpy, irritable tone to them and she was starting to live up to her self-professed title of 'Most moaning traveller in the world'.[32] Her verdict on Milwaukee's Prestige Hotel was 'To hell with prestige – let's have some comfort around here'.[33] Work on Skiathos was progressing slowly: Sir Basil Spence had sent an architect called Isoceles to look at the house and reported back that the drains had been started. Meanwhile she was trailing round America, lecturing for up to an hour at a time, earning much-needed money that the Skiathos house was eating up as fast as she could amass it. In between lectures, she was working on the 'Escape Book', which she now found 'an irritating title',[34] although 'For a long time this book seemed a catalogue of escapes. Escape into the theatre, into reading, into friendship, into love affairs (either with cities, landscapes, personalities), drinking, adventures, travel'.[35] No wonder she wrote back to Joanna Scott-Moncrieff, 'in my loneliness, I long for the touch of a vanished hand and the sound of a voice that is still . . . '.[36]

But there was encouraging news from home. On 20 November, Nick had the first of several operations on his injured hand. Joan told Nancy that the hospital staff had been astonished by his powers of recuperation: 'He'd come round from the anaesthetic even before he got back to the ward, and by the time I phoned was wanting to get up and have a look round, and was complaining strongly about hunger'.[37]

She had received an interesting assortment of presents for her forty-first birthday:

> Tom managed a card and a letter (did you fix?) and Sheila gave me chicly discreet gold cufflinks and Michael a Sellotapeserver . . . and the office brandy cherries. Granny hasn't got around to it yet but promises pyjamas. . . . So I was not neglected, bless 'em all.[38]

Nancy left New York on the *Queen Elizabeth* on 23 November and arrived in England six days later, in time for a *My Word* recording. On the journey home, she had finished the first draft of what had been called the 'Escape Book' and was now entitled *A Funny Thing Happened on the Way*. She also wrote her column for the February *She*, sharing the juiciest nuggets of gossip she had picked up in America:

> Oh boy, what a trip I had. I've eaten cheese with Claudette Colbert, sole with ace astrologer Carol Richter, curry with Ian Fleming, scrod in Boston, Mass., and hamburgers and club sandwiches everywhere. I have yacked at the ladies' club, the university graduates, the girls of Chatham Hall School, Chatham, Virginia, and had corsages pinned to my Maidenformed bosom in Michigan, Andrews Air Force Base, Maryland . . . and it's all been a bit bewildering.[39]

Stafford Somerfield had some rather less glamorous, but also less bewildering, assignments for her on her return. Impressed by what she had previously written about the North of England, he asked her to do a series of articles on the North-East. The result was a number of unusually impassioned, politically aware and prophetic pieces about what was being done to the region's industries and the subsequent social effects. She went to the Pallister Park Estate in Middlesborough and met the Hawkins family. 'How long will it be before life on the dole reduces these fine men to chronic hulks?', she wrote. 'I saw Jarrow murdered. I saw the hunger marches'.[40] Then she went to Greenock, Clydeside and talked to a group of unemployed shipbuilders in Renfrew.

She also visited Norah several times during December. She had had a cataract operation and was convalescing at home. Nancy saw her when she could, but it was not an ideal situation. 'I wish she'd move South', she wrote to Beaverbrook, 'however it's selfish of me'.[41]

By the end of December, she had completed 90,000 words of her 'sort of memoir' and Joan '(that stern critic) insists I re-write the first 30,000 words'.[42] On the back of an envelope, Joan had scribbled some suggestions and observations: a passage about Nancy's seasickness was 'dull'; the last paragraph on page 93 was 'clumsy', and so forth. This first draft contained much more about her adventures in America, and featured Lena Horne, Laurence Olivier and Joan Plowright. These passages were edited out before Nancy handed her final draft to Hutchinson's, and she may have intended to turn them into a separate book. 'My love for America forms another book, which I may one day write',[43] she explained.

Her last book for children, *The Beaver Annual*, was published in time for Christmas. Edited by Nancy, and published by Fairhaven Books, in co-operation with Hanna-Barbera Comics, it featured two of their most popular strips, *The Flintstones* and *Huckleberry Hound and Friends*. In between the cartoons were 'So you want to be a . . . ' articles, written by various friends and acquaintances who had been roped in by the editor. There was Sheila van Damm on being a racing driver; Harry Carlisle on life as a television producer; how to be a cyclist by Eileen Sheridan and how to be famous, by Tony Warren. And, of course, how to be a journalist, by Nancy Spain. She also contributed 'The Juke Box Jury Mystery' short story and the text for a cartoon story, 'The Adventures of Billy Beaver'. Full of colour, action and, above all, people 'doing things', what was most remarkable about this book was that, unlike most of the other annuals of the time, it didn't appear to be aimed specifically at boys or girls – simply any child interested in unusual activities.

She had had another brainwave for a book, though it was not exactly original. While she was in New York in November, she had lunch with Alan Koehler, the author of the *Madison Avenue Cook Book – For People Who Can't Cook and Don't Want Other People to Know It*.[44] When she returned to England, she decided there was a gap in the market for *The Nancy Spain Colour Cookery Book*, a user-friendly, practical culinary guide – and, since it was Nancy, it would contain as much big-name gossip as recipes. Her cookbook, she said, would not be for 'the ever-growing legion of "Experts"'. Indeed, there are still legions of 'non-Experts' using it in the 1990s, even though it has been out of print for thirty years.

According to Nick Laurie, much of the material for the book was easy to obtain: 'She wrote to the various embassies, and asked if they could give her their national recipes and colour transparencies – and they did'. Nancy provided her own tips on presentation and parties, complemented by celebrity anecdotes and advice. 'The Duchess of Windsor once told me . . . ', opened a typical story, and there were also plenty of references to Mrs

Beeton. But if the Spain cookbook had plenty of colour, it also had plenty of camp, and was worth buying for Nancy's gossip and thinly veiled references alone.

She seasoned the recipes and vivid photographs with tales of taking tea in Paris with Alice B. Toklas and Thornton Wilder; of serving fish and lamb chops 'à la Marlene'; and how Lena Horne spent days preparing her favourite dish, chilli con carne. There were stories about her days in the Kilburn bedsit, where she had to cook without an oven, and of cooking while camping in Greece. Joan and Sheila were accorded plenty of mentions, too: Joan got special praise for the presentation of her cooking, especially salads and Sunday lunches, while she included details of Sheila's recipe for mayonnaise. What did you need to make the party go with a swing? Why, 'a gorgeous Windmill Girl and a lot of balloons'. If you were going to invite stars to your party – and it was a good idea to – make sure you invited at least five non-celebrities per star, to balance things out. Parties could have international themes and, as they had with Nancy, embassies would be happy to provide information. The Finnish legation, for instance, had sent her precise instructions on how to smoke sprats. 'Of course, if with this you can manage to entertain a pretty Finnish girl in national costume, you're home and dry', she teased. The *Colour Cookery Book* was a feast of fun, and became one of the most successful books she ever produced.

She had more fun – but less success – with her next departure. She was to appear as herself in a Rank film, 'helping David Hemmings to fame'.[45] *Live It Up* was a short (74 minutes) B movie, written by Lyn Fairhurst and directed and produced by Lance Comfort. Shot in just fifteen days on a low budget, Nancy's appearance as an unnamed, but obviously famous, columnist comes near the very end of the picture. The music, including the title song, was written by Joe Meek, and his protégé, platinum-blonde Heinz Burt – of 'Just Like Eddie' fame – played Ron. There are also several other fresh-faced young stars to recognize: David Hemmings, as Dave Martin; the late Steve Marriott, pre-Small Faces; and Jennifer Moss (Jill), just prior to her joining the cast of *Coronation Street* to play Lucille Hewitt, its first rebellious teenager.

The typical teen-story involves four young lads who are all GPO messenger boys and (of course) have formed their own group, The Smart Alecks. They make a demo tape and Hemmings tries to bring it to the attention of producer Mark Watson (David Bauer), who is making a teen-music film at Pinetree Studios, featuring singers Patsy Ann Noble and Gene Vincent. Hemmings manages to mislay the tape and it is later discovered by technicians at the studios. They love the song – but who *are* The Smart Alecks? Watson's assistant, Kay (Veronica Hurst), decides to enlist the help of the press and suggests to her boss that they speak to some journalists who will be at the Supper Club where Kenny Ball and his Jazzmen are playing that night. 'There's one, just one, who might play ball', she says. They take a taxi to the club – which just happens to be one from Jill's firm. Now The Smart Alecks know where Watson is, but getting his attention is another matter.

Meanwhile, Nancy enters the club, accompanied by Watson and Kay. She is wearing a dark dress and stiffly carrying a handbag. She waves at Kenny Ball and then the trio head for their table. They tell Nancy the story of the mystery tape. 'Well, the editor of *She* will never believe that, but the editor of the *News of the World* might. I'll see what I can do ... '.

Dave Martin comes up with a spiffing wheeze: Jill sends a taxi to collect Watson and his party from the club and they play 'Live It Up' to him through the driver's radio It works: Kay recognizes the song and Watson tells the driver to 'follow that music'. 'How about that for a story?' he asks Nancy. 'Story?' she retorts. 'Do you *mind*? Do you expect them to believe that in Scunthorpe?' The cab drives off into the night and a happy ending ensues.

Live It Up was a crude attempt to take advantage of the growing teenage cinema audience and its obsession with pop music, with a predictable storyline and merely cursory attempts at acting. But some critics enjoyed its lack of pretension. Richard Whitehall of *Films and Filming* said *Live It Up* was 'noisy, brash, fast-paced and very entertaining . . . but, even more important, is the script's fresh and sympathetic approach and its utter lack of condescension'.[46] He also singled out Nancy's appearance as herself 'to deliver one real pip of a line'.[47]

As ever, the *News of the World* columns were keeping her busy. She began the year with a series on 'Hits and Myths' – personalities who, she considered, had become legends in their own time. They included Ian Fleming, Danny Blanchflower, Sir Compton Mackenzie and Barbara Cartland. In the spring, she started a series on 'Young Men at the Top'. It began with a piece on Tony Warren who had, apparently, now told her that they could relax their promise not to write about each other. 'You can write about me as much as you like now!'[48] Nancy had said.

In February, she went on another tour of ladies' luncheon clubs – this time, a little closer to home. The Maurice Frost agency booked her a string of dates in the North of England: Preston, Wigan, Lytham St Annes, Birmingham and Leeds. Then the angle of her column was altered slightly, with readers invited to write to 'Auntie Nance's Postbag'. As usual, her correspondents veered from one extreme to the other. A Mr Stanley of Bristol composed this timeless ode:

> The reign of Spain
> Lays mainly in her brain
> I'd get to grips
> With her hips
> But Nance
> Might lead me a dance.[49]

A Mrs Johnson of Blandford Forum demanded to know, 'Are your talks as boring and egotistical as your newspaper outpourings?'[50] Nancy was also taken aback by the way she was perceived by other members of the public. 'Many of you said I was a cynic', she revealed. 'You assumed (why I wonder?) that I had never done anything for love in my life, but only for money. . . . Strange'.[51]

By now, work on the Skiathos house was actually nearing completion and so Nancy decided another visit was in order. Discovering that sister Liz had also been bitten by the Greece bug the year before, she invited her to join her in Skiathos, possibly in late May. They hadn't spent a holiday together since the cruise to Tenerife in early 1949. Nevertheless, they arranged to meet in Milan and drive to Greece from there.

Nancy set off from England in her new convertible Hillman Superminx and drove through France to Italy, arriving a day ahead of Liz. She met her at the airport and they caught the Brindisi–Patras ferry, on which they shared a de luxe double cabin. In Greece, there were numerous stops along the way, including Xylokastron and Naflion, where they stayed in a hotel on the small island out in the bay, and from where they caught another ferry. In Skiathos, they immediately went to see the house. The road had been finished and Nancy and Liz were taken up, by motorbike, to where Nancy's completed, chalk-white house stood. Unfortunately, the water tank on the roof hadn't been filled and Nancy discovered that they had omitted to build a staircase which led up there.

During the two weeks she was there, carpenters spent days hammering and sawing, installing cupboards in the kitchen and bedrooms. However, the infamous drains were in perfect working order.

On their return journey, Nancy and Liz discussed the local folklore which said that Skiathos was the victim of an ancient curse of witches in Thessaly which caused blindness and lameness. Nancy dismissed it, but remembered that 'Roy Rutterford and his temperamental friend had both broken their legs after their trip to the island'.[52] According to Liz, the trip had finally persuaded Nancy to call an end to her costly island adventure:

'I think she bought the land on an impulse and started building the house, but I don't think she would have had time to go there. She found it all very expensive. I think she couldn't afford it, really – it was too much and a long way to go. She wanted to give the house to me. But I said, 'Oh I don't want it'. I'd never have got my husband out there – it was a terrible journey'.

After the sisters went their separate ways, Nancy drove on alone to Delphi and paid her respects to the temples of Apollo and Athena. Then she headed back to England – her love affair with Greece and the island was over.

While she had been away, all hell had broken loose at the *News of the World*. They had bought up the exclusive rights to the *Confessions of Christine* – Keeler, of course. Every Sunday, millions had read of the exploits of Stephen Ward, Mandy Rice-Davies, the 'Man in the Mask', Johnny Edgecombe and John Profumo. Nancy returned to an England convulsed with righteous indignation and tittering over the breakfast table as the misguided Keeler kissed and told. She had, of course, met Profumo's wife, Valerie Hobson, many years before when a film of Mrs Beeton's life had been mooted. She decided to write a sympathetic piece about the woman who, as *the* sex scandal of the 1960s unfolded, maintained her dignity and pledged her loyalty to her husband. Though under no obligation to do so, she sent Valerie Hobson a copy of the article before it was published, to check for any factual errors. Hobson altered only the opening quote, which was not direct, and asked for another quote to be removed, as it gave the impression she had given an on-the-record interview, which she refused to do – either then or in the future. Nancy made the changes accordingly.

As well as sorting out the problems of a house several thousand miles away, there was the business of moving house in London to contend with.

Since they had lived there, Nancy and Joan had made various attempts to buy 7 Clareville Grove. However, its owners refused all offers and were quite content to continue renting the house. In 1962, a chance came to buy a house in the same street, at number 15, and Joan went to talk to their bank manager about getting a mortgage to meet the asking price of £28,000. However, neither were convinced that borrowing what was then an enormous sum would be wise. 'Seemed to me that in 20 years in our doddering 60s we'd still have the mortgage festooned around our withering necks', Joan told Nancy. 'VERY disappointing darling, but we'll start again soon and aim for something at not a farthing over £15,000'.[53]

It took them nearly a year before they found something that suited both their needs and their budgets. 'Once they'd decided to go and buy a house of their choosing', says Nick Laurie, 'they wanted something quite tasty with a decent garden. If you went north, like Hampstead, you could have that at a severe price, whereas if you went south you could find perfectly reasonable areas without going too far from central London'.

So, south of the river they went, to 59 Sudbrooke Road, a large, rather idiosyncratic detached house in a quiet residential street near Wandsworth Common, which could have been mistaken for a municipal building. 'Joan and I are about to buy a house on mortgages in Clapham', she told Beaverbrook. 'We were sick of our rented property and we both wanted a house with a garden in which we felt we could live, decently and with dignity in our prime with HER children and in our old age'.[54] She gave his name as a reference to the Kent County Building Society from whom they were getting the mortgage. By the beginning of July, she was able to report to their referee that 'Laurie and I are demented with excitement over the new house ... plan to move in about a month's time'.[55]

Nancy and Joan were, indeed, thrilled with their new home, although Dick Laurie did not share their excitement:

'It was dismal and really ugly. You went down a driveway to the front door. Inside the house, it was full of very dark panels and it had a strange smell to it. In the basement there was a huge snooker table; then there was a breakfast room, a huge kitchen, reception room and a huge garden. There was an office for Nancy on the ground floor and upstairs, five big rooms. So they were planning accommodation for Joan, Nancy, Sheila and the boys'.

According to Nick Laurie, Nancy and Joan wanted to convert the basement into a swimming pool.

Tony Warren went to Clapham one afternoon to lend a hand with getting the new house in order:

> 'I took down some awful net curtains that were very un-Nancy – they were spotted net with frills round the edge'.

When Nancy tried to arrange the connection of all the various essential services, she discovered several anomalies. Sudbrooke Road was in three different boroughs: the north side was in Battersea, the east in Clapham and the south-west in Wandsworth. It took her some time, and a good many phone calls, to unravel where the offices for the various services covering the house were: water, Tulse Hill; telephone, Wimbledon; gas, Streatham; and electricity, Balham. 'Please be a pal', she told her *Woman's Hour* listeners. 'Don't ask me where I live – I don't know'.

But, despite all the outward signs of unity, Dick Laurie sensed that the emotional structure of this remarkable household was changing rather radically:

> 'My own feeling was that they were splitting up. Sheila was already installed in Clareville Grove and there were plans for accommodating her in Clapham. They weren't *physically* splitting up but emotionally – living different lives but in the same house. If they were going to split up, they wouldn't have bought the house. But there again, Clareville Grove was too small and the house in Clapham was huge. . . . They were planning for the future, especially for the children'.

But by that time, Nancy was involved with Dolly Goodman, while still seeing Ginette in Paris, and had also, apparently, begun a relationship with Marlene Dietrich.

Earlier that summer, they spent time together in Paris, when Dietrich's grandson, Paul Riva, was staying with her. She gave the little boy copies of some of the 'Tiger' books, which she read to him. In October, while Nancy was in New York and Dietrich was in London to perform at the El Alamein gala and the Royal Command Performance, she wrote that someone had asked her, 'I wonder how you can bear to be here when she is in England'. She replied, 'All I can do from 3,000 miles away is to send my love'.[56] In London, Dietrich was staying with her daughter, Maria, and her grand-children, and when Nancy returned from America, she was a frequent visitor. According to Maria Riva, 'this lady appeared often at our door during the holidays'.[57]

But, despite the obvious attractions of a complicated, inter-continental lovelife, Nancy euphemistically pledged her allegiance in her last memoirs.

> London is my home. . . . It has my heart and is my true love for always. But in the early stages of my passion for Paris I couldn't fail to see the contrast between the tension of my London day and the supernatural relaxation of my day in Paris. And I could not fail to observe them through a fog of romance.

From being 'in love' with Paris I passed through seven years of change and began to love her … I suppose I had put down suckers in Paris as well as London.[58]

In September, *The Nancy Spain Colour Cookery Book* was unleashed on the world, as was its author. She embarked on a vigorous national promotional tour of signings and television appearances. The cookbook, she announced, was 'a practical guide for people like myself who enjoy cooking and eating. You won't find any over-elaborate or timewasting dishes in my book'.[59] The tour had to be planned around recordings of the twelfth series of *My Word*, which also started in September and continued through until the end of the year. But, as usual, Nancy straddled her complicated, hectic personal and professional commitments with the agility and balance of a bareback rider.

For once, Tom was not in Angmering, Loxwood or another usual holiday destination, and so Nancy took him along on most of her promotional events. 'I got to know her – or thought I got to know her – that summer', he says. In August, she took him with her when she went to Stavanger in Norway for a week with the Federation of Deep-Sea Anglers.

The cookbook was launched at the Dorchester, where Frank Muir and Jimmy Edwards gave speeches. On 11 September, Nancy and Tom travelled to Norwich, accompanied by Lionel Cordell, sales director of World Distributors. In the afternoon, she did a book-signing at Jarrold's department store and then gave a talk to 300 members of the Norwich Townswomen's Guild in the shop's restaurant. Later, she was interviewed on *East Anglia at Six* and gave a demonstration of how to prepare her recipe for chicken fricassee.

The following week, on September 26, she combined visiting Norah with a book-signing at Fenwick's, and took the opportunity to praise her fellow Geordies again. 'Newcastle people are very canny', she said. 'They obviously recognize me but never stop me in the street'.[60] The *Evening Chronicle* declared her latest publication to be 'one of the brightest cook books of the age'.[61] The tour also included visits to Manchester, Birmingham and Liverpool, where Nancy took Tom to the Cavern Club.

In early October, she left for America once again, for another tour of lectures on the 'Nine Lives of a Lady of Letters'. Two days before she flew back to England, America was engulfed by the Kennedy assassination.

And Still There Were Cabbages in That Awful Field

To christen their new home, Nancy and Joan threw a particularly spectacular New Year party. The 150 guests included Paul McCartney and, according to Nancy, 'two awful young men who were thoroughly objectionable. They made it quite plain from the outset that they had come for as much free drink as possible, and they insulted everyone in so wholesale a fashion that they were as good as a star turn'.[1] It spawned an idea for her next *Woman's Hour* programme, recorded on 10 January. She decided to call it 'The Party's Over'.

A few days later, it must have seemed like it really was. On 14 January, Norah died of heart failure, in the Northern Hospital, Osborne Road, Jesmond, aged seventy-seven. Her health had been failing for some time and Nancy was in Newcastle when she died. Liz joined her there, to help make the necessary arrangements. The undertakers, of course, removed all Norah's jewellery prior to the funeral, but Nancy decided this was not right. 'I went back to her coffin, raised the lid and put her ring back on her finger', she told Stafford Somerfield. 'I know she was happy'.[2] The cremation took place on 16 January and Norah's ashes were taken to be placed with her husband's in Horsley. In her will, she had stipulated that Nancy and representatives of the National Provincial Bank act as executors for her estate, which was valued at £17,535. Everything was to be divided between Nancy and Liz.

While they were still in Jesmond, the two sisters discussed their own respective financial arrangements and wills. But Liz was bemused by what Nancy told her: 'I said to her, "I'll leave you all my money; that'll be alright." And she said, "I can't leave you mine, I've got to leave it to Miss Laurie's children." I said, "Whatever for?"' Though no explanation was forthcoming at that moment, it wouldn't be too long before the reasoning behind Nancy's arrangements revealed itself.

For the time being, life went on at its usual breathless pace. That week, the big news was that a pop group from Tottenham had had the temerity to knock the Beatles off the top of the singles chart, and so Nancy went off to interview the leader of the Dave Clark Five. Coincidentally, Clark had made a one-line appearance in *Live It Up*, playing a recording engineer. Nancy spent the best part of a week trailing round with the new pop sensations as they prepared to 'become the new threat to the Beatles on their plinth'.[3]

Less successful was her attempt to get an interview with Valentina Nikolayev, the first woman in space, who was due to visit Britain. However, Nikolayev's trip was postponed, owing to exhaustion. Nancy sympathized: 'It's the hammer, hammer, hammer on the hard high road of public appearances, good-will missions and Lord Mayor banquets that destroys',[4] she said.

She was well acquainted with 'the hard high road': a few weeks after Norah's funeral, she returned to Newcastle again, this time to address a meeting of the Newcastle Tea Club on 'The Nine Lives of a Lady of Letters'. As part of yet another national tour of Ladies' Clubs, organized by Maurice Frost, she travelled to Lancashire, Yorkshire, Cheshire and Dorset. The tours were becoming longer: 'the Luncheon Club Movement has grown out of all imagination', she noted. 'By leaps, as they say, and bounds. (Ever seen a women's club bounding? It's a great sight . . . '.[5]

For most of the lectures, she wore the same dress and shoes she had chosen for *Live It Up*. But, on her way to her engagements in Cleckheaton and Burnley, she realized her outfit was lacking something. 'I discovered to my horror that the only footgear I had was a pair of beige ankle boots!'[6] she exclaimed. 'So the ladies of Cleckheaton had to put up with me in my kinky boots'.[7] However, in Burnley, she was lent a pair of stilettos by Florence Rawlinson, the florist at the Keirby Hotel where she was staying. It provided her with another column for the *News of the World*, complete with suitable headline: 'Teetering with the Bishop on Borrowed Stilettos'.[8]

On 14 March, she went to Broadcasting House to record a 4-minute talk on 'Daydreaming', for the series *A Slice of Life*. The next day, she had another 'royal' article in the *News of the World*: this time, it was to mark the birth of Prince Edward and compared the lives of the Queen's children with those of Victoria. According to Nancy, 'the new generation of Royalty will grow all the more successfully as leaders because there is a chance they will know how their people will feel'.[9]

The week before, she had rung Stafford Somerfield to discuss her next assignment. Before he could suggest anything, she put forward her own idea. 'I could cover the Grand National. From the spectators' point of view. I'll fly. Know Mirabelle Topham well. Will land on the course'.[10] Somerfield was happy with this and reminded her not to be late with her copy on the Saturday, as the clocks were going forward and everything had to go to press earlier.

She rang Mirabelle Topham to see if the plan was feasible; it was, and she and Joan were invited to be her personal guests at Aintree and watch the race from her box. It was decided to turn the assignment into a family outing. Sheila was invited along and Nancy also decided to ask Dolly Goodman and her husband, Leon. Joan said she would make all the flight arrangements; she had contacts in the business from last year, when *She* ran an article on getting about by private plane. Nancy would arrange a food hamper and some champagne from Fortnum's for the journey.

Joan contacted the racing driver Ian Walker, who was managing director of Westway Air Taxis Ltd. She arranged to charter a six-seater, twin-engined Piper Apache for a return flight from Luton to Aintree; it would cost £60 plus £7 pilot's fee. Walker contacted the Aintree management for permission to land on a strip at the course.

They duly contacted the Lancashire County police who advised Walker that the plane would have to land between 11.15 a.m. and 11.30 a.m. on a straight section of a motor racetrack, 35 feet wide, 1,800 feet long, and running parallel to Melling Road, Aintree. Walker was also given an alternative landing site, at nearby Woodvale aerodrome. The police sent Walker a plan of the racecourse, with the landing strip clearly marked, to give to his pilot, Owen Stevenson. Australian-born Stevenson was the perfect man for the job: the director and chief pilot of Westway, he had clocked up nearly 3,000 hours' experience of flying single-engine aircraft. Since the journey would take approximately 56 minutes, Joan was told that the time of departure from Luton would be at 10 a.m. on the Saturday morning.

It was all settled, then.

However, the arrangements began to go slightly awry. There were some problems at the Windmill that needed Sheila's urgent attention, and therefore she decided not to travel in the plane with the others. Instead, she said, she and Nona would stay overnight with friends in Chester and then meet up with them at Aintree on Saturday afternoon. Nancy rang round various people to see if they wanted to fill the spare sixth seat on the plane. She had asked Tony Warren earlier if he would like to come on the trip – now there was room, perhaps he still wanted to? In the end, Tony decided to stay in London. Laon Maybanke had also been canvassed, but decided against joining them. Nancy then called a young actress she had recently befriended, but she too declined. Then she contacted Clive Graham, racing correspondent for the *Sunday Express*, to see if he wanted the spare place, but Graham had already made his arrangements for the day. It seemed a waste of a seat, and a splendid day out, but there it was – they would only be five, after all.

And Nancy had more pressing matters to hand that week. She had decided to go to Paris again the following week and booked her Air France ticket. She had also promised to deliver the final, polished draft of *A Funny Thing Happened on the Way* to the Hutchinson office on Friday, but it now looked as if that would be impossible. She rang them to ask if they could collect it from the *She* office, where Joan would have it. That would be fine, she was told; the manuscript could be read over the weekend.

On the Friday morning, Joan and Sheila took a taxi into town together. Sheila got out at Bond Street and Joan continued on to the *She* offices. At Luton Airport, the blue and white Piper PA-23 G-ASHC was refuelled and its oil tested, ready for its flight to Aintree the next morning.

Later in the day, Joan spoke to Sheila on the phone, to see how things were going at the theatre, and to sort out roughly what time they would meet at Aintree. They were both looking forward to the day out.

★ ★ ★

Before Nancy and Joan drove to Luton Airport on Saturday morning, there was plenty to be got ready. It would be fairly cold on the plane, so Nancy decided to put on a pair of thick woollen socks and a green scarf, and wore a cardigan over her pink shirt, with (of course) brown trousers and a zip-up windcheater jacket. She would also take her hooded white duffle coat, in case it turned really cold later. She put on her sapphire-studded gold cufflinks, her gold cocktail watch and bracelet and her heart-shaped gold 'N.S.' medallion.

Like any good racing punter, she made sure she had plenty of cash with her – £40 – and her lucky black hand charm. The occasion called for her smartest brown leather briefcase, into which went other things she thought she might need: notebooks, her two pairs of glasses, some binoculars for watching the race, her Polaroid camera and some film, headache and asthma powders. For less practical reasons, she also took two small leather photo frames containing pictures of Nick and Tommy and, in a pink silk purse, a pair of brown suede baby bootees.

Joan also packed a curious assortment of practical and personal items for the trip. Like Nancy, she too decided to take some lucky charms: apart from the cat talisman on her key ring, she had a four-leaf clover, preserved in a plastic bag. She took her binoculars, her Zeiss camera and her 'JWL' initialled pocket knife. To avoid any problems, she thought it best to take the letter she had received from Owen Stevenson at Westways, outlining the arrangements for the flight. She also thought it wise to take her press card, diary and appointments book. And, just in case, in her wallet was a 'last will and testament' she had scribbled out the year before.

Into her car, they loaded the Fortnum's hamper, the champagne and some cutlery that a waiter at the Ivy had given Nancy for the trip. Originally, she was going to buy some more practical, but less grand, camping cutlery from the Scouts' Association Shop. They arrived at Luton shortly before 10 o'clock. The food, drink and bags were put on the plane. Nancy and Joan posed for a picture on the steps of the little plane – with Joan, camera in hand, standing a step above a notebook-clutching Nancy – for a *News of the World* photographer, and then Dolly and Leon Goodman got on board. Nancy got into the right-hand rear seat; Joan, who had had a few flying lessons herself, decided she wanted to sit in the co-pilot's seat. Dolly and Leon sat in the two passenger seats immediately behind the two front seats. Ian Walker wished them all a pleasant day and waved them off at 10.05 a.m.

Their route took them over Daventry, Lichfield and Whitegate. The champagne was opened and Nancy started to take notes for her article.

★ ★ ★

Sheila and Nona van Damm set off on the bus from Chester to Liverpool: they had planned to arrive at Aintree by no later than three o'clock.

★ ★ ★

Liz Hulse was at home in Bramer, Hampshire.

★ ★ ★

The Seyler boys were both at their respective boarding schools: Tom in North Wales and Nick, in the middle of his final A-level term, was at Abbot's Home in Derbyshire.

★ ★ ★

Noel Coward was having a miserable time in New York. He was there on account of his play *The Girl Who Came to Supper* which, days before, he had been told was to finish its Broadway run. To add to the gloom, he was also in great pain from a recently diagnosed stomach ulcer. He was looking forward, he said, to returning home to Jamaica and lying in the sun by his pool.

★ ★ ★

In London, Alan Freeman was looking forward to meeting a friend for lunch at a restaurant on Edgware Road.

★ ★ ★

Lord Beaverbrook was at home in Cherkley. He was expecting two rather contrasting guests for dinner that evening: John Junor and Michael Foot.

★ ★ ★

Jackie Forster was in Toronto, staying with a friend, Patsy Gallagher, a producer with CBC. Aware that it was Grand National day back in England, Jackie had decided to put a big bet on. She went to bed on Saturday night and set her alarm for seven o'clock, Canadian time, so she could hear the results.

★ ★ ★

Tony Warren was at his home in Albermarle Street, which he shared with the actor Ernst Walder, who played Ivan Cheveski in *Coronation Street*.

★ ★ ★

Marlene Dietrich was at home, in the rented apartment at 12 Avenue Montaigne that was her Paris base.

★ ★ ★

Ginette Spanier was also in Paris but, that morning, had decided she needed to get out of the city for the weekend. She and Paul-Emile abruptly left for Trouville without leaving a contact number.

★ ★ ★

At 11.07 a.m., Owen Stevenson radioed Liverpool airport radar control and asked them to assist in making a cloud-break descent. Ten minutes later, the plane appeared out of the clouds, about 800 feet up. Stevenson told the controller he would head north-west for Aintree. 'I will remain on this frequency and if I can't find it I'll be coming back here'. Five minutes later, he told them he would be arriving 'somewhere near Aintree in about two minutes' time'. As Stevenson began circling the racecourse, looking for the large 'H' on the landing strip, Joan started taking photographs and Nancy made some notes about the aerial view of Aintree. The second time round,

Stevenson spotted it. 'OK then, I will be landing', he told Liverpool, 'and I'll give you a call just on short finals to confirm it'. 'Roger. If you listen out for a time there may be a radar approach', they told him. 'Would appreciate it if you didn't butt in please'. 'Roger, will do'.

The plane approached the racecourse from the south and then made a low, left-hand circuit of the area. Eddie Arcaro, a retired American jockey, saw it come back again. 'It looked as if the passengers were being shown the course',[11] he said. It made another approach from the south and then continued in a north-easterly direction towards the landing strip. Captain Derek Graham, a BEA pilot on attachment to a police helicopter post at the strip, watched it pass overhead at about 300 feet, continue north and turn right, towards fields between Bull Bridge Lane and Wango Lane.

As it passed over nearby houses, one eyewitness thought they heard the engines spluttering. The undercarriage was down. Thomas Smith, doing some work on the rear of one of the houses, saw the plane flying over the field, about 250 feet in the air. Then it made a sudden, sharp left-hand turn. About 300 yards ahead of it was a line of electricity pylons. On the ground, Jack Franklin and Tommy King saw the pylons, too, and thought the plane had turned to avoid them.

Suddenly, the plane's left wing dipped steeply, its tail rose, and the nose tilted down. Now almost vertical, it moved from side to side, spiralling slowly several times, and, according to one onlooker, 'plummeted from the sky like a shot bird'.[12]

★ ★ ★

At their hotel in Trouville, Ginette and Paul-Emile had enjoyed a lunch of warm shrimps and fish, with a bottle of cool Muscadet. Afterwards, Ginette decided to take a nap, while Paul-Emile went for a walk.

★ ★ ★

At 11.34 a.m., a police wireless car received instructions to go to the scene of an aircrash in a cabbage field near Bull Bridge Lane, belonging to Johnson's Farm. The Aintree course doctor, Dr M.G. Garry, was sent for and three fire engines were also called to the scene.

An ambulance arrived in the field at 11.35 a.m. The plane was lying the right side up and had not caught fire. But the nose and cabin had ploughed into the edge of the field; the cabin roof was crushed and the tail, buckling sharply in the middle, was hanging backwards into the next field. Fortunately, it had narrowly avoided crashing onto houses only 300 yards away.

The emergency teams could tell immediately that no one had survived. Owen Stevenson, still strapped into his seat, was sprawled across the controls, head first through the plane's window. Leon Goodman was found in the cabbage field, a few feet behind the right wing; Joan and Dolly were half-lying across the wing. They had not been strapped into their seats.

Incredibly, the plane's engines were still running and one of the police-men leaned in to switch them off. Then he saw that there was a passenger at the back, slumped forward, who was still strapped into a seat. The ambu-lancemen were called and, in a last desperate attempt to find signs of life, started to administer oxygen. There was no response.

Nancy was pronounced dead at 12.05 p.m.

★ ★ ★

Paul-Emile had just set off from the hotel for his walk when the bellboy came tearing after him; there was a person-to-person telephone call for him, from Marlene Dietrich. She had been trying to track him and Ginette down for hours. Knowing only that they had gone to Trouville, she had system-atically gone through the telephone directory and rung all the town's hotels in alphabetical order until she found them. Paul-Emile went back up to their room to take her call. After a few seconds, his face began to register the dreadful news he was hearing. 'She'll call you back', he told Marlene, gently put the receiver back and looked at his wife.

★ ★ ★

At 12.15 p.m., the Accidents Investigation Branch at the Ministry of Aviation received a phone call from the Northern Air Traffic Control Centre in Preston. They were told a team of inspectors would be needed in Liverpool the next day.

The firemen used crowbars to disentangle Nancy, Owen Stevenson and Dolly Goodman from the wreckage. All five bodies were then taken, under police escort, to Ormskirk and District General Hospital mortuary. A cine film of the crash scene was shot by an officer from the Traffic Patrol HQ.

★ ★ ★

In Bramer, the telephone rang. It was a friend of Liz Hulse's, who was at Aintree. 'They said, "I've got something terrible to tell you ... "'.

★ ★ ★

In Derbyshire, Nick heard the crash mentioned on the radio news and promptly phoned the *News of the World* newsroom for confirmation.

★ ★ ★

In North Wales, Tom was ushered into the headmaster's study. 'I thought, "Gosh, what have I done now?"' He was told that there had been an accident. '"They were on their way to the Grand National. But don't worry, they didn't feel a thing"'.

★ ★ ★

Alan Freeman was sitting at the restaurant table:

> 'All of a sudden, this woman came over to me and said, "Mr Freeman, I'm terribly sorry to hear about your terrible loss". I said, "What are you talking about?" She said, "Nancy Spain has just died in a plane crash". At the top of my voice, I called her a "fornicating" liar. .... It was horrible – just awful'.

★ ★ ★

The secretary of Tony Warren's agent rang him at home, and asked him if he had got any brandy in the house. 'Well, of course, I always had brandy in the house. She said, "Go and get yourself a glass. A plane has crashed over Aintree racecourse – I've just heard it on the radio – and they think one of the dead is Nancy Spain . . . "'.

★ ★ ★

Jackie Forster was lying in bed, listening to her radio in Toronto, waiting to hear how her flutter on the National had fared. But news from Aintree was not about the race. 'I was out of bed in a shot. . . . I said, "Patsy, Nancy Spain's been killed with her lover . . . "'.

★ ★ ★

Paul-Emile told Ginette what had happened. He also told her that the *News of the World* had been trying to ring her in Paris and, failing, had rung Marlene in Paris to see if she could find her.

★ ★ ★

Sheila and Nona arrived at Aintree shortly before 3 p.m. and began to look for Nancy and Joan. Rumours were circulating about some sort of plane accident, but it never occured to either of them that it might involve anyone they knew, especially as a policeman had told Sheila that he had seen Nancy in one of the enclosures at 1.30 p.m. So they continued to wander through the crowds, searching for them.

At 3 p.m., Sheila switched on her portable radio to hear the hourly news. 'My God, it's them!' she cried. 'Sheila, pull yourself together', said Nona.[13]

★ ★ ★

At first, Tom didn't realize it was both of them. 'They said, "Your mother's dead". Only they didn't say it in so many words. I thought, "Right, that's Jonnie. So what about Nancy?" "Nancy's dead too"'.

★ ★ ★

Tony Warren was in a daze.

> 'I remember rushing through Mayfair. I thought I need another drink and I went to the Rose and Crown on Park Lane – that's how far I'd run. I just didn't know what I was doing. I was thrown, I was all over the place. I got into the Rose and Crown, just after opening time. I thought I could ring the Press Association, so I rung them and got unconfirmed reports. I went to go towards the counter and I heard Nancy's voice saying the name of a horse . . . we'd always said if there's anything in dying, and it's possible to come back in the process, we'd promised one another we would do it so we would prove it once and for all. It was quite serious. I knew nothing about backing horses, so I went up to these guys at the counter and asked if there was a horse running in the National called Team Spirit. They said it was a rank outsider. I asked them how to back a horse. I put £5 on it each way'.

★ ★ ★

Back at Aintree, the Grand National of 1964 was not without further incident. At the Chair, jockey Paddy Farrell broke his back when his horse, Border Flight, fell. Then, with a storming finish, the smallest horse in the 33-strong field won by half a length. It was an American-owned horse called Team Spirit.

But none of the hundreds of television, radio or newspaper journalists present were under any illusions as to what the real story of the day was. As soon as news of the accident started to filter through, reporters, photographers and film crews rushed to the scene, gathering quotes from eyewitnesses and pestering Chief Superintendent William Roberts, head of Lancashire CID, for details. How had he been certain about who was in the plane? Without a hint of recognition of the grim irony in what he was saying, Roberts told them, 'A driving licence identified Miss Laurie ... I recognized Miss Spain by her mode of dress'.[14]

The *News of the World* began to elicit quotes from the great and the good. Marlene Dietrich told them, 'This is so strange and shattering. She was so full of life. I can't believe it'. Ginette merely said, 'Nancy was the most wonderful person I've met. She gave life to all her friends'.[15]

Roy Rutherford, Nancy's companion on many of her raunchiest adventures, was told the news by his mother. According to Frank Ellul, he never spoke about it again. By his bedside table remained the photograph taken of him and Nancy that accompanied *The Public Life of Nancy Spain*, an advertising campaign for pubs that he had been roped into by her.

★ ★ ★

To add to her appalling shock and grief, it was the very public nature of Nancy's death, rather than the manner of it, that horrified her sister. 'I found that terrible. ... But at least with an air crash ... I think it's the way to go – good and quick, rather than hanging on with some terrible thing. But it was all absolutely dreadful'.

★ ★ ★

But some couples would have loved such a dramatic ending. When Gertrude Stein died of cancer in 1946, Alice B. Toklas wrote to a friend, 'I wish to God we had gone together as I always so fatuously thought we would – a bomb – a shipwreck – just anything but this'.[16]

She might well have envied Nancy and Joan their ending – together, till the end.

★ ★ ★

Sheila and Nona made their way to Orsmkirk police station. When they arrived they were met by one of the patrol cars from Aintree. Sheila told them who she was – to their relief. 'They said, "Thank goodness, at last someone who can help us. Will you come for the identifications?"' She said she would.

She was driven to the mortuary at Ormskirk Hospital where she faced the grimmest, most unenviable of tasks. Once inside the building, 'I remember saying to a great hulking policeman, "Do you mind if I hold your hand?" He was very sweet. I nearly broke it'.[17]

When Sheila had recovered sufficiently, she rang Dick Laurie at home in Putney.

★ ★ ★

At the crash site, the wrecked plane was covered with a sheet. Since there was still a considerable amount of fuel in its tanks, the fire crews sprayed foam around it and connected a hose to a hydrant. The site was guarded overnight by police officers, both to stop any ghoulish visitors and to ensure that the wreckage, which might hold clues to the accident's cause, was not interfered with.

★ ★ ★

Ginette and Paul-Emile returned to Paris, where the BBC called to ask if she would give a tribute for *Woman's Hour* over the phone. Ginette agreed. On the day of the programme, Noble Wilson, the head of BBC Paris, handed her a glass of whisky to drink just before she began, and held her hand throughout the broadcast.

★ ★ ★

Tony Warren woke up suddenly in the middle of Saturday night:

'I saw somebody standing in the middle of the room in a white polo-neck jersey that I'd never seen before. I said, "Darling, what are you doing here?", and she said, "Where am I meant to be?" I said, "You're meant to be there", and she said, "Oh baby, it's not as easy as that . . . ", and she melted away'.

Nick and Tom Seyler, trying to come to terms with what had happened, were well aware of exactly what had gone from their lives. For Tom, 'Nancy's death was a real blow. She was a real childhood pal. The very best'. Nick also felt Nancy's loss deeply:

'I never liked Mum, but I liked Nancy. And I was much more upset about her being killed. I didn't see a lot of Mum. Putting the magazine together, especially in the early days, meant a lot of late nights. But Nancy was always there when I was there, because she worked from home and she was the person I saw every day. She was the person who fulfilled the role of the mother. Essentially, Nancy was the mother figure for me, whereas Tom didn't get a mother figure at all . . . or a father. He really lost out all round'.

Unfortunately, there was further loss yet to come.

Sheila van Damm had arranged both funerals to take place at Golders Green Crematorium, one after the other, so that everyone attending could simply wait for the second ceremony. The notices she put in *The Times* stipulated that the funerals would be private and requested no flowers.

However, some floral tributes did arrive on the day, as did a number of people who wanted a chance to say goodbye. In the end, about eighty turned up, transforming the short ceremony into a more public affair.

Laon Maybanke rang Tony Warren to tell him where the funerals were taking place. Tony wondered whether they should go: 'I was in two minds, but he said he was going and thought I should too. I did want to go and say goodbye to her. I wore a grey suit and black tie.' Dick Laurie and Granny steeled themselves: 'My mother and I decided the only way to get through the whole thing was to have a couple of stiff gins . . . '.

Tony Warren met Laon Maybanke outside the chapel: 'I was feeling very dazed and Laon took my arm, and I thought, "I wish he wouldn't do that, it looks silly". He had a big mauve satin tie on'.

Dick, Granny and Nick were there, as was Liz Hulse, but Tom wasn't. And, one paper noticed, 'None of the big names and none of the show-business personalities who filled Nancy Spain's colourful life were there.'[18]

There were, however, certainly some colourful characters, according to Dick Laurie:

'There were certainly two, maybe more, ladies in dungarees hovering behind the pillars who'd come to pay their last respects to Nancy. One of them had a cigar going outside the chapel. My mother said to me, go and ask them if they want to come back and have a drink. I said I don't think that would be a very good idea. We discovered that one of them was a long-distance lorry driver who Nancy had somehow met on one of her trips'.

The funeral service was brief. Stafford Somerfield nervously read the twenty-third Psalm and broke down: 'the page in my shaking fingers wouldn't turn over and I choked'.[19] Nick put a bunch of violets on Nancy's coffin.

Tony Warren had never attended a cremation before:

'I had no idea how it worked. Suddenly, a bank of flowers started to move sideways and I realized it was the coffin and was totally thrown.

Granny was nice to me on the way out – I heard her say to Nick, "Does Tommy know everything and does he understand?" But I didn't know what that meant. I can remember her sister looking so like Natasha it was ridiculous. Mostly I remember Laon trying to take my arm and everybody just standing there. I'd better offer Laon a lift – I had a hire car – and he said, "We're waiting for Jonnie's service", and I said, "She never liked me and I think it would be wrong for me to stay". He let go of my arm quite quickly, and off I went'.

Instead, he told his driver to take him to the Hilton: 'It had a certain glamour then, and so I went and raised a glass to her on my own'.

There were no flowers for Joan's service, and fewer mourners. Some, like Tony Warren, had gone specifically for Nancy's. Again, the service was brief: Psalm 23 was read again and, within minutes, it was all over. Joan's ashes were later scattered at Golders Green. Liz collected Nancy's and took them back to Horsley, where they were scattered on the Spain family grave.

On the morning of Wednesday 13 May, the inquest into the accident was resumed. Charles Lawson QC represented Westways Ltd., John Briggs represented the Goodmans' executors and David Jacobs also attended.

In all, there had been twenty-one witnesses to the accident, but not all of them were called to give evidence. Those who were included Gilbert Jameson from the Ministry of Aviation; John Harvey, who been standing on Bull Bridge and watched the Piper Apache's final manoeuvres; Ian Walker, who gave details about his instructions to Owen Stevenson; Frederick Pinchin, the other director of Westways; George Stevenson, who testified to his brother Owen's previous experience as a pilot; Captain Derek Graham, the police helicopter pilot at the landing strip; Dick Laurie; and Mrs Margaret Allen, who had also witnessed the crash.

When Frederick Pinchin took the witness stand, Charles Lawson put to him a theory that had also occurred to others. Was it possible, Lawson suggested, that 'as the dual-control plane flew near the racecourse at only 200 feet the passenger in the co-pilot's seat might have turned round to speak to a companion and inadvertently put her hand on the control column?' And, he continued, would the pilot 'have any chance of getting out of the situation?' 'I suppose it could be that the controls could be jammed in some way where he could not recover in time', replied Pinchin.[20]

This theory was also picked up on by the Stevenson family lawyer, perhaps sniffing the chance of a possible suit for damages from the Werner Laurie estate. Coroner Bolton tried to clarify the situation by asking Gilbert Jameson if it had been possible to fingerprint the controls of the aircraft. Jameson said, no, it hadn't been possible, because the controls had disintegrated and what was left was covered in fuel. Bolton also said that a blood test carried out on Stevenson's body to ascertain whether he had been drinking had proved negative.

When the photographs taken by the police of the wreckage and the bodies were passed around the court, Sheila, wishing to spare Dick the terrible sight she had had to witness at Ormskirk mortuary, took them out of his hands before he could look at them. 'She said, "I don't think we need to see them" . . . I sort of thank her for that, in a way'.

In the end, the seven-person jury returned the only verdict possible based on the evidence given: misadventure. But the press picked up on the theory put forward by Charles Lawson: 'Passenger May Have Touched the Controls'.[21]

On Wednesday 8 April, at 12.15 p.m., Joan's memorial service was held in London, at St Michael's Church, Chester Square. Those attending included Liz Hulse, Michael Griffiths, Roy Rutherford, Dick Laurie and his mother, Noel Streatfeild, Denise Robins, Sheila van Damm, Vyvyan and Thelma Holland and editorial and production staff from *She* and the rest of the National Magazine Company. 'It was rather a mournful affair',[22] recalled Holland. The Reverend Joseph McCulloch gave an address and Marcus Morris read the lesson.

On Wednesday 22 April, nearly four hundred people packed St Bartholomew's for Nancy's memorial service, a rather grander affair, which had been organized by Liz and was presided over by the Reverend Dr N.E. Wallbank:

'I said to Geoffrey [Wright], "Where on earth can I have it; what's a good church?" And he suggested St Bartholomew's, which is a beautiful church. The *Express* wanted to do the memorial service card – it was done in awful printing, but I just had to let them do it'.

This time, her husband, Sir Westrow Hulse, and members of his family attended. As well as Dick, Granny, Sheila, Noel, Roy and the Hollands, the congregation included the Duke and Duchess of Bedford, Cyril Lord, Frank Muir, Denis Norden, Tony Warren, Dilys Powell, Francis Goodman, Tony Shryane, Edward J. Mason and Geoffrey Wright. There were also representatives from every sphere of her life, including Tom Blackburn, chair of Beaverbrook Newspapers, and Peter Aitken, who represented the employer she had loved and respected above and beyond the call of duty. Edward Pickering and Robert Edwards also attended from the *Express*.

Other representatives included H. Mason, the director of the *News of the World* organization, together with many members of the paper's staff. The editorial director of Hutchinson's attended, along with Max Parrish and W.G. Gibbins of John Murray Ltd. Joanna Scott-Moncrieff of *Woman's Hour* was there, and Maurice Frost of the Frost Lecture Agency, too. Representing her previous military connections were Lieutenant-Colonel C.W. Holdsworth from the Royal Northumberland Fusiliers Comrades Association and Mrs F. Foster from the Association of WRNS. There were also considerable numbers of the people who had loved her at least as much as anyone present – the public: 'Clippies, housewives, women who served with Nancy in the Wrens during the war'.[23] And, tucked away amongst the more glittering names, was one who had, unbeknownst to them all, played a brief but significant part in her life: Philip Youngman Carter.

The congregation sang Psalm 23 and the Navy's traditional hymn, 'For Those in Peril on the Sea', and listened to Bach's 'Jesu, Joy of Man's Desiring'. Jack Longland gave the address:

> She became a personality because of that self-renewing spring of vitality; because she squandered the energy that most of us prudently conserve. Because she gave so much more than she could have ever hoped to receive. And when the public image is filed away and half-forgotten, it is Nancy's warmth, her wide smile, her joy of living and her love of her friends that we shall remember.[24]

Once again, Stafford Somerfield read the lesson – 1 Corinthians 13:

> If I speak in the tongues of men and of angels, but have not love, I am a noisy gong or a clanging cymbal. . . .
> Love bears all things, believes all things, hopes all things, endures all things. Love never ends . . .
> So faith, hope, love abide, these three; but the greatest of these is love.

After the service, Vyvyan and Thelma Holland went to Wheeler's for a lunch of oysters, scallops and Chablis – Nancy would surely have approved.

Funny Things Happened

There were many things to be taken care of in the immediate aftermath of the accident, but the most pressing was to find Nancy and Joan's wills. At Sudbrooke Road, Sheila and Dick were faced with the task of sorting out Nancy and Joan's other papers and belongings. Granny Laurie came to help out, too. Sheila told Dick that it would be a good idea to destroy some of the more private papers – for other people's sakes. And so, in an incinerator in the back garden, they started a fire, into which went most of the documentation of their daily lives, shared for fourteen years. At one point, a small sealed brown envelope fell out of a pile of papers. Dick opened it and found fifty dollars in cash. 'You'd better keep that', said Sheila.

Later, when he went through Joan's wallet, he found something even more useful – or so he thought. 'I've found a will', he told David Jacobs. 'Oh, thank God!' exclaimed a relieved Jacobs. But, as Dick recalls, when he showed him what he had found, their hopes of a clear-cut settlement were dashed:

> 'It was on the back of a compliments slip or something from a publisher. It said, "In some haste, my last will and testament. I leave everything to Nancy to distribute as she thinks fit for the children; to Michael, I leave my stationery with a grin; to my mother", something or other, "with all my love; Nancy, don't grieve too much, darling". It was signed but unwitnessed. Then written across the top was, "right leg – aneurysm?" [an abnormal dilation of a blood vessel, usually an artery, which can be remedied by surgery]. For a competent, reasonably efficient and aware lady, it was ridiculous'.

What they did have was Nancy's final will, made barely a month before the accident – leaving everything to Joan. Eventually, a copy of Joan's will, signed and witnessed in July 1952, was unearthed: this, of course, stated that everything was to be left to Nancy. Since she was dead, it was now invalid.

All the careful plans they had hatched together over the years – making provisions for the boys' future, even planning to build them a holiday home and, finally, getting their first mortgage to buy their new home – had been done on the basis that one of them would be around to take care of it all. This, then, was the basic flaw in their arrangements. And it was to add a final, tragic twist to the unfolding repercussions of their deaths.

Dick Laurie, David Jacobs and an accountant, Dennis Blake, acted as trustees for Nancy's estate. Everything had to be sold off – the new house, the Greek house, cars – lock, stock and barrel.

Nancy did not die a millionaire. Even so, her estate was £28,250 gross, £14,755 net. Joan's was valued at £28,118 gross, £20,358 net. On the rare occasions when two people, having interchangeable wills, die together, the law decrees that whoever was the oldest at the time of their deaths did, in fact, die first. Therefore, the law said that Nancy, being forty-six, had died before Joan, who was forty-three. Nancy's estate then passed to Joan; the total of both estates subsequently passed to her eldest child, Nick.

Though this situation was legally correct, the flaw in Nancy and Joan's plans opened up a loophole, through which fell Tom Seyler: he was left nothing. And the complexity of the situation did not improve, according to Dick Laurie:

'After about two years, we got this letter from a lady in Newcastle saying she wanted to sell the flat she had her in her name and Nancy's – could she please sell it? There was another property, one was abroad somewhere, that she had taken out in her name – she had these love-nests, tucked away. They were sold off: we couldn't just give them away, because we were trustees of the estate and looking to get as much money as we could for Nick and Tom. I can promise you that, two years after their deaths, nothing surprised me. Absolutely nothing. Another thing was my mother's cottage in Sussex. She had given it to Jonnie to avoid death duties. So Jonnie dies and we had to say to my mother, "buy up or get out", and she'd been living there for years. That was a fairly unhappy time, but she was financially OK in the end'.

Eventually, Granny Laurie sold up and went to live in Canada with her daughter, Sally. Nick still feels that this business was handled badly:

'I tried hard to hang on to my grandmother's cottage. It was set in three acres, with building permission. The cottage was falling apart. I thought what we should have done was let the house fall down eventually and keep the land, and then we'd be very rich out of it one day. But they wanted everything wrapped up as quickly as possible. They sold the cottage and the land for something like £5,000'.

The money Nick was to inherit from the two estates was put into a trust fund, which he would receive when he turned twenty-one. A trust fund was also overseen by Liz Hulse, the National Magazine Company and the *News of the World* to see Tom through his education.

Liz was appalled by the enormous secret that Nancy had kept from her and her parents: 'She was very impulsive – she never really thought anything out, just kind of got on with it'. And, given that Nancy had clearly never intended Tom to be her responsibility, Liz was uncertain of what she was expected to do:

'In a way, I was very glad Nancy didn't tell me about him, because I would have felt I had to be his guardian. It was difficult – he was not my responsibility, I just did what I could do. I went to see Nick and said I'm going to see that he gets some of this money, and I was very stern with him. Then the solicitor got half of the money and bought a house for him. It was very complicated. Luckily I had my husband, so I could discuss it all with him'.

For a brief time, she took Tom back to Hampshire with her: 'I thought it was very bad for him to be in this kind of milieu – and he was a very difficult and strange little boy. He stayed in some place near Bramer, some kind of home for a bit'.

Eventually, however, it was decided that Tom would be better off under the guardianship of Margaret Layton and her husband in North Wales and for him to continue his education at boarding school there. But Liz Hulse was not oblivious to the cumulative effect the peculiar circumstances of his upbringing would have on Tom: 'It must have done an awful lot of damage to him'.

A Funny Thing Happened on the Way was published in May 1964. In the foreword, Hutchinson's offered readers an explanation: 'If, in the circumstances, the title seems inappropriate to some people, it should be said that this was the title she had chosen and we did not think it should be altered'.[1]

As expected, each review in turn became more of an obituary, taking an overview of Nancy's life and achievements. The *Times Literary Supplement* observed:

Nancy Spain had many talents which remained unrevealed in her books, her journalism and her public appearances. What she always managed to transmit was an untiring enjoyment of the ups and downs of life at VIP level. And it is interesting to see what goes to the making of that human phenomenon of the 1960s, the 'television personality'. She certainly had the gift of arousing the admiration and affection of an impressive number of widely different people, who grieved at her death as people do only at the loss of someone whose company they always enjoy. [The book] is an honest, strangely contradictory account of success and self-criticism, floodlights and hard work, celebrity friendships and underlying loneliness . . . [2]

In the *Daily Telegraph*, Lord Kinross said that her personality

seemed to be sometimes unreal, as such personalities will. There was a soft centre within the hard shell. It was, anyway, the struggle in life she enjoyed, not the achievement.

Nancy Spain was a human catalyst who, in her forthright Tyneside way, overrode prejudices of age and class and taste to attract a varied public of viewers and listeners and readers . . . her last work . . . provides them with a high-spirited projection of the admired and lamented image.[3]

Under the headline 'Always Gay', Felicia Lamb of the *Sunday Telegraph* wrote:

The book is a bit of a potboiler, and none the worse for that. The scanty material is skilfully assembled . . . it is the obituary of this child of our time, and the cheerful throwaway comments on her character have to be taken seriously.

Her spontaneous seeming broadcasting, writing and lecturing caused as much nervous strain as the newest amateur.[4]

In the *Sunday Times*, Jeremy Clive described the book as 'her last recording – full of fun, and that zest of intelligence that never left her. ... Sharing her own feelings of happiness was Nancy's art and privilege, a rare one in this day and place'.[5] Simon Raven, in the *Observer*, wrote: 'Her writing could be almost intolerably brash, and this last book is no exception; but it is lively, generous and humane; and above all, so to speak, it wishes us pleasure'.[6] In the *Evening Standard*, Anthony Hern appreciated the qualities of both book and author: 'high spirited, name-dropping, warm, alive'.[7]

The April issue of *She*, which had gone to press before the accident, carried Nancy's last 'Newshound' column. It contained pieces about Millicent Martin, Stirling Moss and one about The Searchers, eerily titled 'The Liverpool Kasbah'. The first post-accident issue, in May, contained a two-page tribute to Joan and Nancy, under the heading 'She Mourns'. There was a full-page photograph of Joan, taken by Michael Griffiths himself, who was now acting editor. Marcus Morris said, 'SHE will be Joan's memorial to many hundreds of thousands of her readers. It will be kept as such. Under Michael Griffiths's guidance it will remain what it is – the creation of a unique and lovable person'.[8] The National Magazine Company itself announced that 'as a token of appreciation of Miss Laurie's work', it would 'endow a permanent reminder through the Chailey Heritage Craft School and Hospital':

> We shall provide for the creation of a landscape garden to adjoin the swimming pool there, which will carry Miss Laurie's name. Her mother has suggested it should be called the Joan Werner Laurie Memorial Garden.

Readers were invited to send donations to the Joan Werner Laurie Chailey Fund.

In the September issue, the magazine was proud to announce that the swimming pool at Chailey Heritage had been opened and that *She* readers had contributed an astonishing £12,500 towards the £40,000 it cost. On one side there was a glass wall overlooking the grounds, which were to incorporate the memorial garden. A plaque commemorating the *She* readers' contributions had been installed on one of the outside walls.

It was not until May 1965 that J.D. Rose's report on the accident was submitted to the Minister of Aviation. Amongst his official conclusions were that the aircraft's total 'all-up-weight' was higher than the authorized limits allowed, both at take-off and at the time of the accident; and that the length of the landing strip was less than required under the Air Navigation (General Regulations), 1960. Most significant, though, was his official opinion:

> The aircraft stalled when the pilot made a steep turn at a low height to line up with the landing strip. The possibility that the stall may have developed due to a decrease of engine power resulting from carburettor icing *or due to accidental interference with the aircraft's controls by the passenger in the co-pilot's seat cannot be entirely dismissed.* [author's italics]

But what sort of 'passenger interference' could this mean? We know Joan was in the co-pilot's seat, and she didn't have her seat belt on. It is virtually beyond doubt that Stevenson was flying north one final time before turning left and lining up with the landing strip, prior to landing. Could it have been that, as several witnesses to the accident observed, he saw the pylons less than 500 yards ahead of the plane and had to make a sharp turn earlier than he had anticipated? And that this sudden, acute lurch to the left resulted in the person nearest the controls, who was not secured in their seat, leaning against or grabbing something which made the plane drop 'like a shot bird'?

Again, J.D. Rose did not rule it out:

> In the circumstances of the subject accident it was possible for the passenger to have accidentally grasped one of the aircraft's controls for support while turning around to speak, or while attempting to secure her safety harness, or due to an involuntary sideway movement in the seat which may have occurred during the aircraft's final turn. This must remain a matter of speculation but the possibility cannot be entirely eliminated.

As the jury rightly decided at the inquest, it was simply a case of 'misadventure': no finger of blame could be pointed at any individual. It was a sequence of unfortunate events that, with hindsight, could all have probably have been avoided – but then hindsight is a wonderful thing. And no one ever thinks such things could happen to them.

All through her life, Nancy was lucky enough to be in the right place with the right people at the right time. On Saturday 21 March 1964, her luck finally ran out.

★ ★ ★

Ginette Spanier continued to live in Paris and work for Balmain until Paul-Emile died. She then left France and lived in Chelsea for the rest of her life. In 1976, a third book was published, *Long Road to Freedom*, which dealt with the Seidmanns' wartime experiences. In 1980, during a radio interview, she said plaintively, 'I miss Noel Coward every day, I miss Nancy Spain every day'. She died in London on 18 April 1988, aged eighty-four. Tony Warren remains in no doubt: 'Ginette Spanier loved Nancy the most; she adored her – still did. I saw her once more before her death and it was still "Nancy" . . . she'd been to seances to try and contact her'.

Warren also felt the loss deeply. 'I couldn't go into the Ivy for a long time after she died – I just saw it as her picture frame'. Like Ginette, he also tried to make some sort of contact. 'I would go to psychics and none of them provided anything. But driving round Belgrave Square one day, something inside my head told me to get a medium'. He went to a group sitting at the British Association of Mediums:

> 'The man suddenly said, "Who died in a plane crash? It was a private plane". Then he started to describe this gentleman. I said, "Are you absolutely sure?" He said, "Well, I don't want to embarrass you. . . . Wait, I know their face. . . . She must have been a card . . . was she blind? Only she keeps drawing round her eyes – and she's got a jersey on. Was she a nun when she was in the body?

Only she's holding up a picture of a nun and pointing to it". Suddenly my blood ran cold'.

He had remembered one afternoon he'd spent with Nancy:

'She'd done this advert for Interdent and said to me, "I'll take you out and buy you anything you like – you're gong to be lavishly kept this afternoon." I said, "I'd like a copy of *The Sound of Music* – as long it's got a picture of Olive Gilbert as a nun on the front". So we spent the afternoon searching for this'.

Now he knew why the medium was seeing 'a picture of a nun' – and why whoever was pointing at it was also drawing round her eyes. Nancy, of course, was extremely short-sighted, as Warren recalls:

'She told Laon Maybanke I looked like Garbo ... I used to say to her, "take those glasses off", because when she had them on she didn't look like Nancy Spain. In fact, she looked bloody awful in them. And she wore them a lot. Whenever she saw me, she'd take them off and let out a deep sigh'.

He asked the medium if the person he could see had their glasses on:

'He said, "She is delighted you've finally got it. But, no, she hasn't got her glasses on". Then she told me a whole load of things – he was getting voice and he was able to get her exact words. She said in four years, I was going to have a serious illness and everyone will despair – and I did. Then he suddenly shouted, "Will the pair of you please lower your voices!", and then I knew it was genuine'.

Tony Warren found phenomenal success with *Coronation Street* and then rather lost his way. After spending many years in America during the 1970s, where he enjoyed all the drink and drugs money could buy, he returned to England. He beat the drink, the drugs and the doldrums and, in the 1980s and 1990s, became the author of a string of hugely enjoyable, best-selling novels, including *The Lights of Manchester*, *Foot of the Rainbow* and *Behind Closed Doors*. The latter featured a cameo appearance by Nancy.

★ ★ ★

'One never quite gets over a thing like that', says Alan Freeman. 'I'm a better person for knowing them, even for a short time. All they showed to me was kindness – Nancy used to send me up something rotten; I sent her up rotten and we'd laugh and giggle, but it was very much family. I'm very proud and happy to have counted them among my friends. I have a photo of myself and Nancy and Joan, sitting on my mantelpiece, so I always see it ... I like to imagine Nancy and Marlene having great little rows somewhere up in Heaven ... '.

★ ★ ★

The Windmill Theatre did, at last, close its doors – on 31 October 1964. It completed a disastrous year for Sheila van Damm, in which she had lost her business, her new home and two of the most important people in her life. She went to live with her sister, Nona, in Sussex, where they ran a farm, country house and stables near Pulborough. She wrote another volume of memoirs, *We Never Closed*, in 1967. She retired from public life and 'confined her driving to country lanes'.[9] She died on 23 August 1987, aged sixty-five.

★ ★ ★

Lord Beaverbrook also died that year. In 1962, cancer of the bladder had been diagnosed, and within a year, machines had been fitted into all his main homes to take him up and downstairs. On 25 May, he managed to attend a banquet held at the Dorchester, in honour of his eighty-fifth birthday. Six hundred and fifty-eight guests were invited; none of them were women. He died at Cherkley on 9 June 1964.

By that time, Express Newspapers had already begun its slow decline. In the 1970s and 1980s, the *Daily Express* – now a tabloid – found itself caught in no man's land, carved up by a brutal circulation and price war waged largely between the *Sun* and the *Daily Mirror*. Though it was still selling 2 million copies a day in 1977, its then editor put his finger on the problem when he was asked where all its readers had gone: 'Largely to the cemetery'.[10]

Like all its main tabloid rivals and broadsheet neighbours, the *Daily Express* left Fleet Street for new premises – not quite as far upriver as *The Times* at Canary Wharf, but just south of the river, on the other side of Blackfriars Bridge. The old *Express* building became a sorry sight, lying empty and half-derelict. The pub where Beaverbrook's finest would gossip over a drink in Poppins Court died with them.

By the end of 1995, the *Express*'s circulation had slumped to around a million, the group's management made hundreds of staff redundant and its longtime editor, Nick Lloyd, resigned. However, a new editor, Richard Addis, was brought on board and attempted to kick some new life into the Beaver's old warhorse. Part of the revamp involved a redesign of the entire paper – based on Stanley Morrison's typographic innovations created for it in the 1940s. Out went columnists like Esther Rantzen and Robert Kilroy-Silk; in came biographer Philip Norman who, in good old-fashioned *Express* style, made an interesting contrast alongside fellow-columnists, Mary Kenny and Sir Bernard Ingham (himself a character who could have come straight out of the Beaverbrook mould). The 'William Hickey' gossip column was revived, as was 'Beachcomber', where more offbeat, humorous items could flourish. New sections were also introduced, including a Health section aimed at women, while 'Express Women' was changed into 'Life'. By reintroducing some of what had contributed to the *Express*'s domination of the 1940s and 1950s, Addis slowly began to make it into a paper for the 1990s – but with no likely candidate to fill the role of a latter-day Nancy Spain.

Her former boss, Sir Edward Pickering, became executive vice-chairman of Times Newspapers, home of the *News of the World*. Having seen an assortment of 'personality' journalists come and go on Fleet Street, he remains unequivocal about the impact Nancy had. 'In the time that she'd been in Fleet Street, she really had created a sort of myth. Lots of people still talk about her. She was, without any doubt, an enormous personality'. And, he thinks, of a type that British newspapers can no longer produce:

'An awful lot of talent that used to come straight into newspapers now gets dissipated and goes into television. It's interesting to think about what paper Nancy would go to now. She might have fitted on the *Sunday Times*. She wouldn't fit in on the tabloids now and I don't think she would have enjoyed herself on them – not that she'd have been snobbish about it'.

★ ★ ★

Like the *Express*, *She* enjoyed mixed fortunes after 1964. Pamela Carmichael was chosen as Joan's successor in the editor's seat and, under her and Michael Griffiths's guidance, its circulation was holding steady, a year later, at 299,000. Their partnership was also a success on a personal level: they subsequently married and continued to work for the National Magazine Company until they retired to live quietly in Wales.

After their departure, the magazine's circulation slumped: by 1985, it had fallen to 228,000. In the late 1980s, it was revamped and billed as the magazine 'for women who juggle their lives', under the inspired editorship of Linda Kelsey. It took on the needs of women who were both working mothers and wives, even launching several campaigns on issues of importance to them, such as more child-friendly public places. The magazine gave an annual award to a woman deemed to be the 'Juggler of the Year'. Its circulation rose from 208,000 to 273,000 in five years. But, by the beginning of 1996, this catchline was dropped and Kelsey herself, exhausted by juggling her own life, stepped down. She was succeeded by Alison Pylkkanen, former editor of *Good Housekeeping*. The magazine was redesigned and its content, it was announced, would concentrate on health, relaxation, stress therapies and leisure, as well as improving its cookery coverage. 'As She smartens up, it is also coming down to earth',[11] observed Maggie Brown in the *Guardian*.

★ ★ ★

Jackie Forster's life changed rather drastically in the 1960s. She divorced, came out as a lesbian and co-founded Britain's first publication for gay women, *Arena Three*. This eventually became *Sappho* and a social group bearing the same name became a vital meeting place for lesbians, especially those who, for various reasons, were unable to be as out as Jackie. One of the most visible lesbians in Britain, she has made numerous appearances on television and radio in defence of gay rights and served as the lesbian representative on the GLC Women's Committee for several years. In the early 1980s, she and Gillian Hanscombe co-authored the ground-breaking book, *Rocking the Cradle – Lesbian Mothers: A Challenge in Family Living*. She was flabbergasted when she learned that Nancy herself had rocked the cradle several decades before.

★ ★ ★

In 1965, Laon Maybanke published his book of portraits, *Second Faces* (Arlington Books). It included photographs of Nancy and Dolly Goodman, and the book itself bore this dedication: 'Nancy Spain was a very rare person. I was infinitely privileged to have known her friendship. To her, with love, this book of photographs'. It also included tributes from Lord Boothby, Dilys Powell, Jack Longland and David Jacobs.

★ ★ ★

Nancy's lawyer, the 'other' David Jacobs, did not survive the decade, either. He still had an impressive roster of big-name clients, but it was his dealings with the biggest 1960s names of all that would, ultimately, be his professional and personal undoing. Larry Parnes introduced Jacobs to Brian Epstein, just before the Beatles conquered America.

In 1964, Epstein hired Jacobs to oversee the licensing of Beatles merchandise potentially worth millions of dollars to the group. Jacobs botched the deal, signing away 90 per cent of the profits to the American licensee, Seltaeb, resulting in years of ugly litigation on both sides of the Atlantic. Incredibly, Epstein saw this as his own failure, rather than Jacobs's, and continued to use his legal services.

By 1968, it was all getting too much for Jacobs. On call twenty-four hours a day to his clients, the pressures of years of overwork proved too much and he suffered a nervous breakdown. He began spending more time at Hove, but his private life was also in a mess – there was speculation that a troublesome boyfriend, much younger than Jacobs, was threatening to blackmail him. On Saturday 14 December, Jacobs unsuccessfully tried to poison himself. The next day, Malcolm Duke, described in the press as Jacobs's 'houseman', found him dead in the garage. He had hung himself. Incredibly, he did not leave a will.

★ ★ ★

Philip Youngman Carter died on 30 November 1969. Margery Allingham had died just three years before and 'Thereafter he was but half himself'.[12]

★ ★ ★

As of the summer of 1995, the children of Chailey Heritage were still using the swimming pool opened in 1964. On a wall in the Joan Werner Laurie Memorial Garden, a plaque still read, 'This garden was made to commemorate the generosity of the readers of the magazine *She* who subscribed nearly £12,000 towards the cost of this pool'.

★ ★ ★

Somewhere in Japan, a private collector has the manuscript of 'Kat Dressed to Kill', bought from a bookseller in 1992. It remained unpublished, its exact whereabouts unknown.

At some point, Sheila van Damm must have had second thoughts about destroying all Nancy's and Joan's papers. In 1995, at a book trade sale in the West Country, author and collector W.J. West bought a job lot of literary papers. Amongst them were several brown carrier bags with 'Spain' written on them. They contained an early draft of *A Funny Thing Happened on the Way*, the unfinished draft of the 'Snobbery' book and letters exchanged between Nancy and Joan when Nancy went on her American tours. How they survived, and how they ended up in carrier bags in a lot at a book sale, separated from the *Kat* novel, remained a mystery.

On 30 January 1977, the *Sunday Times* brought out a special Jubilee issue, celebrating Britain at work from 1952 to 1977. Nancy Spain – 'gifted, funny, ebullient TV panellist, broadcaster and writer' – was picked out as one of the faces of the previous twenty-five years. 'She was 10 years ahead of her time in being openly a Lesbian', it said, 'but she'd also have brought to the non-Lesbian women's movement (late 1960s) a lot of fun and good sense'.[13]

One of the items Joan took with her on the trip to Aintree was an application form for King's College Hospital medical school for Nick. She had wanted him to become a doctor, but he had rather different ideas. In 1967, he officially changed his name from Nicholas Laurie Seyler to Nicholas Werner Laurie: 'The court made me wait until I was twenty-one, though I started using it earlier'. That year, of course, he received the money from the joint estates, held in trust, though 40 per cent of it had been swallowed up by death duties. However, 'Tom and I managed to come out of it with a house each'. Roy Rutherford had contacted him, about the possibility of going into business together: namely, opening a restaurant in Malta. But a little legal trouble, involving possession of marijuana, put paid to that.

It was Dick Laurie who told him that his brother was so in name only: 'I wasn't surprised'.

He married in 1972 and he and his family settled in the West Country. The Werner Laurie publishing tradition continued, with his business, NWL Editorial Services.

Dick Laurie's appearance on *Nancy Spain's Woman's Hour* in 1955 was oddly prophetic, in that he turned reporter for the day to interview his favourite jazz musician. Subsequently, he became a professional jazz clarinettist, as well as editing a number of small publications, including the *Soho Clarion*. He also became an avid collector of T. Werner Laurie books and ephemera.

Tom Seyler also settled in the West Country, except he became 'Tom Carter': 'The reason why I originally took the surname "Carter", apart from it being my father's name, was because it was easier to pronounce than "Seyler". And maybe I wanted to show Pip Carter up'.

He and Nick Laurie have different recollections of exactly when he was told the truth about his real parentage: Tom thinks it was when he started university, while Nick believes it was earlier: 'I know that Tom knew it while he was at school. He may have taken it in one ear and out the other'. It was the redoubtable family GP, Dr Norman 'Nelly' Newman, who could give him all the details, Tom was told.

'When I saw him he was seventy-four. He thought I wanted to see him about something else entirely. I told him who I was and he said, "You're the boy from Wales, aren't you?"' Then Tom asked him the $64,000 question. Yes, Nancy was his mother. As to his father, Newman couldn't remember the exact name, but he knew who he meant: '"It's on the tip of my tongue. He was married to a famous writer. They are both dead now. Got it! Margery Allingham. Whoever is Margery Allingham's husband is your father"'. He was far from being angry at finding out who his real mother had been; it rather explained why he had always regarded Nancy with more affection than Jonnie.

But while he remains philosophical about the effects this may have had on him, Nick Laurie is less circumspect: 'Once they died, there was nobody to pick him up and say, "This is what you do". He was kind of out of sight, out of mind at public school'. The Laytons took over care and custody of Tom. 'I stayed in their household until I went up to university. Which was rather tense'. Nick Laurie, however, has some sympathy for the Laytons:

'They had already raised their own family. They didn't put a lot of effort into raising Tom. He got very little of that family background to grow up with, and develop with. And university is not the greatest educator of social graces – and he came out of that a very muddled person'.

At eighteen Tom became a student at the London University School of Slavonic and East European Studies:

'I got my degree, a 2.2. Then I bummed around and came down here because Nick was here, and bought my house with the last of Nancy's cash. Since then there have been a whole series of nervous breakdowns. Delayed reaction? Who knows? I reckon I think too hard'.

By the 1990s, he remained unemployed, but became very involved in the Bosnia Solidarity Campaign, and keenly interested in all matters relating to the former Yugoslavia. In the 1970s, he completed a course in journalism at the London College of Printing. Before that, he had written for the London student newspaper, *Senate*.

'I was actually the beer correspondent – being keen on real ale, I wrote about pubs for the next three years. I was told by a lot of people it was the only thing worth reading. . . . But my journalistic career hasn't exactly flourished since then'.

Nick Laurie believed that, apart from the question of money, he actually inherited more from Nancy than her own natural son:

'I think to Tom it's a bit more like discovering you've got a famous ancestor. His life with Nancy was a relatively small amount of his time. The direct influence of Nancy on him was considerably less than it was on me. It was a shame for Tom that she never acknowledged him, but she did rather live for the day. And that was the sort of thing that she could put off until tomorrow and tomorrow and tomorrow . . . until it was too late. I suspect when she saw the aeroplane going down, she probably thought of him'.

Any suggestion that Nancy had a death wish is complete nonsense. Since the car accident in 1958, she had been acutely aware of her own mortality, but not to an excessively morbid degree. As with anyone who has had a brush with death, the issue came up from time to time in conversation. In 1962, she had a discussion with James Jones about survival. What she had wanted to say, she wrote, was

> That I would love something that I wrote to survive, but that for myself I didn't care. That I had already seen almost enough, lived almost enough, and that I only really minded for Jonnie's sons, Nick and Tom, and all the other kids who hadn't yet had a chance to live as I had. And that the whole of life and education was really as nothing compared with half an hour's lying under a tree in the sun, knowing that the people I loved were safe and happy.[14]

In the end, though, she was not able to do this.

Though some areas of her life were kept strictly compartmentalized and clandestine, most of the threads interwove with each other remarkably harmoniously. The protracted relationship with Ginette, for instance, did not preclude her becoming part of the extended family; and in a peculiar way, the emergence of Sheila van Damm in their lives steadied things more than unbalanced them. What held the fragments of Nancy's life together was that sense of 'belonging', engendered within her own constructed family – which, despite all the champagne, the travelling and the celebrity, she always seemed to be yearning for. It was the glue that kept her wings on during her flights of fancy, and ensured she came safely back to earth.

Joan Werner Laurie was more admired than liked. She did not elicit the widespread and deep affection that Nancy did. Her talents were not as high-profile and flamboyant as her more famous partner. But, whatever we believe her motives may have been – money, love, ambition, security or a hybrid of all of these elements – the truth is that the Nancy Spain who so entertained and enchanted her public, her colleagues, her friends and her lovers, would not have succeeded in quite the way we know it without her.

'Joan was like an anchor to Nancy', says Jackie Forster. 'She never budged from Nancy. She is the most intriguing character in the whole set-up'.

Of course, a trouser-wearing character called N. Spain would have existed, as she had always done, in one form or another. But having her own customized, affirming family – complete with a chosen, rather than imposed, authority figure at its helm – kept her finely balanced while she strode along the high wire of life at the very top. Quite simply, without Joan, it wouldn't have happened.

It is difficult to speculate what Nancy, with so many possible strings to her bow, would have done through the 1960s and 1970s. During that time, the late Jean Rook became assistant editor of the *Daily Express*; then, a 'stunt/personality' journalist, whose assignments included training a circus tiger, driving a chariot and interviewing stars like George Best. She was also the paper's chief columnist and became known as 'The First Lady of Fleet Street'. One thing is certain: if Nancy had lived, that title would have become hers, and hers alone.

Of course, there was much more to her than stunt journalism and columns – that was the secret of her success. Her surviving family, friends and colleagues have suggested a variety of things she might have gone on to do: she would have done more television and less print journalism; she would have become a travel writer, perhaps focusing on America again or, perhaps, India; she might even have ended up with her own chat show. She could certainly have turned her hand to any or all of these and, by sheer dint of her unique personality, might just have been one of the few who managed to ride the waves stirred up by the 1960s. It was said of Gilbert Harding that he would not have emerged in another place or time other than 1950s Britain, when it was still being called 'dear threadbare Britain'. His frankness and unconventionality burst through the drabness of early 1950s life but, by the time of his death in 1960, were looking increasingly out of step with the times.

Lady Docker – another product of her times – hated what the 1960s represented: when the Beatles were awarded their MBEs, she declared it was the end of Britain's 'age of elegance'. For Tony Warren, that's where Nancy belonged:

> 'It was a much more frivolous age. That's why she was more extraordinary in the middle of it – in a sheepskin coat, striding out, with her Robert James haircut. She belonged to the period where the lights of Shaftesbury Avenue were dimmed for Lawrence – that's when she was at her height, as a person. She loved a West End that doesn't exist any more. She longed for all that glamour, and she got it'.

The question most frequently asked about Nancy Spain in the 1990s was 'Who is there like her now?' Who indeed? Even if you crossed Jean Rook with, say, Sue Lawley, Sandi Toksvig and Cilla Black, you still wouldn't end up with a Nancy Spain.

Over thirty years after her death, it is remarkable how this deceptively frivolous, lightweight personality still provoked extreme feelings of affection or acrimony. People who met her can remember what they disliked about her as though they had only seen her fifty minutes ago, and not fifty years. Those with more affectionate memories can recall the way she laughed, sang, dressed, worked and loved. Members of the public who loved what she represented to them forty years ago have kept the fading cuttings about her death pressed carefully in the pages of scrapbooks. Her face still stares out of photo albums kept by other former Wrens. Walkers on the cliffs outside Brighton point at Roedean School and remember it only as the school 'where Nancy Spain went'. Dozens still remember where they were and what they were doing when they heard she had been killed.

Denis Norden still has the image of a trouser-wearing character, punting off down the river with a beautiful young woman in tow, vividly etched in his memory. But one of his most enduring recollections of Nancy is one of the last poems she wrote, published posthumously in *A Funny Thing Happened on the Way*:

> Good, There's a pang of passion in my heart
> Confusing and surprising me. Something
> Of how I lost my ignorance. And art
> Acquired taught me the way to swim. Remembering

Old joys that grown-ups hold in cool derision.
Faith in myself. Belief in human good –
Youth. Childhood. If you like: ambition.

Where did I lose it? Somewhere on the way
In the gay gritty gutter of the world, The Street,
Where nine-day wonders only last a day
Before they sink un-noticed in the Fleet?
Yes, I ran grinning then because I knew so much
(Unprintable of course) which News Boys shout,
Rustproof and galvanized because in touch
With all the lads whose lust is finding out.

Ambition lost but innocence intact,
Here I am, battered to my bleeding knees
Feeling eighteen but forty-six in fact
Finding I still react to every breeze.
Finding in spite of all I know that I still *care*,
That after all these years I've no defence,
Proving that life is something we can share,
Our only sin a bored indifference.[15]

N.B.S. ('For the Middle-aged', 1963)

'The one attitude that one would least associate with her is bored indifference', reflects Norden. 'There are some people that go in and out of your life, and some you lose early, but she's the one person that I still miss and it's hard to define why. Also, as you pile up the decades, you become conscious that the same people come round again – but she hasn't. There hasn't been a replication of her'.

★ ★ ★

Notes

Introduction

1. *Sunday Times*, 10 May 1964, p. 38.

1. 'Nancy ... A Gipsy Name'

1. Nancy Spain, *A Funny Thing Happened on the Way* (London: Hutchinson, 1964), p. 45.
2. *Ibid.*, p. 64.
3. *Ibid.*, p. 65.
4. *Newcastle Journal*, 11 September 1906, p. 5.
5. *News of the World*, 22 October 1961, p. 8.
6. Nancy Spain, *Why I'm Not a Millionaire* (London: Hutchinson, 1956), p. 92.
7. *Daily Express*, 3 September 1953, p. 6.
8. Nancy Spain, *Mrs Beeton and Her Husband* (London: Collins, 1948), p. 253.
9. Aileen Smiles, *Samuel Smiles and His Surroundings* (London: Robert Hale, 1956), p. 13.
10. *Ibid.*, p. 68.
11. *Ibid.*
12. *Daily Express*, 16 June 1956, p. 4.
13. Thomas B. Green, *Life and Work of Samuel Smiles* (Bettement of London, 1904), p. 22.
14. Spain, *Millionaire*, p. 14.
15. *Ibid.*
16. Sarah Freeman, *Isabella and Sam* (London: Gollancz, 1977), p. 37.
17. Spain, *Millionaire*, p. 23.
18. Spain, *A Funny Thing*, p. 30.
19. *Archaeologia Aeliana*, 31 January 1917.
20. Spain, *A Funny Thing*, p. 30.
21. Charles Williams, *The Greater Triumphs* (1932).
22. Nancy Spain, *A Funny Thing Happened on the Way* (draft; W.J. West collection), pp. 165–8.
23. Spain, *Millionaire*, p. 7.
24. *Hebden Bridge Times and Gazette*, 14 February 1964, p. 8.
25. Spain, *Millionaire*, p. 8.
26. *Archaeologia Aeliana* 4th series vol. xl, p. 283.
27. *Ibid.*
28. New Library, L720 1930, Newcastle Central Reference Library.

29. *Newcastle Journal*, July 1993.
30. Spain, *A Funny Thing* (draft), pp. 165–8.
31. *Ibid.*, pp. 227–8.
32. *Archaeologia Aeliana* 4th series vol. xl, p. 287.
33. *News of the World*, 22 January 1961, p. 8.
34. Spain, *Millionaire*, p. 12.
35. Spain, *A Funny Thing*, p. 30.
36. *Ibid.*, p. 62.
37. Spain, *Millionaire*, p. 8.
38. Spain, *A Funny Thing*, p. 22.
39. *Ibid.*, p. 29.
40. *Ibid.*
41. *Woman's Hour*, 25 January 1954.
42. *Ibid.*, 25 April 1955.
43. Spain, *A Funny Thing* (draft), pp. 165–8.
44. Spain, *Millionaire*, p. 15.
45. Interview with Tony Warren, 18 November 1994.
46. Spain, *A Funny Thing* (draft), pp. 209–18.
47. Spain, *Millionaire*, p. 17.
48. Spain, *A Funny Thing*, p. 23.
49. *Ibid.*, p. 26.
50. Spain, *A Funny Thing* (draft), p. 49.
51. *Ibid.*, p. 48.

2. 'School of Love and School of Might'

1. Nancy Spain, *A Funny Thing Happened on the Way* (London: Hutchinson, 1964), p. 38.
2. Dorothy E. De Zouche, *Roedean School 1885–1955* (Brighton: Dolphin Press, 1955), p. 84.
3. Leslie Comford and F.R. Yerbury, *Roedean School* (Brighton: Ernest Benn, 1927), p. 10.
4. *Good Housekeeping*, June 1951, p. 150.
5. Nancy Spain, *Why I'm Not a Millionaire* (London: Hutchinson, 1956), p. 23.
6. *Good Housekeeping*, June 1951, p. 149.
7. *Ibid.*, p. 43.
8. Spain, *A Funny Thing*, p. 38.
9. *Evening Standard*, 30 September 1954, p. 12.
10. *Good Housekeeping*, June 1951, p. 149.
11. Spain, *A Funny Thing*, p. 38.
12. *Woman's Hour*, 20 March 1956.
13. Spain, *A Funny Thing*, p. 37.
14. Spain, *Millionaire*, p. 19.
15. Spain, *A Funny Thing*, p. 18.
16. *Ibid.*, p. 34.
17. *Ibid.*, pp. 37–8.
18. *The Times*, 12 June 1933, p. 8g.
19. *Woman's Hour*, 20 March 1956.
20. *The Times*, 27 July 1935, p. 14b.
21. *Ibid.*
22. *Ibid.*

23. *Guardian*, 4 February 1994, p. 4.
24. *Daily Express*, 13 February 1959, p. 3.
25. Spain, *Millionaire*, p. 25.
26. *Ibid.*
27. Nancy Spain, *A Funny Thing Happened on the Way* (draft; W.J. West collection), p. 52.
28. Spain, *Millionaire*, p. 26.

3. Miss Sargeant Appeared in a Class of Her Own

1. Nancy Spain, *Why I'm Not a Millionaire* (London: Hutchinson, 1956), p. 28.
2. *Ibid.*
3. *Ibid.*, p. 29.
4. *Ibid.*, p. 27.
5. *Newcastle Journal*, 16 November 1935, p. 14.
6. *Ibid.*, 23 December 1935, p. 12.
7. *Ibid.*, 16 January 1936, p. 4.
8. *Ibid.*, 11 March 1938, p. 10.
9. *Ibid.*, 12 February 1936, p. 12.
10. Spain, *Millionaire*, p. 30.
11. *Ibid.*
12. *Newcastle Journal*, 27 July 1936, p. 7.
13. *Newcastle Journal*, 2 December 1936, p. 13.
14. *Ibid.*
15. *Ibid.*, 5 December 1936, p. 13.
16. *Ibid.*
17. *Ibid.*
18. *Ibid.*, 23 December 1936, p. 13.
19. *Ibid.*, 9 December 1936, p. 12.
20. *Ibid.*, 6 January 1937, p. 13.
21. *Ibid.*, 16 February 1937, p. 12.
22. *Ibid.*, 25 March 1937, p. 13.
23. *Ibid.*, 2 July 1937, p. 13.
24. *Ibid.*, 3 July 1937, p. 13.
25. *Ibid.*, 14 July 1937, p. 13.
26. *Ibid.*, 2 August 1937, p. 9.
27. *Ibid.*, 17 September 1937, p. 12.
28. *Ibid.*, 11 October 1937, p. 11.
29. *Ibid.*, 12 October 1937, p. 12.
30. *Ibid.*, 17 September 1937, p. 3.
31. *Newcastle Evening Chronicle*, 28 October 1937, p. 14.
32. *Newcastle Journal*, 29 October 1937, p. 20.
33. *Observer*, 31 October 1937, p. 29.
34. *Newcastle Journal*, 19 November 1937, p. 4.
35. *Ibid.*, 16 November 1937, p. 11.
36. *Ibid.*, 19 November 1937, p. 13.
37. *Ibid.*, 25 November 1937, p. 11.
38. *Ibid.*, 30 November 1937, p. 12.
39. *Ibid.*, 3 January 1938, p. 12.
40. *Ibid.*, 1 February 1938, p. 9.
41. *Ibid.*, 21 January 1938, p. 14.

42. *Ibid.*, 1 February 1938, p. 12.
43. *Ibid.*, 3 February 1938, p. 13.
44. *Ibid.*, 1 March 1938, p. 12.
45. *Ibid.*, 3 March 1938, p. 12.
46. *Ibid.*, 16 March 1938, p. 14.
47. *Ibid.*, 9 July 1938, p. 13.
48. *Ibid.*, 2 September 1938, p. 3.
49. *Ibid.*
50. *Ibid.*
51. *Daily Chronicle*, 5 September 1938, p. 10.
52. *Newcastle Journal*, 1 September 1938, p. 8.
53. *Ibid.*
54. *Ibid.*, 16 September 1938, p. 9.
55. *Ibid.*, 30 September 1938, p. 14.
56. *Ibid.*, 11 November 1938, p. 13.
57. *Ibid.*, 16 November 1938, p. 12.
58. *Ibid.*, 2 December 1938, p. 15.
59. *Ibid.*, 9 December 1938, p. 11.
60. *Ibid.*, 24 January 1939, p. 11.
61. *Ibid.*, 27 January 1939, p. 13.
62. *Ibid.*, 3 February 1939, p. 5.
63. *Ibid.*, 19 June 1939, p. 12.
64. *Ibid.*, 30 June 1939, p. 5.
65. *Ibid.*, 8 July 1939, p. 8.
66. *Ibid.*, 7 July 1939, p. 8.
67. *Ibid.*, 8 July 1939, p. 8.
68. *Ibid.*, 10 July 1939, p. 9.
69. *Ibid.*, 16 August 1939, p. 14.
70. Nancy Spain, *A Funny Thing Happened on the Way* (London: Hutchinson, 1964), p. 50.
71. *Newcastle Journal*, 26 August 1939, p. 14.
72. Spain, *A Funny Thing*, p. 49.

4. Proper Navy

1. Nancy Spain, *Why I'm Not a Millionaire* (London: Hutchinson, 1956), p. 38.
2. Nancy Spain, *Thank You – Nelson* (London: Hutchinson, 1945), p. 9.
3. *Ibid.*
4. *Woman's Hour*, 1 November 1957.
5. Spain, *Nelson*, p. 14.
6. *Ibid.*
7. Jack Cassin-Scott, *Women at War* (London: Osprey Publishing, 1980), p. 9.
8. Shelley Saywell, *Women in War* (Grapevine, 1986), pp. 99–106.
9. Spain, *Nelson*, p. 36.
10. *Ibid.*, p. 16.
11. *Sunday Chronicle*, 4 February 1945, p. 2.
12. *Ibid.*
13. Spain, *Nelson*, p. 55.
14. *Ibid.*, p. 62.
15. *Ibid.*, p. 63.
16. *Newcastle Journal*, 8 February 1940, p. 7.

17. Spain, *Nelson*, p. 64.
18. Dame Vera Laughton Mathews, *The Blue Tapestry* (London: Hollis and Carter, 1948), p. 100.
19. Spain, *Nelson*, p. 74.
20. *Newcastle Journal*, 1 January 1940, p. 3.
21. *Ibid.*
22. *Woman's Hour*, 25 January 1954.
23. Spain, *Nelson*, p. 74.
24. *Northern Daily Mail*, 24 December 1939, p. 2.
25. Spain, *Millionaire*, p. 34.
26. Nancy Spain, *A Funny Thing Happened on the Way* (London: Hutchinson, 1964), p. 57.
27. Spain, *Nelson*, p. 84.
28. *Ibid.*, p. 93.
29. *Ibid.*, p. 103.
30. *Ibid.*, p. 109.
31. *Ibid.*, p. 117.
32. *Ibid.*, p. 125.
33. *Ibid.*, p. 129.
34. *Amenities and Welfare Conditions in the Three Women's Services* (MOD report), p. 43.
35. Spain, *Millionaire*, p. 39.
36. *Ibid.*, p. 44.
37. *Ibid.*, p. 45.
38. BBC, RCONT1 Nancy Spain – Talks File 1: 1942–57, 5 April 1943.
39. *Ibid.*
40. *Ibid.*
41. Spain, *Millionaire*, p. 53.
42. BBC, RCONT1 Nancy Spain – Talks File 1: 1942–57, 6 March 1942.
43. *Ibid.*
44. Michael Elliman and Frederick Roll, *Pink Plaque Guide* (London: GMP Publishers Ltd, 1986) p. 110.
45. Spain, *Millionaire*, p. 53.
46. Joanna Scott-Moncrieff (ed.), *The Book of Woman's Hour* (London: Ariel Productions, 1953), p. 203.
47. *Ibid.*, p. 204.
48. Spain, *Millionaire*, p. 62.
49. *Ibid.*, p. 63.
50. *Ibid.*, p. 66.
51. *Ibid.*, p. 67.
52. *Ibid.*, p. 69.
53. *Ibid.*, p. 71.
54. *Ibid.*, p. 72.
55. *Ibid.*, p. 73.
56. *Ibid.*, p. 74.
57. *Sunday Chronicle*, 4 February 1945, p. 2.
58. *Woman's Hour*, 1 November 1957.
59. Spain, *Millionaire*, p. 77.
60. *Sunday Times*, 28 January 1945, p. 3.
61. *Newcastle Journal*, 30 January 1945, p. 2.
62. *Observer*, 4 February 1945, p. 3.

63. *Sunday Chronicle*, 4 February 1945, p. 6.
64. Spain, *Nelson*, p. 44.
65. Spain, *Millionaire*, p. 78.
66. *Ibid.*, p. 80.
67. Nancy Spain, *Poison in Play* (London: Hutchinson, 1946), p. 16.

5. To Please Myself

1. *Newcastle Journal*, 4 January 1934, p. 5.
2. Lawrence du Garde Peach, *Meet Mrs Beeton* (London: H.F.W. Deane & Sons, 1934), p. 1.
3. *Ibid.*, p. 17.
4. *Ibid.*, p. 18.
5. *Ibid.*, p. 24.
6. Nancy Spain, *Why I'm Not a Millionaire* (London: Hutchinson, 1956), p. 87.
7. *Ibid.*
8. Isabella Beeton, *Beeton's Book of Household Management* (London: Jonathan Cape, 1968), preface.
9. Nancy Spain's notes from Mrs Beeton's diaries, 8 March 1860, p. 4.
10. *Tribune*, 10 February 1950, p. 18.
11. *Sunday Times*, 24 February 1946, p. 4.
12. Spain, *Millionaire*, p. 88.
13. BBC, RCONT1 Nancy Spain – Copyright File 1: 1945–62, 13 August 1946.
14. Nancy Spain, *A Funny Thing Happened on the Way* (London: Hutchinson, 1964), pp. 161–2.
15. *Daily Express*, 29 July 1955, p. 4.
16. *Woman's Hour*, 2 May 1957.
17. Spain, *Millionaire*, p. 94.
18. *Daily Express*, 12 January 1959, p. 4.
19. *Observer*, 1 December 1946, p. 3.
20. *Sunday Times*, 3 November 1946, p. 3.
21. Nancy Spain, *The Beeton Story* (London: Ward, Lock & Co., 1956), p. 11.
22. *Ibid.*
23. *Evening Standard*, 28 February 1946, p. 1.
24. *Empire News*, 6 July 1947, p. 8.
25. Nancy Spain, *Murder, Bless It* (London: Hutchinson, 1948), p. 20.
26. *Ibid.*, p. 47.
27. Spain, *Millionaire*, p. 107.
28. *Ibid.*, p. 109.
29. *Ibid.*
30. *Observer*, 27 June 1948, p. 3.
31. *Sunday Times*, 18 July 1948, p. 3.
32. BBC, RCONT1 Nancy Spain – Talks File 1: 1942–57, 16 August 1948.
33. *Observer*, 22 August 1948, p. 3.
34. *Sunday Times*, 22 August 1948, p. 3.
35. *Times Literary Supplement*, 11 September 1948, p. 507.
36. BBC TV TALKS, 21 September 1948.
37. *Ibid.*, 1 October 1948.
38. Nancy Spain, *Death Goes on Skis* (London: Hutchinson, 1949), p. 37.
39. *Ibid.*, p. 38.

40. Nancy Spain, *Poison for Teacher* (London: Hutchinson, 1949), p. 30.
41. *Ibid.*, p. 39.
42. *Woman's Hour*, 13 September 1956.
43. Nancy Spain, *Cinderella Goes to the Morgue* (London: Hutchinson, 1950), p. 54.
44. May Sarton, *A World of Light* (New York: W.W. Norton & Co., 1976), p. 197.
45. *Books of Today*, June 1949, p. 8.
46. *Observer*, 12 June 1949, p. 8.
47. *Tribune*, 22 July 1949, p. 20.
48. *Tatler and Bystander*, 22 June 1949, p. 428.
49. *Tribune*, 23 September 1949, p. 26.
50. *Ibid.*, 25 November 1949, pp. 28–9.
51. *Ibid.*, 27 January 1950, p. 18.
52. BBC, RCONT1 Nancy Spain – Talks File 1: 6 December 1949.
53. *Tribune*, 9 December 1949, p. 21.
54. *Tatler*, 30 November 1949, pp. 449–50.
55. *Books of Today*, January 1950, p. 28.
56. Nancy Spain, *'R' in the Month* (London: Hutchinson, 1950), p. 168.
57. Spain, *Millionaire*, p. 127.
58. *The Times*, 27 July 1944, p. 7e.
59. *Books of Today*, May 1950, p. 1.
60. *Ibid.*
61. Spain, *Millionaire*, p. 132.
62. Letter from Joan Werner Laurie to Vivyen Bremner, c. 1947, p. 1.
63. *Ibid.*
64. Spain, *Millionaire*, p. 132.
65. *Ibid.*, p. 133.
66. *Ibid.*, p. 134.
67. *Ibid.*, p. 135.
68. *Ibid.*, p. 136.
69. *Ibid.*, p. 135.
70. Spain, *A Funny Thing*, p. 55.
71. Bremner letter, c. 1947.
72. Spain, *A Funny Thing*, p. 39.
73. *Daily Express*, 13 April 1950, p. 6.
74. *Sunday Times*, 9 April 1950, p. 3.
75. *Observer*, 23 April 1950, p. 7.
76. *Books of Today*, April 1950, p. 30.
77. BBC, RCONT1 Nancy Spain – Copyright File 1: 1945–62, 2 June 1950.
78. *Ibid.*, 10 May 1950.
79. *Woman's Hour*, 15 October 1950.
80. *Observer*, 29 October 1950, p. 8.
81. *Sunday Times*, 12 November 1950, p. 3.
82. Nancy Spain, *Not Wanted on Voyage* (London: Hutchinson, 1951), p. 35.
83. *Ibid.*, p. 55.
84. *Ibid.*, p. 207.
85. *Good Housekeeping*, January 1951, p. 56.
86. Spain, *Millionaire*, p. 142.
87. *Books of Today*, April 1951, p. 1.
88. *Radio Times*, 7 January 1955, p. 27.

89. *Good Housekeeping*, November 1951, p. 150.
90. *Books of Today*, August 1951, p. 30.
91. *Sunday Times*, 29 July 1951, p. 3.
92. *New York Times*, 6 January 1957, p. 24.
93. Nancy Spain, *Out, Damned Tot* (London: Hutchinson, 1952), p. 18.
94. *Ibid.*, p. 17.
95. *Ibid.*, p. 36.
96. *Ibid.*, p. 45.

6. Nobody Told the Truth in Those Days

1. Logan Gourlay (ed.), *The Beaverbrook I Knew* (London: Quartet, 1984), p. 5.
2. *Daily Express*, 30 September 1938, p. 1.
3. *Ibid.*, 1 October 1938, p. 1.
4. Anne Chisholm and Michael Davie, *Beaverbrook: A Life* (London: Hutchinson, 1992), p. 39.
5. Gourlay, *Beaverbrook I Knew*, p. 15.
6. Chisholm and Davie, *Beaverbrook*, p. 524.
7. Gourlay, *Beaverbrook I Knew*, p. 6.
8. *Ibid.*, p. 2.
9. *Ibid.*, p. 169.
10. *Ibid.*, p. 240.
11. Robert Allen, *Voice of Britain: Inside Story of the Daily Express* (Wellingborough: Patrick Stephens, 1983), p. 39.
12. Arthur Christiansen, *Headlines All My Life* (London: Heinemann, 1961), p. 147.
13. Hugh Cudlipp, *At Your Peril* (London: Weidenfeld & Nicolson, 1967), p. 37.
14. Christiansen, *Headlines*, p. 166.
15. *Ibid.*, p. 163.
16. Edward Francis Williams, *Dangerous Estate* (London: Longmans, Green & Co., 1957), p. 219.
17. Gourlay, *Beaverbrook I Knew*, p. 246.
18. *The Times*, 1 April 1982, p. 12g.
19. *Ibid.*
20. Christiansen, *Headlines*, p. 249.
21. *Ibid.*, p. 148.
22. *Ibid.*, p. 164.
23. *Ibid.*, p. 150.
24. *Books of Today*, February 1951, p. 2.
25. *Daily Express*, 13 March 1952, p. 4.
26. *Ibid.*, 3 July 1952, p. 4.
27. *Ibid.*, 20 March 1952, p. 4.
28. *Ibid.*, 3 April 1952, p. 4.
29. *Ibid.*, 17 April 1952, p. 4.
30. *Ibid.*, 7 August 1952, p. 4.
31. *Ibid.*
32. *The Times*, 9 December 1969.
33. HLRO, Hist. Coll. 184, Beaverbrook Papers, C/300, NS to LB, 8 June 1960.
34. *Home for the Day*, 29 March 1953.
35. *Sunday Times*, 22 March 1964, p. 3.

36. *Getting to Know You*, 13 January 1955.
37. Nancy Spain, *Why I'm Not a Millionaire* (London: Hutchinson, 1956), p. 185.
38. *Ibid.*
39. BBC, RCONT1 Nancy Spain – Talks File 1: 1942–57, letter to NS, 1 July 1952.
40. Joanna Scott-Moncrieff, *The Book of Woman's Hour* (Ariel Productions, 1953), p. 9.
41. Joyce Grenfell, *In Pleasant Places* (London: Macmillan, 1979), p. 226.
42. *Daily Mail*, 20 October 1925.
43. BBC, RCONT1 Nancy Spain – Talks File 1: 1942–57, letter to JQ, 31 August 1952.
44. Spain, *Millionaire*, p. 233.
45. BBC, RCONT1 Nancy Spain – Talks File 1: 1942–57, 22 September 1952.
46. *Ibid.*, 18 September 1952.
47. *Ibid.*, 9 October 1952.
48. *Woman's Hour*, 2 December 1952.
49. *Ibid.*
50. BBC, RCONT1 Nancy Spain – Talks File 1: 1942–57, 12 December 1952.
51. *Ibid.*, 13 January 1953.
52. *Ibid.*, 7 January 1953.
53. HLRO, Hist. Coll. 184 BBK C/300 SPAIN N. 1952–63, NS to LB, 18 December 1952.
54. *Daily Express*, 13 February 1953, p. 6.
55. *Ibid.*, 12 March 1953, p. 6.
56. *Ibid.*, 25 June 1953, p. 6.
57. *Ibid.*, 8 October 1953, p. 4.
58. *Ibid.*, 22 October 1953, p. 4.
59. John Hadfield, ed., *Saturday Book* (Hutchinson & Co., 1955), p. 78.
60. HLRO, Hist. Coll. 184 BBK 1953 A-W NS to LB 27 May 1953.
61. Sandy Wilson, *I Could Be Happy* (London: Michael Joseph, 1975), p. 212.
62. *Times Literary Supplement*, 17 July 1953, p. 466.
63. *Sunday Times*, 28 June 1953, p. 4.
64. *Good Housekeeping*, December 1953, p. 86.

7. When Gilbert Met Nancy

1. *Independent*, 9 January 1993, p. 46.
2. Stephen Grenfell (ed.), *Gilbert Harding By His Friends* (London: André Deutsch, 1961), p. 103.
3. *Ibid.*, p. 139.
4. Dicky Leeman, *What's My Line?: The Story of a Phenomenon* (London: Allan Wingate, 1955), p. 7.
5. *Ibid.*, p. 2.
6. *Ibid.*, p. 17.
7. Wallace Reyburn, *Gilbert Harding* (London: Angus & Robertson, 1978), p. 64.
8. Grenfell, *By His Friends*, p. 120.
9. Andrews, Eamonn and Andrews, Grainne with McGibbon, Robin, *For Ever and Ever Eamonn* (London: Grafton, 1989), p. 109.
10. *Ibid.*, p. 126.
11. *Ibid.*, p. 108.

12. Leeman, *What's My Line?*, p. 126.
13. Andrews, *For Ever and Ever Eamonn*, p. 108.
14. Grenfell, *By His Friends*, p. 19.
15. Leeman, *What's My Line?*, p. 131.
16. *Ibid.*
17. *Ibid.*, p. 132.
18. Grenfell, *By His Friends*, p. 123.
19. *Daily Express*, 29 February 1956, p. 4.
20. Reyburn, *Gilbert Harding*, p. 98.
21. Leeman, *What's My Line?*, p. 140.
22. *Ibid.*
23. *Sunday People*, 11 December 1960, p. 5.
24. Gilbert Harding, *Master of None* (London: Putnam, 1958), p. 99.
25. Reyburn, *Gilbert Harding*, p. 87.
26. Harding, *Master of None*, p. 138.
27. *Ibid.*
28. Grenfell, *By His Friends*, p. 163.
29. 'Face to Face', BBC TV, 1960.
30. Roger Storey, *Gilbert Harding* (London: Barrie & Rockcliff, 1961), p. 45.
31. *Evening Standard*, 4 September 1956, p. 13.
32. *Daily Express*, 8 March 1954, p. 4.
33. HLRO, Hist. Coll. 184 BBK C/300 1953 A–W, NS to LB, 9 July 1953.
34. *Ibid.*
35. *Ibid.*
36. *Ibid.*
37. HLRO, Hist. Coll. 184 BBK C/300 SPAIN N 1952–63, NS to LB, 11 July 1953.
38. *Woman's Hour*, 13 September 1956.
39. Denise Robins, *Stranger than Fiction* (London: Hodder & Stoughton, 1965), p. 190.
40. *Woman's Hour*, 8 March 1954.
41. Nancy Spain, *Why I'm Not a Millionaire* (London: Hutchinson, 1956), p. 206.
42. *Evening Standard*, 10 September 1953, p. 11.
43. *Ibid.*
44. Spain, *Millionaire*, p. 206.
45. *Evening Standard*, 24 September 1953, p. 11.
46. *Ibid.*, 1 October 1953, p. 11.
47. *Radio Times*, 11 September 1953, p. 45.
48. *Ibid.*
49. *Ibid.*
50. BBC, RCONT1 Nancy Spain – Talks File 1: 1942–57, JQ to NS, 21 September 1953.
51. *Ibid.*, NS to JQ, undated 1953.
52. *Daily Express*, 23 December 1953, p. 4.
53. *Ibid.*, 3 March 1954, p. 5.
54. *Ibid.*, 11 February 1954, p. 4.
55. *Daily Sketch*, 19 March 1954, p. 8.
56. *Daily Express*, 18 March 1954, p. 4.
57. Harding, *Master of None*, p. 133.
58. Reyburn, *Gilbert Harding*, p. 102.
59. Harding, *Master of None*, p. 133.

60. *Evening Standard*, 4 September 1956, p. 13.
61. Grenfell, *By His Friends*, p. 163.
62. *Ibid.*, p. 58.
63. *Daily Express*, 1 April 1954, p. 6.
64. *Woman's Hour*, 19 April 1954.
65. *Ibid.*
66. *Ibid.*
67. *Daily Express*, 22 November 1955, p. 3.
68. HLRO, Hist. Coll. 184 BBK C/300 H/178, NS to LB, 6 December 1955.
69. *Daily Express*, 24 December 1955, p. 3.
70. HLRO, Hist. Coll. 184 BBK C/300 H/178, NS to LB, 6 December 1955.

8. I Am Not a Star. I Am What They Call a Personality

1. Nancy Spain, *The Tiger Who Couldn't Eat Meat* (London: Max Parrish, 1954), p. 20.
2. Nancy Spain, *The Tiger Who Went to the Moon* (London: Max Parrish, 1956), p. 25.
3. *Times Literary Supplement*, 19 November 1954.
4. *Ibid.*, 23 November 1956.
5. *Ibid.*, 19 November 1954.
6. Nancy Spain, *Why I'm Not a Millionaire* (London: Hutchinson, 1956), p. 218.
7. *Daily Express*, 16 January 1954, p. 4.
8. HLRO, Hist. Coll. 184 BBK C/300 H/170, NS to LB, 6 August 1954.
9. *Ibid.*, LB, 30 August 1954.
10. *Ibid.*, NS to LB, undated 1954.
11. *Daily Express*, 14 August 1954, p. 4.
12. HLRO, Hist. Coll. 184 BBK C/300 H/170, NS to LB, 28 December 1954.
13. *She*, March 1955, p. 18.
14. *Ibid.*
15. *She*, May 1964, p. 35.
16. Denise Robins, *Stranger than Fiction* (London: Hodder & Stoughton, 1965), p. 190.
17. Brian Braithwaite, *Women's Magazines: The First 300 Years* (London: Peter Owen, 1995), p. 23.
18. *She*, June 1964, p. 35.
19. *Radio Times*, 31 October 1963, p. 705.
20. *Ibid.*
21. *Sunday Times*, 29 March 1964.
22. Pat Scott, *The Fifties* (London: Franklin Watts, 1991), pp. 3–4.
23. *She*, April 1955, p. 18.
24. *Ibid.*
25. *Ibid.*
26. *She*, December 1955, p. 74.
27. *Radio Times*, 31 December 1954, p. 25.
28. BBC, RCONT1 Nancy Spain – Talks File 1: 1942–57, JSM to JQ, 20 December 1954.
29. *Woman's Hour*, 4 December 1955.
30. *Ibid.*, 5 October 1955.
31. BBC, RCONT1 Nancy Spain – Talks File 1: 1942–57, CMG to HLE, 13 June 1955.

32. BBC TV ART 2 FILE, 13 June 1955.
33. BBC TV ART 2 FILE HC to NS, 21 July 1955.
34. Spain, *Millionaire*, p. 244.
35. Nancy Spain, *The Kat Strikes* (London: Hutchinson, 1955), p. 70.
36. *Ibid.*, p. 75.
37. *Ibid.*, p. 60.
38. *Ibid.*
39. *Ibid.*, p. 138.
40. HLRO, Hist. Coll. 184 BBK C/300 H/178, NS to LB, 19 July 1955.
41. *Ibid.*, JBW to LB, 22 July 1955.
42. *Ibid.*, LB to NS, 22 July 1955.
43. *She*, August 1956, p. 17.
44. *Sunday Times*, 6 November 1955, p. 4.
45. *Times Literary Supplement*, 23 December 1955, p. 773.
46. *Sunday Times*, 13 November 1955, p. 4.
47. *Observer*, 20 November 1955, p. 12.
48. *Tribune*, 4 November 1949, p. 19.
49. *Woman's Hour*, 13 September 1956.
50. *Gay News*, 6 September 1979, p. 18.
51. *Woman's Hour*, 9 May 1962.
52. *She*, December 1963, p. 32.
53. Nancy Spain, *A Funny Thing Happened on the Way* (London: Hutchinson, 1964), p. 85.
54. *Ibid.*, p. 86.
55. *She*, December 1963, p. 32.
56. Talks File 1 1956–9 M25/982 B'HAM, 13 March 1957.
57. Spain, *A Funny Thing*, p. 102.
58. *Ibid.*, p. 89.
59. *Ibid.*, p. 90.
60. *She*, December 1963, p. 32.
61. *Daily Express*, 27 April 1956, p. 6.
62. Charlotte Mosley (ed.) *Love from Nancy: The Letters of Nancy Mitford* (London, Hodder & Stoughton, 1993), p. 276.
63. *Daily Express*, 27 October 1956, p. 4.
64. *Ibid.*, 1 May 1956, p. 6.
65. *Ibid.*
66. *Ibid.*, 2 May 1956, p. 3.
67. *Ibid.*, 24 May 1957, p. 10.
68. *Ibid.*, 12 June 1956, p. 6.
69. *Ibid.*, 28 December 1956, p. 4.
70. *Ibid.*, 1 May 1957, p. 3.
71. Frances Partridge, *Hanging On: Diaries 1960–1963* (London: Collins, 1990), p. 42.
72. *The Times*, 22 April 1988, p. 18j.
73. Spain, *A Funny Thing*, p. 68.
74. Ginette Spanier, *And Now It's Sables* (London: Robert Hale, 1970), p. 14.
75. *She*, December 1956, p. 30.
76. Spanier, *Sables*, p. 64.
77. Spain, *A Funny Thing*, p. 68.
78. *Ibid.*, p. 72.

79. Nancy Spain, *A Funny Thing Happened on the Way* (draft; W.J. West collection), p. 80.
80. BBC, RCONT1 Nancy Spain – Talks File, 1: 1942–57 JSM to NS 16 October 1957.
81. *Daily Express*, 1 May 1957, p. 3.
82. *Ibid.*, 2 May 1957, p. 8.
83. *Ibid.*, 8 May 1957, p. 8.
84. *Daily Express*, 31 August 1956, p. 4.
85. *Ibid.*
86. *Evening Standard*, 4 September 1956, p. 13.
87. *Sunday Times*, 9 September 1956, p. 4.
88. *Times Literary Supplement*, 21 December 1956, p. 768.
89. *The Times*, 6 September 1956, p. 13.
90. BBC TV ART 2 File Nancy Spain – 1: 1942–57, RW to CMG, 22 October 1956.
91. HLRO, Hist. Coll. 184 BBK C/300 H/193, NS to LB, undated 1956–7.
92. *Ibid.*
93. BBC, RCONT1 Nancy Spain – Copyright File 1: 1942–57, MT, 18 December 1956.
94. BBC, RCONT1 Nancy Spain – Talks File 2: 1958–62, SW to Copyright Dept, 5 February 1958.

9. The Waugh to End All Wars

1. HLRO, Hist. Coll. 184 BBK H/193 NS to LB, undated, 1956–7.
2. *Ibid.*, 22 January 1957.
3. Francis Wheen, *Tom Driberg: His Life and Indiscretions* (London: Chatto & Windus, 1990), p. 492.
4. Anne Chisholm and Michael Davie, *Beaverbrook: A Life* (London: Hutchinson, 1992), p. 494.
5. *Spectator*, 3 July 1953, p. 24.
6. HLRO, Hist. Coll. 184 BBK H/159, July undated.
7. *Sunday Express*, 15 May 1955, p. 4.
8. Lady Frances Donaldson, *Portrait of a Country Neighbour* (London: Weidenfeld & Nicolson, 1967), p. 87.
9. Nancy Mitford, *Love from Nancy: The Letters of Nancy Mitford*, p. 341, letter to Evelyn Waugh, 2 August 1955.
10. Andrew Barrow, *Gossip 1920–1970* (London: Hamish Hamilton, 1978), p. 167.
11. *Spectator*, 15 July 1955, p. 94.
12. *Daily Express*, 23 June 1955, p. 6.
13. *Spectator*, 15 July 1955, p. 94.
14. *Daily Telegraph*, 20 February 1957, p. 9.
15. *Daily Express*, 23 June 1955, p. 6.
16. *Letters of Evelyn Waugh* (London: Weidenfeld & Nicolson, 1976), p. 207 (letter of 14 July 1955).
17. *Spectator*, 15 July 1955, p. 94.
18. *Ibid.*, 22 July 1955, p. 121.
19. *Ibid.*
20. *Spectator*, 29 July 1955, p. 167.
21. *Ibid.*, 22 July 1955, p. 122.

22. *Daily Express*, 31 December 1955, p. 4.
23. *Ibid.*
24. *Ibid.*
25. *Letters of Evelyn Waugh*, p. 468 (letter of 17 March 1956).
26. Christopher Sykes, *Evelyn Waugh: A Biography* (London: Collins, 1975), p. 381.
27. *Letters of Evelyn Waugh*, p. 236 (letter of 24 February 1957).
28. HLRO, Hist. Coll. 184 BBK H/186, NS to LB, 9 May 1956.
29. *Ibid.*, undated 1956.
30. *The Times*, 20 February 1957, p. 5.
31. *Daily Express*, 20 February 1957, p. 5.
32. *The Times*, 20 February 1957, p. 6.
33. *Ibid.*
34. *Ibid.*
35. *Ibid.*
36. Donaldson, *Country Neighbour*, p. 88.
37. *Daily Telegraph and Morning Post*, 20 February 1957, p. 9.
38. *The Times*, 20 February 1957, p. 6.
39. *Ibid.*, 21 February 1957, p. 13.
40. *Ibid.*
41. *Ibid.*
42. *Daily Express*, 16 October 1956.
43. *Letters of Evelyn Waugh*, p. 486.
44. HLRO, Hist. Coll. 184 BBK H/190 February–April, JC to TB, 20 February 1957.
45. *Woman's Hour*, 13 September 1956.
46. HLRO, Hist. Coll. 184 BBK H/193, NS to LB, 29 May 1957.
47. *Daily Express*, 21 May 1957, p. 6.
48. *Ibid.*
49. Nancy Spain, *A Funny Thing Happened on the Way* (London: Hutchinson, 1964), paperback, p. 135.
50. HLRO, Hist. Coll. 184 BBK H/193 NS to LB 19 August 1957.
51. *Ibid.*, NS to LB 21 August 1957.
52. *Ibid.*, LB to NS 10 August 1957.
53. *Daily Express*, 17 August 1957, p. 6.
54. *Ibid.*, 27 September 1957, p. 10.
55. BBC RCONT1 Nancy Spain – Copyright File 1: 1945–62, PD to H. Cop, 8 February 1957.
56. *Daily Express*, 1 March 1957, p. 8.
57. *Ibid.*, 1 November 1955, p. 6.
58. *Ibid.*, 1 March 1957, p. 8.
59. *She*, August 1957, p. 27.
60. Daily Express, 27 December 1957, p. 6.
61. Nancy Spain, *A Funny Thing Happened on the Way* (draft; W.J. West collection), p. 216.
62. HLRO, Hist. Coll. 184 BBK H/193, NS to LB, undated 1956–7.
63. *She*, October 1957, p. 58.
64. HLRO, Hist. Coll. 184 BBK H/193, NS to LB, 18 September 1957.
65. *Woman's Hour*, 3 November 1957.
66. HLRO, Hist. Coll. 184 BBK H/193, NS to LB, 3 January 1958.
67. *Ibid.*
68. *Daily Express*, 27 December 1957, p. 6.

10. Ace Newshound

1. HLRO, Hist. Coll. 184 BBK H/193, NS to LB, 3 January 1958.
2. Nancy Spain, *A Funny Thing Happened on the Way* (London: Hutchinson, 1964), p. 65.
3. *The Times*, 17 December 1968.
4. *She*, June 1958, p. 32.
5. *Daily Express*, 22 February 1958, p. 1.
6. *Ibid.*, 24 February 1958, p. 8.
7. *Ibid.*, 14 April 1958, p. 10.
8. *Ibid.*
9. *Ibid.*
10. HLRO, Hist. Coll. 184 BBK H/199, NS to LB, 18 April 1958.
11. *Daily Express*, 28 April 1958, p. 6.
12. *She*, May 1958, p. 37.
13. *Ibid.*, March 1958, p. 32.
14. *Ibid.*
15. *Ibid.*, May 1958, p. 20.
16. *Ibid.*, September 1958, p. 39.
17. *Ibid.*, July 1958, p. 67.
18. *Ibid.*, March 1958, p. 23.
19. *Daily Express*, 1 March 1958, p. 2.
20. *Ibid.*, 27 May 1958, p. 1.
21. *Ibid.*, 12 July 1958, p. 6.
22. 'My ABC of Snobbery' (draft ms.), W.J. West collection, p. 1.
23. Letter from IML to JWL, 7 August 1958, W.J. West collection.
24. 'Snobbery', p. 1.
25. *Ibid.*
26. *Ibid.*, p. 4.
27. BBC, TV ART 2 NS TV MISC 1948–62, Ed. W.P. to Mag., 1 September 1958.
28. HLRO, Hist. Coll. 184 BBK H/198, AC to LB, 25 August 1958.
29. HLRO, Hist. Coll. 184 BBK 1952–63, NS to LB, 31 August 1958.
30. *Ibid.*, LB to NS, 3 September 1958.
31. *Ibid.*, NS to LB, 9 September 1958.
32. *Daily Express*, 17 November 1958, p. 8.
33. HLRO, Hist. Coll. 184 BBK 1952–63, NS to LB, 22 December 1958.
34. Sheila van Damm, *We Never Closed* (London: Robert Hale, 1967), p. 178.
35. *Woman's Hour*, 12 March 1963.
36. HLRO, Hist. Coll. 184 BBK 1952–63, NS to LB, 22 December 1958.
37. *Ibid.*
38. *Ibid.*
39. *Ibid.*
40. *She*, September 1959, p. 69.
41. Spain, *A Funny Thing*, p. 62.
42. Ginette Spanier, *And Now It's Sables* (London: Robert Hale, 1970), p. 63.
43. *Daily Express*, 31 March 1959, p. 7.
44. *Ibid.*, 3 April 1959, p. 9.
45. *Ibid.*, 4 April 1959, p. 4.
46. *Ibid.*, 18 July 1959, p. 5.
47. *Ibid.*, 13 May 1959, p. 9.

48. *Ibid.*, 25 September 1959, p. 11.
49. *Ibid.*, 12 May 1959, p. 9.
50. *Ibid.*, 30 May 1959, p. 7.
51. *Ibid.*, 26 September 1959, p. 7.
52. *Ibid.*, 20 August 1959, p. 7.
53. *Ibid.*, 19 August 1959, p. 6.
54. *Ibid.*
55. *Ibid.*, 4 December 1959, p. 11.
56. *Ibid.*, 21 August 1959, p. 6.
57. HLRO, Hist. Coll. 184 BBK 1952–63, NS to LB, 16 July 1959.
58. *Daily Express*, 10 June 1959, p. 9.
59. *She*, December 1959, p. 22.
60. *Ibid.*
61. *Daily Express*, 8 December 1959.
62. *Ibid.*, 2 October 1959, p. 11.
63. *Ibid.*, 3 October 1959, p. 7.
64. *She*, October 1959, p. 19.
65. *Daily Express*, 9 October 1959, p. 11.
66. *Times Literary Supplement*, 4 December 1959, p. 705.
67. *Daily Express*, 12 November 1959, p. 14.
68. Spanier, *Sables*, p. 71.
69. *Daily Express*, 2 June 1959, p. 9.
70. *Ibid.*, 9 June 1959, p. 7.
71. FH to NS, 16 March 1963, W.J. West collection.
72. *Pink Paper*, 25 March 1994, p. 17.

11. The Nine Lives of a Lady of Letters

1. *Daily Express*, 4 February 1960, p. 7.
2. *Ibid.*, 5 February 1960, p. 1.
3. Noel Coward, *Diaries*, ed. Graham Payn and Sheridan Morley (London: Weidenfeld & Nicolson, 1982), p. 429 (19 February 1960).
4. *Daily Express*, 16 February 1960, p. 6.
5. *Ibid.*, 7 March 1960, p. 17.
6. *Ibid.*, 25 March 1960, p. 10.
7. *Ibid.*, 2 April 1960, p. 9.
8. HLRO, Hist. Coll. 184 BBK C/300 SPAIN 1952–63, NS to LB, undated 1960.
9. *Ibid.*, 8 June 1960.
10. *Daily Express*, 16 February 1960, p. 6.
11. Noel Coward, *Plays: Five*, 'Waiting in the Wings', p. 279.
12. *Ibid.*, p. 280.
13. *Ibid.*, p. 281.
14. *Ibid.*, p. 282.
15. *Ibid.*, p. 283.
16. *Ibid.*, p. 294.
17. *Ibid.*
18. *Ibid.*, p. 324.
19. *Ibid.*, p. 325.
20. *Ibid.*

21. Graham Payn (with Barry Day) *My Life with Noel Coward* (New York and London: Applause Books, 1994), p. 164.
22. *Play Parade*, Vol. VI, June 1961.
23. *She*, April 1960, p. 28.
24. HLRO, Hist. Coll. 184 BBK C/300 SPAIN N 1952–63, undated telegram.
25. HLRO, Hist. Coll. 184 BBK H/208 1960 Max Aitken, EP to MA, 28 October 1960.
26. *Ibid.*, MA to LB, 1 November 1960.
27. NS to JWL, 29 October 1960.
28. *Ibid.*
29. *Ibid.*, 31 October 1960.
30. *Ibid.*, 29 October 1960.
31. *Ibid.*, 31 October 1960.
32. *Ibid.*
33. *Ibid.*, 1 November 1960.
34. *Ibid.*
35. *Ibid.*
36. *Ibid.*
37. *Ibid.*
38. *Ibid.*
39. *Ibid.*
40. *Ibid.*, 5 November 1960.
41. *Ibid.*
42. *Ibid.*
43. *Ibid.*, 9 November 1960.
44. Nancy Spain, *A Funny Thing Happened on the Way* (draft; W.J. West collection), p. 256.
45. NS to JWL, 9 November 1960.
46. *Ibid.*
47. *Ibid.*
48. *Ibid.*
49. *Ibid.*
50. Spain, *A Funny Thing* (draft), p. 269.
51. NS to JWL, 9 November 1960.
52. *Ibid.*
53. *Woman's Hour*, 20 December 1960.
54. NS to JWL, 10 November 1960.
55. *Ibid.*
56. *Ibid.*
57. *Ibid.*
58. *Ibid.*
59. *Ibid.*, 14 October 1960.
60. *Ibid.*, 18 November 1960.
61. *Ibid.*
62. *Ibid.*
63. *Ibid.*
64. *Ibid.*
65. BBC, RCONT1 Nancy Spain – Talks File 2: 1958–62, JSM to NS, 30 November 1960.
66. *The Gramophone*, December 1960, pp. 353–4.

67. Wallace Reyburn, *Gilbert Harding* (London: Angus & Robertson, 1978), p. 2.
68. *People*, 6 October 1960.
69. *Ibid.*, 30 October 1960.
70. *Ibid.*, 13 November 1960.
71. *Ibid.*, 20 November 1960, p. 12.
72. NS to RS, 4 December 1960, Roger Storey collection.
73. *Daily Express*, 1 December 1959, p. 6.
74. Spain, *A Funny Thing* (draft), pp. 214–15.
75. *The Times*, 3 October 1989, p. 18f.
76. *Ibid.*
77. *Sunday Mirror*, 22 March 1964, p. 1.
78. *News of the World*, 29 April 1963, p. 8.
79. Spain, *A Funny Thing* (draft), pp. 217–18.
80. HLRO, Hist. Coll. 184 BBK C/300 SPAIN N 1952–63, NS to LB, 6 January 1961.
81. *Ibid.*
82. Spain, *A Funny Thing* (draft), p. 181.
83. HLRO, Hist. Coll. 184 BBK C/300 SPAIN N 1952–63, NS to LB 10 February 1961.
84. Spain, *A Funny Thing* (draft), p. 213.
85. HLRO, Hist. Coll. 184 BBK C/300 SPAIN N 1952–63, LB to NS, 26 May 1961.
86. *News of the World*, 22 March 1964, p. 12.
87. *Woman's Hour*, 29 April 1962.
88. Stafford Somerfield, *Banner Headlines* (London: Scan Books, 1979), p. 111.
89. *Ibid.*
90. *News of the World*, 22 March 1964, p. 12.
91. *Ibid.*, 26 February 1961, p. 8.
92. HLRO, Hist. Coll. 184 BBK C/300 SPAIN N 1952–63, NS to LB, 4 July 1961.
93. Nancy Spain, *Why I'm Not a Millionaire* (London: Hutchinson, 1956), p. 232.
94. Spain, *A Funny Thing* (draft), p. 271.
95. *Ibid.*
96. *Noel Coward Diaries*, p. 471 (4 June 1961).
97. *Ibid.*
98. Somerfield, *Banner Headlines*, p. 117.
99. *News of the World*, 20 August 1961, p. 4.
100. *Ibid.*
101. *News of the World*, 10 September 1961, p. 8.
102. *Ibid.*
103. *Newcastle Evening Chronicle*, 16 October 1961, p. 3.
104. *News of the World*, 22 October 1961, p. 8.
105. HLRO, Hist. Coll. 184 BBK C/300 SPAIN N 1952–63, LB to NS, 28 October 1961.
106. *Ibid.*, NS to LB, 7 December 1961.
107. Sheila van Damm, *We Never Closed* (London: Robert Hale, 1967), p. 142.
108. *She*, October 1961, p. 26.
109. NS to JWL, 2 December 1961.

110. *She*, February 1962, p. 14.
111. *News of the World*, 31 December 1961, p. 5.

12. Island of Dreams

1. *News of the World*, 4 February 1962, p. 4.
2. Nancy Spain, *A Funny Thing Happened on the Way* (London: Hutchinson, 1964), p. 98.
3. *Ibid.*, p. 15.
4. *Ibid.*, p. 102.
5. *Ibid.*, p. 105.
6. *She*, July 1962, p. 22.
7. *Ibid.*, January 1963, p. 14.
8. Nancy Spain, *A Funny Thing Happened on the Way* (draft; W.J. West collection), p. 329.
9. *Ibid.*, p. 330.
10. *Ibid.*, p. 331.
11. *Ibid.*, p. 250.
12. *Ibid.*, p. 328.
13. *The Times*, 18 May 1962, p. 15c.
14. Spain, *A Funny Thing*, pp. 129–30.
15. HLRO, Hist. Coll. 184 BBK C/300 SPAIN N 1952–63, NS to LB, 1962.
16. Spain, *A Funny Thing* (draft), p. 332.
17. *Ibid.*, p. 333.
18. *News of the World*, 29 July 1962, p. 6.
19. *Ibid.*
20. Spain, *A Funny Thing*, p. 58.
21. *Woman's Hour*, 26 July 1963.
22. *News of the World*, 2 September 1962, p. 6.
23. JJ to NS, 16 September 1962.
24. *News of the World*, 23 September 1962, p. 9.
25. *Ibid.*, 30 September 1962, p. 6.
26. JWL to NS, 16 October 1962.
27. *Ibid.*
28. *Ibid.*
29. JWL to NS, 24 October 1962.
30. *Ibid.*
31. *Ibid.*
32. *News of the World*, 1 April 1962, p. 8.
33. BBC, RCONT1 Nancy Spain – Talks File 2: 1958–64, NS to JSM, 2 November 1962.
34. Spain, *A Funny Thing* (draft), preface, p. 2.
35. *Ibid.*
36. BBC, RCONT1 Nancy Spain – Talks File 2: 1958–62, NS to JSM, 13 November 1962.
37. JWL to NS, 20 November 1962.
38. *Ibid.*
39. *She*, February 1963, p. 22.
40. *News of the World*, 9 December 1962, p. 6.
41. HLRO, Hist. Coll. 184 BBK C/300 SPAIN N 1952–63, NS to LB, 28 December 1962.

42. *Ibid.*
43. Spain, *A Funny Thing*, p. 157.
44. *News of the World*, 4 November 1962, p. 8.
45. *She*, August 1963, p. 17.
46. *Films and Filming*, January 1964, p. 28.
47. *Ibid.*
48. *News of the World*, 29 April 1963, p. 8.
49. *Ibid.*, 7 April 1963, p. 18.
50. *Ibid.*, 14 April 1963, p. 6.
51. *Ibid.*
52. Spain, *A Funny Thing*, p. 214.
53. JWL to NS, 16 September 1962.
54. HLRO, Hist. Coll. 184 BBK C/300 SPAIN N 1952–63, NS to LB, 22 May 1963.
55. *Ibid.*, 9 July 1963.
56. *News of the World*, 27 October 1963, p. 13.
57. Maria Riva, *Marlene Dietrich* (London: Bloomsbury, 1992), p. 705.
58. Spain, *A Funny Thing*, p. 66.
59. *Newcastle Journal*, 27 September 1963, p. 8.
60. *Evening Chronicle*, 26 September 1963, p. 3.
61. *Ibid.*, 25 September 1963, p. 9.

13. And Still There Were Cabbages in That Awful Field

1. *Woman's Hour*, 12 January 1964.
2. *News of the World*, 22 March 1964, p. 12.
3. *Ibid.*, 12 January 1964, p. 13.
4. *Ibid.*, 2 February 1964, p. 8.
5. *She*, January 1964, p. 14.
6. *Burnley Express and News*, 15 February 1964, p. 6.
7. *News of the World*, 23 February 1964, p. 8.
8. *Ibid.*
9. *Ibid.*, 15 March 1964, p. 12.
10. *Ibid.*, 22 March 1964, p. 12.
11. *Evening Standard*, 21 March 1964, p. 1.
12. *Sunday Telegraph*, 22 March 1964, p. 1.
13. Sheila van Damm, *We Never Closed* (London: Robert Hale, 1967), p. 179.
14. *Sunday Telegraph*, 22 March 1964, p. 1; *News of the World*, 22 March 1964, p. 1.
15. *News of the World*, 23 March 1964, p. 3.
16. Alice B. Toklas, *Staying On* (New York: Vintage, 1975), p. 88.
17. van Damm, *We Never Closed*, p. 179.
18. *Evening Chronicle*, 26 March 1964.
19. Stafford Somerfield, *Banner Headlines* (Scan Books, 1979), p. 129.
20. *Liverpool Echo*, 13 May 1964, p. 1.
21. *Ibid.*
22. Vyvyan Holland unpublished diaries.
23. *News of the World*, 26 April 1964, p. 12.
24. *Ibid.*

14. Funny Things Happened

1. Nancy Spain, *A Funny Thing Happened on the Way* (London: Hutchinson, 1964), p. 5.
2. *Times Literary Supplement*, 14 May 1964, p. 412.
3. *Daily Telegraph*, 21 May 1964, p. 20.
4. *Sunday Telegraph*, 17 May 1964, p. 18.
5. *Sunday Times*, 10 May 1964, p. 38.
6. *Observer*, 17 May 1964, p. 26.
7. *Evening Standard*, 13 May 1964, p. 13.
8. *She*, May 1964, p. 35.
9. *The Times*, 25 August 1987.
10. Chester Lewis and Jonathan Fenby, *The Fall of the House of Beaverbrook* (London: André Deutsch, 1979), p. 13.
11. *Guardian*, 29 January 1996, p. 13.
12. Philip Youngman Carter, *All I Did Was This* (London: Sexton Press, 1982), prefatory note, p. vii.
13. *Sunday Times* magazine, 30 January 1977, p. 16.
14. Nancy Spain, *A Funny Thing Happened on the Way* (draft; W.J. West collection), p. 318.
15. Spain, *A Funny Thing*, p. [11].

Bibliography

Unless specified otherwise, place of publication is London.

Allen, Robert, *Voice of Britain: Inside Story of the Daily Express*. Patrick Stephens, 1983.

Allsop, Kenneth, *The Angry Decade*. Peter Owen, 1985.

Andrews, Eamonn and Andrews, Grainne with McGibbon, Robin, *For Ever and Ever Eamonn*. Grafton, 1989.

Bainbridge, Cyril and Stockdill, Roy, *News of the World Story*. HarperCollins, 1993.

Banham, M., and Hillier B., *A Tonic to the Nation*. Thames & Hudson, 1976.

Barrow, Andrew, *Gossip 1920–1970*. Hamish Hamilton, 1978.

Barsley, M., *Behind the Screen*. André Deutsch, 1957.

Beeton, Isabella, *Beeton's Book of Household Management*. Jonathan Cape, 1968.

Bigland, Eileen, *Story of the WRNS*. Nicholson & Watson, 1946.

Black, Peter, *The Mirror in the Corner*. Hutchinson, 1972.

Booker, Christopher, *The Neophiliacs*. Collins, 1969.

Bourne, Henry, *History of Newcastle upon Tyne*. Newcastle upon Tyne: F. Graham, 1980.

Braithwaite, Brian, *Women's Magazines: The First 300 Years*. Peter Owen, 1995.

Braybon, Gail and Summerfield, Penny, *Out of the Cage: Women's Experiences in Two World Wars*. Pandora, 1987.

Bridson, Douglas, *Prospero and Ariel*. Gollancz, 1971.

Brighton Ourstory Project, *Daring Hearts: Lesbian and Gay Lives of 50s and 60s Brighton*. QueenSpark Books, 1992.

Burton, Peter, *Parallel Lives*. GMP, 1985.

Caron, Sandra, *Alma Cogan*. Bloomsbury, 1991.

Cassin-Scott, Jack, *Women at War 1939–45*. Osprey Publishing, 1980.

Chester, Lewis and Fenby, Jonathan, *The Fall of the House of Beaverbrook*. André Deutsch, 1979.

Chisholm, Anne and Davie, Michael, *Beaverbrook: A Life*. Hutchinson, 1992.

Christiansen, Arthur, *Headlines All My Life*. Heinemann, 1961.

Cole, George, *Jesmond Dene*. San Francisco: J.H. Nash, 1922.

Coleman, Ray, *Brian Epstein*. Viking, 1989.

Comford, Leslie and Yerbury, F.R., *Roedean School*. Ernest Benn, 1927.

Costello, John, *Love, Sex and War: Changing Values 1939–45*. Collins, 1985.

Coward, Noel, *Diaries*, ed. Graham Payn and Sheridan Morley. Weidenfeld & Nicolson, 1982.

Coward, Noel, *Plays: Five*. Methuen, 1983.

Craig, Patricia (ed.), *Penguin Book of British Comic Writing*. Viking, 1992.

Cudlipp, Hugh, *At Your Peril*. Weidenfeld & Nicolson, 1962.

Davidson, Michael, *The World, the Flesh and Myself*. GMP, 1982.

Dendy, Frederick, *An Account of Jesmond*. R. Robinson & Co., 1904.

De Zouche, Dorothy E., *Roedean School 1885–1955*. Brighton: Dolphin Press, 1955.

Docker, Lady Norah, *Norah*. W.H. Allen, 1969.

Donaldson, Lady Frances, *Portrait of a Country Neighbour*. Weidenfeld & Nicolson, 1967.

Driberg, Tom, *Beaverbrook: A Study in Power and Frustration*. Weidenfeld & Nicolson, 1956.

Edgar, Donald, *Express '56*. John Clare Books, 1981.

Edminson, John, *Newcastle-upon-Tyne*. S.P. Publications, 1991.

Ellison, Emley, *Memories of Jesmond Vale*. Gosforth: Geordieland Press, 1980.

Ferguson, Marjorie, *Forever Feminine*. Heinemann, 1983.

Fletcher, M.H., *The WRNS*. Batsford, 1989.

Founders of Roedean, *Founders*. Farncombe's, Brighton, 1935.

Freeman, Sarah, *Isabella and Sam*. Gollancz, 1977.

Gielgud, Val, *BBC Radio Drama 1922–1956*. Harrap & Co., 1957.

Gifford, Denis, *The Golden Age of Radio*. Batsford, 1985.

Gingold, Hermione, *My Own Unaided Work*. T. Werner Laurie, 1952.

Gingold, Hermione, *How to Grow Old Disgracefully*. Gollancz, 1989.

Glendinning, Victoria, *Elizabeth Bowen*. Penguin, 1985.

Gourlay, Logan (ed.), *The Beaverbrook I Knew*. Quartet, 1984.

Graves, Charles, *Champagne and Chandeliers*. Odhams, 1958.

Gray, Frances, *Noel Coward*. Macmillan, 1987.

Green, Thomas B., *Life and Work of Samuel Smiles*. Bettement of London, 1904.

Greig, Cicely, *Ivy Compton-Burnett: A Memoir*. Garnstone Press, 1972.

Grenfell, Stephen (ed.), *Gilbert Harding By His Friends*. André Deutsch, 1961.

Hackforth, Norman, *Solo for Horne*. Angus & Robertson, 1976.

Hadfield, John (ed.), *The Saturday Book – 15*. Hutchinson, 1955.

Hamilton, Gerald, *The Way It Was With Me*. Leslie Frewin, 1969.

Harding, Gilbert, *Along My Line*. Putnam, 1953.

Harding, Gilbert, *Treasury of Insults*. Weidenfeld & Nicolson, 1953.

Harding, Gilbert, *Master of None*. Putnam, 1958.

Harris, Nathaniel, *The Sixties*. Macdonald, 1984.

Hayes, W.A., *Beaverbrook*. Fitzhenry & Whiteside, 1979.

Holloway, David, *The Fifties*. Simon & Schuster, 1991.

Horsley, E.M., *The 50s*. Bison Books, 1978.

Horsley, James, *Lays of Jesmond*. Newcastle upon Tyne: A. Reid & Sons, 1891.

Howes, Keith, *Broadcasting It: An Encyclopaedia of Homosexuality on Film, Radio and TV in the UK 1923–1993*. Cassell, 1993.

Jordan, Terry, *Growing Up in the 50s*. Optima, 1990.

Leeman, Dicky, *What's My Line?: The Story of a Phenomenon*. Allan Wingate, 1955.

Lesley, Cole, *Noel Coward and His Friends*. Weidenfeld & Nicolson, 1979.

Levin, Bernard, *The Pendulum Years*. Pan, 1977.

Lewis, Peter, *The Fifties*. Heinemann, 1978.

McBean, Angus and Woodhouse, Adrian, *Angus McBean*. Quartet Books, 1982.

Macbride, Vonla, *Never at Sea: Life in the WRNS*. Reading: Educational Explorers, 1966.

Mason, Ursula Stuart, *The Wrens 1917–77*. Reading: Educational Explorers, 1977.

Mathews, Dame Vera Laughton, *The Blue Tapestry*. Hollis and Carter, 1948.

Maybanke, Laon, *Second Faces*. Arlington Press, 1965.

Miall, Leonard, *Inside the BBC*. Weidenfeld & Nicolson, 1994.

Mitford, Nancy, *Love from Nancy: The Letters of Nancy Mitford*. ed. Charlotte Mosley, Hodder & Stoughton, 1993.

Nobbs, George, *Radio Stars*. Wensum Books, 1972.

Norman, Philip, *Shout!* Hamish Hamilton, 1981.

O'Donnell, Desmond, *Newcastle Streets*. Bridge Studios, 1990.

Partridge, Frances, *Hanging On: Diaries 1960–1963*. Collins, 1990.

Payn, Graham (with Barry Day), *My Life with Noel Coward*. New York and London: Applause Books, 1994.

Peach, L. du Garde, *Meet Mrs Beeton*, H.F.W. Deane & Sons, 1934.

Pemberton, N.W., *Battles of the Boer War*. Batsford, 1964.

Reyburn, Wallace, *Gilbert Harding*. Angus & Robertson, 1978.

Riva, Maria, *Marlene Dietrich*. Bloomsbury, 1992.

Robins, Denise, *Stranger than Fiction*. Hodder & Stoughton, 1965.

Ross, Alan, *The Forties*. Haycock Press, 1950.

Russell, Leonard (ed.), *The Saturday Book – 5*. Hutchinson, 1945.

Sarton, May, *A World of Light*. New York: W.W. Norton & Co., 1976.

Saywell, Shelley, *Women in War*. Grapevine, 1986.

Scott, Pat, *The Fifties*. Franklin Watts, 1991.

Scott-James, Anne, *Sketches from a Life*. Michael Joseph, 1993.

Scott-Moncrieff, Joanna (ed.), *The Book of Woman's Hour*. Ariel Productions, 1953.

Scott-Moncrieff, Joanna (ed.), *The BBC Woman's Hour Book*. The World's Work, Kingswood, 1957.

Sleight, John, *Women on the March*. John Sleight, 1986.

Smiles, Aileen, *Samuel Smiles and His Surroundings*. Robert Hale, 1956.

Smiles, Samuel, *History of Ireland*. Samuel Smiles, 1844.

Smiles, Samuel, *Self-Help*. John Murray, 1859.

Smiles, Samuel, *Autobiography*. John Murray, 1905.

Smiles, Samuel Jnr, *A Boy's Voyage*. John Murray, 1871.

Snagge, J. and Barsley, M., *Those Vintage Years of Radio*. Pitman, 1972.

Somerfield, Stafford, *Banner Headlines*. Scan Books, 1979.

Spain, G.L., *Jottings from a Corner*. Mawson, Swan & Morgan, 1910.

Spain, George Redesdale Brooker, 'The Gods of the Isle of Man.' *Museums Journal*, 1929.

Spain, George Redesdale Brooker, *Tyne*. T. & G. Allan, 1929.

Spanier, Ginette, *It Isn't All Mink*. Collins, 1959.

Spanier, Ginette, *And Now It's Sables*. Robert Hale, 1970.

Spanier, Ginette, *Long Road to Freedom*. Robert Hale, 1976.

Spoto, Donald, *Blue Angel: The Life of Marlene Dietrich*. Doubleday, 1992.

Stannard, Martin, *Evelyn Waugh: No Abiding City, 1939–66*. Dent, 1992.

Storey, Roger, *Gilbert Harding*. Barrie & Rockcliff, 1961.

Sykes, Christopher, *Evelyn Waugh: A Biography*. Collins, 1975.

Sylvester, Christopher (ed.), *Penguin Book of Interviews*. Viking, 1993.

Taylor, A.J.P., *Beaverbrook*. Hamish Hamilton, 1972.

Taylor, Eric, *Women Who Went to War 1938–46*. Robert Hale, 1988.

Thorogood, Julia, *Margery Allingham*. Heinemann, 1991.

Thwaite, Anne, *A.A. Milne – His Life*. Faber & Faber, 1990.

van Damm, Sheila, *No Excuses*. Beacon Books, 1957.

van Damm, Sheila, *We Never Closed*. Robert Hale, 1967.

van Damm, Vivian, *Tonight and Every Night*. Stanley Paul & Co., 1952.

Waller, Jane and Vaughn-Rees, Michael, *Women in Uniform 1939–45*. Papermac, 1989.

Warren, Tony, *I Was Ena Sharples's Dad*. Duckworth, 1969.

Waugh, Evelyn, *The Letters of Evelyn Waugh*. Weidenfeld & Nicolson, 1976.

West, Rebecca, *Sunflower*. Virago, 1986.

Wheen, Francis, *The Sixties*. Century/Channel Four, 1982.

Wheen, Francis, *Tom Driberg: His Life and Indiscretions*. Chatto & Windus, 1990.

Whitcomb, Noel, *A Particular Kind of Fool*. Anthony Blond, 1990.

White, Cynthia, *Women's Magazines, 1693–1968*. Michael Joseph, 1970.

Williams, Edward Francis, *Dangerous Estate*. Longmans, Green & Co., 1957.

Wilson, Sandy, *I Could Be Happy*. Michael Joseph, 1975.

Winship, Janice, *Advertising in Women's Magazines*. University of Birmingham, 1980.

Winship, Janice, *Inside Women's Magazines*. Pandora, 1987.

Youngman Carter, Philip, *All I Did Was This*. Sexton Press, 1982.

In order to obtain a full picture of Nancy's journalism, it was necessary to read each issue of the following newspapers, magazines and periodicals covering the dates given below:

Daily Express April 1952 to February 1961 (2,757 issues).

Newcastle Journal September 1935 to January 1940 (1,404 issues).

Good Housekeeping January 1951 to June 1955 (53 issues).

She March 1955 to May 1964 (110 issues).

News of the World February 1961 to March 1964 (160 issues).

Books of Today Nos. 1–12, 1950 and 1951 (24 issues).

Empire News June 1947 to December 1948 (78 issues).

Evening Standard May–October 1953; July–October 1954 (291 issues).

Tribune September 1949 to March 1950 (30 issues).

Books by Nancy Spain

Autobiography

Thank You – Nelson, Hutchinson, January 1945.

Why I'm Not a Millionaire, Hutchinson, September 1956.

A Funny Thing Happened on the Way, Hutchinson, May 1964.

Biography

Mrs Beeton and Her Husband, Collins, August 1948 (republished as *The Beeton Story*, Ward, Lock & Co., 1956).

'Teach' Tennant, T. Werner Laurie, July 1953.

Fiction

(All published by Hutchinson)
Poison in Play, January 1946.
Death Before Wicket, December 1946.
Murder, Bless It, June 1948.
Death Goes on Skis, June 1949.
Poison for Teacher, November 1949.
Cinderella Goes to the Morgue, April 1950.
'R' in the Month, November 1950.
Not Wanted on Voyage, July 1951.
Out, Damned Tot, June 1952.
The Kat Strikes, November 1955.
My Boy Mo, December 1959.

Children's books

The Tiger Who Couldn't Eat Meat, Max Parrish, November 1954.
The Tiger Who Went to the Moon, Max Parrish, November 1956.
The Tiger Who Won His Star, Max Parrish, 1957.
The Tiger Who Saved the Train, Max Parrish, May 1960.
The Tiger Who Found the Treasure, Max Parrish, 1961.
Nancy Spain's Tiger Annual, Max Parrish, 1961.
The Beaver Annual (ed. Nancy Spain), Fairhaven Books, 1962.

The Nancy Spain Colour Cookery Book, World Distributors, September 1963.

Index